Contested Will

by the same author

RIVAL PLAYWRIGHTS

SHAKESPEARE AND THE JEWS

OBERAMMERGAU

1599

Contested Will

Who Wrote Shakespeare?

James Shapiro

faber and faber

First published in 2010
by Faber and Faber Limited
Bloomsbury House
74–77 Great Russell Street
London WC1B 3DA

Typeset by Faber and Faber Limited
Printed in England by TJ International Ltd, Padstow, Cornwall

A CIP record for this book
is available from the British Library

ISBN 978–0–571–23576–6

1 3 5 7 9 10 8 6 4 2

For Luke

PERTH & KINROSS COUNCIL		
05643931		
Bertrams	26/10/2010	
822.33 LAN	£20.00	
IILA		

Contents

List of Illustrations ix

Prologue 1

ONE
Shakespeare
15

TWO
Bacon
91

THREE
Oxford
171

FOUR
Shakespeare
251

Epilogue
297

Bibliographical Essay
317

Acknowledgements
355

Index
357

[vii]

List of Illustrations

'I gyve unto my wief my second best bed,' from Shakespeare's Will, 1616. By permission of the National Archives. 1

George Romney, 'The Infant Shakespeare Attended by Nature and the Passions', engraved by Benjamin Smith, 1799. By permission of the Folger Shakespeare Library. 15

Portrait, from Samuel Ireland, *Miscellaneous Papers and Legal Instruments under the Head and Seal of William Shakspeare* (London, 1796). 17

Letter from Queen Elizabeth, from Samuel Ireland, *Miscellaneous Papers*. 23

Manuscript page of *King Lear*, from Samuel Ireland, *Miscellaneous Papers*. 24

Shakespeare and Anne Hathaway, unknown artist, *c.*1860. By permission of the Folger Shakespeare Library. 57

Francis Bacon, by William Marshall, after Simon De Passe, 1641. By permission of the National Portrait Gallery. 91

Delia Bacon, from Theodore Bacon, *Delia Bacon: A Biographical Sketch* (Boston, 1888). 93

Helen Keller and Mark Twain, 1902, photograph by E. C. Kopp. By permission of the American Foundation for the Blind, Helen Keller Archives. 125

Cipher Wheel, frontispiece to vol. 2 of Orville Ward Owen's *Sir Francis Bacon's Cipher Story* (Detroit, 1894). 136

Edward de Vere, seventeenth Earl of Oxford, by Joseph Brown, after George Perfect Harding, 1848. By permission of the National Portrait Gallery. 171

Sigmund Freud with Otto Rank, Karl Abraham, Max Eitingon, Ernest Jones, Hanns Sachs, and Sándor Ferenczi, 1922. By permission of the Freud Museum, London. 173

John Thomas Looney. By permission of the Shakespeare
Authorship Trust. 186

William Shakespeare, by Martin Droeshout, 1623. By permission
of the National Portrait Gallery. 251

Schoolroom, Guildhall, Stratford-upon-Avon. By permission of
the Shakespeare Birthplace Trust. 253

'By me William Shakespeare,' from Shakespeare's Will, 1616. By
permission of the National Archives. 297

Prologue

This is a book about when and why many people began to question whether William Shakespeare wrote the plays long attributed to him, and, if he didn't write them, who did.

There's surprising consensus on the part of both sceptics and defenders of Shakespeare's authorship about when the controversy first took root. Whether you get your facts from the *Dictionary of National Biography* or Wikipedia, the earliest documented claim dates back to 1785, when James Wilmot, an Oxford-trained scholar who lived a few miles outside of Stratford-upon-Avon, began searching locally for Shakespeare's books, papers, or any indication that he had been an author – and came up empty-handed. Wilmot gradually came to the conclusion that someone else, most likely Sir Francis Bacon, had written the plays. Wilmot never published what he learned and near the end of his life burned all his papers. But before he died he spoke with a fellow researcher, a Quaker from Ipswich named James Corton Cowell, who later shared these findings with members of the Ipswich Philosophic Society.

Cowell did so in a pair of lectures delivered in 1805 that survive in a manuscript now located in the University of London's Senate House Library, in which he confesses to being 'a renegade' to the Shakespearean 'faith'. Cowell was converted by Wilmot's argument that 'there is nothing in the writings of Shakespeare that does not argue the long and early training of the schoolman, the traveller, and the associate of the great and learned. Yet there is

'I gyve unto my wief my second best bed', from Shakespeare's Will

nothing in the known life of Shakespeare that shows he had any one of the qualities.' Wilmot is credited with being the first to argue, as far back as the late eighteenth century, for an unbridgeable rift between the facts of Shakespeare's life and what the plays and poems reveal about their author's education and experience. But both Wilmot and Cowell were ahead of their time, for close to a half-century passed before the controversy resurfaced in any serious or sustained way.

Since 1850 or so, thousands of books and articles have been published urging that someone other than Shakespeare wrote the plays. At first, bibliographers tried to keep count of all the works inspired by the controversy. By 1884 the list ran to 255 items; by 1949, it had swelled to over 4,500. Nobody bothered trying to keep a running tally after that, and in an age of blogs, websites and online forums it's impossible to do justice to how much intellectual energy has been – and continues to be – devoted to the subject. Over time, and for all sorts of reasons, leading artists and intellectuals from all walks of life joined the ranks of the sceptics. I can think of little else that unites Henry James and Malcolm X, Sigmund Freud and Charlie Chaplin, Helen Keller and Orson Welles, or Mark Twain and Sir Derek Jacobi.

It's not easy keeping track of all the candidates promoted as the true author of Shakespeare's plays and poems. The leading contenders nowadays are Edward de Vere (the Earl of Oxford) and Sir Francis Bacon. Christopher Marlowe, Mary Sidney, the Earl of Derby and the Earl of Rutland have attracted fewer though no less ardent supporters. And over fifty others have been proposed as well – working alone or collaboratively – including Sir Walter Ralegh, John Donne, Robert Cecil, John Florio, Sir Philip Sidney, the Earl of Southampton, Queen Elizabeth and King James. A complete list is pointless, for it would soon be outdated. During the time I've been working on this book, four more names have been put forward: the poet and courtier Fulke Greville, the Irish rebel William Nugent, the poet Amelia Lanier (of Jewish descent and thought by some to be the unnamed Dark Lady of the

Sonnets) and the Elizabethan diplomat Henry Neville. New candidates will almost surely be proposed in years to come. While the chapters that follow focus on Francis Bacon and the Earl of Oxford – whose candidates are the best documented and most consequential – it's not because I believe that their claims are necessarily stronger than any of these others. An exhaustive account of all the candidates, including those already advanced and those waiting in the wings, would be both tedious and futile, and for reasons that will soon become clear, Bacon and Oxford can be taken as representative.

Much of what has been written about the authorship of Shakespeare's plays follows the contours of a detective story, which is not all that surprising, since the authorship question and the 'whodunnit' emerged at the same historical moment. Like all good detective fiction, the Shakespeare mystery can be solved only by determining what evidence is credible, retracing steps and avoiding false leads. My own account in the pages that follow is no different. I've spent the past twenty-five years researching and teaching Shakespeare's works at Columbia University. For some, that automatically disqualifies me from writing fairly about the controversy on the grounds that my professional investments are so great that I cannot be objective. There are a few who have gone so far as to hint at a conspiracy at work among Shakespeare professors and institutions, with scholars paid off to suppress information that would undermine Shakespeare's claim. If so, somebody forgot to put my name on the list.

My graduate-school experience taught me to be sceptical of unexamined historical claims, even ones that other Shakespeareans took on faith. I had wanted to write my doctoral dissertation on 'Shakespeare and the Jews' but was told that since there were no Jews in Shakespeare's England there were no Jewish questions, and I should turn my attention elsewhere. I reluctantly did so, but years later, after a good deal of research, I learned that both claims were false: there was in fact a small community of Jews living in Elizabethan London and many leading English writers at that time wrestled in their work with questions of Jewish difference (in an effort to better grasp what constituted English identity). That experience, and the book that grew out of it, taught me the value of revisiting truths universally acknowledged.

There yet remains one subject walled off from serious study by Shakespeare scholars: the authorship question. More than one fellow Shakespearean was disheartened to learn that I was committing my energies to it, as if somehow I was wasting my time and talent, or worse, at risk of going over to the dark side. I became increasingly interested in why this subject remains virtually taboo in academic circles, as well as in the consequences of this collective silence. One thing is certain: the decision by professors to all but ignore the authorship question hasn't made it disappear. If anything, more people are drawn to it than ever. And because prominent Shakespeareans — with the notable exceptions of Samuel Schoenbaum, Jonathan Bate, Marjorie Garber, Gary Taylor, Stanley Wells and Alan Nelson — have all but surrendered the field, general readers curious about the subject typically learn about it through the books and websites of those convinced that Shakespeare could never have written the plays.

This was forcefully brought home not long ago when I met a group of nine-year-olds at a local elementary school to talk about Shakespeare's poetry. When toward the end of the class I invited questions, a quiet boy on my left raised his hand and said: 'My brother told me that Shakespeare really didn't write *Romeo and Juliet*. Is that true?' It was the kind of question I was used to hearing from undergraduates on the first day of a Shakespeare course or from audience members at popular lectures, but I hadn't expected that doubts about Shakespeare's authorship had filtered down to the fourth grade.

Not long after, at the Bank Street Bookstore, the best children's bookstore in New York City, I ran into a colleague from the history department buying a stack of books for her twelve-year-old daughter. On the top of her pile was a young adult paperback by

Elise Broach, *Shakespeare's Secret*, which I learned from those who worked at the store was a popular title. I bought a copy. It's a fascinating and fast-paced detective story about a diamond necklace that once belonged to Queen Elizabeth. The mystery of the necklace is only worked out when another mystery, concerning who wrote Shakespeare's plays, is solved.

The father of the story's young heroine is a Shakespeare scholar at the 'Maxwell Elizabethan Documents Collection in Washington, DC' (whose 'vaulted ceilings' and 'long, shining wood tables' bear a striking resemblance to those of the Folger Shakespeare Library). He tells his curious daughter that there's 'no proof of course, but there are some intriguing clues' that 'Edward de Vere, the seventeenth Earl of Oxford' was 'the man who might be Shakespeare'. When she asks him why people think Oxford might have written the plays, he explains that Oxford had 'the perfect background, really. He was clever, well-educated, well-traveled,' and 'events of his life bear a fascinating resemblance to events in Shakespeare's plays'. He adds that 'most academics still favor Shakespeare', though 'over the years Oxford has emerged as a real possibility'. But it doesn't take her long to suspect that Shakespeare wasn't the author after all; by page 45, after learning that Shakespeare 'couldn't even spell his own name', she decides: 'Okay, so maybe he didn't write the plays.'

An unusual twist to the story is the suggestion that Queen Elizabeth and the Earl of Oxford had a clandestine relationship, which explains why Oxford couldn't claim credit for writing the plays falsely attributed to Shakespeare: 'If there were some connection between Oxford and Elizabeth that meant the royal name would be besmirched by his ambitions as a playwright.' In the end, the secret of the necklace reveals 'that Edward de Vere was Elizabeth's son'. More surprising still is the hint that the relationship between son and mother didn't end there, for when he came of age, Oxford 'might have been her lover' as well.

Elise Broach provides an author's note in which she explains that the 'case for Edward de Vere as Shakespeare is compelling', and that while 'there is no proof that Edward de Vere was the son of Elizabeth I, there is clear evidence of a connection between them, and the notion that he might have been either her lover or her son continues to be discussed'. As for her own views: 'As a historian' (who did graduate work in history at Yale) 'I don't find the evidence to be complete enough – yet – to topple the man from Stratford from his literary pedestal. But as a novelist I am more convinced.'

I put the book down relieved that the nine-year-old boy had stuck to Shakespeare's authorship and not asked me about Queen Elizabeth's incestuous love-life. The question of how schoolchildren could learn to doubt whether Shakespeare wrote the plays may have been answered, but only to be replaced by more vexing ones: What led a writer as thoughtful and well informed as Elise Broach to arrive at this solution? What underlying assumptions – about concealed identity, Elizabethan literary culture, and especially the autobiographical nature of the plays – enabled such a conception of Shakespeare's authorship to take hold? And when and why had such changes in understanding occurred?

In taking this set of questions as my subject this book departs from previous ones about the authorship controversy. These have focused almost exclusively on *what* people have claimed, that is, whether it was Shakespeare or someone else who wrote the plays. The best of these books – and there are a number of excellent ones written both by advocates and those sceptical of Shakespeare's authorship – set out well-rehearsed arguments for and against Shakespeare and his many rivals. Consulting them, or a handful of online discussion groups such as 'The Shakespeare Fellowship' (for a pro-Oxford bias), 'The Forest of Arden' (for a pro-Shakespeare one) and 'Humanities.Lit.Authors.Shakespeare' (for a glimpse of how nasty things can get), will offer a sense of where the battle-lines are currently drawn, but will fail to make clear how we got to where we are now and how it may be possible to move beyond what seems like endless trench warfare.

Shakespeare scholars insist that Christopher Marlowe could

not have written plays dated as late as 1614 because he was killed in 1593, and that the Earl of Oxford couldn't have either, because he died in 1604, before *Lear*, *Macbeth* and eight or so other plays were written. Marlowe's defenders counter that Marlowe wasn't in fact killed; his assassination was staged and he was secretly hustled off to the Continent, where he wrote the plays now known as Shakespeare's. Oxfordians respond that despite what orthodox scholars say, nobody knows the dates of many of Shakespeare's late plays, and in any case Oxford could easily have written them before his death. Shakespeareans reply that there is not a shred of documentary evidence linking anyone else to the authorship of the plays; advocates of rival candidates respond that there is plenty of circumstantial evidence – and, moreover, many reasons to doubt Shakespeare's claim. Positions are fixed and debate has proven to be futile or self-serving. The only thing that has changed over time is how best to get one's message across. Until twenty years ago it was mainly through books and articles; since then the Web has played an increasingly crucial role. Those who would deny Shakespeare's authorship, long excluded from publishing their work in academic journals or through university presses, are now taking advantage of the level playing field provided by the Web, especially such widely consulted and democratic sites as Wikipedia.

My interest, again, is not in what people think – which has been stated again and again in unambiguous terms – so much as why they think it. No doubt my attitude derives from living in a world in which truth is too often seen as relative and in which mainstream media are committed to showing both sides of every story. Groups are locked in opposition, proponents gravitating to their own kind, reinforced in their beliefs by like-minded (and potentially closed-minded) communities. There are those who believe in intelligent design and those who swear by theories of evolution; there are those who believe that life begins at conception and those who don't. Then there are those whose view of the world is shaped for better or worse by conspiracy, so while most are convinced that astronauts walked on the moon, some believe that this was staged. More disturbingly, there are those who survived the Holocaust and those who maintain it never happened. I don't believe that truth is relative or that there are always two sides to every story. At the same time, I don't want to draw a naïve comparison between the Shakespeare controversy and any of these other issues. I think it's a mistake to do so, except insofar that it too turns on underlying assumptions and notions of evidence that cannot be reconciled. Yet unlike some of these other controversies, I think it's possible to get at why people have come to believe what they believe about Shakespeare's authorship, and it is partly in the hope of doing so that I have written this book.

I should say at this point that I happen to believe that William Shakespeare wrote the plays and poems attributed to him, a view left unshaken by the years of study I have devoted to this subject (and toward the end of this book I'll explain in some detail why I think so). But I take very seriously the fact that some brilliant writers and thinkers who matter a great deal to me – including Sigmund Freud, Henry James and Mark Twain – have doubted that Shakespeare wrote the plays. Through their published and unpublished reflections on Shakespeare I've gained a much sharper sense of what is contested and ultimately at stake in the authorship debate. Their work has also helped me unravel a mystery at the heart of the controversy: why, after two centuries, did so many people start questioning whether Shakespeare wrote the plays?

There's another mystery, often and easily confused with this one, that I cannot solve, though it continues to haunt both Shakespeareans and sceptics alike: what led to the playwright's emergence (whoever one imagines he or she was) as such an extraordinary writer? As for the formative years of William Shakespeare – especially the decade or so between his marriage to Anne Hathaway in the early 1580s and his reappearance in London in the early 1590s, by now an aspiring poet and playwright – they are called the 'Lost Years' for a reason. Was he a lawyer, a butcher, a soldier, or teaching in a Catholic household in Lancashire during those years, as some have surmised? We simply don't know. No less inscrutable is the 'contested will' to which the dying Shakespeare affixed his signature in 1616. The surviving three-page document makes no mention of his books or manuscripts. And, notoriously, the only thing that Shakespeare bequeathed in it to his wife Anne was a 'second best bed'. Not only the nature of their marriage but also the kind of man Shakespeare was seems bound up in this bequest. Was he referring, perhaps, to the guest bed or alternatively to the marital bed they had shared? Was he deliberately treating his wife shabbily in the will or did he simply assume that a third of his estate – the 'widow's dower' – was automatically her share? We don't know and probably never shall, though such unanswerable questions continue to fuel the mystery surrounding his life and work.

With these challenges in mind, this book first sets out to trace the controversy back to its origins, before considering why many formidable writers came to question Shakespeare's authorship. I quickly discovered that biographers of Freud, Twain and James weren't keen on looking too deeply into these authors' doubts about Shakespeare. As a result, I encountered something rare in Shakespeare studies: archival material that was unsifted and in some cases unknown. I've also revisited the life and works of the two most influential figures in the controversy, the allegedly 'mad' American woman, Delia Bacon, who first made the case for Francis Bacon, and the schoolmaster J. T. Looney, the first to propose that Edward de Vere, the seventeenth Earl of Oxford, was the true author of the plays. For a debate that largely turns on how one understands the relationship of Shakespeare's life and works, there has been disappointingly little attention devoted to considering how Bacon's and Looney's experiences and worldviews determined the trajectory of their theories of authorship. Scholars on both sides of the debate have overlooked a great deal by taking these two polemicists at their word.

More than any subject I've ever studied, the history of the

authorship question is rife with forgeries and deception. I now approach all claims about Shakespeare's identity with caution, taking into account when each discovery was made and how it altered previous biographical assumptions. I've also come to understand that the authorship controversy has turned on a handful of powerful ideas having little directly to do with Shakespeare but profoundly altering how his life and works would be read and interpreted. Some of these ideas came from debates about biblical texts, others from debates about classical ones. Still others had to do with emerging notions of the autobiographical self. As much as those on both sides of the controversy like to imagine themselves as independent thinkers, their views are strongly constrained by a few powerful ideas that took hold in the early nineteenth century.

While Shakespeare was a product of an early modern world, the controversy over the authorship of his works is the creation of a modern one. As a result, there's a danger of reading the past through contemporary eyes – from what Shakespeare's contested will really meant to how writers back then might have drawn upon personal experiences in their works. A secondary aim of this book, then, is to show how Shakespeare is not our contemporary, nor as universal as we might wish him to be. Anachronistic thinking, especially about how we can gain access to writers' lives through their plays and poems, turns out to be as characteristic of supporters of Shakespeare's authorship as it is of sceptics. From this vantage, the longstanding opposition between the two camps is misleading, for they have more in common than either side is willing to concede. These shared if unspoken assumptions may in fact help explain the hostility that defines their relationship today, and I'll suggest that there may be more useful ways of defining sides in this debate. I'll also argue that Shakespeare scholars, from the late eighteenth century until today, bear a greater responsibility than they acknowledge for both the emergence and the perpetuation of the authorship controversy.

*

The evidence I continued to uncover while researching this book made it hard to imagine how anyone before the 1840s could argue that Shakespeare didn't write the plays. This working assumption couldn't easily be reconciled with the received history of the controversy, one that, as noted earlier, goes back to James Wilmot in 1785, or at least to James Cowell in 1805. Aware of this uncomfortable fact, I held off until the very end of my research on consulting the Cowell manuscript in the Durning-Lawrence Library at Senate House Library in London. Before I called it up I knew as much as others who had read about this unpublished and rarely examined work. It was one of the jewels of a great collection of materials touching on the life and works of Francis Bacon, assembled at great expense by Sir Edwin Durning-Lawrence, and, after his death in 1914, by his widow, Edith Jane Durning Smith, who shared his keen interest in the authorship controversy. Upon her death in 1929, the collection was bequeathed to the University of London, and by 1931 the transfer of materials was complete. A year later the leading British scholar Allardyce Nicoll announced in the pages of the *Times Literary Supplement* in an essay entitled 'The First Baconian' the discovery of Cowell's lectures. It was Nicoll who put the pieces of the puzzle together, relying heavily on a biography written in 1813 by Wilmot's niece, Olivia Wilmot Serres. Serres's account, while not mentioning her uncle's meeting with Cowell or his Shakespeare research, nonetheless confirmed that Wilmot was a serious man of letters, had lived near Stratford, was an admirer of Francis Bacon and had indeed burned his papers. Nicoll was less successful in tracing James Corton Cowell, concluding that he 'seems to have been a Quaker' on the grounds that 'he was in all probability closely related to the well-known Orientalist E. B. Cowell, who was born at Ipswich in 1828'.

Armed with this information, I turned to the lectures themselves, which made for gripping reading – how Cowell began as a confirmed Shakespearean, how his fortuitous encounter with Wilmot changed all that, how Wilmot anticipated a widely accepted reading of *Love's Labour's Lost* by a century, and perhaps most fascinating of all, how Wilmot uncovered stories of 'odd characters living at or near Stratford on the Avon with whom Shakespeare must have been familiar', including 'a certain man of extreme ugliness and tallness who blackmailed the farmers under threat of bewitching their cattle', as well as 'a legend of showers of cakes at Shrovetide and stories of men who were rendered cripples by the falling of these cakes'. I thought it a shame that Cowell had not taken even better notes.

And then my heart skipped when I came upon the following words: 'It is strange that Shakespeare whose best years had been spent in a profitable and literary vocation should return to an obscure village offering no intellectual allurement and take up the very unromantic business of a money lender and dealer in malt.' The sentence seemed innocuous enough; scholars and sceptics alike have often drawn attention to these well-known facts about Shakespeare's business dealings. But having long focused more on *when* than on *what* people thought what they did about Shakespeare, I remembered that these details were unknown in 1785, or even in 1805. Records showing that Shakespeare's household stockpiled grain in order to produce malt were not discovered until the early 1840s (and first published in 1844 by John Payne Collier). And it wasn't until 1806 that the Stratford antiquarian R. B. Wheler made public the first of what would turn out to be several documents indicating that Shakespeare had engaged in moneylending (in this case, how in 1609 Shakespeare had a Stratford neighbour named John Addenbrooke arrested for failing to repay a small sum). While an undelivered letter in which another neighbour asks Shakespeare for a loan had been discovered in the late eighteenth century, the scholar who found it chose not to announce or share his discovery; it remained otherwise unknown until 1821. So Shakespeare's grain-hoarding and money-lending didn't become biographical commonplaces until the Victorian era.

The word 'unromantic' in the same sentence should have tipped me off; though there was a recorded instance of its use before

1800, it wasn't yet in currency at the time Cowell was supposedly writing. Whoever wrote these lectures purporting to be from 1805 had slipped up. I was looking at a forgery, and an unusually clever one at that, which on further examination almost surely dated from the early decades of the twentieth century. That meant the forger was probably still alive – and enjoying a satisfied laugh at the expense of the gulled professor – when Allardyce Nicoll had announced this discovery in the pages of the *TLS*. The forger had brazenly left other hints, not least of all the wish attributed to Cowell that 'my material may be used by others regardless whence it came for it matters little who made the axe so that it cut'. And there were a few other false notes, including one pointed out by a letter-writer responding to Nicoll's article, that Cowell had got his Warwickshire geography wrong. It also turns out that Serres, the author of Nicoll's main corroborative source (the biography of Wilmot) was a forger and fantasist. Much of her biographical account (including the burning of Wilmot's papers) was invented and she later changed her story, asserting she was actually Wilmot's granddaughter and the illegitimate daughter of King George III. Her case was even discussed in parliament and it took a trial to expose her fraudulent claim to be of royal descent. So Olivia Serres, at the source of the Cowell forgery, would also prove to be the pattern of a Shakespeare claimant: a writer of high lineage mistaken for someone of humbler origins, whose true identity deserved to be acknowledged.

I've not been able to discover who forged the Cowell manuscript; that mystery will have to be solved by others. His or her motives (or perhaps their) cannot fully be known, though it's worth hazarding a guess or two. Greed perhaps figured, for there is a record of payment for the manuscript of the not inconsiderable sum of £8 8s – though this document may have been planted and we simply don't as yet know when or how the Cowell manuscript became part of the Durning-Lawrence collection. But, given how much time and care went into the forgery, a far likelier motive was the desire on the part of a Baconian to stave off the challenge posed by supporters of the Earl of Oxford, who by the 1920s threatened to surpass Bacon as the more likely author of Shakespeare's works, if in fact he had not done so already. A final motive was that it reassigned the discovery of Francis Bacon's authorship from a 'mad' American woman to a true-born Englishman, a quiet retiring man of letters, an Oxford-educated rector from the heart of England. Wilmot also stood as a surrogate for the actual author of Shakespeare's plays: a well-educated man believed to have written pseudonymously who refused to claim credit for what he wrote and nearly denied posterity knowledge of the truth.

All of the major elements of the authorship controversy come together in the tangled story of Wilmot, Cowell, Serres and the nameless forger – which serves as both a prologue and a warning. The following pages retrace a path strewn with a great deal more of the same: fabricated documents, embellished lives, concealed identity, calls for trial, pseudonymous authorship, contested evidence, bald-faced deception, and a failure to grasp what could not be imagined.

ONE

SHAKESPEARE

George Romney, 'The Infant Shakespeare Attended by Nature and the Passions', engraved by Benjamin Smith, 1799

Ireland

For a long time after Shakespeare's death in 1616, anyone curious about his life had to depend on unreliable and often contradictory anecdotes, most of them supplied by people who had never met him. No one thought to interview his family, friends or fellow actors until it was too late to do so, and it wasn't until the late eighteenth century that biographers began combing through documents preserved in Stratford-upon-Avon and London. All this time interest in Shakespeare never abated; it was centred, however, on his plays rather than his personality. Curiosity about his art was, and still is, easily satisfied: from the closing years of the sixteenth century to this day, his plays could be purchased or seen onstage more readily than those of any other dramatist.

Shakespeare did not live, as we do, in an age of memoir. Few at the time kept diaries or wrote personal essays (only thirty or so English diaries survive from Shakespeare's lifetime and only a handful are in any sense personal; and despite the circulation and then translation of Montaigne's *Essays* in England, the genre attracted few followers and fizzled out by the early seventeenth

Portrait, from Samuel Ireland, *Miscellaneous Papers and Legal Instruments under the Head and Seal of William Shakspeare* (London, 1796)

century, not to be revived in any serious way for another hundred years). Literary biography was still in its infancy; even the word 'biography' hadn't yet entered the language and wouldn't until the 1660s. By the time that popular interest began to shift from the works themselves to the life of the author, it was difficult to learn much about what Shakespeare was like. Now that those who knew him were no longer alive, the only credible sources of information were letters, literary manuscripts or official documents, and these were either lost or remained undiscovered.

The first document with Shakespeare's handwriting or signature on it – his will – wasn't recovered until over a century after his death, in 1737. Sixteen years later a young lawyer named Albany Wallis, rummaging through the title deeds of the Fetherstonhaugh family in Surrey, stumbled upon a second document signed by Shakespeare, a mortgage deed for a London property in Blackfriars that the playwright had purchased in 1613. The rare find was given as a gift to David Garrick – star of the eighteenth-century stage and organiser of the first Shakespeare festival – and was subsequently published by the leading Shakespeare scholar and biographer of the day, Edmond Malone. Malone's own efforts to locate Shakespeare's papers were tireless – and disappointing. His greatest find, made in 1793 (though it remained unpublished until 1821), was the undelivered letter mentioned earlier, addressed *to* Shakespeare by his Stratford neighbour Richard Quiney.

A neighbour's request for a substantial loan, a shrewd real-estate investment and a will in which Shakespeare left his wife a 'second best bed' were not what admirers in search of clues that explained Shakespeare's genius had hoped to find. What little else turned up didn't help much either, suggesting that the Shakespeares secretly clung to a suspect faith and were, moreover, social climbers. Shakespeare's father's perhaps spurious Catholic 'Testament of Faith' was found hidden in the rafters of the family home on Henley Street in Stratford-upon-Avon in 1757, though mysteriously lost soon after a transcript was made. And the Shakespeares' request in 1596 for a grant of a coat of arms –

bestowing on the Stratford glover and his actor son the status of gentlemen – surfaced in 1778, and was published that year by George Steevens in his edition of Shakespeare's plays. Contemporaries still had high hopes that 'a rich assemblage of Shakespeare papers would start forth from some ancient repository, to solve all our doubts'. For his part, a frustrated Edmond Malone blamed gentry too lazy to examine their family papers: 'Much information might be procured illustrative of the history of this extraordinary man, if persons possessed of ancient papers would take the trouble to examine them, or permit others to peruse them.'

Some feared that Shakespeare's papers had been, or might yet be, carelessly destroyed. The collector and engraver Samuel Ireland, touring through Stratford-upon-Avon in 1794 while at work on his *Picturesque Views on the Upper, or Warwickshire Avon*, was urged by a Stratford local to search Clopton House, a mile from town, where the Shakespeare family papers might have been moved. Ireland and his teenage son, William-Henry, who had accompanied him, made their way to Clopton House, and in response to their queries were told by the farmer who lived there, a man named Williams,

By God I wish you had arrived a little sooner. Why it isn't a fortnight since I destroyed several baskets-full of letters and papers; . . . as to Shakespeare, why there were many bundles with his name wrote upon them. Why it was in this very fireplace I made a roaring bonfire of them.

Mrs Williams was called in and confirmed the report, admonishing her husband: 'I told you not to burn the papers, as they might be of consequence.' All that Edmond Malone could do when he heard this dispiriting news was complain to the couple's landlord. The unlucky Samuel and William-Henry Ireland went back to London.

They didn't return empty-handed, having purchased an oak chair at Anne Hathaway's cottage. It was said to be the very chair in which Shakespeare had wooed Anne, and it's now in the possession of the Shakespeare Birthplace Trust. Samuel Ireland added it to his growing collection of English heirlooms that included the cloak of the fourteenth-century theologian John Wyclif, a jacket owned by Oliver Cromwell and the garter that King James II wore at his coronation. But the great prize of Shakespeare's signature continued to elude him. It probably didn't help Ireland's mood that his lawyer and rival collector Albany Wallis, who thirty years earlier had discovered Shakespeare's signature on the Blackfriars mortgage deed, had recently regained access to the Fetherstonhaugh papers and located a third document signed by Shakespeare, the conveyance to that Blackfriars transaction.

As the eighteenth century came to a close, the long-lost cache of Shakespeare's papers – and not just legal transactions, but more revelatory correspondence, literary manuscripts and perhaps even commonplace books (in which Elizabethan writers recorded what they saw, heard and read) – still awaited discovery. And crucial information about the Elizabethan theatrical world, which might have illuminated Shakespeare's professional life, was only fitfully coming to light. A major find in 1766 – a copy of *Palladis Tamia*, Francis Meres's published account of the Elizabethan literary world in 1598 – confirmed that by then a 'honey-tongued Shakespeare' was already prized as the leading English writer of both comedies and tragedies. While the contours of Shakespeare's professional world were slowly becoming visible, his personal life remained obscure. Though unsuccessful in his search for Shakespeare's notebooks, a dogged Edmond Malone did find the record-book of one of the Jacobean Masters of the Revels in a trunk that hadn't been opened for over a century. It was a discovery, Malone wrote, 'so much beyond all calculation or expectation, that, I will not despair of finding Shakespeare's pocket-book some time or other'.

Despite the belated efforts of eighteenth-century scholars and collectors, no document in Shakespeare's hand had as yet been found that linked him to the plays published under his name or attributed to him by contemporaries. The evidence for his authorship remained slight enough for a foolish character in a play staged in London in 1759 – *High Life Below Stairs* – to wonder aloud, 'Who Wrote Shakespeare?' (when told that it was Ben Jonson, she replies: 'Oh no! Shakespeare was written by one Mr Finis, for I saw his name at the end of the book'). And in 1786 an anonymous allegory called *The Learned Pig* was published, a story that turns on the Pig's various reincarnations, including one in Elizabethan times when the Pig encountered Shakespeare – who then took credit for the animal's work, or so the Pig claims: 'He has been fathered with many spurious dramatic pieces: *Hamlet, Othello, As You Like It, The Tempest,* and *A Midsummer Night's Dream,*' of 'which I confess myself to be the author'. Both of these fictional works joke about authorship, but do so with a slightly uneasy edge, testifying to the growing divide between Shakespeare's fame and how little was known for sure about the man who wrote the plays.

Young William-Henry Ireland, eager to please his disappointed father, continued hunting for Shakespeare's papers among the various documents he came across as a law clerk as well as among the wares of 'a dealer of old parchments' whose shop he 'frequented for weeks'. In November 1794 he was invited to dinner by a family friend, at which (to quote Malone's account) William-Henry made the acquaintance of 'Mr H.', a 'gentleman of large fortune, who lived chiefly in the country'. Their 'conversation turning on old papers and autographs, of which the discoverer said he was a collector, the country-gentleman exclaimed, "If you are for *autographs,* I am your man; come to my chambers any morning, and rummage among my old deeds; you will find enough of them."' The young man did just that, discovering in a trunk a mortgage deed, written at 'the Globe by Thames' and dated 14 July 1610, with the seal and signature of William Shakespeare.

Mr H., in whose home it was found, preferred to remain anonymous; he made a gift of it to his young visitor and two weeks later, on 16 December, William-Henry gave his father an early

Christmas present. An overjoyed Samuel Ireland took it to the Heralds' Office for authentication, where Francis Webb declared that it bore 'not only the signature of his hand, but the stamp of his soul, and the traits of his genius'. Webb had difficulty deciphering the seals, so Ireland consulted with the economist Frederick Eden. Eden also confirmed the document's authenticity and explained to the Irelands that Shakespeare's seal contained a quintain – a device used to train knights in handling lances – wittily suited to 'Shake-spear'.

Samuel Ireland, along with friends who viewed this deed, hoped that 'wherever it was found, there must undoubtedly be all the manuscripts of Shakespeare so long and vainly sought for', and urged William-Henry to return to the gentleman's house and search more thoroughly. William-Henry did so, and further searches produced a treasure-trove of papers, including a receipt from Shakespeare to his fellow player John Heminges, Shakespeare's own Protestant 'Profession of Faith', an early letter from Shakespeare to Anne Hathaway, a receipt for a private performance before the Earl of Leicester in 1590, an amateurish drawing depicting an actor (possibly of Shakespeare as Bassanio in *The Merchant of Venice*), articles of agreement with the actor John Lowin, a 'Deed of Trust' dating from 1611, and Shakespeare's exchange with the Jacobean printer William Holmes over the financial terms governing the publication of one of his plays (in the end, Shakespeare rejected Holmes's ungenerous offer: 'I do esteem much my play, having taken much care writing of it . . . Therefore I cannot in the least lower my price'). Books with Shakespeare's name and annotations were also discovered, including copies of Thomas Churchyard's *The Worthiness of Wales*, John Carion's Protestant-leaning *Chronicles* and Edmund Spenser's *The Faerie Queene*.

Among the discoveries were a letter to and another from the Earl of Southampton, to whom Shakespeare had dedicated both *Venus and Adonis* and *The Rape of Lucrece*, as well as a note from Queen Elizabeth, signed in her unmistakable hand, thanking

Shakespeare for the 'pretty verses' he had sent her and informing him that 'We shall depart from London to Hampton for the holidays where we shall expect thee with thy best actors that thou mayest play before ourself to amuse us.'

Biographies of Shakespeare would have to be updated and revised. As a column in the newspaper *The Oracle* announcing these remarkable finds made clear, this royal letter in particular showed that previous, anecdotal accounts of Shakespeare's start in the theatre were 'degrading nonsense' and 'utterly fictitious'. The papers revealed a different aspect, a 'new character' of Shakespeare's, one that combined 'an acute and penetrating judgment with a disposition amiable and gentle as his genius was transcendent'.

London's leading men of letters descended on the Ireland household on Norfolk Street, eager to view and verify these extraordinary papers. Among the first were two men knowledgeable in matters

Letter from Queen Elizabeth, from Samuel Ireland, *Miscellaneous Papers*

Shakespearean: the literary critic Joseph Warton and the classics scholar Samuel Parr, who were especially impressed by Shakespeare's 'Profession of Faith': 'Our litany abounds with beauties, but here is a man has distanced us all,' and they, as well as others, congratulated young William-Henry on having afforded 'so much gratification to the literary world'.

An even greater discovery emerged in early February 1795, when William-Henry Ireland's further searches turned up a long-lost manuscript of *King Lear*. The invaluable find confirmed what editors and critics had suspected: Shakespeare's original had been carelessly treated in the playhouse; the printed editions were littered with actors' cuts, interpolations and scurrility. By comparing the manuscript (or transcripts of its now difficult to decipher secretary hand) with printed versions of Lear's final speeches, critics were able to see the great difference between what Shakespeare had originally written:

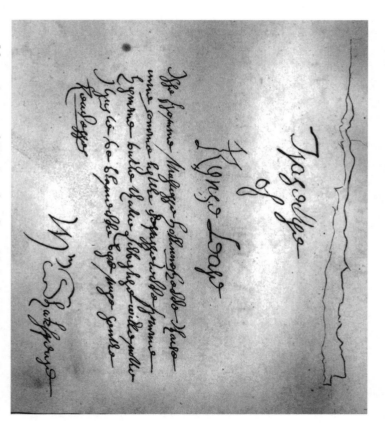

Manuscript page of *King Lear*, from Samuel Ireland, *Miscellaneous Papers*

What is't thou sayst? Her voice was ever soft
And low, sweet music o'er the rippling stream,
Quality rare and excellent in woman.
O yes, by Heavens, 'twas I killed the slave
That did round thy soft neck the murderous
And damned cord entwine. Did I not, sirrah?

and what the actors had done to these lines, as evident in the butchered version that appeared in the edition of the play printed in 1608:

What is't thou sayst? Her voice was ever soft,
Gentle and low, an excellent thing in woman.
I killed the slave that was a-hanging thee.

The excessive cuts made clear why in his 1611 'Deed of Trust' Shakespeare requested that if his plays 'be ever again imprinted', it should be done from his manuscripts and not from the corrupt versions 'now printed'. No less important for understanding the author's intentions was a note on the first page of the *Lear* manuscript, which underscored that Shakespeare wrote not only for the stage but also, if not primarily, for his 'gentle readers'.

The excitement in London's literary community was justifiably great. James Boswell, famous for his *Life of Johnson*, perused the manuscripts and documents in mid-February, then kissed them, kneeled, and declared, 'How happy am I to have lived to the present day of discovery of this glorious treasure. I shall now die in peace.' Boswell went to his grave three months later, having lived to see and hold the manuscript of Shakespeare's great tragedy. The playwright and biographer James Boaden recalled his own excitement: 'I remember that I beheld the papers with the tremor of purest delight – touched the invaluable relics with reverential respect, and deemed even existence dearer, as it gave me so refined a satisfaction.' The press to view the Shakespeare papers was so great that two weeks after Boswell's celebrated visit, Samuel Ireland had to restrict access and even charge an entry fee of two guineas: 'Any gentleman, on sending his address in writing, on being introduced by a subscriber, may view the manuscripts at Number 8, Norfolk Street, on Monday, Wednesday, and Fridays, between the hours of twelve and three.' The Prince of Wales – the future King George IV – invited Samuel Ireland to Carleton House to show him Shakespeare's papers in person. Britain's newspapers and magazines were filled with stories about the discoveries.

Samuel Ireland decided to make transcriptions and even some facsimiles of the papers available in a sumptuous volume, and leading scholars, heralds, dramatists and men of taste testified to their conviction that 'these papers can be no other than the production of Shakespeare himself.' The *Miscellaneous Papers* appeared in print right before Christmas 1795, prefaced by a list of over a hundred prominent subscribers. Contemporaries would have noted, perhaps with a smile, the absence of two names from these lists, the greatest living authorities on Shakespeare's life and work: Edmond Malone and George Steevens. Malone must have been jealous; despite his intense interest in documents in Shakespeare's hand, he had not even deigned to visit the house on Norfolk Street to view the papers. Steevens, too, had not gone to see them, though his reticence may have been more understandable. While his reputation was built upon editing Shakespeare's plays, it had been sullied by his attempt to defraud the public with a forged letter from the Elizabethan playwright George Peele to Christopher Marlowe, a transcription of which he published in the *Theatrical Review* (Steevens had Peele describe how the actor Edward Alleyn teased Shakespeare about borrowing his words in the scene in which Hamlet advises the players).

Shortly after the *Miscellaneous Papers* were published, a tantalising report of new and even more exciting material came to light. William-Henry Ireland informed a committee of twenty-four authorities convened by his father that he had learned of additional finds, including whole or partial manuscripts of *Julius Caesar* and *Richard the Second*, as well as of a hitherto unknown Shakespeare play, *Henry the Second*. A manuscript of another

Shakespearean history, *Vortigern* – drawn from Holinshed's *Chronicles*, on the tumultuous life of Vortigern, the fifth-century ruler of the Britons who fell in love with the Saxon princess Rowena – had also been discovered. The script of *Vortigern* appeared promising enough to restage; a four-hundred-line excerpt circulated and negotiations were begun with the managers of Drury Lane and Covent Garden theatres, both of whom were eager to present the long-lost play. A catalogue of books in Shakespeare's own hand had also been found, along with his annotated copies of Chaucer's *Works*, Holinshed's *Chronicles* and the Bible, a 'deed by which he became partner of the Curtain Theatre', two drawings of the Globe, verses to Elizabeth I, Sir Francis Drake and Walter Ralegh, along with the most tantalising discovery of all: Shakespeare's 'brief account of his life in his own hand'.

It was all a fraud. William-Henry Ireland would eventually confess to having forged every single document (including the old drawing of a young Jacobean man, reproduced at the beginning of this chapter, that he had purchased on Butcher Row and doctored to resemble Shakespeare). The mysterious 'Mr H.' didn't exist. Reports of finding other lost plays or Shakespeare's memoirs were pure fantasy. So too were additional forgeries, including one in which Shakespeare thanks a fellow Elizabethan (coincidentally named William Henry Ireland) for saving him from drowning in the Thames. The remnants of Shakespeare's library, with its forged catalogue listing over a thousand volumes, consisted of rare books that William-Henry found in London's bookstalls and then inscribed with Shakespeare's signature and annotations. To produce authentic-looking documents he purchased bookbinder's ink that looked old and faded, then filched paper and ancient seals from his law office. The random choice of a seal displaying a quintain (hinting at Shakespeare's name) was a happy accident. When he ran out of paper he obtained more from London booksellers who sold him blank endpapers torn out of rare books. His rendering of Shakespeare's signature proved convincing because he had

CONTESTED WILL

traced it from a version that had recently appeared in facsimile in Malone's edition of Shakespeare's works. William-Henry, barely out of his teens, had done it all without an accomplice, and with incredible speed. He had deceived nearly everyone in literary London, including his own father.

His labours sparked what might be called the first Shakespeare authorship controversy, an instructive episode that ought to be better known, for it introduced a set of arguments familiar to anyone acquainted with subsequent disputes over who wrote Shakespeare's plays. Mortified contemporaries should have known better, even as the Irelands themselves should not have fallen for the cock-and-bull story that Mr and Mrs Williams of Clopton House – toying with the expectations of tourists hunting for curios – told them about having recently burned Shakespeare's papers. One reason why the *Miscellaneous Papers* succeeded in duping so many is because the collection read like a documentary life, one that refracted the profile of Shakespeare through the expectations of the time. The good husband, loyal subject, devout Protestant and all-round contemporary man of letters perfectly matched what people hoped to discover about Shakespeare, and established a precedent for future claims about the identity of the author of the plays, which would turn out to be no less grounded in fantasy, anachronism and projection.

Ireland's most notorious attempt at passing his own words off as Shakespeare's – the chronicle history of *Vortigern* – was performed on the London stage on 2 April 1795, on the eve of the exposure of the forgeries. It was a disaster. The most humiliating moment for the Irelands may well have been the ten-minute uproar, much of it consisting of raucous laughter, that followed John Philip Kemble's pointed delivery of the unfortunate line, 'And when this solemn mockery is ended.' Had the Irelands held off on seeing it staged and refrained from publishing 'Shakespeare's papers', the controversy over the documents' authenticity would likely have gone on for years.

[28]

Shakespeare Deified

William-Henry undertook these forgeries not long after the author of *Hamlet* and *Lear* had begun to be regarded as a literary deity, a crucial precondition for this and all subsequent controversies over his identity. It also helps explain why Drury Lane had won out over Covent Garden for the right to stage *Vortigern*, given how heavily invested that playhouse had been in promoting a divine Shakespeare. In April 1794, the newly rebuilt Drury Lane had been rededicated as a 'monument' to Shakespeare, a 'shrine more worthy of his fame we give, / Where unimpaired, his genius still may live'. The opening-night performance of *Macbeth* concluded with an epilogue spoken by the popular actor Elizabeth Farren, who called for the 'Genius of Shakespeare' roaming in the air to spread his 'broad wings' over their 'new reared stage'. As a larger-than-life sculpture of Shakespeare was revealed onstage, Farren proclaimed:

And now the image of our Shakespeare view
And give the Drama's God the honour due.

This divine image of Shakespeare was surrounded by a group of his literary creations along with the Muses of Comedy and Tragedy, and the performers onstage burst into song:

Behold this fair goblet, 'twas carved from the tree,
Which, O my sweet Shakespeare, was planted by thee;
As a relic I kiss it, and bow at the shrine,
What comes from thy hand must be ever divine!
All shall yield to the mulberry-tree.
Bend to thee,
Blest mulberry,
Matchless was he
Who planted thee,
And thou like him immortal be.

Audience members would have known that the 'relic' they were celebrating could be traced back to 'Drama's God' himself – a wooden chalice carved from the famed mulberry tree that the playwright had reportedly planted at New Place, the large house he had purchased in Stratford-upon-Avon. It was the closest thing to a literary Holy Grail. The old tree had been cut down in 1756 by the owner of New Place, who had grown tired of all the souvenir hunters disturbing his peace. A savvy local tradesman named Thomas Sharp saw his chance, bought most of the logs and spent much of the next half-century enriching himself by selling off countless carvings from it, far more than one tree, no matter how miraculous its origins, could ever produce. No one at Drury Lane that evening objected to a spectacle that a former age would have found sacrilegious. The great anti-theatrical preachers of Elizabethan England may have been turning in their graves, but Shakespeare's divinity was now taken for granted.

The process that had led to his deification was a curious one. In his own day Shakespeare was typically equated with rivals, both classical and contemporary. Francis Meres likened him to Ovid, and ranked him with the best of English tragedians and comedians. In his Epistle to *The White Devil* in 1612, John Webster grouped him with Thomas Dekker and Thomas Heywood as one of England's most prolific playwrights, notable for their 'right happy and copious industry'. And when Edmund Howe added a brief account of 'our modern, and present excellent poets', in the fifth edition of John Stow's *Annales* in 1615, Shakespeare's name predictably appears along with those of a score of other distinguished Elizabethan poets and dramatists. Examples could easily be multiplied.

It was only posthumously that Shakespeare was finally unyoked from the company of rivals or mortals. This occurred in the prefatory verses to the collection of his plays put together by fellow actors John Heminges and Henry Condell, who had worked alongside Shakespeare for over twenty years. They published the collected plays in 1623 in a folio edition (and the decision to publish them in a large and costly folio format – in which the printed sheet of paper was only folded once – the equivalent of the modern 'coffee-table' book rather than the paperback-sized and inexpensive quartos or octavos in which plays typically appeared, and in which the printed sheet was refolded to produce a considerably smaller page – was itself an indication of his distinction). Before this, only Ben Jonson had published plays in a folio-sized volume, and he had been mocked for presuming to do so. For Jonson, who contributed a pair of poems to the First Folio in praise of his rival, Shakespeare 'did far outshine' Marlowe, Thomas Kyd and John Lyly (though not, presumably, Jonson himself). But in the same poem, Jonson also recycled a trope he had used so effectively in his 'Ode to Cary and Morison', where the heroic dead live on in the heavenly firmament:

But stay, I see thee in the hemisphere,
Advanced and made a constellation there!
Shine forth thou star of poets.

In a similar vein, James Mabbe wrote that 'We thought thee dead', but like a good actor, Shakespeare has managed to 'die, and live'. For Leonard Digges, it was the works that would prove immortal: 'every line, each verse, / Here shall revive, redeem thee from thy hearse'. Ben Jonson wrote much the same thing:

Thou art a monument, without a tomb,
And art alive still, while thy book doth live.

These are all lovely and probably heartfelt sentiments, but nobody at the time would have mistaken hyperbolic claims about Shakespeare's immortality for anything but a literary device. So too, when in the late seventeenth century John Dryden spoke of Shakespeare's 'sacred name', or 'professed to imitate the divine Shakespeare', his words were never meant to be taken literally.

Yet referring to Shakespeare as divine had become so habitual that by 1728 a sharp-eared foreigner like Voltaire couldn't help but notice that Shakespeare 'is rarely called anything but "divine" in England' – to which Arthur Murphy proudly retorted that 'With us islanders, Shakespeare is a kind of established religion in poetry'.

What had begun as a literary trope became a widely shared conviction after David Garrick mounted a Shakespeare festival – a three-day 'Jubilee' with all its religious overtones – in Stratford-upon-Avon in September 1769, Garrick, who had risen to fame thanks to Shakespeare, had few rivals as a bardolator. By this time he had appeared in a score of Shakespearean roles and had produced many of the plays. Acknowledged in his day for having done much to revive interest in Shakespeare onstage, he would be buried at the foot of Shakespeare's statue in Westminster Abbey, the words on his tomb declaring that 'Shakespeare and Garrick like twin stars shall shine.'

Garrick had even built a temple to Shakespeare on his estate in Hampton on the banks of the Thames. The treasures contained within the octagonal shrine drew admirers from Horace Walpole to the King of Denmark: Roubiliac's statue of Shakespeare (now housed in the British Museum, and for which Garrick himself was almost certainly the model), various carvings from the famed mulberry tree, and even some of Shakespeare's personal effects, including 'an old leather glove, with pointed fingers and blackened metal embroidery', an old dagger and a 'signet ring with W.S. on it'. For detractors like Samuel Foote the heresy was a bit much: Mr. Garrick had 'dedicated a temple to a certain divinity ... before whose shrine frequent libations are made, and on whose altar the fat of venison, a viand grateful to the deity, is seen often to smoke'. Others found nothing strange in this at all.

Even Garrick admitted that the rain-soaked Stratford Jubilee had been a 'folly'. It set him back £2,000 and he never again set foot in Shakespeare's native town. Locals were apparently confused by the Jubilee (including a labourer from Banbury hired to deliver a double-bass viol to the event, who reportedly thought that it was to be used at 'the resurrection of Shakespeare'). Stratford's tourist industry as well as the proliferation of Shakespeare festivals around the world can trace their roots back to that extravaganza. The Jubilee, according to Christian Deelman, the best historian of the event, also 'marks the point at which Shakespeare stopped being regarded as an increasingly popular and admirable dramatist, and became a god'.

By all accounts, its climax was Garrick's recitation of an 'Ode to Shakespeare', a shameless appeal to Shakespeare's divinity:

'Tis he! 'tis he – that demi-god!
Who Avon's flowery margin trod.

In case anyone missed the point, Garrick was happy to repeat it: "'Tis he! 'Tis he! / The god of our idolatry!' One gushing eyewitness wrote afterwards that the audience 'was in raptures'. Garrick avidly promoted mulberry relics, of which he owned a considerable supply, including the very goblet that reappeared as a prop in the Drury Lane celebration of 1794.

Garrick recouped his Stratford losses four times over by restaging a version of the events at Drury Lane, in a play simply called *The Jubilee*. It was a sensation and ran for a record ninety-two nights. His 'Ode' was not only published and circulated widely, but also recited on provincial stages from Canterbury to Birmingham. The Jubilee tapped into larger cultural currents, for no 'other topic in the century inspired quite such a surge of stage plays and poems'. Word spread quickly beyond England's shores, and two Jubilees were held in Germany, modelled on Garrick's. After Garrick's death, William Cowper celebrated him as 'Great Shakespeare's priest', underscoring the ways in which the celebration of Shakespeare was now most fittingly described in religious terms:

For Garrick was a worshipper himself;
He drew the liturgy, and framed the rites
And solemn ceremonial of the day,
And called the world to worship on the banks
Of Avon famed in song.

Contemporary painters were quickly drawn to the idea of a divine Shakespeare, and did much to popularise this conceit. In 1777 Henry Fuseli sketched out plans, much talked of but never

[33]

realised, for a Shakespeare ceiling modelled on that of the Sistine Chapel: even as Michelangelo portrayed the story of Creation, Fuseli would render Shakespeare's creations in his predecessor's style, including characters from *The Tempest*, *Twelfth Night*, *Lear* and *Macbeth*. In his 'Ode' Garrick had described how 'the Passions' wait upon Shakespeare and 'own him for their Lord'; George Romney would capture this image in an exceptional painting – *The Infant Shakespeare Attended by Nature and the Passions* – completed around 1792, reproduced at the beginning of this chapter. As critics have noted, the infant Shakespeare is cast in a pose familiar from Nativity scenes, while Nature and the Passions substitute for the Magi and Shepherds. Other artists picked up on similar themes, depicting, for example, the poet in clouds of glory in 'The Apotheosis of Shakespeare'. By the end of the eighteenth century the idea of a divine Shakespeare had become commonplace. Still, it wasn't as if anyone was paying homage to his image in a house of worship. Another century would pass before that happened.

It was William-Henry Ireland's misfortune to have forged what amounted to divine writ at a time when the first fully-fledged Shakespeare experts, most prominent among them Edmond Malone, had appeared on the scene (though the word 'expert' itself wouldn't enter the vocabulary for another quarter-century). Malone's exposure of the Ireland forgeries struck a nerve: who had the expertise to decide such matters? And what knowledge did such experts possess that well-versed amateurs lacked?

Malone did not weigh in until he had his hands on Samuel Ireland's *Miscellaneous Papers* and was able to examine the documents closely. He obtained a copy of the book immediately after its publication in late 1795 and worked without pause for the next three months. At the end of March 1796 he published *An Inquiry into the Authenticity of Certain Miscellaneous Papers and Legal Instruments . . . Attributed to Shakespeare*. It was an overnight best-seller. His verdict was devastating: the documents and manuscripts were second-rate forgeries and the subscribers dupes. The evidence was damning. Malone demonstrated that the spelling and language of the documents in the possession of the Irelands were wildly at variance with Elizabethan usage. Words that Ireland attributed to Shakespeare weren't in currency until the eighteenth century (one of his most damning examples was the word 'upset', originally a nautical term, not employed in the now familiar sense of 'distressed' or 'troubled' until two centuries after Shakespeare's day). Malone also showed that the dates affixed to many of Ireland's documents were off the mark; Queen Elizabeth's letter addressed to Shakespeare at 'the Globe' in the late 1580s, for example, anticipated the building of that playhouse by over a decade. He also established that surviving autographs of the Earl of Southampton looked nothing like the ones that appeared in the Ireland papers.

Malone's *Inquiry* made clear that those who had examined the manuscript of *Lear* and confirmed its legitimacy had no clue what Elizabethan dramatic manuscripts looked like. Only a few other scholars and editors used to handling old papers were in a position to recognise that these playscripts did not in the least resemble the documents Ireland had forged. And they knew this because they had bought, consulted and borrowed (in Malone's case often refusing to return) as many of these as they could get their hands on. 'I am myself', Malone writes in the *Inquiry*, 'at this moment surrounded with not less than a hundred deeds, letters, and miscellaneous papers, directly or indirectly relating to Shakespeare.'

The handful of dramatic manuscripts that had survived – and few were extant, since there was no need to keep them once a play was printed – were written in a mix of secretary and italic script (in part to distinguish speaking parts from stage directions). Professional dramatists and scribes prepared these documents in a kind of theatrical shorthand, indicating that they were intended for playhouse use rather than for publication. And, unlike Ireland's manuscript of *Lear*, these scripts typically bore the mark of the censor, since a copy would have to pass through the hands of the Master of the Revels, who had to signify on each script his official approval before it could be publicly staged. In contrast to the Ireland forgeries, the Elizabethan manuscripts Malone had at hand weren't written on both sides of the page or 'trimmed' or 'ornamented in any way, but stitched in covers and well embrowned with dust and age'. And unlike Ireland's manuscripts, none included line numbers in the margin.

Yet Ireland succeeded by making the language of his forged texts seem sufficiently strange – in a pseudo-Elizabethan way – to pass as genuine. Among his tricks was omitting all punctuation and then spelling words in a way that seemed old-fashioned, doubling as many consonants as possible and adding a terminal 'e' whenever possible. The prefatory words to *Lear* are typical: 'Iffe fromme masterre Hollinshedde I have inne somme little departedde fromme hymme butte thattte libbertye will notte I truste be blammedde bye mye gentle readerres.'

One reason why the forgeries struck contemporaries as authentic was that their portrait of Elizabethan literary culture felt so familiar. Like a typical eighteenth-century author, Ireland's Shakespeare accumulated a sizeable library, negotiated terms with his publishers and took great care in disposing of what he had written, for it was his property, to do with as he pleased. He was also a writer on familiar terms with members of the elite, as we see in the forged correspondence with the Earl of Southampton (in which Shakespeare refuses half the money that his 'friend' and patron offers) as well as in his exchange with Queen Elizabeth (who attended command performances of his plays at the public playhouses a dozen times 'every season', as eighteenth-century royalty might). What neither the Irelands nor those men of letters who testified to the authenticity of the documents understood was that such conventions and behaviour were almost unimaginable in Shakespeare's day.

These and other anachronisms underscore how irrevocably the nature of authorship had changed since Elizabethan times (though they have changed comparatively little since then, so that we stand much closer to Ireland's contemporaries than they do to Shakespeare's). It wasn't just authorship that had changed, but the most basic social customs as well: one of Ireland's forgeries, a poem Shakespeare addresses to Queen Elizabeth, describes how 'Each titled dame deserts her rolls and tea'. Only Malone seems to have been aware that tea, that quintessential English beverage, was as yet unavailable in England in Shakespeare's day.

Many at the time felt that Malone had engaged in overkill. Had his main target been William-Henry Ireland, that accusation would have been justified. Ireland was quite young, for one thing; for another, it was obvious that he wasn't profiting directly from the forgeries, and, at least at the outset, was motivated by a desperate wish to win a withholding father's approval. Malone, though, had a greater objective than attacking the Irelands, and that was putting in their place amateurs who thought they knew enough about Shakespeare to judge such matters and who on the basis of this authority had declared the forged documents to be authentic. Many chafed at this; a critic in the *St James's Chronicle* spoke for many when he derided Malone's efforts to dominate Shakespeare scholarship as an act of a 'Dictator *perpetuo*'. But Malone had made his point: the Ireland incident had turned out to be a perfect way to distinguish those who knew enough to pass judgement about Shakespeare's authorship from those who didn't. The most enduring lesson of this episode is that some people will persist in believing what they want to believe – in this case that Shakespeare really was the author of the Ireland documents.

As far as Samuel Ireland and his closest supporters were concerned, Malone, who had for so long tried and failed to find the lost Shakespeare archive, was jealous and delusional, convinced that 'everything that belonged to Shakespeare was his own exclusive property'. Others picked up on this point, wondering how Malone or anyone else knew precisely how Shakespeare wrote: 'How are they to be proved not genuine? From conjecture!' From their perspective, the dispute over the authorship of these documents had to end in a standoff; each side had its own story to tell, for 'conjecture may be answered and contradicted by conjecture equally as fair and forcible'. Samuel Ireland questioned Malone's authority in a new book, *An Investigation of Mr Malone's Claim to the Character of Scholar, or Critic*, concluding that Malone's case 'is by no means established by that mode of proof which he has adduced and the arguments he has used'. Did Malone have 'in his possession any of the original manuscripts of Shakespeare, to show the specific usage of the bard?' Lacking that crucial evidence, 'upon what ground does his inference rest?'

Others who remained convinced of the documents' authenticity rallied to the Irelands' cause. For Francis Webb, the fact that all the documents 'reciprocally illustrate and confirm each other' surely trumped Malone's objections: 'Shakespeare's genius, character, life, and situation, connect them all.' 'After frequent inspection and careful perusal of these papers,' Webb concludes, 'duly weighing their claims to my belief, founded on their own evidence, I am not only fully satisfied of their authenticity: but also ... that no human wisdom, cunning, art, or deceit, if they could be united, are equal to the task of such an imposture.'

Some others hedged their bets: while willing to concede that the *Lear* and *Vortigern* manuscripts were probably forged, they maintained that the contemporary deeds and letters were genuine. The critic and scholar George Chalmers was also convinced that some of these documents could not have been faked, especially the letter from Queen Elizabeth thanking Shakespeare for his 'pretty verses'. And there were those who still refused to accept William Henry's confession at face value and hinted darkly at a wider collusion over the authorship of the works – conspiracy theories that implicated Samuel Ireland, Albany Wallis and even George Steevens.

'Like a Deceived Husband'

The story would take another and unexpected turn. Malone prided himself on exposing those who tried to dupe the literary world.

He had even attacked the beloved ninety-one-year-old actor William Macklin for having decades earlier circulated a forged Elizabethan document. Malone felt it his duty to ridicule those so desperate for clues to Shakespeare's personality that they had allowed themselves to be seduced by Ireland's falsehoods. Yet his own desire to imagine what Shakespeare was like proved no less overwhelming. As a scholar he was adept at distinguishing archival fact from biographical fiction; but in accounting for Shakespeare's life he confused the two, and in doing so cleared the way for those following in his footsteps to do the same. While justly celebrated for having resolved one authorship controversy, Malone bears much of the blame for ushering in far more divisive ones.

This occurred not in a bold polemic like the *Inquiry*, but quiet-ly, in his textual annotations, which first appeared in a two-volume 1780 supplement to Samuel Johnson and George Steevens's 1778 edition of *The Plays of Shakespeare*, and then again in his solo edi-tion of Shakespeare's works in 1790. This 1790 edition broke sharply with longstanding traditions going back to the First Folio of 1623 and continuing up through the great eighteenth-century editions of Rowe, Pope, Theobald, Johnson, Capell and Steevens. Malone parted company with his predecessors in two key ways. First, he tried to present the plays chronologically rather than as Heminges and Condell had originally arranged them in 1623, by genre, with no attention to the order in which they were written, under the headings of Comedies, Histories and Tragedies. Secondly, he included Shakespeare's poems alongside the plays; his edition was the first to be called *The Plays and Poems of William Shakespeare*. Today these innovations seem unremarkable but at the time they were unprecedented and would have unforeseen consequences for how Shakespeare's works were read and his life and authorship imagined.

Before the plays could be arranged chronologically the order of their composition needed to be worked out. Nobody had ever done this and it's unclear when anyone first thought it worth doing. In 1709 Nicholas Rowe wondered which was Shakespeare's first play – he couldn't even hazard a guess – but thought it a mistake to assume that Shakespeare necessarily improved over time: 'We are not to look for his beginnings in his least perfect works.' A half-century later, Edward Capell, who was also curious about how Shakespeare had 'commenced a writer for the stage, and in which play', took things a step further, proposing that someone ought to investigate 'the order of the rest of them'. Capell was well aware of how daunting a task this would be, requiring comprehensive knowledge of everything from versification to the printing history of the plays and the sources that Shakespeare drew upon. While Capell himself in his *Notes and Various Readings* broke fresh ground in this field, it would be left to Malone to attempt a full account of the plays' chronology.

Malone made a fair number of mistakes in his *Attempt to Ascertain the Order in Which the Plays of Shakespeare Were Written* in 1778, dating several plays far too early (his claim that *The Winter's Tale* was written in 1594 was off by nearly twenty years) while placing others too late. But after a decade of additional research he was able to fix some of his more glaring errors, and his efforts spurred others to improve upon his chronology. It's next to impossible to arrange plays in their order of composition without seeing a pattern, and the one that Malone believed in superseded the open-minded one offered by Rowe. Citing the authority of Pope and Johnson, Malone offered his readers a more comforting Enlightenment portrait, one in which an industrious Shakespeare steadily 'rose from mediocrity to the summit of excellence; from artless and sometimes uninteresting dialogues, to those unparalleled compositions, which have rendered him the delight and wonder of successive ages'. Malone hastened to add that he wasn't really arguing for 'a regular scale of gradual improvement', only that Shakespeare's 'knowledge increased as he became more conversant with the stage and with life, his performances *in general* were written more happily and with greater art'.

A few – surprisingly few – lines in Shakespeare's plays refer explicitly to contemporary events, such as the allusion in *Henry the Fifth* to the Earl of Essex's Irish campaign in the spring and summer of 1599, which allowed Malone to date that play with considerable precision. They were so few in number that their absence seems to have been a deliberate choice on Shakespeare's part. But once Malone began sifting the plays for allusions to contemporary events and court intrigue, he found many more of them, or thought he did, reinforcing in a circular fashion his account of the plays' chronology. While his primary aim was a working chronology, his sense of what counted as topical allusions, as well as his interpretation of them, led readers to believe that specific political messages were encoded in the plays.

So, for example, when Malone came upon the comic scene in *Antony and Cleopatra* where the Egyptian queen strikes a servant who brings her news of Antony's remarriage, he recalled reading in Elizabethan chronicles that Queen Elizabeth had once boxed the Earl of Essex on the ear for turning his back on her. Malone decided that Shakespeare may have been attempting in this scene to 'censure' Elizabeth – who at this point had been dead for three or four years – 'for her unprincely and unfeminine treatment of the amiable Earl of Essex'. Why stop there? A few scenes later, when the same servant describes to Cleopatra her rival's features, Malone interprets it as 'an evident allusion to Elizabeth's inquiries concerning the person of her rival, Mary Queen of Scots'. There's so much wrong about this it's hard to know where to begin. For one thing, it implies that conversations onstage shouldn't be taken at face value; they are really about something else, if only we could connect the dots and identify that something. For another, why Shakespeare, a member of the King's Men, would want to alienate his monarch by introducing into this scene a discussion of how unattractive James's dead mother, Mary, Queen of Scots, had been is unfathomable, though it didn't give Malone pause.

Reductively identifying topical moments as Malone had, a byproduct of trying to line up the life, works and times, became an easy and tempting game. Malone's obsession with the Earl of

Essex carried over into his interpretation of *Hamlet*. He had read the penitent earl's last words from the scaffold, before Essex was beheaded in 1601 for treason: 'send thy blessed angels, which may receive my soul, and convey it to the joys of heaven'. The dying man's conventional prayer sounded to Malone sufficiently like Horatio's words spoken over the dying Hamlet: 'flights of angels sing thee to thy rest'. Malone suspected that *Hamlet* had been staged before Essex was executed, but even that didn't stop him. So eager was he to suggest that 'Lord Essex's last words were in our author's thoughts' that Malone supposes that the 'the words here given to Horatio may have been one of the many additions to the play'. Are we then to conclude that *Hamlet* is Shakespeare's secret lament for the defeated earl, who, like his play's protagonist, would be king?' This is shoddy criticism and bad editing. Moreover, the history that Malone draws upon in making these topical corres-pondences was limited to chronicles, centred on the court, mostly from the reign of Elizabeth. That's understandable enough: he didn't have access to the kind of gritty social history that's now a bedrock on which our understanding of Shakespeare's drama and culture rests. But it badly skews the plays, turning them into court allegories, in which a Jacobean Shakespeare seems stuck in an Elizabethan past, unable to get out of his mind a slap administered by his queen, in a very different context, many years earlier.

I dwell on this at such length because Malone helped institu-tionalise a methodology that would prove crucial to those who would subsequently deny Shakespeare's authorship of the plays (after all, the argument runs, how would anybody but a court insider know enough to encode all this?). First, however, this approach would influence traditional accounts of the plays, such as George Russell French's *Shakespeareana Genealogica* (1869), which assures us that 'nearly all Shakespeare's *dramatis personae* are intended to have some resemblance to characters in his own day'. Such readings turned the plays into something other than comedies, histories and tragedies: they were now coded works, full of in-jokes and veiled political intrigue for those in the know. And given the great number of characters in Shakespeare's plays and the many things that they say and do, the range of topical and biographical applications was nearly limitless. I don't think that Malone really thought this through – he was just trying to bolster a shaky chronology and show off his knowledge of Elizabethan culture. But in doing so he carelessly left open a fire door.

The problems with Malone's topical assumptions pale in comparison with those precipitated by his biographical ones. Until Malone had established a working chronology of Shakespeare's plays, no critic or biographer had ever thought to interpret Shakespeare's works through events in his life. About the closest anyone had come to reading the plays biographically was suggesting that Shakespeare had modelled comic characters such as Falstaff and Dogberry on local folk he had known. But such claims were never meant to reveal anything about Shakespeare's character, other than perhaps suggesting that he had a bit of a vindictive streak.

Where earlier eighteenth-century editors such as Nicholas Rowe and Alexander Pope had prefaced the plays with a brief and anecdotal 'Life', Malone chose to fuse life and works through extended notes that appeared at the bottom of each page of text. So, for example, when Malone first discovered in the Stratford archives that Shakespeare's son Hamnet had died in 1596, he thought it likely that Constance's 'pathetic lamentations' about the loss of her son Arthur in *King John* (which Malone dated to this same year) were inspired by Shakespeare's own recent loss. Perhaps they were. Perhaps the play had been written before Shakespeare learned of his son's death. Perhaps he waited until composing *Hamlet* to unpack his heart. Or perhaps Shakespeare had been thinking of something else entirely when he wrote these lines. We'll never know.

Malone's argument presupposed that in writing his plays Shakespeare mined his own emotional life in transparent ways, and for that matter, that Shakespeare responded to life's surprises much as Malone and people in his own immediate circle would have. So that for Malone, Shakespeare was not the kind of man who could suffer such a loss without finding an outlet for his grief in his work: 'That a man of such sensibility, and of so amiable a disposition, should have lost his only son, who had attained the age of twelve years, without being greatly affected by it, will not be easily credited.' There was no corroborating evidence in any case to confirm or refute Shakespeare's amiability (an anachronistic term, not used in this sense until the mid-eighteenth century), how hard the death of his son hit him, and how or even whether he transmuted loss into art. Indeed, there was no effort to consider that even as literary culture had changed radically since early modern times, so too had a myriad of social customs, religious life, childhood, marriage, family dynamics and, cumulatively, the experience of inwardness. The greatest anachronism of all was in assuming that people have always experienced the world the same way we ourselves do, that Shakespeare's internal, emotional life was modern.

Malone's decision to include the Sonnets and other poems alongside the plays proved even more consequential. As Margreta de Grazia has eloquently put it,

Malone's pursuit from the externally observed to the inwardly felt or experienced marked more than a new type of consideration: it signalled an important shift in how Shakespeare was read. Shakespeare was cast not as the detached dramatist who observed human nature but as the engaged poet who observed himself.

Nowhere was this revised portrait of the artist more apparent than in the notes Malone first appended to the opening lines of 'Sonnet 93' in 1780, which set the direction of Shakespeare biography – and debates over authorship – on a new and irreversible course.

'Sonnet 93' begins with its speaker comparing himself to a familiar type, the cuckolded spouse: 'So shall I live, supposing thou art true, / Like a deceived husband.' There's nothing especially difficult in the meaning of these opening lines that warrants an explanation; Malone's interest in providing an explanatory note was solely biographical. To this end, he collapses the very real distinction between the elusive persona of the speaker and Shakespeare himself (for we have no idea to what extent Shakespeare is writing out of his own experience or simply imagining a situation involving two fictional characters). By doing so, Malone gives himself licence to treat the sonnet as something that gave him direct and unmediated access into Shakespeare's emotional life.

Malone tried to justify his novel approach by explaining that he had come across a manuscript of the biographer William Oldys, who had written that these lines 'seem to have been addressed by Shakespeare to his beautiful wife on some suspicion of her infidelity'. That's not actually something that Oldys had uncovered in some now lost papers. Oldys's manuscript notes on Shakespeare, now housed in the British Library, are almost all dryly factual and bibliographic, except for one stray and gossipy remark that 'Shakespeare's poem called *A Lover's Affection* seems to be written to his beautiful wife under some rumour of inconstancy'. Oldys was clearly misled by the title under which 'Sonnet 93' had appeared in John Benson's 1640 edition of the Sonnets: 'A Lover's Affection though his Love Prove Unconstant'. Seizing on this hint, though knowing it's the only one like it in Oldys's notes, Malone wondered whether 'in the course of his researches' Oldys had 'learned this particular' about Shakespeare's marriage – intimating that there was some archival underpinning here, though it's obvious to even a casual reader of his notes that Oldys couldn't be less interested in Shakespeare's marriage or inner life. Malone then offers a few scraps of supporting evidence, including that contested will in which Shakespeare had chosen his daughter Susanna as his executor and had further slighted his wife by bequeathing her 'only an old piece of furniture'. Early biographers were so disturbed by what they interpreted as Shakespeare's graceless decision to leave his widow a 'second best bed' that when reprinting the document some silently emended the phrase to 'brown best bed'.

Malone found further evidence of Shakespeare's jealous resentment of his wife – expressed in the will and confirmed in 'Sonnet 93' – in several of the dramatic works, for 'jealousy is the principal hinge of *four* of his plays', especially *Othello*, where 'some of the passages are written with such exquisite feeling, as might lead us to suspect that the author had himself been *perplexed* with doubts, though not perhaps in the *extreme*'. A mistaken identification of the Sonnets' author with their speakers, a strained reading of a poem's opening lines and a fundamental misunderstanding of the conventions of early modern wills, confirmed, if further confirmation were needed, by what occurred in play after play, added up for Malone to a convincing case.

Knowing that his account crossed a boundary, one that had been strictly observed by every previous editor and critic of Shakespeare's plays, Malone retreated a half-step, admitting that the case was built on 'an uncertain foundation' and explaining that all he meant 'to say is, that he appears to me to have written more immediately from the heart on the subject of jealousy, than on any other; and it is therefore not improbable that he might have felt it'. Recognising that this semi-retraction didn't go quite far enough, he added: 'The whole is mere conjecture.' But he refused to reword or remove what he had written.

As noted earlier, Malone's annotations appeared in an edition of Shakespeare's *Works* edited by George Steevens. Steevens, an established scholar, had warmly welcomed the younger Malone into the world of Shakespeare editing three years earlier, even as Dr Johnson had welcomed him; but when he read Malone's note to 'Sonnet 93', he insisted on adding a rejoinder. Steevens knew and feared where this kind of speculation could lead. It was a very slippery slope, with conjecture piled upon conjecture. He too had consulted Oldys's notes and saw through Malone's ploy, insisting that whether 'the wife of our author was beautiful or otherwise was a circumstance beyond the investigation of Oldys'. Steevens added that whether 'our poet was jealous of this lady is likewise an unwarrantable conjecture'. Steevens was especially offended by

Malone's reductive view that just because one of Shakespeare's characters experienced something, the poet must have felt it too: 'That Shakespeare has written with his utmost power on the subject of jealousy is no proof that he ever felt it.' For if this were so, given the nearly limitless range of Shakespeare's characters, it would be possible to claim virtually anything and everything about Shakespeare's own feelings. Because Timon of Athens hates the world, Steevens asked, does it follow that Shakespeare himself 'was a cynic or a wretch deserted by his friends'? And because Shakespeare so vividly conveys the 'vindictive cruelty of Shylock', he added, driving the point home, 'are we to suppose he copied from a fiend-like original in his own bosom?'

Steevens was unforgiving. He recognised that Shakespeare scholarship stood at a crossroads, foresaw that once Malone pried open this Pandora's box it could never be shut again. He would not have been surprised to learn that two centuries later a leading scholar would write (and a major university press publish) a book called *Shylock Is Shakespeare* that answered his rhetorical question in the affirmative. Steevens's response to the kind of biographical flights of fancy Malone was both engaged in and inviting could not have been clearer:

As all that is known with any degree of certainty concerning Shakespeare is – that he was born at Stratford upon Avon – married and had children there – went to London, where he commenced actor, and wrote poems and plays – returned to Stratford, made his will, died, and was buried – *I must confess my readiness to combat every unfounded supposition respecting the particular occurrences of his life.*

Malone, more comfortable criticising others than being taken to task himself, was stung by Steevens's response. Steevens was clearly threatened by his upstart collaborator and now rival, and the wounds opened in this latest exchange would never heal. When Steevens died in 1800, Malone didn't even attend his funeral and continued to harp on the 'incessant malignity and animosity' that Steevens had directed at his annotations years earlier.

An overlong note to 'Sonnet 93' got longer still when Malone again insisted that the works described what Shakespeare himself had gone through: 'Every author who writes on a variety of topics will have sometimes occasion to describe what he has himself felt.' He then turned on Steevens for imagining that Shakespeare could have shared Timon's cynicism, let alone 'the depravity of a murderer'. To argue this 'would be to form an idea of him contradicted by the whole tenor of his character'. Since Malone knew what Shakespeare's character was like, he had no difficulty identifying which of his dramatic creations embodied it.

The unprofitable game of profiling what could or couldn't be true of Shakespeare's character, based on what his characters said or did, had begun. So too had the baseless tradition that Shakespeare was unhappily married. Trying to extricate himself from charges that this was idle speculation, Malone further entangled himself in the intricacies of Shakespeare's love-life. While willing to concede that 'it does not necessarily follow that because he was inattentive to her in his Will, he was therefore jealous of her', Malone didn't believe that Anne Hathaway was good enough for Shakespeare: 'He might not have loved her; and perhaps she might not have deserved his affection.' Malone was a bachelor when he wrote these words – in fact, he would never marry, though he wanted to (he seems to have wooed far too aggressively, and two years after this edition appeared would write to a woman he had wanted to marry but who had rejected him, words that echo his sentiments here: 'How, my dear,' he complained, 'have I deserved that you should treat me with such marked unkindness?'). Malone's biographical note to 'Sonnet 93' thus introduced yet another centrepiece of modern Shakespearean biography: the tendency to confuse the biographical with the autobiographical, as writers projected onto a largely blank Shakespearean slate their own personalities and preoccupations.

Malone, who had trained as a lawyer, was, unsurprisingly, convinced that Shakespeare too had legal training, and 'not merely such as might be acquired by the casual observation of even his all-comprehending mind'. Malone even suspected that Shakespeare 'was employed, while he yet remained at Stratford, in the office of some country attorney'. The evidence? Not anecdotal reports, which claimed that he had been a butcher or a schoolteacher, but rather internal evidence from the plays, most notably *Hamlet*. Malone was uncomfortable enough with this line of argument to add that Shakespeare 'may be proved to have been equally conversant with the terms of divinity or physic'. If others could come along and show that Shakespeare knew as much about religion or medicine as he did about the law, Malone concluded, then 'what has been stated will certainly not be entitled to any weight'.

Underlying his reasoning here was the presumption that Shakespeare could only write about what he had felt or done rather than heard about, read about, borrowed from other writers or imagined. The floodgates were now open and others would soon urge, based on their own slanted reading of the plays, that Shakespeare must have been a mariner, a soldier, a courtier, a countess and so on. By assuming that Shakespeare had to have experienced something to write about it with such accuracy and force, Malone also, unwittingly, allowed for the opposite to be true: expertise in the self-revealing works that the scant biographical record couldn't support – his knowledge of falconry for example, or of seamanship, foreign lands or the ways that the ruling class behaved – should disqualify Shakespeare as the author of the plays.

Yet another precondition for challenging Shakespeare's authorship had now been established, one that would be trotted out more often than all the others combined. From now on, consensus would be impossible, and writing the life of the author of Shakespeare's works a game that anyone with enough ingenuity and conviction could play. When desire outpaced what scholars could turn up, there remained only a few ways forward: forgery, reliance on anecdote, or turning to the works for fresh evidence about the author's life. The impulse to interpret the plays and poems as autobiographical was a direct result of the failure to recover enough facts to allow anyone to write a satisfying cradle-to-grave life of Shakespeare.

Malone's commentary on 'Sonnet 93' was a defining moment in the history not only of Shakespeare studies but also of literary biography in general. What has emerged in our own time as a dominant form of life writing can trace its lineage back to this extended footnote. While the sixteenth and seventeenth centuries had seen a handful of literary biographies, the genre didn't come into its own until the eighteenth century, spurred by an intense interest in life writing, swept along not only by a torrent of biographies and memoirs, but also by great collaborative efforts such as the multi-volume *Biographia Britannica* of 1747–66. The *Biographia Britannica* marked a conceptual leap forward, recognising that accurate biographies could act as a check on self-interested memoirs:

the work before us becomes both a supplement and a key, not only to our general histories, but to particular memoirs, so that by comparing the characters of great men, as drawn by particular pens, with their articles in this *Biographical Dictionary*, we see how far they are consistent with, or repugnant to, truth.

William Oldys was one of the principal contributors to the *Biographia Britannica*. He was possessed of a prodigious memory, an obsession with uncovering biographical facts and a familiarity with the many archives where he might find them. He'd sort his notes into separate parchment bags, one for each biographical subject. His patience and tenacity were rewarded by many biographical discoveries, and he went on to write the lives of over a score of major figures, including William Caxton, Michael Drayton, Richard Hakluyt, Edward Alleyn and Aphra Behn. Oldys was content with just the facts and unearthed a great many of them. But facts alone were not enough to breathe life into his subjects. Writers like James Boswell (in his *Life of Johnson*) and Dr Johnson himself, who relied heavily on the *Biographia Britannica* (which covered a majority of the poets treated in his four-volume *Lives of* the *Most Eminent English Poets*), understood this, and went on to redefine how lives were written and read.

Yet even Dr Johnson drew the line at reading individual poems or plays autobiographically. Though deeply interested in writers' lives, he understood well enough that authorial and personal identity were not one and the same, and he refused to collapse the two. In fact, he went out of his way to ridicule those who did so, as he makes clear in his life of James Thomson. Johnson had read that an earlier Thomson biographer (probably Patrick Murdoch) had carelessly 'remarked, that an author's life is best read in the works' – and pointed out the folly of such a claim. He recalled how the author Richard Savage (friend to both Thomson and Johnson himself) had once told him 'how he heard a lady remarking that she could gather from [Thomson's] works three parts of his character, that he was a *great Lover, a great Swimmer, and rigorously abstinent*. Savage set the record straight: the lady's reading of *The Seasons* as autobiographical was wrong on all three counts – Thomson was not the kind of devoted lover she imagined, was 'never in cold water in his life', and 'indulges himself in all the luxury that comes within his reach'. So much for reading backwards from the works.

Johnson was even wary of using letters as evidence, mocking the notion that 'nothing is inverted, nothing distorted' in writers' correspondence, and he made little use of them in his biographies. He was no less distrustful of so-called autobiographical poetry, sidestepping the confessional verse of Milton, Otway, Swift and Pope, and saying in reference to the latter that 'Poets do not always express their own thoughts', and notes, as an example of this, that for all Pope's 'labour in the praise of music', he was 'ignorant of its principles, and insensible of its effects'.

With Malone's decision to parse the plays for evidence of what an author thought or felt, literary biography had crossed a Rubicon. Fictional works had become a legitimate source for biographies, and Shakespeare's plays and poems crucial to establishing this new approach. In 1790 Malone had announced that his long-promised life of Shakespeare was well along; he had already 'obtained at very different times' a great deal of material, though 'it is necessarily dispersed'. At 'some future time', though, he would 'weave the whole into one uniform and connected narrative'. He still had faith that Shakespeare's commonplace book or personal correspondence would surface, which would enable him to flesh out the many lost years and mysteries of the life. As late as 1807, five years before his death, Malone was still reassuring friends that only a third of the *Life* 'remained to be written', that 'all the materials for it are ready', and that he even had £300 worth of paper 'lying ready at the printing house', to save time when it was ready to be published. It had taken Malone fewer than ninety days to write and publish a four-hundred-page book about the Ireland forgeries. Yet after decades of labour, his *Life of Shakespeare* remained unfinished, a puzzle still lacking most of its largest pieces. Even the works failed to supply the missing evidence. When James Boswell the Younger was given the unenviable task of gathering the disjointed remains and moulding them into a *Life* after Malone's death, he saw soon enough that he was faced not with some tidying up of loose ends but with a 'chasm'.

Those who write about the history of Shakespeare studies cast Malone as an early hero and Ireland as one of the first villains of the story. I've been trained to think this way too and it's difficult getting beyond it. It's easy to see why: Malone, much like the scholars who tell his story, spent much of his life surrounded by old books and manuscripts, strained his vision poring over documents in archives, and struggled to complete his life work on Shakespeare. Ireland cheated, took a short-cut. But in truth, they were in pursuit of the same goal – which may account for the viciousness of Malone's attack on his young rival. Both were committed to rewriting Shakespeare's life; one forged documents, the other forged connections between the life and the works. In retrospect, the damage done by Malone was far greater and longer-lasting. He was the first Shakespearean to believe that his hard-earned expertise gave him the right, which he and many scholars have since tried to deny to others, to search Shakespeare's plays for clues to his personal life. By the time that Boswell brought out an updated edition of Malone's *Shakespeare's Plays and Poems* in 1821, it was already 'generally admitted that the poet speaks in his own person' in the Sonnets.

Malone had failed in his decades-long quest because every thread leading directly back to Shakespeare's interior life had been severed. Most likely each had been cut for well over a century. Sufficient materials for a comprehensive biography were no longer available. One possibility is that Shakespeare went out of his way to ensure that posterity would find a cold trail. In any case, expectations about what evidence might reasonably have survived were wildly inflated. There may well have been bundles of letters, theatrical documents and even a commonplace book or two that outlived Shakespeare, but if so they have never been found and the extinction of the family line by the end of the seventeenth century and the sale and subsequent demolition of Shakespeare's home, New Place, helped ensure their disappearance.

Then again, if one goes through Francis Meres's list of the best English dramatists in 1598 one quickly discovers that commonplace books and early drafts of published plays don't survive for *any* of these popular Elizabethan playwrights. The memorials best befitting Shakespeare's stature and accomplishments were in fact created and preserved by those who honoured his legacy: a monument and a gravestone in Stratford's church; and, seven years after his death, a lavish collection of his plays, prefaced by commendatory verses and his portrait. At the time, no English playwright had ever been posthumously honoured with such a collection. Clearly, this was the way his fellow players thought fitting, and sufficient, to remember Shakespeare.

Shakespeare had no Boswell – but neither did Marlowe, Jonson, Webster or any other contemporary dramatist. While there had been 'Lives', there were not as yet full-length literary biographies. For that reason it's especially unfortunate that one of the earliest efforts in this genre – *The Lives of the Poets, Foreign and Modern* – doesn't survive. It was written (or at least contemplated) by Shakespeare's fellow dramatist Thomas Heywood, and had been mentioned in 1614 and then again in 1635; but it was either left incomplete, lost or never published.

Assuredly, there had to have been witnesses to Shakespeare's daily life, including boy actors born before the turn of the century who may have lived until the 1670s or 1680s, and who had acted for the King's Men and worked with Shakespeare before he retired from the company around 1614. Immediate family members, had they been interviewed, might also have cast considerable light on his personality. Shakespeare's sister Joan lived until 1646. His elder daughter Susanna died in 1649 and his younger one, Judith, was still alive in 1662; a local vicar with an interest in Shakespeare made a note to seek her out and ask her about her father, but she died before this conversation could take place. Nobody thought to seek out Shakespeare's granddaughter Elizabeth, who was eight years old when Shakespeare died; she was the only one of his four grandchildren to live past the age of twenty-one or wed, but she bore no children in her two marriages and the family line ended with her death in 1670.

There were family friends and in-laws, too, who might have been questioned, including Thomas Combe, to whom Shakespeare bequeathed his sword and who lived until 1657. Stratford neighbour Richard Quiney was alive until 1656. His son, Shakespeare's son-in-law Thomas Quiney, who married Judith, lived until 1663. Both men knew him well. So did Shakespeare's brother-in-law Thomas Hathaway, who could have been questioned until the mid-1650s. Shakespeare's nephew William, his namesake, became a professional actor in London and may have been privy to wonderful theatrical anecdotes; he died in 1639.

One of the most tantalising lost connections to Shakespeare's personal life was through his son-in-law John Hall, who married Susanna in 1607. The two men seem to have been close: Hall had travelled with Shakespeare to London and had been appointed by him as co-executor of his will. Hall was a prominent physician in Stratford who kept notes in abbreviated Latin on those he treated. After Hall's death, Dr James Cooke sought out his widow about Hall's books, and Susanna was willing to sell him some (he called on her at New Place, which she and her husband had inherited). Cooke's interests were medical rather than literary, so he apparently did not ask Susanna about her father or *his* books – and he subsequently published a translation of one of Hall's medical notebooks. Among the patients Hall treated was Shakespeare's fellow playwright, the Warwickshire native Michael Drayton. Unfortunately, Hall's other notebook was lost before its contents could be transcribed or printed and unless it turns up some day we will never know whether it contained any information about his father-in-law.

There's one more story about Hall and Shakespeare, less well known than it ought to be, though James Orchard Halliwell-Phillipps reported it over a century ago. On 22 June 1616, two months after his father-in-law died, John Hall paid a visit to the registry of the Archbishop of Canterbury, located near St Paul's in London, to prove Shakespeare's will. Among the documents he produced was 'an inventory of the testator's possessions. Whatever valuable books, manuscripts or letters Shakespeare owned and was bequeathing to his heirs would have been listed in this inventory rather than in the will itself (which explains, as Jonathan Bate has observed, why the surviving wills of such Elizabethan notables as the leading theologian Richard Hooker and the poet Samuel Daniel fail, like Shakespeare's, to list any books at all). Had the inventory that John Hall brought with him to London survived – or if by some miracle it ever surfaces – it would finally silence those who, misunderstanding the conventions of Elizabethan wills and inventories, continue to insist that Shakespeare of Stratford didn't own any books and was probably illiterate.

By the time those in search of Shakespeare finally made the pilgrimage to Stratford in the mid-seventeenth century, led by

Thomas Betterton, John Aubrey and Thomas Fuller, all that remained were secondhand anecdotes. We've learned from these that Shakespeare had apprenticed as a butcher. That he drank heavily. That he poached deer. That he didn't enjoy carousing and wasn't a company keeper. That he died of a fever after a bout of drinking with Ben Jonson and Michael Drayton. That he died a Catholic.

The eighteenth-century editor Edward Capell was the first to recognise that a biography about Shakespeare's private life – rather than his public and professional one – was a lost cause: 'those who alone had it in their power' to record what Shakespeare was like had failed to do so. Further efforts to unravel the mystery of Shakespeare were pointless: 'our enquiries about them now must prove vain', and 'the occurrences of this most interesting life (we mean, the private ones) are irrevocably lost to us'. The search may have been over for Capell, but for others it was just beginning.

'With This Key'

In his own day, and for over a century and a half after his death, nobody treated Shakespeare's works as autobiographical. But after Malone did so a mad dash was on, and by the 1830s it seemed like nearly everyone was busy searching for clues to Shakespeare's life in the works. The Sonnets, long ignored, suddenly became popular. Unlike Shakespeare's other major poems – *Venus and Adonis* and *Lucrece* – the Sonnets had never been reissued during Shakespeare's lifetime, and there are surprisingly few allusions to them following their publication in 1609. In 1640 they were finally reprinted by John Benson, who cropped the prefatory material, changed the gender of pronouns where he saw fit, invented titles and freely rearranged and combined 146 of the 154 sonnets into seventy-two or so longer poems, then mingled Shakespeare's poems with those of others falsely attributed to him in the 1612 edition of *The Passionate Pilgrim*. But even these modifications failed to generate much

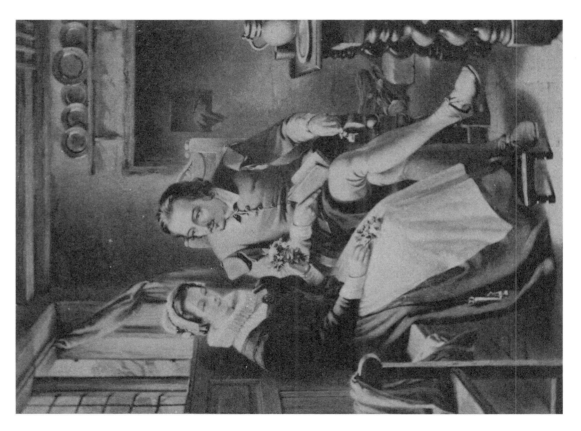

Shakespeare and Anne Hathaway, unknown artist, c.1860.

interest in this outdated genre, and while Shakespeare's plays went through four Folios in the course of the seventeenth century, the Sonnets remained largely inaccessible to new generations of readers. When available, it was almost exclusively in Benson's version – a situation that remained unchanged until Malone published them in his Supplement as they had first appeared. If Steevens thought that he could squelch Malone's autobiographical approach by excluding the Sonnets from his next Shakespeare edition in 1793, he was wrong. Still, he tried his best, declaring 'the strongest act of Parliament that could be framed, would fail to compel readers into their service'. 'Had Shakespeare produced no other works than these,' Steevens added, 'his name would have reached us with as little celebrity as time has conferred on that of Thomas Watson, an older and much more elegant sonneteer.'

German critics were among the first to seize on the potential of Malone's approach. August Wilhelm von Schlegel took the English to task in his Viennese lectures of 1808 for never having 'thought of availing themselves of [Shakespeare's] Sonnets for tracing the circumstances and sentiments of the poet' and for failing to recognise that they contained the 'confessions of his youthful errors'. His equally famous brother Friedrich von Schlegel seconded and extended this view: 'It is strange but delightful to scrutinise, in his short effusions, the character of Shakespeare.' Heinrich Heine would confirm that the Sonnets are 'authentic records of the circumstances of Shakespeare's life'.

William Wordsworth soon spread the word that in the Sonnets, 'Shakespeare expresses his own feelings in his own person.' He made this point more memorably in his poem 'Scorn not the Sonnet' where he writes, 'with this key, Shakespeare unlocked his heart'. Wordsworth saw no contradiction between his belief that these Elizabethan poems were thoroughly autobiographical and his admission that he had held off publishing his own autobiographical poem, *The Prelude*, because it was 'a thing unprecedented in literary history that a man should talk so much about himself'. He had found a Romantic precursor in this newly minted Shakespeare.

Others scrambled aboard. A contributor to *Blackwood's Magazine* confidently claimed in 1818 that the Sonnets are 'invaluable, beyond any thing else of Shakespeare's poetry, because they give us little notices, and occasional glimpses of our own kindred feelings, and of some of the most interesting events and situations of his life'. A long piece on the Sonnets in *New Monthly Magazine* in 1835 – 'The Confessions of William Shakespeare' – took things a step further, calling the Sonnets 'personal confessions' and breathlessly describing their triangular love-plots. Who could resist such voyeuristic pleasures? With the Sonnets, 'we seem to stand by the door of the confessional, and listen to the most secret secrets of the heart of Shakespeare'.

Word spread to America, where Emerson, in his influential *Representative Men* (1850), wondered: 'Who ever read the volume of the Sonnets without finding that the poet had there revealed, under masks that are no masks to the intelligent, the lore of friendship and of love?' By the mid-nineteenth century, the critical heavyweights on both sides of the Atlantic – the Schlegels, Wordsworth, Coleridge, Heine and Emerson – had all embraced the position first suggested by Malone. According to John Keats's close friend Charles Armitage Brown, author of *Shakespeare's Autobiographical Poems* (1838), the Sonnets were 'pure uninterrupted biography'. The Bard's life was now an open book.

A handful of dissenters struggled, with little success, to challenge this new consensus. Thomas Campbell complained in 1829 that the Sonnets were 'insignificant as an index' to Shakespeare's biography, and rejected the argument that 'they unequivocally paint his passions, and the true character of his sentiments'. He tried again a few years later, this time more bluntly: 'Shakespeare's sonnets give us no access to his personal history.' His words fell on deaf ears, as did Robert Browning's rebuttal of Wordsworth's 'Scorn Not the Sonnet':

> *With this same key*
> *Shakespeare unlocked his heart*," once more!'
> Did Shakespeare? If so, the less Shakespeare he!

By 1856, the battle was all but over. As David Masson put it in that year, 'Criticism seems now pretty conclusively to have determined . . . that the Sonnets of Shakespeare are, and can possibly be, nothing else than a poetical record of his own feelings and experience.' There was no longer any doubt that the poems 'are autobiographic – distinctly intensely, painfully autobiographic'.

Once critics began reading the Sonnets as confessional, they began to turn their attention to the unnamed shadowy figures alluded to in the poems on the assumption that Shakespeare had actual people in mind when the various speakers of the Sonnets complained about dark ladies, young men and rival poets. George Chalmers, an enemy of Malone and a believer in the Ireland forgeries, got this biographical competition off to a strong start by arguing in 1797 that *all* the Sonnets had been addressed to Queen Elizabeth herself. Countless others soon went about uncovering the identity of the 'only begetter' of the Sonnets, the mysterious 'W.H.'; at least they had initials to go by, and the dedication apparently had a real, if elusive, individual in mind.

Malone himself was among the earliest to hazard a guess as to the identity of that 'better spirit' of 'Sonnet 80', the talented literary rival 'to whom even Shakespeare acknowledges himself inferior'. Malone concluded that it had to be Edmund Spenser, and to support this claim devoted over a third of his unfinished biography of Shakespeare to the relationship of the two poets. George Chalmers, who could never bring himself to agree with Malone, did so this time. Others weren't so sure, and placed bets on Samuel Daniel, Michael Drayton, George Chapman, Christopher Marlowe, Ben Jonson and a host of others. Another insisted that they were all wrong: surely Chaucer was the great rival Shakespeare had in mind.

The lists of Elizabethan Dark Ladies, Young Men, and those with the initials W.H., H.W., W.S., or some similar combination were even longer. The parlour game that began with Malone is still avidly played, with hardly a year going by without another fresh name trotted out. It would take pages to list them all, the equivalent of an Elizabethan census. The most innocent and metaphorical utterances of the fictive speakers of Shakespeare's poems were interpreted as biographical fact. Was Shakespeare syphilitic, as hinted at in 'Sonnet 144'? Did the author of 'Sonnet

37' (which speaks of being 'made lame by Fortune's dearest spite') walk with a limp? Did Shakespeare hate prostituting his talents onstage, as Malone claimed he confessed in 'Sonnet 111'? Who needed to wrestle with the Sonnets' dense language, when it was possible to make one's literary reputation unlocking the biographical secrets they contained?

By the mid-nineteenth century, the obsession with autobiographical titbits had all but displaced interest in the aesthetic pleasures of the poems themselves. Wordsworth had famously described the Sonnets as a 'key'. Coleridge suggested that one of the poems (probably 'Sonnet 20', the most explicitly homoerotic) was a 'purposed blind'. Emerson spoke of these poems as 'masks that are no masks to the intelligent'. And following the invention of the telegraph and Morse code, a new and ominous metaphor was introduced to describe the way in which Shakespeare deliberately concealed autobiographical traces: for Robert Willmott, writing in 1858, the 'Sonnets are a chapter of autobiography, although remaining in cipher till criticism finds the key'.

The best contemporary explanation I have come across for this frenzy of biographical detection – and it is worth quoting at length – is offered by Anna Jameson, in her *Memoirs of the Loves of the Poets*, published in 1829. Jameson was at least honest about her motives, admitting that it's 'natural to feel an intense and insatiable curiosity relative to great men, a curiosity and interest for which nothing can be too minute, too personal'. Yet the few facts of Shakespeare's life left her hungry for more:

I felt no gratification, no thankfulness to those whose industry had raked up the very few particulars which can be known. It is too much, and it is not enough: it disappoints us in one point of view – it is superfluous in another: what need to surround with the common-place, trivial associations, registers of wills and genealogies, and I know not what.

Missing was the only thing that really mattered: that which could connect us to 'a presence and a power . . . diffused through all time, and ruling the heart and the fancy with an incontrollable and universal sway!' The desire to feel that presence, experience a sense of intimacy with Shakespeare, was not going to go away simply because not enough facts about his personal life were known. It was easier for critics who shared that desire to make stuff up rather than admit defeat.

Soon enough, what started with the Sonnets migrated to the plays, though the claim that Shakespeare was speaking for himself through his dramatic characters was more difficult to sustain. John Keats was among the first to do when he wrote that Shakespeare's 'days were not more happy than Hamlet's, who is perhaps more like Shakespeare himself in his common everyday life than any other of his characters'. It was but a short step from here to Keats's self-identification with both Hamlet and Shakespeare: 'Hamlet's heart was full of such misery as mine is when he said to Ophelia, "Go to a nunnery, go, go!"' Coleridge made the case more simply and directly: 'I have a smack of Hamlet myself, if I may say so.' Over-identification on the part of Shakespeare's biographers had mutated into an over-identification on the part of his readers.

Critics began identifying moments when Shakespeare accidentally slips out of writing in character and into self-revealing auto-biography. Coleridge, for example, was sure that this was the case with Capulet's lines in *Romeo and Juliet*:

Such comfort as do lusty young men feel
When well-appareled April on the heel
Of limping winter treads, even such delight
Among fresh female buds shall you this night
Inherit at my house.

(1.2.26–30)

'Other passages more happy in illustrating this', he adds, 'might be adduced where the poet forgets the character and speaks in his own person.' Coleridge was also the first to suggest that Prospero, the great image of artistic authority in the nineteenth century, 'seems a portrait of the bard himself' – a claim that would echo, with increasing volume, through the rest of the nineteenth century.

Coleridge was also the first to take the ultimate biographical leap: reading the trajectory of the entire canon of Shakespeare's plays as a story of the poet's psychological development. For as Coleridge himself recognised, he was 'inclined to pursue a psychological, rather than a historical, mode of reasoning' (and in doing so, was not only the first to use this new term 'psychological' in its modern sense, but also one of the first to engage in psychobiography). In February 1819, Coleridge sketched out before an audience at the Crown and Anchor Tavern on the Strand his theory of the five eras of Shakespeare's creative life, scrambling the established chronology of the canon to suit this more psychologically compelling biographical narrative. According to Coleridge, Shakespeare began with the late romances (*Pericles, The Winter's Tale, Cymbeline*) as well as a few of the comedies (*Comedy of Errors, A Midsummer Night's Dream* and, surprisingly, *All's Well*), then worked through the history plays, before arriving at his major era in which he 'gives all the graces and facilities of a genius in full possession and habit of power' – and this mixed group includes *The Tempest, As You Like It, The Merchant of Venice* and *Twelfth Night*. In the end, a triumphant Shakespeare climbs to the 'summit', the great run of tragedies, *Lear, Hamlet, Macbeth* and *Othello*. Following this great climb is the inevitable descent, 'when the energies of intellect in the cycle of genius were though in a rich and potenziated form becoming predominant over passion and creative self-modification' – and to this final stage of Shakespeare's career Coleridge consigns *Measure for Measure*, as well as most of the classical and Roman plays: *Timon of Athens, Coriolanus, Julius Caesar, Antony and Cleopatra and Troilus and Cressida.*

Others would modify or build upon this model, including Henry Hallam, who in 1837 turned this into a more melodramatic story: 'There seems to have been a period of Shakespeare's life when his heart was ill at ease, and ill content with the world or his own conscience.' As 'the memory of hours misspent, the pang of affection misplaced or unrequited . . . sank down into the depths of his great mind', they 'seem not only to have inspired into it the character of Lear and Timon, but that of one primary character, the censurer of mankind' – a version of Shakespeare's self which is projected through a series of characters, from Jaques in *As You Like It*, up through Hamlet, Lear and Timon.

It wasn't long before an autobiographical canon-within-a-canon had emerged, with a half-dozen works attracting almost all the attention of those wishing to trace the life in the works, from Shakespeare as lover in *Romeo and Juliet* and the Sonnets, to the brooding, depressed and misunderstood Jaques, Timon, Lear and especially Hamlet of Shakespeare in the depths, to the triumphant and serene artist, Prospero, whose decision to break his staff and abandon his art prefigures Shakespeare's own retirement to Stratford. It was a great story and would have a long half-life, even if it didn't leave much room for characters or plays that couldn't be shoehorned into this plot, so that *Titus Andronicus*, *Pericles*, *The Comedy of Errors* and a couple of dozen others were left largely untouched by biographical speculators. Scholarship had stumbled off course the moment that Malone used 'Sonnet 93' to introduce conjectural readings of both life and work, and the Romantics who followed in Malone's errant footsteps rapidly and irrevocably transformed how Shakespeare's poems and plays would be read.

Only one thing could have arrested all of this biographical specu-lation: admitting that a surprising number of the plays we call Shakespeare's were written collaboratively. For there's no easy way to argue that a co-authored play, especially one in which it's hard to untangle who wrote which part, can be read autobiographical-ly. The problem of collaboration has bedevilled Shakespeare stud-ies for over three hundred years, ever since the editors of the second impression of the Third Folio, published in 1664, added seven plays to the thirty-six included in the First and Second Folios of Shakespeare's collected works: *Pericles*, *The London Prodigal*, *The History of Thomas Lord Cromwell*, *Sir John Oldcastle*, *The Puritan Widow*, *A Yorkshire Tragedy* and *The Tragedy of*

Locrine. Though some readers may have believed that these plays didn't feel Shakespearean, there was corroborative evidence for at least some of them on the title pages of quarto editions published during Shakespeare's lifetime.

Things got even messier when editors began to question Shakespeare's authorship of some of the plays that Heminges and Condell had published under his name, and his name only, in 1623. The first to do so was the Restoration dramatist Edward Ravenscroft, who in his 1678 adaptation of Shakespeare's *Titus Andronicus* wrote that he had 'been told by some anciently conversant with the stage, that it was not originally his, but brought by a private author to be acted, and he only gave some master-touches to one or two of the principal parts or characters'. When the poet Alexander Pope brought out a major edition of Shakespeare's plays in 1725, he rejected as spurious all seven of the plays that had been added to the Third and Fourth Folios – and admitted to doubts even about some of the canonical plays: 'I should conjecture of some of the others (particularly *Love's Labour's Lost*, even *The Winter's Tale*, *Comedy of Errors*, and *Titus Andronicus*), that only some characters, single scenes, or perhaps a few particular passages were of his hand.' Pope concluded that these plays long attributed to Shakespeare 'were pieces produced by unknown authors'; posterity had assigned these bastard offspring to Shakespeare much 'as they give strays to the Lord of the manor'.

For a while, at least, the canon continued to shrink. Lewis Theobald questioned the legitimacy of *Henry the Fifth* in 1734. Thomas Hanmer did the same with *Two Gentlemen of Verona* in 1743. Two years later Samuel Johnson deemed *Richard the Second* suspect and soon after Richard Farmer rejected *The Taming of the Shrew*. The *Second* and *Third Part of Henry the Sixth* were challenged as well, with some, like Capell, excusing them (and *King John*) as 'first drafts', while others, like Bishop Warburton, urged that they be excluded from the canon. While editors at this time knew from the title pages of a handful of mostly Jacobean plays that some non-Shakespearean drama had been jointly written, the thought never seems to have occurred to them that Shakespeare could have willingly collaborated with other playwrights. Disputed plays, then, were either in or out, Shakespeare's or someone else's.

Malone, like every other editor in his day, was keenly interested in authorship and attribution. He published a dissertation in 1787 on the *Henry the Sixth* plays in which he concluded that the early versions of these plays that survive in quarto – *The Contention* and *The True Tragedy* – were probably written by Robert Greene and George Peele respectively. Committed to examining the disputed plays in a thorough way, he edited and republished for the first time the seven disputed plays appended to the Third Folio. His objective was to distinguish the counterfeit from the real Shakespeare: 'Though nearly a century-and-a-half have elapsed since the death of Shakespeare, it is somewhat extraordinary, that none of his general editors should have attempted to separate his genuine poetical compositions from the spurious performances with which they have been so long intermixed.' The works were mixtures then, not compounds, easily separated into what was Shakespeare's and what was not. Inclusion in the canon should be based on a principle of how much could be deemed Shakespearean. *Pericles* was included, since 'if not the whole, at least the greater part of that drama was written by our author', while on similar grounds, *Titus* was definitely out, since Malone didn't believe a single line of it to be Shakespeare's.

Malone stood head and shoulders above his predecessors in his response to the challenge posed by disputed plays – at least until 1790, the year he published his first solo edition of Shakespeare's works. For in that year, just as he was submitting final pages to the press, the greatest discovery ever made about the Elizabethan stage fell into his hands: the records of Philip Henslowe, owner of the Rose Theatre. Henslowe's *Diary* contained almost everything we now know about the staging of plays in Shakespeare's day: how frequently the repertory changed, how many plays a company bought and performed every year, how much was spent on costumes, even how long it took to write a play. It was an amazing document, and nobody knew it better than Malone, into whose hands it was delivered from Dulwich College, where it had been discovered. The most significant revelation contained within the *Diary* concerned the collaborative nature of Elizabethan playwriting, at least for the rivals of Shakespeare's company, the Admiral's Men, for the overwhelming majority of plays were co-authored, by two, three, four or more playwrights working together.

Malone excitedly turned its pages looking for evidence that might cast light on the disputed plays that had been attributed to Shakespeare – and was delighted to see that his hunch that *Oldcastle* was not by Shakespeare had been right: the Dulwich papers proved that it was 'the joint production of four other poets' – Michael Drayton, Anthony Munday, Richard Hathway and Robert Wilson. Malone was now in sole possession of evidence that could extend to Shakespeare the possibility of joint authorship. But he couldn't bring himself to change his mind about Shakespeare's singularity, free himself from the fantasy that the plays were easily separated mixtures, not compounded on occasion by a pair or more of talented writers working together, one of whom was Shakespeare. Malone even imagined that if a similar 'account book of Mr Heminge shall be discovered, we shall probably find in it – "Paid to William Shakespeare for mending *Titus Andronicus*."'

Even when confronted with the overwhelming evidence from Henslowe's *Diary*, Malone couldn't break the habit of seeing plays composed by one playwright, then subsequently mended or repaired by another, and so concludes: 'To alter, new-model, and improve the unsuccessful dramas of preceding writers, was I believe, much more common in the time of Shakespeare than is generally supposed.' It followed then, that *Pericles* was 'new modelled by our poet' rather than jointly composed. By the same logic, the *Second* and *Third Part of Henry the Sixth* are 'new-modelled' and 'rewritten' by Shakespeare. Malone hastily appended some excerpts from Henslowe's *Diary* as his 1790 edition was at the press. But he had not had a chance to really digest the implications of this find for his understanding of how Shakespeare collaborated, and never seems to have done so.

I have been hard on Malone in these pages, perhaps unduly so. But I find his inability to step back and see how Henslowe's *Diary* might have altered his thinking about authorship deeply frustrating. Malone was clearly committed to a vision of Shakespeare as an Enlightenment figure, always working toward improving, perfecting, the unsuccessful efforts of others — a Mozart to the Salieris of the theatrical world. But what was truly unforgivable was that Malone made sure that nobody else had a chance to read the *Diary* and offer an alternative account of the stage and of how Shakespeare himself might have written. He not only refused to share the *Diary*, he wouldn't even return it to Dulwich. Only after his death many years later would his literary executor find these materials among his papers and return them to their rightful owner — minus a number of literary autographs, which Malone had cut out.

A great opportunity was lost. Malone should have known better about collaboration. In fact, he was actively engaged at just this time in an intense collaborative writing project, helping Boswell write and revise his *Life of Johnson*, busily refining the prose, altering the tone, eliminating Scotticisms and so on, going back and forth on a daily basis, in close company with his needy friend. Yet he somehow couldn't imagine Shakespeare and Thomas Middleton working closely like this on *Timon of Athens*, or Shakespeare actively collaborating with Fletcher on *Henry the Eighth*, *Cardenio* and *The Two Noble Kinsmen*.

The likeliest explanation for Malone's refusal to consider the possibility that Shakespeare worked in similar ways — through 'joint production' or 'in concert' with other writers, to use his own terms — is that such a view could not be reconciled with his conviction that Shakespeare's works were autobiographical and that Shakespeare himself, if not divine, was at least singular, so much so that a good editor should be able to separate the dross of lesser mortals from Shakespearean gold. By the time that Henslowe's *Diary* was finally viewed by others – it was eventually transcribed and published by John Payne Collier in 1845 – it was too late. By that point, the notion that Shakespeare was autobiographical, singular and divine was indelibly imprinted on readers and theatregoers. Just how hardened this view became by the mid-nineteenth century is clear when a writer like Henry Tyrrell, in *The Doubtful Plays of Shakespere*, can reject a collaborative ascription on the grounds that 'It is not probable that the great Shakespeare, the acknowledged poet of the age, the friend of nobles, and the pet of princes, should have united with a dramatist of third-rate reputation.' Joseph C. Hart, one of the earliest to doubt Shakespeare's authorship of the plays, was similarly influenced by the evidence offered in the 'old Diary' (which he believed in 1848 to have been 'discovered but a few years ago'). Based on his reading of the *Diary*, Hart concluded that some of the plays attributed to Shakespeare must have been collaborative – but that Shakespeare could therefore have had no hand in them. The critical tradition that extends from Malone through Tyrrell and Hart persists to this day, and the conviction that Shakespeare was a solitary writer whose life can therefore be found in his works cannot comfortably accommodate the overwhelming evidence of co-authorship.

Moneylender and Malt Dealer

The hunt for information about Shakespeare's life didn't end with Malone. Others soon followed up on his suggestions about where to look for fresh biographical details – so successfully, that in the decades following Malone's death more new facts about Shakespeare's life were discovered than ever before or since. The first were located in Stratford-upon-Avon by a local antiquarian who had time on his hands and the inexhaustible patience to pore through so many old records. R. B. Wheler was rewarded for his efforts with four significant discoveries. Two concerned complicated and profitable real-estate transactions: the unexecuted counterpart of the conveyance of the old Stratford freehold to Shakespeare by William and John Combe in 1602; and a record of Shakespeare's purchase three years later of half a leasehold interest in a parcel of tithes in Stratford for the huge sum of £440 (what an Elizabethan schoolteacher could expect to earn in a lifetime).

Wheler also uncovered a pair of writs, documents noted earlier, that cast light on Shakespeare's moneylending. In 1609, in pursuit of a comparatively minor debt, Shakespeare had John Addenbrooke, a Stratford neighbour, arrested after failing to repay £6 and demanded an additional twenty-six shillings in damages. Addenbrooke was released upon providing a surety. A jury was probably empanelled and a verdict was reached in Shakespeare's favour, since, when payment was still not made, a second writ was issued by the Stratford Court of Record – this time against Addenbrooke's surety, Thomas Horneby, a local blacksmith, who was now responsible for both debt and damages. We don't know more than this. Why Shakespeare was so eager to prosecute neighbours over a loan is not known, but it was not the kind of story that pleased his admirers – and coupled with the belated publication of that undelivered letter discovered by Malone decades earlier, in which Richard Quiney asked Shakespeare for a £30 loan, a case was building that Shakespeare cared more about cash than art.

The pressure to find the right biographical materials – documents that reinforced rather than undermined what people wanted to believe about Shakespeare – led to new fakes and forgeries, including, in 1811, Richard Fenton's anonymously published *Tour in Quest of Genealogy* in which he describes purchasing at an auction in southwest Wales some books and a manuscript that had been in the possession of 'an eccentric and mysterious stranger'. The purchase turned out to include 'a curious journal of Shakespeare, an account of many of his plays, and memoirs of his life by himself'. One of Shakespeare's journal entries answered the question that had long puzzled those who wondered how a young man from rural Stratford could have mastered foreign languages and was familiar with leading Italian authors:

Having an earnest desire to lerne foraine tongues, it was mie goode happ to have in my father's howse an Italian, one Girolamo Albergi, tho he went by the name of Francesco Manzini, a dyer of wool; but he was not what he wished to pass for; he had the breeding of a gentilman, and was a righte sounde scholar. It was he who taught me the little Italian I know, and rubbed up my Latin; we read Bandello's Novells together, from the which I gathered some delicious flowers to stick in mie dramatick poseys.

It may have been taken as a jest by knowing readers at the time – but excerpts were still being republished as fact as late as 1853.

It came as a considerable relief to Shakespeare's admirers when in the 1830s the ambitious young researcher John Payne Collier began publishing pamphlets outlining a series of biographical finds, drawn especially from a new and untapped source: the papers of Sir Thomas Egerton, a well-placed Elizabethan official who had served as Solicitor General as well as Lord Keeper of the Great Seal to Elizabeth I, and then as Lord High Chancellor to James I. Collier had become friends with Egerton's descendant, Lord Francis Egerton, who then employed him to publish a catalogue of the ancestral holdings. Collier's first pamphlet, *New Facts Regarding the Life of Shakespeare* (1835), offered twenty-one new documents related to Shakespeare's life, nine of them from this collection.

At long last, someone had discovered something having to do with Shakespeare's life in London. Collier's most exciting find was a certificate listing Shakespeare as a shareholder in Burbage's company at the Blackfriars Theatre as early as 1589. The problem of the 'Lost Years' was half-solved – so much for the old canard, beloved even by Samuel Johnson, that Shakespeare had spent the late 1580s holding horses for gentlemen playgoers outside the theatre. Collier's discoveries also pulled back the veil on Shakespeare's final years in London. By then, another document revealed, Shakespeare's stake in the Blackfriars Theatre had grown to over £1,400, a monumental sum. Another great find was a warrant from King James, dated January 1610, appointing Shakespeare and three others to train 'a convenient number of children who shall be called the Children of her Majesties Revels' in the art of 'playing Tragedies, Comedies &c.' As exciting as these documents were, they were also somewhat impersonal. The same could not be said for the letter in an elegant hand, signed H.S. – most likely the Earl of Southampton – asking that Egerton 'be good to the poor players of the Blackfriars', and mentioning in passing 'two of the chief of the company' – Burbage and Shakespeare – the latter 'my especial friend, till of late an actor . . . and writer of some of our best English plays which as your Lordship knoweth were most singularly liked of Queen Elizabeth.' The letter also contains a lovely detail: Burbage is praised as 'one who fitteth the action to the word and the word to the action most admirably' – clearly echoing *Hamlet*.

Collier worked rapidly, publishing the finds as fast as they came to hand, following up his first pamphlet with *New Particulars Regarding the Works of Shakespeare* in 1836 and three years later with *Further Particulars Regarding Shakespeare and His Works*. The former contained transcriptions of an eyewitness account of contemporary performances of *Macbeth*, *Cymbeline* and *The Winter's Tale* by the famous Elizabethan astrologer and physician Simon Forman. Collier also found a document confirming that *Othello* had been performed before Queen Elizabeth in 1602 (which overturned Malone's late dating of the play), a letter by fellow poet Samuel Daniel indirectly alluding to Shakespeare, and a tax record indicating that Shakespeare resided in Southwark as late as 1609. A workhorse, Collier even found the time to publish Henslowe's papers and *Diary*, discovering an allusion there to 'Mr Shakespeare of the Globe' that Malone had overlooked.

Collier's many discoveries in the 1830s and 1840s provided a counterweight to a documentary base weighted too heavily toward Stratford and financial preoccupations. While Shakespeare's personal life remained a mystery, evidence of his theatrical career, both early and late, as well as evidence of some of his more important relationships with fellow writers and actors, had been greatly enhanced. Almost overnight – and we will soon see why this proved disastrous – these findings found their way into what seemed like an endless stream of popular biographies of Shakespeare. Eager to claim credit, Collier decided to write the great Shakespeare biography of his day. In the early 1840s he offered a preview of this 'Life' as part of a planned new edition of Shakespeare's works. This edition included even more recent discoveries made in the Stratford archives, including the notes of the Stratford Town Clerk, Thomas Greene, on Shakespeare's freehold of unenclosed fields in 1614, as well as the document showing that Shakespeare's household had hoarded malt in 1598, during a period of dearth in Warwickshire.

The 1830s and 1840s were boom years for historical and antiquarian societies committed to researching England's past. The Hakluyt Society began disseminating English travel narratives; the Parker Society, religious texts; the Camden Society and Percy Society literary ones. In 1840, Collier, along with twenty or so others, founded a Shakespeare Society, dedicated to 'the purpose of collecting materials, or of circulating information, by which [Shakespeare] may be thoroughly understood and fully appreciated', drawing on materials 'in private hands and among family papers, of the very existence of which the possessors are not at present aware'. Three of the leading members were also Collier's rivals as biographers of Shakespeare: Alexander Dyce, Charles Knight and James Orchard Halliwell-Phillipps. All three knew how deeply they were indebted to Collier's finds, especially Halliwell-Phillipps, who chose as the frontispiece for his first biography, *The Life of William Shakespeare*, published in 1848, a facsimile of the letter found by Collier in which 'H.S.' pays tribute to Shakespeare as his 'especial friend'.

But it wasn't long before these competitors began to question some of Collier's discoveries. To charge someone with forgery was a sensitive business, and it wouldn't be easy proving the case against so prominent a figure. Dyce was the first to do so in print in his *Memoir of Shakespeare* (1832). Knight expressed his scepticism a decade or so later in his *William Shakespeare: A Biography* (1843). Halliwell-Phillipps chose to publish his *Observations on the Shaksperian Forgeries at Bridgewater House* privately, in 1853. For Halliwell-Phillipps, this was an especially delicate matter, as he himself had been accused of tampering with and then reselling manuscripts from Trinity College, Cambridge in his younger days — and even of stealing and disfiguring one of the two extant copies of the First Quarto of *Hamlet*.

By now the word was out. Collier was an incredibly skilled forger. How much had he faked? Some of his finds, such as Forman's playgoing accounts, were without question genuine. Yet Collier had handled virtually every key document in Stratford as well as London and Dulwich, indeed had got to many of them first, making it next to impossible to determine whether he had added materials to otherwise genuine documents (and, in fact, he had). Every Collier discovery had to be suspected – and scholars would spend decades going over every biographical claim he had advanced. As a rule of thumb, the claims that Collier made regarding Shakespeare of Stratford, or Shakespeare's business transactions, were true; those having to do with Blackfriars, or Southampton, or the Globe, or in fact anything to do with Shakespeare's creative life were fabricated, especially all that rubbish about Shakespeare's early affiliation with Blackfriars, yet one more effort to satisfy the bottomless need to provide the evidence, now all but lost, of Shakespeare's early years and professional associations. The rest – and there are many other finds – are genuine. Collier had discovered more documents about Shakespeare than anyone before or since; they just weren't the ones he had hoped to find. Those, he made up.

Collier hadn't left much to discover, and most of the remaining scraps were just what researchers least hoped to find. Joseph Hunter learned that Shakespeare defaulted in 1598 on taxes of thirteen shillings four pence, while Halliwell-Phillipps discovered that Shakespeare had taken the apothecary Philip Rogers to court in 1604 for repayment of twenty bushels of malt as well as a small sum. Apparently, Rogers, who had many mouths to feed and was often in debt, had only paid back six shillings on a bill of £2.

Much was made of Shakespeare's dealings in malt, revealing how little Victorians understood about daily life in late sixteenth-century Warwickshire. When viewed through a nineteenth-century lens, Shakespeare's financial activities made him appear to be a rapacious businessman. The hoarding of malt is a particularly good example of what's lost when actions are severed from their cultural contexts. For in late sixteenth-century Stratford-upon-Avon, where malting was the town's principal industry, anybody with a bit of spare change and a barn was storing as much grain as possible. Shakespeare's holdings were about average; a dozen men, including the local schoolmaster, had stored more. When local officials protested at restrictions made on their hoarding malt, they explained that 'our town hath no other special trade, having there-by only time beyond man's memory lived by exercising the same, our houses fitted to no other use, many servants among us hired only to that purpose'. Their defence was self-serving, but it was also true. In addition, it's likely that a good many of the local records concerning Shakespeare's business activities in Stratford were actually the affair of his wife, Anne Hathaway, who would have been responsible (though as her husband, Shakespeare would have been officially involved in cases going to court). This is not to exonerate the Shakespeares for hoarding malt while impoverished Warwickshire neighbours starved. It is to say that biographical information needs to be understood within its immediate context, not through the bias of another cultural moment. If Shakespeare was a 'grain merchant', as some now began to call him, what man or woman from the middling classes in Stratford wasn't?

Halliwell-Phillipps, more than any of his predecessors, had a knack for finding uninspiring facts about Shakespeare's business dealings, including an assignment of an interest in a lease of tithes from Ralph Huband to Shakespeare in 1605, records of

Shakespeare's involvement in land enclosure in Welcombe in 1614, and a pair of letters by Stratford neighbours that mentioned Shakespeare in connection with other financial dealings. Things hit rock bottom when Halliwell-Phillipps came upon yet another lawsuit, brought by a William Shakespeare in 1600 in the Court of the Queen's Bench against John Clayton; he had lent Clayton £7 in May 1592 and now wanted his money back.

Scholars still can't agree whether this was our Shakespeare and not another who sued Clayton; whether or not it was, it fitted the pattern of a tight-fisted Shylock all too well. There would be a few more dramatic discoveries made in the early twentieth century – including information about Shakespeare's life in a Huguenot household on Silver Street in London in the early years of the seventeenth century (a story wonderfully told in Charles Nicholl's *The Lodger*) – but as matters stood in the 1850s, a biography so heavily weighted to financial dealings profoundly influenced how Shakespeare's life was imagined. Halliwell-Phillipps conceded as much in the most influential biography of the age: 'It must be admitted that nothing whatever has yet presented itself, which discloses those finer traits of thought and action we are sure must have pervaded the author of *Lear* and *Hamlet* in his communication with the more cultivated of his contemporaries.' In the absence of such disclosures, it was best to accept what the evidence does confirm, that Shakespeare was 'a prudent man of the world, actively engaged in the promotion of his fortune, and intent on the foundation and preservation to his posterity of the estates he had won by his writings'.

Halliwell-Phillipps knew how hard this would be to swallow, how it would 'tend to destroy the finely drawn appreciation of Shakespeare's life, which owes its existence to the fiction of later days'. But he chose not to emphasise that all we could *expect* to find at this late date were legal records, rather than more personal ones, so that too much weight should not be placed on quite partial evidence. Unlike his fellow biographers, Halliwell-Phillipps wasn't in the least uncomfortable with his portrayal of his subject as preoccupied with money; that was precisely how he himself experienced the world of the professional writer, and it's telling that late in life he compiled a list of ways in which he was just like Shakespeare. Once again, biography and autobiography were not easily untangled.

Halliwell-Phillipps's verdict was that no doubt 'can exist in the mind of any impartial critic, that the great dramatist most carefully attended to his worldly interests; and confirmations of this opinion may be produced from numerous early sources'. Alexander Dyce put matters even more bluntly in his biography: 'from his earliest days' Shakespeare's 'grand object' was 'the acquisition of a fortune which was to enable him eventually to settle himself as a gentleman in Stratford'. By 1857, when Dyce wrote these words, an unbearable tension had developed between Shakespeare the poet and Shakespeare the businessman; between the London playwright and the Stratford haggler; between Shakespeare as Prospero and Shakespeare as Shylock; between the kind of man revealed in the autobiographical poems and plays, and the one revealed in tax, court and real-estate records; between a deified Shakespeare and a depressingly mundane one. Surely he was either one or the other. Less than a century had passed since Dr Johnson, who would have found the very idea of having to choose between these alternatives ludicrous, had said that 'No man but a blockhead ever wrote, except for money.' The writing life may not have changed much, but assumptions about it certainly had.

A tipping point had been reached; it was only a matter of time before someone would come along and suggest that we were dealing not with one man, but two. An essay called 'Who Wrote Shakespeare?' appeared in 1852 in *Chambers's Edinburgh Journal*. Surveying the field, its anonymous author acknowledged the obvious: 'Is it more difficult to suppose that Shakespeare was not the author of the poetry ascribed to him, than to account for the fact that there is nothing in the recorded or traditionary life of Shakespeare which in any way connects the poet with the man?'

[77]

The biographical facts reveal only a 'cautious calculating man careless of fame and intent only on money-making', while the 'unsurpassed brilliancy of the writer throws not one single spark to make noticeable the quiet uniform mediocrity of the man.' Nothing connects this Shakespeare to *Hamlet*, 'except the simple fact of his selling the poems and realizing the proceeds, and their being afterwards published with his name attached'. We are left, the anonymous author concludes, with equally unhappy alternatives: either Shakespeare employed a poet who wrote the plays for him, or the plays were miraculously conceived, with Shakespeare resorting to a cave to receive by 'divine afflatus' the sacred text.

Homer, Jesus and the Higher Criticism

Back in 1794, even as Londoners were honoring 'Drama's God' at Drury Lane, a German scholar at the University of Halle was completing a book that would forever cast doubt on the authorship – even the existence – of an even greater literary divinity, Homer. The publication of Friedrich August Wolf's *Prolegomena ad Homerum* in 1795 sent shock waves through the world of classical studies and well beyond. Wolf argued that the oral composition of the *Iliad* and *Odyssey* could be traced as far back as 950 BC, well before the Greeks were acquainted with literary writing (though Wolf proved to be wrong about this detail). Close philological analysis showed that these long poems could not have been the unchanged words of an ancient bard, preserved and transmitted orally from generation to generation for four hundred years. It was no longer possible, though, to recover exactly when the *Iliad* and *Odyssey* arrived at their final form or the identity of those involved in their composition and revision. According to Wolf, if there had been a Homer, he was no more than an illiterate and 'simple singer of heroic lays'. The conventional biography of Homer – accepted almost without question from Herodotus and Aristotle on down through the Renaissance – was suddenly and permanently overthrown. As Emerson put it a half-century later, 'From Wolf's attack upon the authenticity of the Homeric poems dates a new epoch of learning.' Authorship would never be the same.

Admittedly, there had been rumblings about Homer going back to antiquity, when Josephus had claimed, without citing any evidence, that Homer was illiterate. More widespread scepticism began in earnest in the late seventeenth century, when the French critic François Hédelin attacked the *Iliad*'s bad style, morality and inconsistencies; citing 'ancient reports of Homer's illiteracy', he concluded that 'there had never been such a person as Homer, and the *Iliad* and *Odyssey* were the patchwork creations of a later and incompetent editor'. Giambattista Vico expressed similar doubts in 1730: 'Homer was the best poet ever, but he never existed.' In England, Robert Wood added that 'the Greek alphabet was a late invention', and that Homer's works had only reached their current form because of the 'deliberate intervention of learned collectors, after centuries of oral transmission as separate ballads'. It was clear what conditions had made the Homeric authorship controversy possible; according to Thomas Blackwell, the Greeks had come 'to persuade themselves that a mind so vast could not belong to a man; that so much knowledge could only flow from a heavenly source; and having once firmly settled his Apotheosis in their own minds, they wanted next that everything about him should appear supernatural and divine'.

What set Wolf's book apart – and made it one of the landmark works of modern scholarship – was not his conclusion, already shared by others, but the philological and historical method by means of which he explored how texts were transmitted over time, a method that would have profound implications for other fields of intellectual enquiry and other revered books and authors. Eighteenth-century readers were not quite ready to accept the conclusion, as one recent classicist has put it, that Homer was no more than 'a discursive effect, the function of institutional apparatuses and practices that developed over time'. Yet these unnerving postmodern implications of Wolf's work were grasped early on by critics like Friedrich Nietzsche, who addressed the problem directly in his inaugural lecture at Basel in 1869, when he asked, regarding Homer: 'has a person been made out of a concept' or 'a concept out of a person?'

Scholars were soon confronted with a troubling set of questions (which would be dusted off and asked of Shakespeare a half-century later). Why were there no surviving contemporary references to so great a poet as Homer? Was 'Homer' a pseudonym? Could authorship be determined by means of internal evidence and consistency (in other words, was there an identifiable style that transcended textual irregularities)? What now was the status of other poems long attributed to Homer, such as *The Battle of the Frogs and Mice* and *The Homeric Hymns*? And why were those with a professional investment in the traditional view of Homeric authorship so resistant to new ways of thinking about these issues?

Controversial theories of authorship were proposed, including one by the English novelist Samuel Butler, author of *Erewhon* and *The Way of All Flesh*, and a trained classicist. Butler, arguably the most autobiographical writer of his day, read the *Odyssey* as a fundamentally autobiographical poem. The Phaeacian episode convinced him that the poem had to have been written by a young and strong-willed Sicilian woman who drew on her own experience – and he published *The Authoress of the Odyssey* in support of this claim. Butler also saw what the Homeric controversy meant for Shakespeare: 'Who would have thought of attacking Shakespeare's existence – for if Shakespeare did not write his plays he is no longer Shakespeare – unless men's minds had been unsettled by Wolf's virtual denial of Homer's?' It was not an isolated view. One of Benjamin Disraeli's characters in his 1837 novel *Venetia* had already wondered: 'And who is Shakespeare? We know of him as much as we do of Homer. Did he write half the plays attributed to him? Did he ever write a single whole play? I doubt it.'

Predictably, Romantic writers drawn to Shakespeare's story were also captivated by Wolf's new theory about Homer. But they

SHAKESPEARE

had to overlook its focus on collaborative authorship, which undermined their conception of artistic creation as the product of solitary and autonomous genius. Coleridge carefully marked up his copy of Wolf, while 'Friedrich Schlegel took it as the model for his own studies in Greek poetry, and his brother August Wilhelm popularised it in his lectures.' Thomas de Quincey wrote three essays on the Homeric question for *Blackwood's* in 1841, not long after he wrestled with the problem of Shakespeare's biography, wondering how 'such a man's history' could have 'so soon and so utterly have been obliterated'. It's difficult today to register how deeply Wolf's arguments unsettled nineteenth-century readers. One last example must suffice: Elizabeth Barrett Browning's *Aurora Leigh* (1856), where Aurora denounces the work of that 'kissing Judas, Wolf'. For Aurora,

Wolf's an atheist;
And if the Iliad fell out, as he says,
By mere fortuitous concourse of old songs,
Conclude as much too for the universe.

When poets hurl around accusations of 'atheist' and 'kissing Judas', it's clear that far more is threatened by Wolf's method than the authorship of a pair of ancient Greek poems.

The battle over Homer's identity, though no longer the struggle it once was, continues to this day. Classicists now have a better understanding of how oral poetry was transmitted; almost all accept that there was no Homer in the traditional sense which readers for over two thousand years had imagined. Happily, since nobody was advancing alternative candidates from ancient Greece – what contemporary rival, after all, could even be named? – there wasn't anything to fuel an authorship controversy, and the problem was more or less ignored; the less said, the better. Still, there are those who refuse to give up on the traditional story, including E. V. Rieu, who translated the Penguin paperback that introduces so many readers to the *Iliad*. Rieu warns there that 'It will astonish people who know nothing of the "Homeric question" to learn

[81]

that these splendidly constructed poems, and especially the *Iliad*, have in the past been picked to pieces' by scholars who argue that 'the *Iliad* is the composite product of a number of poets of varying merit'. Rieu will have none of it, reassuring readers that poems with such 'consistency in character-drawing' could only have been written by one man.

As groundbreaking as Wolf's book proved to be, his method wasn't original. It derived, most immediately, not from work done by other classicists, but from the latest in Biblical scholarship, which had been an especially rich field of intellectual enquiry since the Reformation. Post-Reformation theologians skilled in Semitic languages, familiar with a long tradition of Jewish textual scholarship and attuned to historical changes, recognised that the Old Testament was a very complicated text. Over a century or so, close textual analysis, as well as a richer understanding of the transmission of Scripture, called into question the idea that the words derived in unadulterated form from Moses himself. Some of the finest minds of the sixteenth and seventeenth centuries had addressed the historical problems posed by Biblical texts and laid the foundations for the radical scholarship that followed. Over time, an ever-widening gap opened up between the received understanding of the Bible – especially the books of the Old Testament – and the way that Holy Writ was received by the faithful. Wolf had studied under leading Biblical scholars at the University of Göttingen and was familiar with the path-breaking and controversial work of German Biblical criticism, especially Johann Gottfried Eichhorn's *Einleitung ins Alte Testament*, which had begun to appear in 1780. Eichhorn showed how to reconstruct the history of a text when the original had undergone significant changes over time. The implications for the study of Homer were obvious. As Anthony Grafton has shown, Wolf in essence 'annexed for classical studies the most sophisticated methods of contemporary Biblical scholarship'.

Eichhorn is best remembered today for having coined the term the 'Higher Criticism', a phrase that describes how he and others employed historical methods to study the origins, date, composition and transmission of the books of the Bible, especially the Old Testament (Lower Criticism was devoted to textual minutiae). Over time, the Higher Critics showed that Biblical works were rarely solo-authored. Collaboration of various sorts was the norm: while some books of the Bible have come down to us as composite works (with one author's ideas or writings collected in a single volume), others were more deeply collaborative, combining the words of a number of authors in a single Scriptural text – including the Five Books of Moses.

Arguing that Genesis wasn't written by Moses was one thing; saying that Matthew, Mark, Luke and John could not have written eyewitness accounts of the life of Jesus was far more subversive. But scholars couldn't avert their eyes forever from the Higher Critical problems raised by the Gospels – and in 1835 David Friedrich Strauss, a young lecturer at the Protestant seminary of Tübingen, took on the New Testament much as Eichhorn had the Old Testament and Wolf had Homer. Strauss's book was an immediate sensation, and its heretical implications ensured that Strauss would never again be employed at a German university or seminary. Copies of *The Life of Jesus* quickly made their way to America as well as to England, where it was translated by the young George Eliot.

Strauss focused his attack on biographical facts. He closely examined ninety evangelical stories – especially those recounting the miracles attributed to Jesus – and relentlessly exposed 'the discrepancies, contradictions and mistakes in the Gospel narratives and made the supernatural explanations appear weak and untenable'. He further questioned the truth-value of the Gospels by pointing out that accounts of Jesus' life weren't written down until a generation after his death – so were based on second-hand and anecdotal testimony. After reading fifteen hundred pages of this assault, it was hard for anyone to escape the conclusion that there had been 'no incarnation, no supernatural, divine Christ, no miracles, and no resurrection of the dead'. For Strauss, the life of Jesus was composed in much the same way that children sitting in a circle pass along and inevitably embellish a story as each one whispers it in the next one's ear. Strauss imagined the earliest stories about Jesus 'passing from mouth to mouth, and like a snowball growing by the involuntary addition of one exaggerating feature from this and another from that narrator'. It was all, as Strauss put it (in a term that became a byword for his approach), a 'myth'. Jesus was a remarkable person but he was not divine. Strauss became the most notorious and vilified theologian of his day.

The shock waves of Strauss's work soon threatened that lesser deity, Shakespeare, for his biography, too, rested precariously on the unstable foundation of posthumous reports and more than a fair share of myths. One of the first to recognise the extent to which the Shakespeare authorship question was fuelled by the Higher Criticism was H. Bellyse Baildon, editor of the 1912 Arden edition of *Titus Andronicus*. For Baildon,

the fact seems obvious enough, that the skepticism with regard to Shakespeare's authorship of the works at one time universally attributed to him, is part of that general skeptical movement or wave which has landed us first in the so-called 'Higher-Criticism' in matters of religion and finally in Agnosticism itself.

It's surprising that nearly a century passed before scholars like Charles Laporte (in his fine 2007 essay on 'The Bard, the Bible, and the Victorian Shakespeare Question') paid much attention to the connection between the *Life of Jesus* and the life of Shakespeare. The authorship controversy's theological roots also help explain why those debating Shakespeare's claims slid so quickly into the language of apostasy, conversion, orthodoxy and heresy. Had the impulse to speak of Shakespeare as a literary deity been curbed or repudiated, Shakespeare might not have suffered collateral damage from a controversy that had little to do with him. J. M. Robertson had suspected as much back in 1913, noting that it 'is very doubtful whether the Baconian theory would ever have been framed had not the idolatrous Shakespeareans set up a visionary figure of the Master. Broadly speaking, all error is consanguineous. Baconians have not invented a new way of being mistaken.'

Unfortunately, the conviction that Shakespeare was godlike had by now intensified to the point where his plays could casually be referred to as a 'Bible of Humanity' and a 'Bible of Genius', and his words juxtaposed with those of Holy Writ to underscore their scriptural force in books like J. B. Selkirk's *Bible Truths with Shakespearean Parallels* (1862). Nineteenth-century writers in both England and America were even more devout in their worship of Shakespeare than their forebears had been. Thomas Carlyle, in 'The Hero as Poet', hailed Shakespeare as one of the 'Saints of Poetry', while Herman Melville wrote in *The Confidence Man* that 'Shakespeare has got to be a kind of deity'. Even the unsentimental Matthew Arnold couldn't help himself in his 1844 poem 'Shakespeare', where he addressed his object of adoration in lines better suited to Jesus than to an Elizabethan playwright:

And thou, who didst the stars and sunbeams know,
Self-school'd, self-scann'd, self-honour'd, self-secure,
Didst walk on Earth unguess'd at. – Better so!
All pains the immortal spirit must endure,
All weakness that impairs, all griefs which bow,
Find their sole speech in that victorious brow.

In such a climate, it was only a matter of time before someone would try to do to Shakespeare what Strauss had done to Jesus. The similarities were so striking that by 1854 some – like George Gilfillan – wondered why it hadn't been attempted already:

so deep are the uncertainties surrounding the history of Shakespeare, that I sometimes wonder that the process applied by Strauss to the *Life of Our Saviour* has not been extended to his. *A Life of Shakespeare*, on this worthy model, would be a capital exercise for some aspiring sprig of Straussism!

Gilfillan didn't know it, but in 1848, twenty-four-year-old Samuel Mosheim Schmucker, a fierce critic of Strauss and his fellow 'Modern Infidels', had already published just such a 'capital exercise', in which he demonstrated that the 'historic doubts regarding Christ' are 'equally applicable to Shakespeare'; 'the former existence of a distinguished man in the *literary* world, may be as easily disproved, as infidels have laboured to disprove the existence of an eminent person in the religious world'. But Schmucker (who in the course of his brief life would be a prolific biographer and historian as well as a Lutheran pastor) had done so not to extend Strauss's method to Shakespeare but rather to mock and parody it. The result – *Historic Doubts Respecting Shakespeare: Illustrating Infidel Objections against the Bible* – is almost unknown, but it probably tells us more about the Shakespeare authorship controversy than any other book, though without setting out to. Remarkably, before that controversy even broke out, Schmucker, who never for a moment doubted that Shakespeare was Shakespeare, anticipated and carefully mapped out almost all the arguments subsequently used to question Shakespeare's authorship.

Schmucker wrote *Historic Doubts Respecting Shakespeare* out of a concern that Strauss's ideas were making serious headway in America. He blamed writers like Emerson who were sympathetic to the Higher Criticism for encouraging the 'spirit of learned doubt' and for undermining 'the simple Christianity which has prevailed here, ever since the Pilgrim fathers hallowed these Western climes with their presence and their principles'. Knowing how difficult it was to confront directly the force of Strauss's claim that the life of Jesus as reported in the Gospels is a tissue of myths, Schmucker figured that he could undermine Strauss's entire approach by asking the same questions of the life of Shakespeare, for 'if any one is willing to doubt on their authority, the history and existence of Christ, he must, in order to be consistent, be willing to doubt on the same grounds, the history and existence of Shakespeare'.

Schmucker has a great time of it, mostly because it never entered his head that his readers could seriously imagine that Shakespeare wasn't Shakespeare. It gave him the freedom to push his case hard: Where are the contemporary allusions? Why the muddled claims about the stability of the texts and even their authorship? How can we really trust what contemporaries said about him? How could someone be so great and yet there be so little recorded about him:

If so much may be contrived and urged, to mystify the existing records concerning a person who is dead but several centuries, how much more may be contrived by a perverse ingenuity against the existing records respecting an individual [Jesus] who lived and acted in the world nearly two thousand years ago?

Parodying Strauss's line of attack, Schmucker takes the reader step by step through all the reasons that prove that Shakespeare authorship is suspect. For starters, there is almost no documentary evidence: 'if no such authentic records of Shakespeare were written in his own day, all subsequent histories of him must be without any historical truth or authority. They are founded on supposition.' Indeed, the entire biography is implausible: 'What disinterested witnesses ever lived, whose testimony was sufficiently strong and undeniable, as to overbalance the extraordinary *improbability* of their story?' What little evidence survives, he argues – stealing one of Strauss's favourite terms – remains '*contra-dictory*'. Biographers of Shakespeare, like those of Jesus, not only dispute the facts of the life, they can't even agree on what their subject accomplished: 'They have contended, some for one play, and some for another as genuine. While one critic set up, another pulled down. What one affirmed, another denied.'

Schmucker draws a sharp distinction between Shakespeare the man and Shakespeare the poet, in what would soon be a favourite gambit of those who doubted his authorship: 'Even if we grant the truth of the facts recorded concerning the *man* William Shakespeare, these personal facts have no weight in proving the history of the supposed *author and poet*.' In fact, 'all the incidents of his life as a man, are unfavourable to his character as a writer'. As for his lack of formal education: 'Is it not strange that one individual, so ill prepared by previous education, and other indispensable requisites, should be the sole author of so many works, in all of which it is pretended that such extraordinary merit and rare excellence exist?'

He also anticipates the conspiracy theories later used to explain the elevation of Shakespeare: 'British national pride must needs have some great dramatist to uphold the nation's honour . . . Greatness thus became associated with [Shakespeare's] name. He became, in the progress of time, and from the influence of confirmed prejudice and ignorance and pride, supreme in the literary world,' and 'his power and his title have become consolidated in the hearts of an interested nation, and of an admiring and credulous world'. Shakespeare must have been a fraud, an 'imposture which we have proved to be both *possible and natural*'.

He then suggests how the mistaken belief in Shakespeare first took hold, in a Straussian argument that would soon be used by those who seriously denied his authorship of the plays: How 'did this error . . . originate'? By taking things for granted and 'listening to authority, by giving credence to the assertions of those were most interested in the delusion'. Why was it so 'submissively tolerated'? Apathy, ignorance, and an unwillingness to admit error. And 'how were these delusions exposed?': 'Proofs accumulated in power and in amount, as the investigation proceeded, until at the last, the whole truth was shown up to the astonished gaze of men.' And after Shakespeare is shown to be an impostor, what then? Will true believers concede the point? Never. As a result, 'men will continue to be the willing dupes of a fascinating imposition' – a 'melancholy spectacle of simplicity and weakness'.

It's an exhilarating performance, the last thing one would expect from a young Pennsylvanian writing in 1847, for whom invoking Shakespeare is merely a means to a larger theological end. After a hundred pages or so of this Schmucker suddenly worries that readers might get the wrong idea and perhaps not just doubt Shakespeare but in doing so, come to doubt Jesus as well, and so concludes: 'If the failure of every attempt to invalidate Shakespeare's history . . . only serves to confirm it; so the failure on every past assault on Christ's extraordinary history much more serves to confirm and establish it, beyond all future peril.' Schmucker died at age forty, having lived just long enough to see his farcical arguments taken literally, though he left no account of what he thought of those he would probably have described as Shakespeare infidels.

Schmucker had drafted the sceptics' playbook; but in truth, anybody at the time could have, and some were already thinking and writing in similar terms, for every scheme he proposed was lifted from well-worn arguments – familiar enough to parody – about biography, singularity and literary attribution, issues that had been fiercely contested for over half a century. There's no evidence that any early doubters were influenced by or even knew of Schmucker's strange book. They didn't need to. His book confirms that the competition to identify who was the first to deny that Shakespeare wrote the plays misses the point badly. It's worth adding that those who first sought to topple Shakespeare (though not their successors or their critics) would be painfully aware of the theological source of their arguments – and, as we shall soon see, it's no surprise that the most influential of them only turned to the authorship question after experiencing spiritual crises.

TWO

BACON

Francis Bacon, by William Marshall, after Simon De Passe, 1641

Delia Bacon

The story is familiar: a young and ambitious writer with little formal schooling leaves family behind, moves to the metropolis, writes a tragedy and persuades a star of the London stage to play the lead. But the year is 1837, not 1587, and the writer is not Shakespeare of Stratford but an American named Delia Bacon.

Born in a frontier log-cabin in 1811, Delia Bacon was the youngest daughter of a visionary Congregationalist minister who left New Haven, Connecticut to found a Puritan community in the wilds of Ohio. The venture collapsed, the impoverished family returned to New England and her father died soon after. While money was found to send her eldest brother Leonard to Yale, Delia's formal education ended when she was fourteen, after a year at the Female Seminary in Hartford run by Catherine and Mary Beecher, who were impressed by her 'fervid imagination' and 'rare gifts of eloquence'.

At fifteen, to help support her family, Delia Bacon became a schoolteacher. She continued to read voraciously, added a bit of

Delia Bacon, from Theodore Bacon, *Delia Bacon: A Biographical Sketch* (Boston, 1888)

Greek to her limited Latin, and began writing stories (which she justified to her brother Leonard, now a leading Congregationalist minister in New Haven, as 'fiction only as the drapery to something better – truth'). At twenty she published, anonymously, *Tales of the Puritans* – three longish stories of colonial life. The following year she won a story-writing contest sponsored by the Philadelphia *Saturday Courier*, beating rivals including Edgar Allan Poe for the $100 prize. Her entry, 'Love's Martyr', retold a tragic incident of the Revolutionary War in which a colonist named Jane McCrea was murdered by Indians (in the service of the British General Burgoyne) on the way to meet her royalist lover at Fort Edward; McCrea's death became a rallying cry for the colonial forces and, as tradition had it, helped turn the tide of the war.

Delia Bacon cut an increasingly impressive figure; as one awestruck onlooker described her, 'graceful and intellectual in appearance, eloquent in speech, marvelously wise, and full of inspiration, she looked and spoke the very muse of history'. As her reputation as a teacher grew, she progressed from instructing schoolgirls to teaching adult women, and eventually – something almost without precedent for a woman at the time – to lecturing publicly on world history to audiences of both men and women. Her delivery was especially impressive: an admirer recalled that 'she wrote out nothing – not even notes'. Bacon was a gifted synthesiser. She drew comfortably on literature, art, archaeology, linguistics, science, theology and anything else that helped illustrate her account of how mankind, under Providence's guiding hand, had developed spiritually and intellectually 'from the dawn of history, through the shadowy glimmerings of faith and tradition in successive ages, to the broad daylight of the present era'.

By her mid-twenties Bacon was on her way to cementing a career as a professional lecturer in New Haven, but she was restless, and in 1836, with Leonard's reluctant blessing, moved to New York City. But even lecturing there failed to hold her interest. She sought out leading cultural figures, including James Gates

Percival, Richard Henry Dana and the inventor Samuel Morse, and started going to the theatre. Her timing was fortunate, for one of the leading Shakespeare actors of the day, Ellen Tree, had recently begun performing in New York. Fresh from her successes as Beatrice, Rosalind and Romeo (to Fanny Kemble's Juliet) on the London stage, Tree was appearing at the Park Theatre in lower Manhattan. Bacon met Tree in the winter of 1837 and convinced her to play the leading role in a tragedy she was writing – a theatrical remake of her prize-winning story 'Love's Martyr', renamed *The Bride of Fort Edward*. It promised to be a path-breaking collaboration; like Bacon, Ellen Tree was unmarried and not dependent on any man for support, and, like Bacon, she managed to maintain a reputation as one who was 'impeccably pure and decorous', not all that easy at the time for women connected with the theatre. When Tree left New York for a three-month Southern tour to which she had committed, Bacon settled down to finish her play.

Bacon was convinced that there was money to be made as a playwright; she had heard that another aspiring dramatist had recently won a $1,000 prize for a new play and Ellen Tree was already amassing a small fortune from her three-year American tour. Yet the possibility of wealth and fame as a playwright was not easily reconciled with Bacon's puritanism and her uneasiness about working in the theatre. 'I should be sorry', she wrote to Leonard at the time, 'to do anything unbecoming a lady or a Christian, even for the sake of a thousand pounds.' Bacon also felt compelled to rationalise her work-in-progress to her brother, if not to herself, on moral grounds: 'If the play has any effect at all, it will be an elevating one,' since theatre was 'a form better fitted to strike the common mind' than other kinds of writing. She added, a little desperately, that 'If I can get it introduced into so bad a place as the [Park] Theatre I should count it as great a triumph as if they should tear down the green room and the stage and put up a pulpit and send for you to preach to them.'

In writing a political play about 'a well-known crisis in our national history', Bacon was breaking new ground as an American woman playwright, for her few antebellum predecessors had devoted themselves to comedy and melodrama. Her debt to Shakespeare's tragedies and histories is hard to miss: there's the mix of conversational prose and blank verse as well as the juxtaposition of tragic and comic scenes (including low-life American troops whose banter recalls that of Falstaff's companions). Her main character is modelled on Shakespeare's heroines, which may account for Ellen Tree's interest in the part: she's a composite of Juliet (marrying her household's enemy and dying right after her bridal day), Desdemona (in her intimate scene with a servant before her death as well as in her brief revival before she finally dies) and Ophelia (especially after her death, when her brother and her lover, like Laertes and Hamlet, compete over who can grieve more for her). Politically, the plot reads like an Americanised version of Shakespeare's *Lucrece*, in which the death of the heroine leads to the creation of the Republic (just as, in Shakespeare's poem, the sight of the dead Lucrece leads the Romans to repudiate monarchy). While keenly aware of her English literary roots – not many works about the Revolutionary War mention in passing both Geoffrey Chaucer and Edmund Spenser – Bacon also saw herself as part of a new generation of American writers; even as colonial militia would vanquish the British, so, too, one day, would American authors.

When Ellen Tree left New York to tour in February 1837, most of *The Bride of Fort Edward* was already drafted, and Bacon planned to submit the finished script to Edward Simpson (the formidable manager of the Park Theatre) in April. Then things unravelled. Bacon started getting headaches. She then decided that she'd need the summer to finish the play. After that, she became discouraged when a friend who read the script didn't think it would succeed onstage. In the end, it seems pretty clear, she couldn't reconcile her puritanism with her literary ambitions – so she put what she had written in a drawer. A year later, she retrieved it and sent a finished draft to her brother Leonard. By then, Ellen Tree had moved on. Leonard sat on the script for six months, then criticised it harshly.

Hoping to salvage what she could, determined not to seek Leonard's advice again, and resolved that plays were meant to be read and not seen, she touched up the script and published it anonymously in 1839. Bacon added a defensive preface to make clear that what she had written was 'A dialogue . . . not a play – and 'not intended for the stage'. This wasn't entirely accurate, nor was the distinction Bacon drew between Drama (which captured the 'repose, the thought, and sentiment of actual life') and Theatre (whose capacity to instruct was undermined by 'hurried action, the crowded plot, the theatrical elevation which the Stage necessarily demands'). Bacon turned her back on the stage – including Shakespeare's plays in performance. One of her students later recalled that 'Miss Bacon not unfrequently spoke of having seen Shakespeare in theatrical representation', but she 'always spoke of her experience in theatre-going as a disappointment, and said that she did not care to go again'.

Despite her misgivings, Delia Bacon's first and only play had stage potential; with Ellen Tree in the lead and some skilled pruning it would have commanded attention. The published version was positively reviewed in the *Saturday Courier*, and, as it happened, Edgar Allan Poe wrote about it as well, noting that the anonymous author's 'imagination [is] of no common order' and calling the play's 'design . . . excellent'. The published 'Dialogue' was a commercial failure – only 692 of fifteen hundred copies sold.

Defeated, Bacon returned to New Haven and resumed teaching and lecturing, knowing that she wasn't cut out to be a novelist or a playwright and that she would have to find a different outlet for her intellectual gifts and driving ambition. In the spring of 1845, her winter classes over, Bacon withdrew from society, moved into New Haven's Tontine Hotel and buried herself in her books, on the verge, she was sure, of a revelation about the authorship of Shakespeare's works. Six months later Bacon had at last mapped out her findings, though more likely in her mind than on paper.

She shared the news with Leonard, who recorded in October 1845 that Delia 'has about concluded to publish her new theory of Shakespeare in one or more volumes, to find a place in Wiley and Putnam's *Library of American Authors*'. In fact, over a decade would pass before she published a word of her theory – first in an anonymous article in *Putnam's Magazine* in 1856, and then, a year later, in a strange and rambling book, published simultaneously in England and America, which told a somewhat different story, or at least a different part of the story, Bacon died two years later, following a descent into insanity.

Since Delia Bacon, more than anyone before or after, was responsible for triggering what would come to be known as the Shakespeare authorship controversy, it's helpful to know what drew her to it, how her views changed over time, and what was ultimately at stake for her. Unfortunately, little evidence that might illuminate any of this survives – no manuscript drafts, no diary or journal, not even a record of what books or editions she consulted. Her family disapproved of this project (and blamed her drift into insanity on it), and may have destroyed what evidence once existed. It's no small irony that anyone investigating the development of Delia Bacon's ideas confronts much the same problems as Shakespeare's biographers. In her case, too, critics have been quick to reach conclusions about the work based on anecdotal evidence drawn from the life.

Delia Bacon saw herself living in an age of discoveries, and not just scientific ones. She could see in Biblical and Homeric textual scholarship the extent to which questions of authorship were overturning centuries of conventional wisdom. Perhaps Shakespeare's works deserved a closer look too. Yet at the time there were no departments of English literature, let alone Shakespeare professors, to do so, at either American or British universities. This was her opening, for very few Americans could rival her knowledge of Shakespeare's works. She was familiar with the major criticism, had spent years reading and teaching the plays and had the kind of intimate knowledge of them that could only be acquired from emulating Shakespeare in one's own plays and stories.

The young women under her tutelage in New Haven received a rich grounding in Shakespeare denied their brothers enrolled across town at Yale. Bacon led her charges through repeated close readings of such plays as *Hamlet* and *Julius Caesar*, devoting a good deal of attention to questions of character and searching relentlessly for each play's deeper philosophical meaning – a by-product, no doubt, of her longstanding view that writers hid a deeper 'truth' under fictional 'drapery'. One of her students recalled how Bacon

seemed to saturate herself with the play, as it were; to live in it, to call into imaginative consciousness the loves, hopes, fears, ambition, disappointment, and despair of the characters, and under this intense realization to divine, as it were, the meaning of the play – 'its unity' as she said – its motif.

Bacon showed them how to discover 'intimations in obscure passages, in unimportant utterances, apparently void of significance', and taught them that there '"is nothing superfluous . . in any of these plays, the greatest product of the human mind; nothing which could have been dispensed with. Every character is necessary; every word is full of meaning."'

While her search for the plays' hidden meaning was unusual for the time, Bacon's approach to Shakespearean drama was otherwise typical of the age. She had a hard time believing that these nobly philosophical works were written with popular performance and commercial potential in mind. And thanks to the influence of contemporary biographies of Shakespeare, she found the gap between the facts of his life and his remarkable literary output inexplicable.

The framework within which she imagined the world of the English Renaissance, also typical of her day, was limited to monarchs, courtiers and writers. The rest were written off as ignorant masses (masses . . still unlettered, callous with wrongs, manacled with blind traditions, or swaying hither and thither, with the breath of a common prejudice'). It was history from the top down and limited geographically to London and the court. Her Shakespeare canon was no less restricted and also typical of nineteenth-century readers: at the centre of it were *Hamlet* and *The Tempest*, and it extended to the plays meatiest in philosophical and political content – *Othello, Julius Caesar, Lear, Romeo and Juliet, Richard the Second*, and, unusually, *Coriolanus* – but not much further. While she had surely read the other thirty or so plays, as well as the poetry, they didn't serve her purpose, and for the most part she passed over them in silence.

Nobody before Delia Bacon who had doubts about Shakespeare's authorship had been willing to take the crucial next step and explain, in print, the reasons that the plays should be reattributed to an alternative candidate. Rather than ransack the archives for proof she sought it in the plays themselves, and concluded that the evidence had been there all along. Others had just not read the plays with sufficient attention to obscure and seemingly irrelevant passages. It was no great leap for her to assume that Francis Bacon was somehow behind the plays (and it's not, as many have assumed, because she believed herself to be distantly related).

Francis Bacon was widely celebrated as one of the great men of the Renaissance, the father of modern scientific method, a worldly courtier, a talented writer, a learned jurist and a brilliant philosopher. Born in 1561, he studied at Cambridge and at the Inns of Court, and travelled on the Continent. His long career as a writer and public servant began in the 1580s, and in 1594 Queen Elizabeth appointed Bacon as one of her learned counsel. His literary range was exceptional and included parliamentary speeches, Christmas entertainment, political reports, translations of the Psalms, letters of advice, political tracts, a *History of King Henry the Seventh*, as well as his famous *Essays* and his great philosophical works: *The Advancement of Learning*, the utopian *New Atlantis*, *Instauratio Magna* and *Novum Organum*. About the only thing

Bacon didn't try his hand at were plays or narrative poems. He remained deeply involved in politics throughout his life, and, after much jockeying, finally attained the positions of Attorney General and Lord Chancellor under King James, before falling out of favour in 1621 on dubious charges of corruption. He was briefly committed to the Tower of London. After his release, Bacon chose, as he put it, 'to retire from the stage of civil action and betake myself to letters'. He died in 1626. Bacon was unquestionably one of the great minds of his age. For the next two centuries his reputation was secure and the French *philosophes* did much to promote Bacon as a philosopher dedicated to social reform, his works implicitly an 'attack on the systems and dogmas of traditional institutions'. It is this legacy that most powerfully informs Delia Bacon's conception of him.

While Francis Bacon's stock has declined precipitously in the last hundred years or so, he was still revered in early nineteenth-century Britain and America, his reputation peaking at just the moment that Delia Bacon turned to the authorship question. Ralph Waldo Emerson's audiences in the 1830s would have taken for granted his claim that Francis Bacon, not 'less than Shakespeare, though in a different way . . . may claim the praise of universality'. Emerson also spoke for many at the time when he said that 'no man reads the works of Bacon without imbibing an affectionate veneration for their author . . . We come to regard him as an Archangel to whom the high office was committed of opening the doors and palaces of knowledge to many generations.'

Emerson's hyperbolic praise was comparatively tame in its day. Francis Bacon's works, William Wirt writes in 1803, were 'filled with pure and solid golden bullion' and 'redeemed the world from all . . . darkness, jargon, perplexity and error'. For John Playfair in 1820, Bacon 'has no rival in the times which are past, so is he likely to have none in those which are to come'. Francis Bacon proved equally popular among those eager to resolve the growing tensions between science and religion: Bacon College was founded by the Disciples of Christ in Kentucky in 1836, and a contributor to a religious magazine would claim, in all seriousness, that Baconian philosophy was 'ultimately responsible' for 'the sacredness of the marriage tie, the purity of private life, the sincerity of friendship, charity toward the poor, and general love of mankind'. Not to be outdone, the *American Agriculturalist* hailed Francis Bacon as 'the patron of progress in American farming'.

By the time she had begun to question Shakespeare's author-ship of the plays, Delia Bacon was familiar with Francis Bacon's writings, had been reading and taking notes in Leonard's copy of his works and had befriended one of the leading American advo-cates of Bacon, Professor Benjamin Silliman of Yale. Her interest had also been piqued by her conversations with her old friend from New York, Samuel Morse. Morse, who was experimenting with codes for encrypting messages for the telegraph he had recently invented, told her about Francis Bacon's creation of a secret cipher, something she hadn't known about and which would contribute to her thinking about Bacon's masked authorship of Shakespeare's works.

The pieces started falling into place. Resolving two longstand-ing literary mysteries at once, she could now explain why the fourth part of Francis Bacon's magnum opus, *Instauratio Magna*, was incomplete, the promised sections on 'the New Philosophy' unpublished and presumed lost. Her close reading of Shakespeare's plays revealed that Francis Bacon's missing work had in fact survived under a different name, as the greatest dra-matic works of the Elizabethan era. It made far better sense to accept the likelihood that one mind was behind both great bodies of work than to concede the odds-defying possibility that two geniuses, among the greatest ever, had lived at the exact same time and place and produced work that had so much in common philo-sophically. The challenge she set herself was to figure out why Francis Bacon (and, as her theory developed, others in his extend-ed intellectual circle) had resorted to writing under such a guise.

Delia Bacon could not have foreseen it, but a break with her religious upbringing and Puritan roots was in the offing, one that would profoundly shape her authorship project and delay its publication for many years. But it also enabled her project by fraying the ties that tightly bound her to her family, church and nation. It was the most humiliating thing that ever happened to her and it changed her, making her deeply suspicious of others and more desperate than ever to achieve renown. Her theory can't be easily untangled from this crisis, though questions of cause and effect – as in the case of her later insanity – are impossible to resolve. The following, based on a surprising amount of documentary evidence, remains speculative – as must all claims about the ways in which life experiences shape a writer's work – even that of a modern writer like Delia Bacon.

One of the few people in whom she confided during the months in which she was first working out her Shakespeare theory was a fellow lodger at New Haven's Tontine Hotel, Alexander MacWhorter, a recent theology graduate of Yale. The two spent more and more time together, which soon raised eyebrows, not only because it pressed the bounds of what upstanding unmarried men and women might be seen doing together, but also because of the difference in their ages: she was thirty-four, he twenty-three. Both believed themselves to be on the verge of great discoveries (MacWhorter was engaged in Biblical textual scholarship and was convinced that he had found that the Hebrew Bible's use of the tetragrammaton 'Yahveh' anticipated and signified the Coming of Christ). For a year or so, the two were inseparable. Delia Bacon's family and friends began to worry, as no engagement had been announced.

None would be. People began to gossip. When Leonard encountered MacWhorter in New Haven and demanded to know whether his intentions toward his sister were honourable, MacWhorter replied that he had no idea what Leonard was talking about. Furious, Leonard told his sister never to write to MacWhorter again, and made her, Ophelia-like, return his love tokens. She asked for hers in return, and MacWhorter, who had been much more guarded than Bacon in writing about what he professed to feel, refused to return her love letters and began reading choice bits from them aloud to amused friends. There was no question that she had agreed to marry him; but had he actually proposed? Outsiders were left to wonder whose account of the affair was true. It was beginning to resemble one of those Shakespearean problem comedies, where everything turned on the grammatical fault lines of marital promises.

The gossip and insinuations became intolerable; not just Delia Bacon's reputation was threatened, but her family's as well. Leonard, outraged, had MacWhorter brought up on charges of 'calumny, falsehood, and disgraceful conduct, as a man, a Christian, and especially as a candidate for the Christian ministry'. In the summer of 1847 an ecclesiastical trial of MacWhorter was held. The trial, in which Delia Bacon had to testify, went on for weeks; then, in a 12–11 decision, the ministers ruled in favour of MacWhorter, reprimanding him only for his imprudence. The Bacons continued their appeals through the spring of 1848, to no avail. It left a deep rift among New Haven's Congregationalists and was unbearably humiliating for Delia Bacon, whose faith in her church was badly shaken.

The scandal went national. Catherine Beecher recalled that she was asked about it everywhere she went – 'Not only through New England and the eastern cities, but in Kentucky, Ohio, Indiana, Missouri, Illinois, Wisconsin and Iowa the same topic constantly recurred as a matter of curious inquiry or accidental remark. There was no escape from it.' Outraged by the verdict and hoping to right the wrong, Beecher decided to retell the story in a book – *Truth Stranger than Fiction* – but her intentions backfired. Delia Bacon had begged her not to publish it, to no avail, and after it appeared in 1850 there were few who hadn't read or heard the story, in mortifying detail.

Bacon moved to Boston, conducted her Shakespeare research in libraries there, started a new co-educational lecture series, and quickly acquired a following of some of the most influential women in Boston and Cambridge, including Caroline Healey Dall, Elizabeth Palmer Peabody and Eliza Farrar. But Boston wasn't far enough away and her latest research efforts, while confirming her suspicions about the true authorship of the plays, convinced her that further proofs could only be found in England. While she spoke to friends about lecturing overseas, they quickly saw through the pretence. Eliza Farrar believed that Bacon

had no notion of going to England to teach history; all she wanted to go for was to obtain proof of her theory, that Shakespeare did not write the plays attributed to him, but that Lord Bacon did. This was sufficient to prevent my ever again encouraging her going to England, or talking with her about Shakespeare.

Elizabeth Peabody lent a more sympathetic ear. Bacon eagerly discussed with her the life and works of Shakespeare, Francis Bacon and Walter Ralegh. But Bacon soon became anxious to the point of paranoia about how much Peabody knew about her as-yet-unpublished theory and asked her to swear that she 'would never anticipate her, by even suggesting the discovery, but allow to her the whole glory of this remarkable piece of historical criticism which really belonged to her'. When even that promise failed to placate Bacon, Peabody backed off completely: 'In order not to worry her,' she later wrote, 'I gave the whole thing up and promised her I would – as far as in me lay – not think of it until after she had given it to the public.'

To her credit, Peabody 'was never in the least offended by her jealousy' and saw 'this morbid sensitiveness' as an understandable reaction to Bacon's 'cruel experience' at MacWhorter's hands. Caroline Healey Dall also thought that Delia had never recovered from the crisis of faith, personal and religious, precipitated by the MacWhorter affair: 'a terrible personal experience warped her mind soon after she entered upon her historical studies', and the 'warp was shown when a nature essentially of the noblest turned mean and suspicious'. Yet Dall, who later wrote a book in defence of Shakespeare's authorship, couldn't understand why Bacon was so secretive about 'a theory she nonetheless talked of incessantly': having 'perfected her theory', Bacon 'never communicated it fully to any one; she seemed to fear that her laurels would be stolen if she did'. Bacon had begun trying out parts of her new theory in her lectures and with acquaintances – with decidedly mixed results. Eliza Farrar recalled that Sarah Becker, in whose house Bacon was lodging, put her copy of Shakespeare's works 'out of sight, and never allowed her to converse with her on this, her favorite subject. We considered it dangerous for Miss Bacon to dwell on this fancy, and thought that, if indulged, it might become a monomania, which it subsequently did.'

Delia Bacon was now set on showing the world the difference between surface and deeper meaning. It's a distinction she knew all too well. She had been wrong, after all, about MacWhorter, mistaking his surface expressions for deeper intentions; and in the ensuing scandal she had been profoundly disappointed in her church, which had relied on the surface meaning of the words the two had exchanged in reaching a verdict. It was her mission now, to reveal how *everyone* had been mistaken, had misread the greatest of literary works – had not recognised, as she had, how they were the product of failure and frustration. The pursuit of the authorship question, for Delia Bacon, was both a product of, and illuminated by, personal and religious crisis. But she had not yet abandoned her belief in the workings of Providence, though she remained uncertain whether this would help or hinder her life's work, telling a supporter that 'she feels sure that she has a great object to accomplish, and that Providence is specially busy, not only in what promotes her progress, but in what seems to impede it'.

The Shakespeare Problem Resolved

A radical theory was emerging from Delia Bacon's reflections on the plays, more far-reaching than simply a matter of authorship. But because she never seems to have arrived at a final, definitive account and never managed to fit all the parts together seamlessly, the best that can be reconstructed is a version drawn primarily from details offered in the opening and closing pages of her book, which, in focusing on extended close readings of three plays (*Julius Caesar*, *Lear* and *Coriolanus*) offered what she believed to be decisive internal evidence, amounting to proof, of her theory.

Delia Bacon saw the plays long attributed to Shakespeare as the product of failure. These great works of literature, she writes, were the collective effort of a 'little clique of disappointed and defeated politicians who undertook to head and organize a popular opposition against the government, and were compelled to retreat from that enterprise'. It was a story of tactical defeat and withdrawal: 'Driven from one field, they showed themselves in another. Driven from the open field, they fought in secret.' Having failed in the political realm, these men turned to drama to effect change, if not in the present, then at least in the future. She cast them as romantic heroes, gathered around a 'new Round Table', like King Arthur and his knights of yore. At the centre of this cohort was Francis Bacon. Aligned with him were Walter Ralegh, perhaps Edmund Spenser, Lord Buckhurst and the Earl of Oxford, and maybe others as well – it's hard to know for sure, because she was maddeningly vague on who was involved and her account of membership in the group kept changing. Sometimes it seemed that Francis Bacon was primarily responsible; at other times, the enterprise appeared much more collaborative. Such details seem almost a nuisance for her, distracting from the larger and more compelling story of how a handful of remarkable and frustrated men, led by Bacon, began collaborating, through great drama, to oppose the 'despotism' of Queen Elizabeth and King James.

Reminding us that both Francis Bacon and Walter Ralegh were cast aside and imprisoned by their monarchs, she then exaggerates the brutality of the Tudor and Stuart regimes in order to explain away what would otherwise be seen as cowardice in her heroes: 'Does not all the world know that scholars, men of reverence, men of world-wide renown, men of every accomplishment, were tortured, and mutilated, and hung, and beheaded, in both these two reigns, for writing wherein Caesar's ambition was infinitely more obscurely hinted at – writings unspeakably less offensive to majesty' than a play like *Julius Caesar*? So these 'disappointed and defeated' visionaries were forced to turn from direct political intervention to subversive and pseudonymous writing. They also felt it 'necessary' to 'conceal their lives as well as their works', to 'veil' their 'true worth and nobility' and to 'play this great game in secret'. And, in a passage that feels uncomfortably autobiographical, she imagines that in 'one way or another, directly or indirectly, they were determined to make their influence felt in that age, in spite of the want of encouragement which the conditions of that time offered to such an enterprise'.

They found in playwriting a perfect form, because at the time plays were staged both at court and in the public theatres, then published, which enabled them to speak to rulers and ruled as well as to posterity: they 'wanted some organ of communication with these so potent and resistless rulers – some "chair" from which they could repeat to them in their own tongue the story of their lost institutions, and revive in them the memory of the kings their ancestors'. The closet-dramatist-turned-lecturer Delia Bacon (who, as one observer noted, relied in her lectures on 'maps, charts, models, pictures, and everything she needed to illustrate her subject') can't seem to help recreating this coterie in her own pedagogical image: 'They wanted a school in which they could tell them stories ... they wanted a school in which they could teach the common people *History* (and not English history only), with illustrations, large as life, and a magic lantern to aid them, – "visible history"'.

There could be no mistaking their radical political agenda: these men were committed republicans whose plays were vindications against tyranny by another name, works 'produced for the ostensible purpose of illustrating and adorning the tyrannies which the men, under whose countenance and protection they are produced, were vainly attempting, or had vainly attempted to set bounds to or overthrow'. The only time that their work was actually put to the test was when the Earl of Essex's followers asked for their play *Richard the Second* to be performed on the eve of their revolt in 1601, but this uprising proved a failure. Had that revolutionary effort – inspired by this radical literary enterprise – succeeded, imagine how profoundly the course of Anglo-American history would have been altered: the end of tyrannical monarchy in England would have precluded an English revolution in the 1640s and made that fracture of 1776 that sundered the American colonies from England unnecessary. They had come that close.

Delia Bacon's claim that the plays were politically radical was a century and a half ahead of its time. So, too, was her insistence that some of the plays should be read as collaborative. Had she limited her argument to these points instead of conjoining it to an argument about how Shakespeare couldn't have written them, there is little doubt that, instead of being dismissed as a crank and a madwoman, she would be hailed today as the precursor of the New Historicists, and the first to argue that the plays anticipated the political upheavals England experienced in the mid-seventeenth century. But Delia Bacon couldn't stop at that point. Nor could she concede that the republican ideas she located in the plays circulated widely at the time and were as available to William Shakespeare as they were to Walter Ralegh or Francis Bacon. Offering a new reading of Shakespeare's plays might bring praise but not the fame she clearly craved. The reign of Shakespeare had to be brought to an end.

In making this argument Delia Bacon had an even more revolutionary agenda: overturning the myths of America's founding fathers. Here, for example, is what her brother Leonard, a major proponent of these Puritan traditions, was espousing at the time:

The settlement of New England took place at a time when great changes were obviously impending over the parent country . . . A party had arisen in England, to whom liberty, an ample and well fortified liberty, was indispensable, and of whom some were blindly yearning after, and others were intelligently devising and manfully endeavoring, a large and sweeping reform in the structure of society. But where and how should that reform be realized? Some – the boldest, the most large-hearted, the most enterprising and unflinching of their party – the master spirits of that age, turned their eyes to New England, and after long deliberation, they determined on leaving behind them all the antiquated institutions of the old world, the accumulation of ages of darkness and of tyranny . . . and they hoped to realize under this western sky, the prophet's vision of 'new heavens and a new earth,' in which dwelleth righteousness.

Delia Bacon's theory called all this into question, for if the 'party' of Elizabethan courtiers and aristocrats – the true 'master spirits of that age' led by Francis Bacon – were the proto-republicans she made them out to be, it was they (and not the Puritans who sailed for Plymouth Rock and helped to found the American colonies) who were the original source of the anti-monarchical and anti-tyrannical platform on which America was founded. It was also, then, not Congregationalist preachers like her father and brother (or those who had sided with MacWhorter) who had paved the way, but creative writers like herself, with a deeply pedagogical bent. And who was better placed – as an American, a Congregationalist with Puritan ancestry, a writer and public lecturer – to see it? Her authorship theory was at once heretical and unpatriotic.

It was no wonder she had such difficulty putting these ideas on paper, let alone committing them to print. The great discovery both exhilarated and unnerved her. The best glimpse we have of its psychic toll comes from her conversations with Nathaniel Hawthorne. When they spoke, Hawthorne noted in his journal, Bacon 'was very communicative about her theory, and would have been more so had I desired it; but I thought it best to repress, rather than draw her out. Unquestionably, she is a monomaniac; this great idea has completely thrown her off her balance.' But Hawthorne, formed by the same New England culture, soon recognised that what had thrown her was not the obsession itself, but how it had overturned everything that Delia Bacon had once believed in: 'From her own account, it appears she did at one time lose her reason; it was on finding that the philosophy, which she found under the surface of the plays, was running counter to the religious doctrines in which she had been educated.' Hawthorne, who knew exactly how far her work departed from the evangelical Puritan narrative in which she was raised, didn't know quite what to make of someone advocating a theory so 'at variance with her pre-conceived opinions, whether ethical, religious, or political'.

Delia Bacon's last great obstacle was finding patrons and publishers who might help secure funds for her English research and the publication of her discovery. Brilliant and charismatic in person, she persuaded Charles Butler (a lawyer and banker who had helped found the New York University Law School and the Union Theological Seminary) to cover the cost of her English research. And Elizabeth Peabody, well connected and eager to help, got in touch with Ralph Waldo Emerson on Delia Bacon's behalf and arranged for Bacon to send him a letter and a prospectus. These friendships, late in Bacon's life, confirm how impressive some of the greatest literary minds of the day on both sides of the Atlantic found her. But it wasn't just her intelligence that attracted them: they also saw the extent to which her work was in the radical tradition of the Higher Criticism, to which they were sympathetic.

Emerson, who had just published what remains one of the most influential American essays on Shakespeare in his *Representative Men*, responded graciously, if guardedly, to her claim that the author of Shakespeare's plays was really Francis Bacon: 'You will have need of enchanted instruments, nay alchemy itself,' he replied, 'to melt into one identity these two reputations.' As for the clincher to the argument (the Baconian cipher she spoke of but refused to share): 'If the cipher approve itself so real and consonant to you, it will to all, and is not only material but indispensable.' In many ways, Emerson was, for Delia Bacon, the ideal reader, and not simply because he considered Francis Bacon, no less than Shakespeare, a universal genius, or because he understood that implicit in her argument was that Americans, whose culture was so shaped by republican values, were likely to be better readers of Shakespeare than Englishmen. Emerson also felt that this 'best poet led an obscure and profane life, using his genius for the public amusement'. And he thought that Shakespeare's proximity to men like Bacon, Ralegh, Essex, Drake and Spenser shaped the plays ('It was impossible', Emerson wrote, 'that such an observer as Shakespeare could walk in the same city from year to year with this renowned group without gathering some fruit from their accomplishments and learning').

Over the course of many years of lecturing and reflecting on Shakespeare, Emerson had read nearly every important work of scholarship about him. Yet all that had done was reinforce for him, as it did for so many others, an insuperable divide between what he knew of the man and the works. There simply was no adequate explanation: Shakespeare 'was a jovial actor and manager. I cannot marry this fact to his verse. Other admirable men have led lives in some sort of keeping with their thought, but this man in wide contrast.' Emerson was left to conclude that despite all the research into his life, 'our poet's mask was impenetrable.' Delia Bacon's theory promised to lift that mask, explain the seeming contradiction between transcendent poet and 'jovial actor and manager', show exactly how life and thought dovetailed. Emerson, while reconciled to the seeming paradox that was Shakespeare, was nonetheless willing to entertain a theory that helped resolve it. But he demanded evidence, the kinds of documentary proof (what Delia Bacon dismissively called 'direct historical testimony') that her account annoyingly failed to provide. Bacon, for her part, kept Emerson's interest in her work alive by reporting new and corroborative finds, alluding to the mysterious cipher and arguing that decisive evidence was only to be had in England.

Emerson remained sufficiently intrigued to bear with these evasions. He even visited her in Cambridge, recognising how much was at stake in her work: 'Her discovery, if it really be one, is of the first import not only in English, but in all literature.' Emerson later grew sceptical of the existence of that magical cipher – 'a certain key or method, which she professed to have found'. But he rightly judged the force and originality of her insights into the plays, and in a compliment that meant the world to Delia Bacon, wrote that 'I have seen nothing in America in the way of literary criticism, which I thought so good'. He volunteered to serve as her literary agent and provided her with letters of introduction to leading British scholars, including Thomas Carlyle, James Spedding (the leading Bacon scholar of the day) and Sir Henry Ellis, head librarian at the British Museum. She sailed for England on 14 May 1853.

Delia Bacon never found corroborative evidence for her theory there, nor did she use the letters of introduction that would have given her access to the British Museum or other archives. She did meet with Thomas Carlyle, who shrieked, she wrote to her sister Julia, when first hearing her theory of authorship: 'I wish you could have heard him laugh. Once or twice I thought he would have taken the roof of the house off. At first they were perfectly stunned' and

they looked at me with staring eyes, speechless for want of words in which to convey my sense of audacity. At length Mr Carlyle came down on me with such a volley. I did not mind in the least. I told him that he did not know what was in the plays if he said that, and no one *could* know who believed that that booby wrote them. It was then that he began to shriek. You could have heard him a mile. I told him too that I should not think of questioning his authority in such a case if it were not with me a matter of *knowledge*. I did not advance it as an opinion.

Bacon left a copy of her 'introductory statement' with Carlyle, who with her permission began showing her paper around to those in the literary and publishing worlds.

It's clear from Carlyle's correspondence that, much like Emerson, he was fascinated by Delia Bacon's effort to show that the life of Shakespeare was (in Strauss's sense of the word) as mythic as the life of Jesus. He wrote to his brother of the visit of the

[. . .] Yankee Lady, sent by Emerson, who has discovered that the 'Man Shakespear' is a *Myth*, and did *not* write those plays that bear his name, which were on the contrary written by a 'Secret Associate' (names *unknown*): she has actually come to England for the purposes of examining that, and if possible, proving it . . . *Ach Gott!*

Others were subsequently drawn to the same impulse in the Baconian movement, including Walt Whitman, who would write:

We all know how much *mythus* there is in the Shakespeare question as it stands to-day. Beneath a few foundations of proved facts are certainly engulfed far more dim and elusive ones, of deepest importance – tantalizing and half suspected – suggesting explanations that one dare not put in plain statement.

Because of Bacon's lack of evidence, Carlyle remained highly sceptical, though he strongly encouraged her to consult manuscripts in the British Library, where 'if you can find in that mass of English records . . . *any* document tending to confirm your Shakespeare theory, it will be worth all the reasoning in the world'. She decamped instead to St Albans, 'the great Bacon's place', where, Carlyle reported to Emerson, 'Miss Bacon' is 'working out her Shakespeare Problem, from the depths of her own mind, disdainful apparently, or desperate and careless, of all *evidence* from museums or archives'. Neither man would have been amused to learn that while at St Albans she tried and failed to persuade the caretaker to open Francis Bacon's tomb so that she could unearth the manuscripts hidden there that confirmed her theory.

Delia Bacon was torn between publishing proofs drawn from internal evidence (her close readings of the plays) and offering historical evidence (to substantiate her story of the great collaboration). She never seemed to consider combining the two, and rebuffed repeated suggestions to address counter-evidence in favour of Shakespeare's authorship. When Emerson, for example, asked her about Ben Jonson's explicit praise of his fellow dramatist, she brushed him off: 'I know all about Ben Jonson. He had two patrons besides "Shakespeare." One was Ralegh, the other was Bacon.' The conspiracy was so transparent it didn't merit an explanation. She also couldn't decide whether to publish first in America or in England, or in serialised form or as a finished book. The indecision cost her some excellent opportunities that Emerson had secured. She also didn't understand the book world and considered it outrageous that publishers should make so much profit from her discovery. Her big break finally came in late 1855 when the publishers Dix and Edwards, at Emerson's urging, agreed to the serialising of the work in *Putnam's Monthly* – a leading American periodical that published Longfellow, Lowell and Melville – before bringing it out as a book.

She chose, again, to publish anonymously. Her essay's title was understated: 'William Shakespeare and His Plays; An Enquiry Concerning Them'. The opening cleverly situates the Shakespeare question squarely in the tradition of the authorship challenges to the great works of the past, Homeric and Biblical: 'How can we undertake to account for the literary miracles of antiquity, while this great myth of the modern ages still lies at our door, unquestioned?' We were wrong about these inspired works, why not about Shakespeare's as well? Bacon places blame squarely on those deifying high priests, 'the critics' who 'still veil their faces, filling the air with mystic utterances which seem to say, that to this shrine at least, for the footstep of the common reason and the common sense, there is yet no admittance'. She reminds readers that classical scholarship has come a long way, as critics now 'take . . . to pieces before our eyes this venerable Homer; and tell us how many old forgotten poets' ashes went to his formation'.

The shift from Homer to Shakespeare is deftly handled, and it takes a minute before readers are sure that she is talking about *Hamlet* and *Lear*, not the *Iliad* and *Odyssey*: 'The popular and traditional theory of the origin of these works was received and transmitted after the extraordinary circumstances which led to its first imposition had ceased to exist, because in fact, no one had any motive for taking the trouble to call it in question.' What then of Shakespeare?' 'Two hundred and fifty years ago, *our* poet – our Homer – was alive in the world,' yet as far as his works are concerned, 'to this hour, we know of their origin hardly so much as we knew of the Homeric epics'. How much longer, she wonders, in 'a period of historical inquiry and criticism like this', shall 'we be able to accept . . . the story of the Stratford poacher?'

Throughout, her essay is suffused with the language of the debates over the Higher Criticism and the life of Jesus – though strangely, this feature of her argument has passed almost without notice by critics. It begins to feel like Shakespeare becomes a surrogate for her doubts about her own faith: 'If you dissolve him do you not dissolve with him? If you take him to pieces, do you not undo us also?' Despite surface similarities there remained a significant difference between the Higher Critics and Bacon: they were willing to do the close philological work that showed how Homer's epics and Scripture were the products of different hands and different historical moments. But Bacon wanted to reach a similar conclusion without doing the painstaking philological analysis at the heart of this critical endeavour. She was content to insist, rather than demonstrate, that Shakespeare was as much a myth as Homer or Jesus. When that didn't suffice, she turned to invective.

Anyone still in Shakespeare's corner, she argued, would have to defend a 'pet horse-boy at Blackfriars', an 'old tradesman', an 'old showman and hawker of plays', and an all-round 'stupid, illiterate, third-rate play-actor'. It's bad enough that he couldn't read and was little more than a money-hungry actor; what really disqualifies him is his utter lack of 'the highest Elizabethan breeding, the very loftiest tone of that peculiar court culture'. Authorship could be determined through a process of elimination: whoever wrote the plays had to have had an 'acquaintance with life, practical knowledge of affairs, foreign travel and accomplishments, and above all, the last refinements, of the highest Parisian breeding'.

The real author 'carries the court perfume with him, unconsciously, wherever he goes' and 'looks into Arden and into Eastcheap from the court stand-point, not from these into the court'. Others would fine-tune this taxonomy, but Delia Bacon was the first to propose it: pure motives, good breeding, foreign travel, the best of educations and the scent of the court were necessary criteria for an author of works of 'superhuman genius'. The biographical record confirms that Shakespeare of Stratford fell well short of all these benchmarks. It defied 'common sense' and was 'too gross to be endured' to persist in the false belief that such a sad excuse for a man could have written the plays.

Bacon is relentless, cross-examining the hapless Shakespeare, as she herself had once been cross-examined, and thereby establishing a now venerable tradition of putting Shakespeare on trial for a host of offences so deeply appealing to the judges and lawyers who have swollen the ranks of the sceptics, beginning with Shakespeare's refusal to preserve his manuscripts. Turning to us, as jurors, she asks: 'He had those manuscripts . . . What did he do with them? He gave them to his cook' or perhaps 'poor Judith may have curled her hair to the day of her death with them'. She then turns on Shakespeare himself and demands: 'You will have to tell us what you did with them. The awakening ages will put you on the stand, and you will not leave it until you answer the question, "What did you do with them?" His silence tells us all we need to know. The paltry claim that might be offered in his defence – that he wrote for the stage, not for posterity – is handily dismissed: 'Who is it that writes, unconsciously, no doubt, and without it ever occurring to him that it was going to be printed, or to be read by any one?' Yet this is the man, she reminds us, whose 'bones are canonized', whose 'tomb is a shrine'.

By the time her relentless assault on Shakespeare's character ends, there's only room left for a paragraph or two to limn the real man, or men, behind the mask. Yet Bacon pulls up short at the very moment we expect to learn who in fact wrote the plays. The most she is willing to offer is some vague hints about the actual, unnamed authors having been men 'exercised in the control and administration of public affairs, men clothed even with imperial sway'; 'men who knew what kind of crisis in human history that was which they were born to occupy', and who had to work under 'the censorship of a capricious and timorous despotism', so repressive that anyone speaking one's mind ran the risk of 'cruel maimings and tortures old and new, life-long imprisonment, and death itself'. These were also men who stooped to conquer, who knew that 'in the master's hand' the 'degraded play-house' might 'yet be made to yield, even then, and under those conditions, better music than any which those old Greek sons of song had known how to wake in it'. All of this makes sense in light of what she argues in her book; but the book was not yet published and I suspect that this part of her argument simply bewildered readers.

While the true author or authors remain unnamed, in the mid-nineteenth century there could be no mistaking who is hinted at by 'the Philosopher who is only the Poet in disguise — the philosopher who calls himself the New Magician — the poet who was toiling and plotting to fill the globe with his arts'. And in case *that* was not obvious enough, she quotes from Bacon's *Advancement of Learning*. But she never elaborates here on the great story of how the band of frustrated republicans wrote the plays to counter Tudor and Stuart despotism. Perhaps she planned to turn to that in later instalments.

Her snide tone and reductive logic infuriated Shakespeare's supporters. By the time that Delia Bacon published this essay, the first American Shakespeare expert, Richard Grant White, had arrived on the scene. A quarter-century later White confessed that the editors at Putnam's had sent him Bacon's next article — the second of four she had submitted, and which was already in type — and invited him to write an introduction to it. He not only refused, he denigrated both essay and author, insisting that 'she must be insane; not a maniac, but what boys call "looney"'. White was working on his own Shakespeare book at the time and rather than engage Bacon's ideas found it easier to have her silenced.

Bacon never knew this, but it would probably have confirmed her own notions about the censorship of radical ideas. Even after her death White found it easier to vilify than refute her work, unfairly calling it a product of a disturbed mind, 'a mental aberration which soon after consigned her to the asylum in which she died'. White's intervention persuaded Putnam's to renege on its agreement with Delia Bacon. Before the three unpublished and now rejected instalments made it safely back to her, they were lost. Emerson was at fault – they had been entrusted to him – and his assistance was at an end. She had not made copies so the loss proved irreparable, and no record of their content survives. Bacon was devastated and beginning to worry that others, drawing on her published essay, would claim precedence for her discovery.

What she couldn't understand was that others were independently arriving at similar conclusions. Take, for example, the wonderful anecdote recorded in the journal *Baconiana*, in which R. A. Smith describes how back 'in 1844, at his home in Nashville Tennessee, Mr. Return Jonathan Meigs was reading Bacon's *Instauratio* in the original Latin. He suddenly closed the book and exclaimed: "This man Bacon wrote the works of Shakespeare."' Smith adds, 'Mr. Meigs's son, then a lad of 14 years, who was sitting in the same room with his father, heard his father's remark, and has never forgotten it. In later years they frequently conversed on the subject of Bacon and his writings, and the son became a firm believer in the statement that his father made that day.'

Delia Bacon had more to fear from William Smith, an Englishman. Shortly after her *Putnam's* piece appeared in 1856 Smith published a brief pamphlet, *Was Lord Bacon the Author of Shakespeare's Plays*, in which he argued that the plays pointed to the life of Bacon, not Shakespeare: 'The history of Bacon is just such as we should have drawn of Shakespeare, if we had been required to depict him from the internal evidence of his works.' Smith elaborated on this a year later in a book, *Bacon and Shakespeare*, which claimed, among other things, that the plays were meant to be read, not staged; that the Sonnets were autobiographical (and pointed to Francis Bacon's early life); that a comparison of the works of Bacon and Shakespeare showed striking similarities; and that the works were a product of an aristocrat whose 'daily walk, letters, and conversation, constitute the beau ideal of such a man as we might suppose the author of the plays to have been'.

Accusations flew that Smith had stolen Delia Bacon's conclusions. Hawthorne, in introducing Bacon's book in 1857, intimated as much. Smith wrote to Hawthorne protesting how wrong this was, and Hawthorne wrote back, apologising. But the *Athenaeum*, which had run a piece as early as March 1855 paraphrasing an account of Delia Bacon's ideas that had recently appeared in Norton's *Literary Gazette* of New York, asked incredulously, 'Will Mr. Smith assert that up to September 1856 he was unacquainted with Miss Bacon's theory? If so, we will make another assertion: namely, that Mr. Smith was the only man in England pretending to Shakespeare lore who enjoyed that amount of happy ignorance.' Smith responded that he had been thinking along these lines for some years. He probably had. But it's highly unlikely that Smith's pamphlet or book would have generated anywhere near the kind of interest that Bacon's article and book did – not only because Bacon had behind her some very powerful and visible literary figures, but also because her work (far more than his) was swept along on the powerful tide of the Higher Criticism.

With Hawthorne's quiet subvention *The Philosophy of the Plays of Shakspere Unfolded*, a rambling and almost unreadable book, was at last published in 1857, with five hundred copies for sale in England and another five hundred shipped over to America. The impossibly long title she had earlier proposed to her publishers was scrapped, though it more accurately conveys her argument: *The Advancement of Learning to Its True Sphere as Propounded by Francis Bacon and Other Writers of the Globe School, including the Part of Sir Walter Ralegh*. Hawthorne had been unable to prevail upon her to submit to editing ('Miss Bacon,' he later wrote, 'thrust the whole bulk of inspiration and nonsense into the press in a lump; and there tumbled out a ponderous octavo volume, which fell with a dead thump at the feet of the public'). It was the last thing Delia Bacon would ever publish and the first that bore her name. Her plans to remain in England for another year 'to prosecute the subject in a very different manner from any that I have been able to adopt hitherto' in 'order to make my second volume sustain the promise of this' were never realised. Her health, both mental and physical, had declined markedly during the previous year or so, much of it spent impoverished and in isolation. Shortly after the book came out she lost her wits, was briefly institutionalised in Warwickshire and then brought home to America, where she spent the last two years of her life in an asylum.

While Bacon had Hawthorne to thank for seeing her book at last into print, it was Hawthorne who unfortunately shaped for posterity the unshakable image of Bacon as a madwoman in the attic, a gothic figure who might have stepped out of the pages of his fiction. In 1863 he published an essay about her, 'Memories of a Gifted Woman', that left readers with an indelible image of Delia Bacon haunting Shakespeare's grave, eager to unearth the long sought-for evidence that would prove her theory once and for all, daring the warning carved on Shakespeare's gravestone, 'curst be he that moves my bones':

Groping her way up the aisle and towards the chancel, she sat down on the elevated part of the pavement above Shakespeare's grave. If the divine poet really wrote the inscription there, and cared as much about the quiet of his bones as its deprecatory earnestness would imply, it was time for those crumbling relics to bestir themselves under her sacrilegious feet. But they were safe. She made no attempt to disturb them; though, I believe, she looked narrowly into the crevices between Shakespeare's and the two adjacent stones, and in some way satisfied herself that her single strength would suffice to lift the former, in case of need. She threw the feeble ray of her lantern up towards the bust, but could not make it visible beneath the darkness of the vaulted roof. Had she been subject to superstitious terrors, it is impossible to conceive of a situation that could better entitle her to feel them, for if Shakespeare's ghost would rise at any provocation, it must have shown itself then; but it is my sincere belief, that, if his figure appeared within the scope of her dark lantern, in his slashed doublet and gown, and with his eyes bent on her beneath the high, bald forehead, just as we see him in the bust, she would have met him fearlessly and controverted his claims to the authorship of the plays, to his very face.

Hawthorne didn't know it, but Bacon had designs not only on Shakespeare's grave but also upon his monument. She would have taken that secret to the grave had she not confided in her brother, who then shared this bit of information with her physician: 'her hallucination about Shakespeare has been, I believe, constant'. He adds:

She believes then, I suppose, believes now that the old tomb in the Church at Stratford-on-Avon, if she could be persuaded to take it down, would give conclusive evidence that the authorship of those plays which have been the world's admiration belong to Lord Bacon, Sir Walter Ralegh, and others, and withal a key to the hidden meaning of the Shakespearean Scriptures.

In this respect, too, she would anticipate future tomb-raiders eager to prove that someone other than Shakespeare had written the plays.

Shakespeare scholars have too often found it more convenient to invoke Hawthorne's gothic vision than to take seriously Emerson's posthumous verdict: 'Our wild Whitman . . . and Delia Bacon, with genius, but mad . . . are the sole producers that America has yielded in ten years.' It was easier to dismiss her as a madwoman (this 'eccentric American spinster' really 'was mad', Samuel Schoenbaum insisted), one who led MacWhorter on, and us too, than to admit that she had merely taken mainstream assumptions and biographical claims a step or two further – albeit a dangerously mistaken one – than the scholars themselves had been willing to go. The intensity of the personal attacks begs the question of what was so threatening about her. Schoenbaum called Delia Bacon the first of the deviants – a term rich in religious, psychological, even sexual connotations. Perhaps it wasn't her difference that proved so unnerving, but rather the extent to which her theory built on shared, if unspoken, beliefs.

One of these had to do with the extent to which the personality and temperament of the author of *The Tempest* closely resembled that of Francis Bacon. One of the last things Delia Bacon wrote was an unpublished 'author's apology and claim', now, along with most of her surviving letters and papers, housed in the Folger Shakespeare Library. The long and rambling essay ends with Horatio's words to a dying Hamlet and a hopeful declaration: 'Rest Rest, perturbed spirit! Delia Bacon. Stratford-on-Avon. The Shakespeare Problem Solved.' But it is *The Tempest* that powerfully holds her imagination in this, her own version of Prospero's great speech on how 'our revels now are ended':

The solving of these enigmas, the unraveling of this work, is going to make work and sport for us all; it is going to make a name – a scientific name, a common name, and a proper name, for us all. The name for us each, and the name for us all, scientifically defined, is at the bottom of it. We shall never solve the enigma, we shall never read these plays, till we come to that. '*Untie the spell*' is the word. That is the word on the *Isle of Prosper-O*, that magic isle . . . This discovery was not made, could not have been made, by one impatient for the world's acknowledgements, or by one who loved best, or prized most, the sympathy, the approbation, or – the wisdom of the living. It was made, it had to be, by one instructed, not theoretically only, in the esoteric doctrine of the Elizabethan Age.

Her words and Prospero's – and, for her, Francis Bacon's – merge, are one. Delia Bacon had concluded her great task. She had also touched upon something that deeply resonated with many Victorian readers, a sense that the personality of the author of this last great play was much like that of the serene, learned, bookish Francis Bacon.

Hawthorne famously claimed of *The Philosophy of the Plays of Shakspere Unfolded* that 'it has been the fate the of this remarkable book never to have had more than a single reader'. He was wrong.

Within a year of its publication and the dissemination of its argument in reviews and newspapers in England, Europe and the United States, the Baconian movement became international, with writers weighing in on the controversy in India, South Africa, France, Sweden, Germany, Denmark, Poland, Austria, Italy, Hungary, Holland, Russia and Egypt. Word spread as far as the Mississippi River, where a pair of riverboat pilots vigorously argued the merits of Delia Bacon's case against Shakespeare. One of the pilots moved by her arguments was a young man named Samuel Clemens, soon to be known to the world by his pseudonym, Mark Twain.

Mark Twain

On a chilly Friday afternoon in early January 1909, Mark Twain awaited a trio of weekend guests at Stormfield, his home in Redding, Connecticut. Twain had recently turned seventy-three. Though still spry, he was not in the best of health. He was a widower, his wife and best critic, Livia, having died five years earlier. Isabel Lyon, his forty-five-year-old secretary, did her best to fill Livia's place, while keeping Twain's two surviving children, Clara and Jean, distant from their father and Stormfield. Instead of family, the ageing Twain was surrounded by a doting secretary, a business manager, a resident biographer, stenographers and housekeepers – a host of retainers who called him, with no hint of irony, 'the King'. It cost a lot to maintain this entourage, which meant that Twain, who kept losing money on disastrous business ventures, then earning it back from books and lectures, had to keep writing.

A great final project continued to elude him; there would be no transcendent 'late phase' to his artistic career. Twain's best work, for which he hoped to be remembered, was becoming a thing of the increasingly distant past. His first bestseller, *The Innocents Abroad*, had been published forty years earlier. The torrent of great works that followed – including *Tom Sawyer* in 1876, *The Prince*

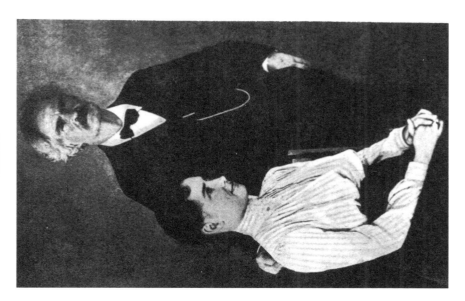

and the Pauper in 1881, Life on the Mississippi in 1883, The Adventures of Huckleberry Finn in 1884, A Connecticut Yankee in King Arthur's Court in 1889 and Pudd'nhead Wilson in 1894 – had, by century's end, slowed to a trickle.

Searching for something to write about, Twain turned to the subject he knew best, one that had always been at the centre of his fictional world: himself. He had been experimenting with autobiography for decades and now seized on a new approach, a kind of free association, recorded by a stenographer: 'Start at no particular time of your life; wander at your free will all over your life: talk only about the things that interest you for the moment.' Twain even invited his recently appointed biographer, Albert Bigelow Paine, to

Helen Keller and Mark Twain, 1902, photograph by E. C. Kopp

sit in while he dictated a half-million words in 250 or so sessions between 1906 and 1909. Twain was convinced that he had stumbled onto something original: 'I intend that this autobiography shall become a model for all future autobiographies when it is published, after my death, and I also intend that it shall be read and admired a good many centuries because of its form and method.'

What he dictated wasn't all that revealing or even necessarily true. Paine, who was familiar with the basic facts of his subject's life, saw soon enough that 'Mark Twain's memory had become capricious and his vivid imagination did not always supply his story with details of crystal accuracy. But it was always a delightful story.' The experiment was a financial, though not critical, success: in 1906 Twain began selling five-thousand-word autobiographical instalments to *The North American Review*, a venture so profitable that he was able to purchase the 248-acre Redding estate and build a villa that he had initially considered naming 'Autobiography House' before settling on 'Stormfield'. He was confident that he could churn out fifty thousand words a month of autobiographical dictation for the rest of his life.

Twain's last book, published in 1909, was subtitled *From My Autobiography*, which at first glance seems peculiar, since the book is titled *Is Shakespeare Dead?* The book is celebrated to this day by those who believe, as Twain came to believe and wittily argued in these pages, that Shakespeare could not have written the plays attributed to him. What's easily overlooked, both by those who hail the book and by those dismayed that such a prominent author could write it, is what led Twain to this conclusion: a conviction that great fiction, including his own, was necessarily autobiographical. It followed that, given what was known about his life, Shakespeare could have no claim to the works. A great deal was riding on this argument for Twain, for if the man from Stratford had indeed written the plays, Twain's mostly deeply held beliefs about the nature of fiction and on how major writers drew on personal experience would be wrong.

Twain's fascination with autobiography coincided with a significant shift in Anglo-American literary culture. By the early twentieth century, autobiography was fast establishing itself as a major form of imaginative writing, a position from which it has yet to be dislodged. When in 1887 Twain's friend William Dean Howells asked him to recommend titles for a series of 'Choice Autobiographies', Twain couldn't name many: 'I didn't know there were any but old [Benjamin] Franklin's and Benvenuto Cellini's. But if I should think of any I will mention them with pleasure.' Many others had in fact been written, but the genre was only beginning to command attention and a reading public; the very term 'autobiography' had only entered the language at the start of the nineteenth century. A hundred years later, major literary figures were turning to the form in increasing numbers. As Twain was dictating his autobiography, Henry James, Joseph Conrad, Arnold Bennett and Henry Adams were writing theirs.

It's not easy to determine how many autobiographies, especially by novelists, were being written in the early twentieth century. But something was clearly happening: one of the few scholars who has tried counting American literary autobiographies concludes that between '1800 and 1880 only twenty-six autobiographies were published by authors, journalists, or novelists, but in the forty years between 1880 and 1920' that number had more than doubled and redoubled again. By the mid-twentieth century, propelled in part by psychoanalytic theories about how we become who we are, the number of those – especially writers – publishing the story of their own lives had skyrocketed, with one scholar counting over five thousand American autobiographies in the thirty-five years following the Second World War. My guess is that figures in Britain followed a similar steep curve.

Fiction, too, was becoming much more autobiographical, and self-consciously so, on both sides of the Atlantic. And at some point along the way it had become a commonplace that writers had always mined their life experiences in furnishing their fictional worlds. Allon White, whose *The Uses of Obscurity* illuminates this development, identifies 'a new kind of reading, a new kind of critical attention in the period, whereby the sophisticated read through the text to the psychological state of the author'. Novelists, meanwhile, were becoming increasingly sensitive to the ways in which fiction-writing was inescapably self-revealing. White quotes as illustrative of these simultaneous developments Joseph Conrad's reflections in *Some Reminiscences*, first published (at the urgings of Conrad's friend Ford Madox Ford) in the pages of the *English Review*:

I know that a novelist lives in his work. He stands there, the only reality in an invented world, among imaginary things, happenings, and people. Writing about them, he is only writing about himself. But the disclosure is not complete. He remains, to a certain extent, a figure behind the veil; a suspected rather than seen presence – a movement and a voice behind the draperies of fiction.

Conrad wrote this in 1908, as this mode of reading and writing was becoming fully established. It's hard, though, to think of a major novelist in England or America much before Mark Twain who could confess, as he did in 1886, that

my books are simply autobiographies. I do not know that there is any incident in them which sets itself forth as having occurred in my personal experience which did not occur. If the incidents were dated, they could be strung together in their due order, and the result would be an auto-biography.

But I suspect that quite a few novelists would soon concede as much. It's surprising that such a major shift in what writers offer – and in what readers look for – has attracted relatively little critical attention. This emerging if largely unexamined conviction that fiction was necessarily autobiographical would affect not only what subsequent novelists would write, but also how previous authors, especially Shakespeare, were read. This, as much as any other factor, explains why so many – Twain included – came to question Shakespeare's authorship of the plays.

For Twain, the notion that great writing had to be drawn from life – rather than from what an author heard, read, or simply imagined – was an article of faith, at the heart of his conception of how serious writers worked. He held himself to this strict standard when, in 1870, in his mid-thirties, he decided to write about mining diamonds in South Africa, but didn't want to risk going there himself. Rather than abandon the idea, he hired a stunt-writer; he would draw on his first-hand experience and write the book 'just as if I had been through it all myself'. His stand-in, James H. Riley, was a journalist who in his younger days had been a gold miner. Twain drew up a detailed contract: Riley was to 'skirmish, prospect, work, travel, and take minute notes . . . for three months, or five or six if necessary'. Twain saw himself in the tradition of Daniel Defoe, drawing on the travails of Alexander Selkirk to create his masterpiece, *Robinson Crusoe* (conveniently forgetting that Defoe hadn't paid Selkirk to be marooned on an island for four and a half years so that he could fictionalise his experiences). Upon his return, Riley was to move into Twain's house for as long as a year and be debriefed for 'one or two hours . . . every day' until Twain had 'pumped [him] dry'. Riley sailed off, had adventures, and took notes. Unfortunately, on the voyage home he 'wounded his mouth with a fork while eating, with ensuing blood poisoning and death soon after his return'. Twain now owed his publisher $2,000 that had been handed over to Riley for expenses, and his publisher preferred repayment with a book rather than cash. So Twain went back to mining his Mississippi boyhood – his views on writing from life hadn't altered – and the death of Riley led to the birth of *Tom Sawyer*, published in 1876.

Retelling his life-story overlapped with Twain's other great preoccupation: ensuring that he would still be read long after his death. A biographical sketch of Twain published in 1899 (signed by his nephew, Samuel Moffett, who touched it up, though it was written by Twain himself) made the case for both at once: 'In the thirty-eight years of his literary activity Mark Twain has seen a numerous succession of "American humorists" rise, expand into sudden popularity, and disappear, leaving hardly a memory behind.' The last phrase echoes one of Twain's favourite lines from Shakespeare, Prospero's description in *The Tempest* of how all

shall dissolve,

And like this insubstantial pageant faded,

Leave not a wrack behind.

(4.1.154–6)

To speak of artistic legacy was inevitably for Twain to invoke the one writer whose reputation had never flagged. As if to reassure readers that he would follow in Shakespeare's footsteps rather than those of the forgotten 'American humorists', Moffett (or rather Twain himself) declares that 'Mark Twain has become a classic, not only at home, but in all lands whose people read and think about the common joys and sorrows of humanity'.

Writers had long engaged in self-promotion; Twain was the first to brand himself. As early as 1873 he had tried to trademark 'Mark Twain', and in 1908 formally established the Mark Twain Company to promote his work and image. Starting in 1909 the company, rather than Twain himself, retained copyright to new works. Mark Twain cigars and Mark Twain whiskey were already on the market. We may struggle to call to mind what Emerson or Hawthorne or Melville looked like, but not Twain. From early on, he made sure that his image remained distinctive and unforgettable – from the shaggy moustache, shock of white hair and ever-present pipe to the white serge suits, worn year-round, that were his signature outfit. Twain had become iconic, his visage almost as familiar as the one staring back at us from the frontispiece of the 1623 Folio. Those invited to his seventieth birthday celebration in 1905 were given 'foot-high plaster busts' of Twain to lug home. He left an extensive photographic trail (making sure to include his picture and autograph in the front of his books), wouldn't talk to unauthorised biographers, and recognised the power of new media, even licensing Thomas Edison's company to film *The Prince and the Pauper*, complete with out-takes of him padding around Stormfield. Twain worked hard at being a celebrity – one of those words that now seems timeless but had first been used to describe 'a famous person' only in the course of his own lifetime.

Another celebrity was visiting Twain that weekend in January 1909: Helen Keller, whose fame was fast approaching his own. She was hailed internationally for having overcome the loss of sight and hearing in early childhood as well as for her widely admired autobiography, *The Story of My Life* (1903). Keller deeply valued her friendship with Twain, who treated her, she recalled, 'not as a freak but as a handicapped woman seeking a way to circumvent extraordinary difficulties'. Looking back on their friendship in *Midstream: My Later Life* (1929), she describes how they first met in 1894, when she was fourteen and he was still 'vigorous, before the shadows began to gather'. They had stayed in touch since then and after Keller had sent him a copy of her second book, *The World I Live In* (1908), Twain wrote back urging her to visit – 'the summons', she recalled, 'of a beloved king'.

Travelling with Keller to Stormfield was her longtime teacher and companion, Anne Sullivan – now Anne Sullivan Macy – famous in her own right for having taught her deaf and blind pupil how to communicate. She had recently accompanied Keller to Radcliffe College at Harvard University, and assisted her there by spelling into her hand the content of classroom lectures. Keller had the good fortune while at Harvard to take two Shakespeare classes with the eminent George Lyman Kittredge, and wrote a thesis on the minor playwright George Peele for a class taught by another Shakespeare expert, William A. Neilson, who soon became her friend. Keller's interest in Shakespeare only intensified after she received her degree. She even corresponded with a leading sceptic, Edwin Reed, whose books – *Francis Bacon Our Shakespeare* and *Bacon and Shake-speare Parallelisms* – had been devastatingly reviewed by her teacher, Kittredge, in *The Nation*. 'It was to Reed', Keller records, 'that I wrote that my Shakespeare was so strongly entrenched against Baconian arguments that he could never be dislodged.'

In the months leading up to her visit to Stormfield, Keller had immersed herself in Shakespeare scholarship, reading everything in Braille she could get hold of, and having other printed works communicated to her by tactile signing onto her hand by Anne Sullivan Macy, her mother and others. Her reading left Keller increasingly disappointed by the way that biographers had deified Shakespeare, whose life, she writes, as 'presented to the public in books and essays composed by scholars and literary men, is a myth of imposing proportions, and is growing every year in volume and fatuity', a 'mysterious, inspired Shakespeare whose godlike head is "lost among the clouds"'.

She began to turn her attention to the literature generated by the authorship controversy and in the weeks preceding her visit to Twain had published on the subject, reviewing George Greenwood's *The Shakespeare Problem Restated* (1908). Keller now admitted to grave doubts:

some years ago I declared that . . . no siege of fact or argument could make me honour another than Shakespeare of Stratford . . . but Mr. Greenwood's masterly exposition has led to the conclusion that Shakespeare of Stratford is not to be even thought of as a possible author of the most wonderful plays in the world.

'How long must we wait', she wondered, 'for the solution of the greatest problem in literature?'

Joining Helen Keller and her teacher on the visit to Stormfield was the man Anne Sullivan had recently and somewhat reluctantly married, John Macy, eleven years her junior. A lecturer at Harvard and a rising star in literary circles, Macy had been recruited to work with Keller on her first book, *The Story of My Life*. Since then, he had been tirelessly promoting Keller's career and, after his marriage to Anne Sullivan, sharing his political and literary enthusiasms – including the authorship question – with them both.

Twain greeted his house guests on the veranda of his Italianate villa dressed in his familiar white suit. Isabel Lyon kept detailed notes as well as snapshots of the memorable visit. Lyon writes of Twain appearing in one photograph 'in an elated mood, yet somewhat wistful', alongside his guests. The photograph only hints at the tensions just beneath the surface. Lyon was struck with how openly John Macy flirted with Helen Keller (she may have heard rumours that Macy had wanted to marry Keller rather than her teacher). Lyon also thought Keller was 'in love with Macy' and watched as Macy 'encourages this emotion'. A 'plaintive and tired' Mrs Macy could only look on and confess her obvious distress to Lyon. Lyon herself was on the verge of a nervous breakdown; Twain's closest companion, she was soon to be banished from Stormfield.

After dinner that first evening Macy announced that he had brought along galley proofs of a forthcoming book, written by an English friend, William Stone Booth, called *Some Acrostic Signatures of Francis Bacon*. Isabel Lyon observed that 'the King was instantly alert'. The following day the conversation returned to the authorship question and Macy announced that Booth had found in every one of the plays published in the First Folio an acrostic, hidden there by Francis Bacon. To prove the point, he pulled out some page proofs and showed the ciphers to Twain, including one from the closing lines of *The Tempest*, where Booth had underlined a dozen key words in the facsimile of Prospero's Epilogue as they appeared in the 1623 Folio. Booth believed that the hidden signature in this play was especially convincing, coming as it did from the play's closing lines, 'the playwright's last word to his audience, and the place where he would be likely to sign his name in cipher if writing either under a pseudonym or anonymously'.

Macy couldn't have chosen a better example to pique Twain's interest – or indeed that of most admirers of Shakespeare's works at the time, since Prospero's departure from the stage was nearly universally read as Shakespeare's own, the most transparently autobiographical moment in the canon. Twain had trouble identifying Booth's seemingly random string cipher. With Macy's help, he was finally able to follow it from the bottom of the page to the top, singing out the first letter of each key word and successfully spelling out the encoded signature: 'FRANCISCO BACONO'. Macy confidently announced that Booth's book was 'going to make a complete establishment of the fact that Shakespeare never wrote the plays attributed to him'.

Those quick to dismiss the possibility that a hidden acrostic signature could be overlooked for centuries may be unaware that a leading scholar had made such a find in a canonical work just a few years before Booth had begun his search. *The Testament of Love* was a medieval prose narrative that had been accepted without question as Chaucer's – by the likes of Shakespeare, Milton, Dryden and Coleridge – since its inclusion in the 532 edition of his collected works. By the early nineteenth century, biographers such as William Godwin were drawing on key details in *The Testament of Love* to flesh out their story of Chaucer's life. Then, in 1897, while freshly editing this work, Cambridge professor Walter Skeat discovered that the first letter of the first word of each chapter formed an acrostic that spelled out: 'MARGARETE: OF VIRTW, HAVE MERCI ON THSKNVI.' 'Margaret of virtue, have mercy' made sense enough to Skeat, but who was 'Thsknui'? The puzzle was solved by his friend Henry Bradley, who pointed out that the order of the closing chapters had been rearranged. The acrostic originally read 'THIN VSK' – 'thine Usk.' After three and a half centuries of false attribution, *The Testament of Love* was at last revealed to have been written not by Chaucer but by his fellow writer and admirer Thomas Usk. If one of Chaucer's works was now shown to have been written by somebody else, why not one or more of Shakespeare's?

A fierce race was on to see who would be the first to prove that Bacon's authorship was encoded in Shakespeare's plays. Booth was a relative newcomer to the contest; his formidable competitors and their teams of assistants had already devoted years of their lives to scanning Folio pages for word ciphers and biliteral ciphers.

By 1909 two of Booth's main rivals had already sailed to England, convinced they were on the verge of finding Bacon's long-buried manuscripts of the plays. For those invested in the authorship question, the excitement was intense. In July 1909, the official Baconian journal, *Baconiana*, excitedly announced 'The Goal in Sight' and held up publication through the autumn to be the first to break the news of the great discovery.

It was Delia Bacon's friend Samuel Morse who had set in motion the age's fascination with codes and ciphers. The effect of the telegraph and Morse code, not only on the popular appreciation of encryption, but also on how knowledge was now imagined as an act of decoding, was profound. Even as readers were searching texts for encoded clues, writers like Edgar Allan Poe (in stories like 'The Gold Bug') were beginning to produce fiction that turned on deciphering codes. At a moment when even children could send coded messages and governments and businesses regularly encrypted communications, the notion that earlier writers had hidden codes in their works no longer seemed far-fetched. And as the world-wide popularity of *The Da Vinci Code* attests, these Victorian assumptions have, if anything, become more deeply entrenched.

Cipher Hunters

A few years after Mark Twain established the publishing house of Charles L. Webster and Company in 1884 he had a chance to publish what promised to be the definitive deciphering of Shakespeare's works. Its author, Ignatius Donnelly – former Lieutenant Governor of Minnesota, then three-term congressman, and a lifelong political reformer – had already won a wide following as a writer with his wildly popular *Atlantis: The Antediluvian World* in 1882, in which he argued that there really had been a lost world of Atlantis hinted at by the ancients. Donnelly followed up that success a year later with *Ragnarok: The Age of Fire and Gravel*, which claimed that a great comet had smashed into the Earth aeons ago, almost destroying the planet. Even before these books came out, Donnelly had turned to a new project: 'I have been working . . . at what I think is a great discovery,' he wrote in his diary, 'a cipher in Shakespeare's Plays . . . asserting Francis Bacon's authorship of the plays . . . I am certain there is a cipher there and I think I have the key.' It took Donnelly six years of exhausting labour to work out the code and publish his findings in the thousand-page *The Great Cryptogram: Francis Bacon's Cipher in the So-Called Shakespeare Plays* (1888).

Twain later recalled that when 'Ignatius Donnelly's book came out, eighteen or twenty years ago, I not only published it, but read it'. That's not quite true. Twain had initially decided against taking it on, but then changed his mind and condemned his partner for failing to publish it. Twain had read Donnelly's book closely and found it 'an ingenious piece of work'. In the end, though, he didn't find the acrostics convincing enough: 'a person had to work his imagination rather hard sometimes if he wanted to believe in

Cipher Wheel, frontispiece to vol. 2 of Orville Ward Owen's *Sir Francis Bacon's Cipher Story* (Detroit, 1894)

the acrostics', and, as a result, the book 'fell pretty flat'. But Twain heartily endorsed Donnelly's argument that writers drew upon what they experienced first-hand, not what 'they only know about by hearsay'.

Donnelly had stumbled onto the authorship question by accident. Flipping through the pages of a volume his son was reading – *Every Boy's Book* – he came across a chapter on cryptography, where he learned that the 'most famous and complex cipher perhaps ever written was by Lord Bacon'. What 'followed, like a flash' for Donnelly was the question: 'Could Lord Bacon have put a cipher in the plays?' He immediately turned to Bacon's late work, *De Augmentis Scientiarum*, to learn more about Baconian ciphers, and was hooked. It didn't take long for Donnelly to conclude that Bacon had embedded 'in the plays a cipher story, to be read when the tempest that was about to assail civilization had passed away'. The story was already taking on the apocalyptic dimensions of Atlantis and Ragnarok. Donnelly supposed that if Bacon had encoded a message, it would read along the lines of 'I, Francis Bacon, of St. Albans, son of Nicholas Bacon, Lord Keeper of the Great Seal of England, wrote these Plays, which go by the name of William Shakespeare.' Lacking a concordance, he set about reading through the complete works in search of something like it.

Having come up empty-handed, Donnelly decided that the encoding must have been far more sophisticated, so complex that Bacon had to have written the code first and the plays almost as an afterthought. As he later explained:

before Francis Bacon put pen to paper to write these plays, he had mapped out the cipher story; and had his pages blocked off in little squares, each square numbered according to its place from the top to the bottom of the page. He next adjusted the length of his columns, and their subdivisions, to enable him to pursue significant words like 'written,' 'playes,' 'shakst,' 'spur,' etc., over and over again, and when all this was in place, he proceeded to write out the plays; using his miraculous ingenuity to bring the right words in the proper positions.

Donnelly didn't have a clue about how compositors worked in Elizabethan printing houses, where such a scheme would have been unimaginable and the layout he describes impossible to reproduce. Even with his complex arithmetical scheme, Donnelly had to fudge his word cipher, which was based on the numerical distance between his arbitrarily chosen key words. Worse still, he constantly miscounted in order to arrive at satisfying results. Cryptologists who have examined his method have concluded that he 'described Bacon's own cipher without understanding it' and 'showed a fatal inclination to seize on whole words which happen to be in both the vehicle and the message to be deciphered'. It also turned out that his cipher could produce virtually any message one wanted to find. Donnelly nevertheless remained confident 'beyond a doubt' that 'there is a Cipher in the so-called Shakespeare Plays. The proofs are cumulative. I have shown a thousand of them.'

Donnelly is notable less for his cryptographic skills than for his belief that there was a grander, autobiographical story buried in the plays. He saw, especially in *The Tempest*, a self-portrait of 'the princely, benevolent and magnanimous' Francis Bacon, who, 'like Prospero, had been cast down'. What began with a disguised author's hidden life blossomed into far-reaching and revisionist history: 'the inner story in the plays', Donnelly writes, makes visible 'the struggles of factions in the courts; the interior view of the birth of religions; the first colonization of the American continent, in which Bacon took an active part, and something of which is hidden in *The Tempest*'.

In the end, finding a disguised signature or an embedded autobiography or even rewriting world history wasn't enough, not for Donnelly and not for most cipher hunters. Like many other doubters, he went in search of that Holy Grail, the lost manuscripts of the plays. He suspected that they were 'buried probably in the earth, or in a vault of masonry, a great iron or brass coffer'. While promoting his book in England he tried and failed to persuade the Earl of Verulam, Bacon's descendant, to allow him to excavate at the estate in hopes of unearthing the long-lost manuscripts, following hints in the cipher.

We can smile at all this now, but in his own day, Donnelly's work won many admirers, among them the poet Walt Whitman, who recommended the book to friends and was inspired by it to write a brief poem – 'Shakespeare Bacon's Cipher' – later included in his *Leaves of Grass*:

I doubt it not – then more, far more;
In each old song bequeathed – in every noble page or text,
(Different – something unrecked before – some unsuspected author,)
In every object, mountain, tree, and star – in every birth and life,
As part of each – evolved from each – meaning, behind the ostent,
A mystic cipher waits infolded.

The poem initially bore the subtitle 'A Hint to Scientists'. For Whitman, there was something not dreamt of in the philosophy of those supposed experts; he found deeply appealing the idea of a hidden, mystical meaning in all things, in all poetry – unseen by the rigid and doctrinaire.

Twain, too, was inspired by Donnelly's approach, enough to try his own hand at deciphering a literary work that had long fascinated him: John Bunyan's 1678 classic, *The Pilgrim's Progress* – though he never developed these ideas beyond a notebook sketch. Even as Donnelly and others had been troubled by the fit between the provincial man from Stratford and the greatness of the plays attributed to him, Twain became convinced that *The Pilgrim's Progress* could never have been written by someone with Bunyan's limited life experience. Twain concluded that *The Pilgrim's Progress*, with its account of the 'Eternal City', could only have been written by somebody who had actually been to Rome; Bunyan, who Twain joked, had never seen 'anything but a canal boat', assuredly hadn't. So Twain reassigned the work to a writer he knew had travelled widely, John Milton, whose 'great Continental Tour enabled him to imagine the travel in the Dream – and no stay-at-home could ever have done it'. Milton, Twain added, 'was a clandestine duck' who 'used to always jerk a public poem to divert attention from what he meant to do some day' in *The Pilgrim's Progress*; 'not knowing' that Milton 'was riddling', readers 'took him at his word' and misread his intentions. Once down the conspiratorial road, it was hard to stop. Twain also suspected that Milton also became involved in the Shakespeare conspiracy, and supposed that the 'furtive Bacon got him and Ben Jonson to play into his hand', persuading Milton to contribute an enthusiastic poem on 'Shakespeare' for the 1632 Second Folio. Knowing and admiring 'Bacon's secret', Twain writes, Milton 'afterward borrowed the idea without credit'. As tempting as it is to dismiss this sketch as a parody on Twain's part, he seems far too invested, researched it too thoroughly and draws too many connections for it to simply be a joke: *The Pilgrim's Progress*, he concludes, 'must be read between the lines'. 'This has never been suspected before,' he concludes, but 'the cipher makes it plain.'

While *The Great Cryptogram* failed to resolve the authorship question, there were those who believed that its premise was sound; it was only Donnelly's grasp of Baconian ciphers that was faulty. Orville Ward Owen, a prosperous physician from Detroit who had most of Shakespeare committed to memory, took up the challenge in the 1890s. Like Donnelly, he was convinced that Bacon had probably employed a word code, though one based on a different set of 'guide' or 'key' terms, including 'fortune', 'honour', 'nature' and 'reputation'.

Owen had a great advantage over Donnelly, for in his search for how to discover Bacon's cipher, he claimed he had stumbled upon a forty-three-page instruction manual, in verse, that Bacon had left for his future 'decipherer'. Owen never elaborated on this discovery, nor did he ever explain how he managed to decode the manual (a critic complained that it was a bit 'like picking the lock of a safe, only to find inside the key to the lock you have already picked'). Bacon, Owen wrote, had instructed his decipherer to

Take your knife and cut all our books asunder,
And set the leaves on a great firm wheel
Which rolls and rolls, and turning the
Fickle rolling wheel, throw your eyes
Upon FORTUNE, that goddess blind, that stands upon
A spherical stone, that turning and incessant rolls,
In restless variation.

Owen faithfully followed Bacon's instructions and built a decoding machine consisting of two large drums on which revolved a two-foot-wide and thousand-foot-long canvas sheet. He pasted onto this long loop the pages of each book attributed to Bacon – which, the cipher told him, included not only Bacon and Shakespeare's works, but also those written under Bacon's other masks: Christopher Marlowe, Robert Greene, Edmund Spenser, Robert Burton and George Peele. Owen and his capable assistants would spin the drums and as the cut-and-pasted writing revolved, key words would reveal themselves. Adjacent lines or phrases would then be transcribed and textual messages reconstructed. Since his key terms appeared over ten thousand times on the pasted script, and the coded message could appear dozens of lines away from that word, there was a good deal of interpretive latitude about which phrases or lines Owen could claim as part of the cipher message.

The story that emerged in the six volumes he and his assistants produced – *Sir Francis Bacon's Cipher Story* – was breathtaking, and explained why Bacon had been so careful to conceal his story in code. Embedded within the plays (and the other works attributed to Bacon) was an autobiography that overturned a great deal of received wisdom and made Donnelly's discoveries seem tame in comparison. Queen Elizabeth was no virgin queen and Francis Bacon no son of Lady Anne and Sir Nicholas Bacon. Bacon only belatedly learned that he was the bastard child of the Earl of Leicester and Elizabeth herself – making him the rightful heir to the English throne. Hamlet could now be properly read as the poet's lament at being denied the throne. Elizabeth had taken the

[141]

play as a personal attack by her natural son and banished Bacon to France after telling him:

I am thy mother.
Thou mightst be an emperor but that I will not
Bewray whose son thou art;
Nor though with honourable parts
Thou art adorned, will I make thee great
For fear thyself should prove
My competitor and govern England and me.

But before Elizabeth had a chance to acknowledge Bacon as her son and heir, Robert Cecil strangled her to death. The plays, for Owen, were clearly the by-product of their author's tumultuous life and, once again, a key to the suppressed history of the age.

One of Owen's most capable assistants, Elizabeth Wells Gallup, now entered the competition. While sympathetic to Owen's word cipher and to the autobiographical account he had uncovered, she also believed that Bacon had embedded a biliteral cipher in his writing — the type of cipher Bacon had himself described at length in 1622. This ingenious code depended on the writer using two fonts that looked alike but that a practised eye could see were not identical. Convinced that Bacon had used this cipher in the First Folio and other works and eager to make fresh discoveries, Gallup abandoned the Cipher Wheel in favour of close and meticulous analysis of alternating fonts. George Fabyan, a wealthy Bostonian who had supported Owen's research, now financed hers as well.

Another ally, Kate Prescott, leaves behind a revealing portrait of Gallup at work, overcoming a particularly knotty decoding problem:

One morning I entered the room where Mrs. Gallup was working and found her 'floored.' She had gone far enough to feel convinced that she had made no mistake, that her alphabet was working, but here she had eleven consonants without one vowel: W S G P S R B C M R G. It was some days before she solved the riddle. The letters resolved themselves into the initials of the names William Shakespeare, George Peele, Spenser, Robert Burton, Christopher Marlowe, Robert Greene – Bacon's masks . . . From then on all was clear sailing.

Prescott's account of Gallup piecing together names from a string of letters recalls nothing so much as the scene in *Twelfth Night* in which Malvolio is spied on as he decodes an unsigned letter with its cryptic message 'M.O.A.I. doth sway my life'. Malvolio gets off to a promising start – "M." Malvolio. "M" – why that begins my name'. But he runs into trouble when he sees that 'there is no consonancy in the sequel', since '"A" should follow, but "O" does'. Malvolio, the patron saint of hopeful decipherers, resolves the matter in his own favour by fiddling with the anagram: 'yet to crush this a little, it would bow to me,' for 'every one of these letters are in my name'. The first decoder of Shakespeare's words, Malvolio would not be the last to crush an anagram to fit the name he so badly wanted to find.

The biliteral cipher revealed secrets denied to Owen. While Gallup, like her former employer, found evidence confirming that Bacon was Queen Elizabeth's son, she was able to add a crucial biographical detail: the Earl of Essex was also Elizabeth's child and therefore Bacon's younger brother (making far more poignant the clash between the two, when Bacon had to prosecute his brother after Essex's abortive coup in 1601 – a source of 'unhappiness and ever-present remorse' forever after for Bacon). There would be even greater revelations, for the plays turned out to contain, like a set of Chinese boxes, still other plays encoded in them. These were truly plays-within-plays, unlike their pale shadows in *A Midsummer Night's Dream* and *Hamlet*.

The fantasy of extending the canon, a dream that had led young William-Henry Ireland to forge *Vortigern*, had at last been legitimately realised. Five long-buried tragedies, all drawn from the author's circle – *Mary Queen of Scots*, *Robert the Earl of Essex*, *Robert, Earl of Leicester*, *The Death of Marlowe* and *Anne Boleyn* – confirmed that embedded within Shakespeare's art was a personal story as well as a necessarily suppressed history of his times. Unfortunately, Gallup only provides plot summaries and the occasional extract of these encoded works. But based on her findings she was able to conclude that Bacon had used these works as 'a receptacle of his plaints' and 'the escape valve of his momentary passions'. Collectively, they provided a rich biographical record of 'his lost hopes, and the expression of those which he still cherished for the future'.

The discoveries did not end there, nor could they, for there was still the matter of the lost manuscripts. Here, too, Gallup got ahead of Owen, after decoding Bacon's message that the hidden manuscripts could be found in 'certain old panels in the double work of Canonbury Tower' in Islington. To find their exact location, Bacon instructed: 'take panel five in B's tower room, slide it under fifty with such force as to gird a spring. Follow A, B, C, therein. Soon will the Mss. so much vaunted theme of F's many books be your own.' In sole possession of this revelation, Gallup set sail for England in 1907 and made her way directly to Islington.

She soon faced renewed competition from Owen, who had temporarily returned to his medical practice but was drawn back into the fray when he forwarded a copy of a decoded transcription that Kate Prescott and her husband had made of a 1638 edition of Sir Philip Sidney's *Arcadia* (it's not entirely clear how or why Bacon embedded this message in a book published long after he was dead and buried). Owen wrote back excitedly with '"an astounding message" that he had decoded their material and he now knew "where the manuscripts are!"' What enabled his discovery was a new kind of decoding, the 'King's Move Cipher', by which Owen began at one letter and moved from there in any direction, one space, much as a king moves in chess. This cipher soon revealed where Bacon had hid his literary treasures: 'two and a half miles above where the Wye River joins the Severn' near the Welsh border. There the decoder would find a 'pretty dell' near 'Wasp Hill', a cave and a castle. With the financial backing of the

Prescotts, Owen sailed to England to oversee the final stage of his great find – the unearthing of Bacon's books and manuscripts. His great Cipher Wheel was nothing compared with the dredging machinery rented by Owen to search the bottom of the Severn River for the buried manuscripts, sealed in waterproof lead containers. His search was international news, and stories and photos of his venture appeared in the British and American press. It was an exhilarating time for Baconians. It remained to be seen who would be the first to strike gold – he near Wales, or she in Islington.

Helen Keller chose this promising moment to add her voice to the growing chorus of sceptics. Five weeks after her visit to Twain in January 1909, she wrote to her long-time publisher at *Century Magazine*, Richard Watson Gilder, explaining that for 'months I have been interested in a subject of great moment, it seems to me, in the history of the literary world, and I write to ask if you would care to publish an article on Shakespeare and Baconian authorship'. She had been won over, she wrote, by Booth's string cipher, and hoped to be in print by the time his book would appear in April: the 'signatures are perfect, unmistakable, obvious acrostics. I have some right under my fingers in braille. I have traced and checked them, and I know that there is no accident, no imposture, no conjecture about them. No evidence given and sworn to in court could be more overwhelming than this.' She put it even more vividly in the article she was now drafting;

It was the experience of tracing out the acrostic signatures with the ten eyes of my fingers that opened this subject to me. When I found Francis Bacon's name clear and secure, I felt like a swimmer who, with no sense of danger, stands suddenly upright on a rock, and then sees in what a treacherous current he has been floating.

Keller was sure, she wrote to Gilder, that Booth's book 'will be the talk and the wonder of the literary world. It will surely make the ears of men tingle! My fingers tingle indeed at the mere thought of it. The beloved poet of Avon is dissolving in a mist.' Keller was not ignorant of the resistance she faced:

I realize that, like most of our poets and literary men, you belong to the 'true' faith; you worship Shakespeare of Stratford. I know that at first blush you will think I have deviated into a windy heresy. But believe me, I am telling you plain matters of fact which you can verify yourself. You will be among the first to admit the evidence of Bacon's authorship of the plays when you see it.

Gilder's response to the article she forwarded to him was disheartening: 'The whole subject is one which grieves me beyond words', he wrote, 'to think of your devoting your beautiful mind to.' The last thing he wanted was for Keller to take such a stance: 'For you to come out with a partisan article on the subject will not be impressive to the public mind and only involves you in controversy which alienates you for the time being from a true literary career.' Gilder, in his patronising way, was trying to protect a very successful product, the steady and profitable supply of autobiographical works from Helen Keller, which the reading public couldn't get enough of.

But Keller was fed up with churning out autobiographical chapters and with being 'utterly confined to one subject – myself', and felt that she had already 'exhausted it'. The previous summer, in the preface to her latest book, *The World I Live In*, she had confessed as much to her readers: 'Every book is in a sense autobiographical. But while other self-recording creatures are permitted at least to seem to change the subject, apparently nobody cares what I think of the tariff, the conservation of natural resources, or the . . . Dreyfus' case. Her 'editorial friends' had met her every attempt to reach beyond memoir with the words, "That is interesting. But will you please tell us what idea you had of goodness and beauty when you were six years old."

Keller was also irked by Gilder's insinuation that her interest in Bacon had been foisted on her by others. It was the same old story: those who didn't really know her or what she was capable of assumed that because she couldn't see or hear for herself, she couldn't think for herself either. She already had to deal with reviewers who claimed that the works published under her name were ghosted, could never have been written by someone who hadn't seen or heard what she described. Keller was uncharacteristically sharp with Gilder: 'Evidently you think I have been unhappily misled into this controversy. I do wish editors and friends could realize that I have a mind of my own.' She added, for good measure, that if 'there is anything to be troubled about, it is the ignorance of the public at large concerning the genuine data of Shakespeare's life, and this ignorance can be dispelled if an editor and teacher will examine the matter'.

Ironically, in her desire to move beyond autobiography, Keller joined a movement committed to the belief that literature was ultimately confessional. Yet Keller was living evidence that a great writer didn't need to see or hear things herself to write about them. Though she knew this, she remained unable to accept that it was Shakespeare's ability to imagine things that mattered – and that what he found in books, as much as or more than what he experienced first-hand, stimulated his imagination, as it had hers. In late May, Keller wrote to Booth, who had sent her a copy of his new book, apologising for having been unable to help get it 'the fair, unbiased consideration which it deserves'. Twain wrote to Keller a month later, urging her to give over 'the expectation of convincing anybody that Shakespeare did not write Shakespeare'. But if Gilder wouldn't run her piece, he added, somebody else would.

'Is Shakespeare Dead?'

Recalling her visit to Stormfield, Helen Keller writes that Twain 'was at first skeptical' about Booth's cipher 'and inclined to be facetious at our expense'. That facetiousness was either a pose or quickly vanished. Lyon remembered how Twain was galvanised by what he saw and 'seized upon it with a destroying zeal. He is as keen about it as Macy is; and you'd think that both men had Shakespeare by the throat righteously strangling him for some hideous crime.' Twain paced 'the long living room with his light quick step, flushed and excited', while Macy, seeing his obvious enthusiasm, 'promised to send to England' for a copy of the book that Keller had recently reviewed, Greenwood's *The Shakespeare Problem Restated*. For the rest of the weekend Twain held 'long searching enthusiastic talks' with Macy who was 'egging him on to write his own book "which will be timely"'.

Ordinarily, Twain didn't have the energy to write after seeing off house guests. Lyon recalled that this day 'was different. There was silence in his room all morning.' We have Twain's own words for what he excitedly confided that day to posterity in his auto-biographical dictation:

Two or three weeks from now a bombshell [will fall upon us] which may possibly woundily astonish the human race! For there is secretly and privately a book in press in Boston, by an English clergyman, which may unhorse Shakespeare permanently and put Bacon in the saddle. Once more the acrostic will be in the ascendant, and this time [it may be that] some people will think twice before they laugh at it. That wonder of wonders, Helen Keller, has been here on a three day's visit [*sic*] with her devoted teachers and protectors Mr. and Mrs. John Macy, and Macy has told me about the clergyman's book and bound me to secrecy. I am divulging the secret to my autobiography for distant future revealment, but shall keep the matter to myself in conversation.

'Distant future revealment' is a lovely notion, precisely what he thought Bacon had in mind by the acrostic. Twain could barely contain his excitement:

I am to have proof-sheets as fast as they issue from the galleys, and am to behave myself and keep still. I shall live in a heaven of excited anticipation for a while now. I have allowed myself for so many years the offensive privilege of laughing at people who believed in Shakespeare that I shall perish with shame if the clergyman's book fails to unseat that grossly commercial wool-stapler.

This was no parlour game for Twain, nor was his interest in Shakespeare and the authorship question a passing fancy. Quite the contrary; no writer of his day had wrestled longer with both. He was a regular theatregoer (as well as a dramatist in his own right) and familiar with Shakespeare's plays in performance – from Edwin Booth's *Hamlet* and Edwin Forrest's *Othello* to the rough-and-tumble frontier productions he had witnessed growing up and so brilliantly recaptures in *Huck Finn*. Twain not only reread Shakespeare's plays as preparation for *The Prince and the Pauper*, but also echoed and quoted Shakespeare in *A Connecticut Yankee in King Arthur's Court*, and even tried his hand in 1876 at Elizabethan prose in the bawdy *1601*, set at Queen Elizabeth's fireside, in which Shakespeare himself figures as a character.

When Twain visited Shakespeare's birthplace during a trip to England in 1872, he was already sceptical that the man from Stratford could have written these plays: 'It is curious there is not a scrap of manuscript in the shape of a letter or note of Shakespeare in the present day except the letter of someone trying to [borrow] £30 from him.' Twain's doubts in fact stretched back even further than that, to a time before he became a writer. His scepticism was less a deathbed conversion by an ageing writer obsessed with his legacy (though that too is part of it) than the confirmation of what he had half-suspected for over fifty years.

The heady days following the visit of Helen Keller and the Macys led Twain to admit what he had long left unspoken: from 'away back towards the very beginnings of the Shakespeare–Bacon controversy I have been on the Bacon side, and have wanted to see our majestic Shakespeare unhorsed'. When Twain asked himself what led him to side with Bacon, he couldn't quite say: 'My reasons for this attitude may have been good, they may have been bad, but such as they were, they strongly influenced me.'

Twain began working feverishly on a new project – part autobiography, part authorship polemic – and his reflections on Shakespeare's authorship took him back to the publication of 'Delia Bacon's book – away back in that ancient day – 1857, or 1856' when he was an apprentice steamboat pilot on the Mississippi River under the tutelage of George Ealer. Ealer, Twain recalls, was 'an idolator of Shakespeare' and would often recite Shakespeare, 'not just casually, but by the hour, when it was his watch, and I was steering'. Ealer didn't just take pleasure in reciting Shakespeare; he enjoyed arguing about him too. He had strong opinions about the controversy stirred up by 'Delia Bacon's book' and shared them with Twain. Ealer even 'bought the literature of the dispute as fast as it appeared', Twain recalled, 'and we discussed it all through thirteen hundred miles of river'.

Ealer 'was fiercely loyal to Shakespeare and cordially scornful of Bacon and all the pretensions of the Baconians', and so was Twain – 'at first'. But Twain got fed up with Ealer's arguments and went over to the other, Baconian, side. He recognised from the start 'how curiously theological' the controversy was – and soon became 'welded to my faith' and 'looked down with compassion not unmixed with scorn, upon everybody's else's faith that didn't tally with mine'. Twain admits that he got the better of his formidable pilot-master only once, when he wrote out a passage from Shakespeare, then 'riddled it with his wild steamboatful interlardings' – capturing what he actually heard as Ealer both steered and recited while guiding the steamboat downriver. He handed the passage to Ealer to read aloud and, as Twain expected, Ealer made the 'thunderous interlardings . . . seem a part of the text', made 'them sound as if they were bursting from Shakespeare's own soul'.

Twain then sprang his trap, insisting that 'Shakespeare couldn't have written Shakespeare's works, for the reason that the man who wrote them was limitlessly familiar with the laws and the law courts.' Ealer replied that Shakespeare could have learned about the law from books, at which point Twain 'got him to read again the passage from Shakespeare with the interlardings'. Ealer was forced to concede that 'books couldn't teach a student a bewildering multitude of pilot-phrases so thoroughly and perfectly that he could talk them off in book and play or conversation and make no mistake that a pilot would not immediately discover'. Twain thought his argument irrefutable: 'A man can't handle glibly and easily and comfortably and successfully the argot of a trade at which he had not personally served.'

It's hard to know how much of this account is true. Ealer had indeed been Twain's instructor on the Mississippi in November 1857 and then again from February to June 1858, when news about Delia Bacon's book, and the book itself, were already in circulation. If Twain's recollections are to be trusted, he and Ealer were probably familiar with Delia Bacon's argument from an article that had run in June 1857 in a newspaper they read, the *New Orleans Daily Picayune*. The 'interlarding' passage sounds fictional, a re-creation, based on the burlesques of *Hamlet*, *Macbeth* and other plays that Twain in later years would perfect; yet there is a ring of truth in Lyon's account of how 'the King told how . . . Ealer used to read Shakespeare aloud, all interrupted with river talk, and piloting orders', and how 'splendid' it was 'to hear and see' Twain 'read it, for he acted it, and threw in plenty of river profanity'.

It's extremely unlikely, though, that Twain had argued back in 1857 that only a lawyer could have written the plays; some years had to pass before a procession of lawyers would pick up on Malone's hint and strongly urge that case. But what does sound like authentic Twain is the argument that you can only write convincingly about what you know about and have experienced first-hand. There's no substitute for that, he was convinced, no way to learn from books alone. Anyone who tries 'will make mistakes' and 'will not, and cannot, get the trade-phrasings precisely and exactly right'; 'the reader who has served that trade will know the writer hasn't.'

In what sounds like another apocryphal episode that would be recycled in his book on the Shakespeare authorship controversy, Twain tells the story of how, as a seven-year-old boy, he had tried to write a biographical account of Satan's life, and ran into all sorts of trouble with his schoolmaster, given how little factual evidence there was about the devil. The moral: Shakespeare and Satan 'are the best-known unknown persons that have ever drawn breath upon the planet'. More likely he had Jesus, not Satan, in mind, though it would have been near heretical to say so publicly. But he confessed as much to Paine at this time, who writes that Twain's 'Shakespeare interest had diverging by-paths. One evening, when we were alone at dinner, he said: "There is only one other illustrious man in history about whom there is so little known," and he added, "Jesus Christ." Twain 'reviewed the statements of the Gospels concerning Christ, though he declared them to be mainly traditional and of no value'. Paine adds that Twain 'did not admit that there had been a Christ with the character and mission related by the Gospels. "It is all a myth," he said, tellingly. "There have been Saviours in every age of the world. It is all just a fairy tale."' Once again, the Higher Criticism had left its mark.

After dredging up these memories from his childhood and time as a cub pilot in his autobiographical dictations, Twain briefly lost interest in the project. But he was re-energised a month later when the long-promised copy of Greenwood's *The Shakespeare Problem Restated* finally arrived. It 'so fired the King', Isabel Lyon recalled, 'that he has started again at his article, which he had dropped, on the Life of Shakespeare'. Twain wrote to his daughter Jean that 'I am having a good time . . . dictating to the stenographer (Autobiography) a long day-after-day scoff at everybody who is ignorant enough and stupid enough to go on believing Shakespeare ever wrote a play or a poem in his life.' And his copy of Greenwood's book was soon 'splattered' with notes and fresh ideas.

His biographer, Paine, who couldn't understand why Twain kept insisting that he knew 'that Shakespeare didn't write those plays', asked how him how could be so sure. Twain replied: 'I have private knowledge from a source that cannot be questioned.' Paine thought that Twain was joking and, 'asked if he had been consulting a spiritual medium', but Twain was 'clearly in earnest'. Paine finally learned that Twain's confidence was based on the string cipher and Twain insisted that Booth's book 'was far and away beyond anything of the kind ever published; that Ignatius

Donnelly and others had merely glimpsed the truth, but that . . . Booth, had demonstrated, beyond any doubt or question, that the Bacon signatures were there'. Paine was about to set sail for Egypt and begged for more information before his departure, but Twain refused, assuring him that the news would come by cable to his ship 'and the world would quake with it'. Paine was so excited by this imminent revelation that, he writes, 'I was tempted to give up my trip, to be with him at Stormfield at the time of the upheaval.' In the end he sailed off and upon arriving in Cairo 'looked eagerly through English newspapers, expecting any moment to come upon great head-lines; but I was always disappointed. Even on the return voyage there was no one I could find who had heard any particular Shakespeare news.'

Twain kept writing about the authorship of the plays because he cared about something other than what he believed Booth had already proven. Left unanswered by the cipher solution were questions that bore directly on Twain's unshakeable belief that writers could only successfully write about what they had experienced first-hand. Nowhere is this clearer than in the marginal notes he scrawled throughout the copy of Greenwood's book that Macy had sent him. One of those annotations reveals a great deal about the prism through which Twain now saw Shakespeare: 'Certain people persisted to the end in believing that Arthur Orton was Sir Roger Tichborne. Shakespeare is another Arthur Orton – with all the valuable evidence against him, and not a single established *fact* in his favor.' Arthur Orton, known in his own day almost universally as the Claimant, is no longer a household name, though he was one of the wonders of the Victorian age. The controversy that raged over his identity goes back to 1854, when the young heir to one of the Britain's oldest aristocratic titles, Sir Roger Charles Tichborne, disappeared, reportedly drowned at sea off the coast of South America. His body was never recovered. The story had all the trappings of Shakespearean romance: families torn asunder by tempests, long searches for lost children, and, in the end, long-desired reunion. Roger Tichborne's mother refused to accept the news that her son had died and began making enquiries abroad about his whereabouts. In 1866 a man arrived from Australia claiming to be her long-lost son and heir. He didn't look much like her son (he was a huge man, while her son, when she last saw him, was quite skinny, and Sir Roger's distinctive tattoo had somehow disappeared). Nonetheless, Lady Tichborne immediately identified him as the long-lost son, as did several other family friends and servants. Relatives, keen on protecting the family title and lands, thought the ill-educated Claimant a fraud. It would take litigation to settle the matter and in 1872 the longest and most celebrated British trial for imposture began. It generated tremendous interest, cutting across class boundaries and stirring up many of the same reactions as the authorship controversy did at this time: how could a low-class, unschooled provincial possibly be mistaken for a well-travelled, worldly man, one naturally knowledgeable about the ways of the aristocracy?

The story captivated Twain, who managed to attend the trial when visiting London and found it 'the most intricate and fascinating and marvelous real-life romance that has ever been played upon the world's stage'. Twain kept newspaper reports on the case, for a future sketch, though he never used this material, many years later in *Following the Equator* he describes how he had been invited to observe the Claimant after a day at court at 'one of his showy evenings in the sumptuous quarters provided for him from the purses of his adherents and well-wishers. He was in evening dress, and I thought him a rather fine and stately creature.' Twain, like so many others, was taken in. The court subsequently declared that the Claimant was named Orton; he was a butcher from the Australian provinces, and an impostor. Despite this ruling, the Claimant continued to insist that he was indeed Roger Tichborne, even after his release from prison ten years later. When the impoverished Claimant died in 1898 his funeral was attended by thousands. The name placed on his coffin was 'Sir Roger Charles Doughty Tichborne'. For Twain, Orton's supporters – like Shakespeare loyalists – continued to believe in their man long after the facts proved otherwise.

Twain, feeling as duped by Shakespeare as he had by the Claimant, was now intent on exposing the man from Stratford as the 'Arthur Orton of literary "Claimants".' If anyone understood what it meant to be a 'Claimant' it was Samuel *Clemens* – who enjoyed punning on the resemblance of the words. He had been writing under an assumed identity from almost the outset of his literary career, and it's a critical commonplace that no writer has ever been more obsessed with twinning, doubling, pseudonyms, and imposture and the confusion of identity. Part Clemens, part Twain, he couldn't help seeing others in this light as well; when he wrote a thank-you note to Helen Keller he called her 'a wonderful creature, the most wonderful in the world – you and your other half together – Miss Sullivan, I mean, for it took the pair of you to make a complete and perfect whole'. He was preoccupied with twins and impostors in his fiction, too, from *The Prince and the Pauper* and *Those Extraordinary Twins* to *Pudd'nhead Wilson*. It's hardly surprising that a writer whose own identity was split in twain came to believe that one of the greatest of writers also wrote under an assumed identity.

Living in a world in which imposture was more pervasive than anyone imagined motivated Twain to seek out instances of it elsewhere. So it was in 1894, his friend Henry W. Fisher reports, that Twain 'thought he might have turned up . . . a bombshell' and asked Fisher 'to assist him in gathering evidence to prove that Queen Elizabeth was in fact a man. "Mark my word," Twain told him, "Elizabeth was a he."' Fisher, who was on his way to England, dug around a bit, interviewed some people, and after a fortnight returned to Paris, where Twain was staying, to report back what he had learned. He passed along anecdotes he had heard about how Elizabeth as a girl had caught 'malignant fever and died', and, fearful of Henry VIII's anger, her governess, who 'knew that her life depended upon finding a substitute for Elizabeth', found one in the 'late Princess' boy playmate'. The story was just what Twain had hoped to hear, and he assured Fisher that Elizabeth 'was a male character all over – a thousand acts of hers prove it.' Twain found corroboration in an entry in the *Encyclopaedia Britannica* which suggested that there was "some physical defect" in Elizabeth's make-up' and that she was 'masculine in mind and temperament'. Twain refused to believe that a woman could have the experience or character to accomplish what Elizabeth did, from enriching her kingdom to writing sophisticated letters to King Philip of Spain. 'Wasn't that a man's game?' Elizabeth's success, which he thought well beyond the capabilities of a woman, had, for Twain, a simpler if conspiratorial explanation.

Twain wrote a good deal more in the margins of Greenwood's book; its argument seems to have unleashed in him a kind of running tirade about how writing works:

Men are developed by their *environment* – *trained* by it. Consider Shakespeare's

Did ever a man move the world by writing solely out of what he had learned from schools & books, & leaving out what he had *lived and felt*?

It is environment, & environment alone, that develops genius or strangles it

To write with powerful effect, a [sic] must write out *the life he has led* – as did Bacon when he wrote Shakespeare

Time and again Twain reaffirms the intrinsic link between powerful writing and an author's life experience. Twain simply could not accept that a young man from the provinces, at age twenty-one, 'without any qualifying preparation in the way of training and experiences' could bring 'forth great tragedies like a volcano'.

One of the oddest things about *Is Shakespeare Dead?* – the book Twain had been writing since the visit of Helen Keller and the Macys – is Twain's insistence that Shakespeare couldn't have written the plays because he couldn't have mastered the legal language that appears in the plays. Twain himself didn't have such knowledge either, but Greenwood did, and it was the central claim of

The Shakespeare Problem Restated. Twain was so taken by Greenwood's argument that he made it his own, lifting and pasting unaltered into his book, without attribution, most of Greenwood's chapter on Shakespeare and the law (even leaving instructions in his copy of *The Shakespeare Problem Restated* where to begin lifting Greenwood's words on page 371, and where, sixteen pages later, to 'stop'). Greenwood was furious when he learned of this and threatened legal action. Again, the ironies were great: Twain plagiarised Greenwood's words in a work subtitled *From My Autobiography* in order to challenge Shakespeare's claims to authorship, on the grounds that you had to know something about law to speak with authority about it. Yet in doing so, Twain does what Shakespeare himself had done: appropriated what others said or wrote, using their words to lend authority to his own – something that Twain had argued wasn't possible.

The *New York Times* and other newspapers picked up on the mild scandal, and Twain, who first brushed off his theft as an oversight, was forced to insert a leaf after the copyright notice that read: 'Chapter VIII, "Shakespeare as a Lawyer," is taken from *The Shakespeare Problem Restated* by George G. Greenwood.' Despite his protests, Twain understood exactly what he was doing in folding Greenwood into his autobiography, and felt that even through Greenwood might have written it, it was still his. Writing to Macy in late February to thank him for sending along Greenwood's book, he admitted that he had 'stolen meat enough from it to stuff yards and yards of sausage-gut in my vast autobiography and make it look like my own.' And, he underscored, 'really the gut is <u>mine</u>'.

Is Shakespeare Dead? was published in April 1909. It was Twain's final chance to air his views about the difference between major writers who drew on 'experience' and inferior ones who depended on 'listening'. He also couldn't resist making a case for the fame that would surely have been Shakespeare of Stratford's had he written the plays: 'If Shakespeare had really been celebrated, like me,' he adds in a postscript to the book, his neighbours in 'Stratford could have told things about him; and if my experience goes for anything, they'd have done it.'

The book's title was based on an old joke, one that he had told in *Innocents Abroad*. The question was Twain's way of needling tour guides who had 'exhausted their enthusiasm pointing out to us . . . the beauties of some bronze image'. Twain and his fellow tourists would 'look at it stupidly and in silence' for as long as they could 'hold out' before asking: 'Is he dead?' Actually, as Leslie Fiedler has pointed out, the title should have been *Is Shakespeare Shakespeare?* But the death of the author had always been a subject near and dear to Twain, and his own demise, he knew, couldn't be far off. In that sense, the title is shadowed by another, used by one of its reviewers: 'Is Twain Dead?', and calls to mind as well the title of Twain's unsuccessful play *Is He Dead?* (in which an artist pretends to be dead in order to ensure his posthumous success). Behind it all was an echo of Twain's famous response to an erroneous report in 1897 in the *New York Journal*, that the 'report of my death was an exaggeration'. A few months after Twain died in 1911 the executors of his estate 'dispersed much of his private library at an urgent sale in New York City', as though intending to capitalize on what could be fleeting fame'. Twain himself had mockingly scribbled in his copy of Greenwood's book that Shakespeare 'Left no books – "doubtless" hadn't any.'

Baconian reports of Shakespeare's demise were also exaggerated – and the publication of Twain's book coincided with the deathknell of Baconianism. After a half-century the movement had peaked and was now in decline, though Baconian diehards soldiered on (including those at *Baconiana* who announced in July 1911, with no irony, that they were 'Nearing the End'). The case for Francis Bacon's authorship of the plays continues to find new supporters to this day, though they are fewer in number, less prominent, and less vocal. *Baconiana* is still published and a steady trickle of books maintaining that Bacon wrote the plays continue to appear, mostly rehearsing familiar arguments.

William Stone Booth's book fell on deaf ears, as did his subsequent and increasingly desperate *Marginal Acrostics and Other Alphabetical Devices, A Catalogue* in 1920 and his *Subtle Shining Secrets Writ in the Margents of Books* in 1925. A year later, John Macy reported Booth's death to a friend: 'I fancy his ghost arguing with Shake and Bake until they both wish they were in Hell.' Helen Keller failed to persuade a publisher to run her piece on the authorship question. Her thirty-four-page manuscript sits unpublished in the archives of the American Foundation for the Blind in New York City. She never revisited the subject.

Ignatius Donnelly kept writing to the very end, though failed to find a publisher for his last discovery, *Ben Jonson's Cipher*. Orville Ward Owen continued digging, right up to 1920, though never found those hidden manuscripts. On his deathbed in 1924 he warned an admirer to avoid the 'Bacon controversy', for

you will only reap disappointment. When I discovered the Word Cipher, I had the largest practice of any physician in Detroit. I could have been the greatest surgeon there . . . But I thought that the world would be eager to hear what I have found. Instead, what did they give me? I have had my name dragged in the mud . . . lost my fortune, ruined my health, and today am a bedridden almost penniless invalid.

Owen's Cipher Wheel, recently rediscovered in a warehouse in Detroit, is now housed at Summit University, in Montana.

Elizabeth Wells Gallup never found the hidden manuscripts either. And when her benefactor, Colonel Fabyan, had experts in typography examine her work, they found it to be fundamentally flawed: she had been working under the assumption that the compositors of all the works she had been examining alternated two distinct typefaces to create the biliteral cipher. It turned out that in the trays of Elizabethan compositors were dozens of fonts, with slight differences, mixed together. Her project was doomed from the start.

The cipher story had one positive, if unintended, consequence. William Friedman, a talented young geneticist who was teaching part-time at Cornell University, was lured away by Colonel

Fabyan to a job at his Riverbank Laboratories, where Fabyan also supported the cipher hunters. Expecting to work there on Mendelian genetics, Friedman was enlisted instead to help Mrs Gallup and was soon appointed 'Head of Ciphers'. The cipher department at Riverbank became the primary recruiting ground for the cryptanalytic training of American officers during the First World War, and after that, for the National Security Agency. In 1921 Friedman left Riverbank to work for the government, armed with the knowledge of cryptography that during the Second World War would enable him to lead the team that cracked the seemingly unbreakable Japanese machine cipher, providing the intelligence that helped Allied forces to prevail in the Pacific, including the decisive battle at Midway. Donnelly, Owen and Mrs Gallup never achieved the fame they sought, but their work on ciphers helped win a war.

Henry James

Is Shakespeare Dead? won few admirers and Twain's retainers did their best to shield him from what Lyon describes as 'sour bitter letters . . . more of censure than of praise'. In surviving correspondence a defensive Twain retreated from his advocacy of Francis Bacon: 'all I want', he insisted, 'is to convince some people that Shakespeare did not write Shakespeare. Who did, is a question which does not greatly interest me.' In this, he was moving toward the position of another major writer of the day, Henry James.

Pinning down Henry James's scepticism about Shakespeare's authorship isn't easy. Unlike Twain, James wasn't willing to confront the issue publicly or directly. We don't know when he became interested in the subject or how much his views changed over time. His position has to be pieced together from tantalising bits of evidence: a handful of letters, a journal entry, a short story, an essay and a passing allusion in his fiction. It's not a lot to go by, and any claims are further qualified by James's maddeningly elliptical and evasive style. Still, there are good reasons to pursue this as far as it leads, for James is representative of what I suspect were many artists who questioned Shakespeare's authorship but were fearful of the ridicule that might follow if they expressed their reservations publicly. He also succeeded, far better than any other writer, in finding a creative outlet for his doubts, first in a twenty-thousand-word story, 'The Birthplace', and then, a few years later, in a remarkable essay on *The Tempest*.

James was no stranger to Shakespeare. As a child he had been given a copy of Charles and Mary Lamb's *Tales from Shakespeare*, and even called his first story 'A Tragedy of Errors'. James knew the plays and poems intimately, owned several editions of them, reviewed a dozen or so productions, had engaged with Shakespeare's plays in his fiction and frequently cites them in his letters, notebooks and criticism. There were few periods in his creative life when James didn't find himself responding in one way or another to Shakespeare or reflecting on the mystery of his genius. This was certainly the case in the early years of the twentieth century, when James was approaching sixty, at the pinnacle of his career, beginning to write both biography and autobiography, planning a trip to America where he would revisit his own birthplace, and fashioning what might be described as a modern-day equivalent to the First Folio – the landmark New York Edition of his novels and stories. Everywhere James turned, Shakespeare's example loomed large. Two years before he died, anxious about how biographers would treat his life and work, and having already condemned to the flames manuscripts and thousands of letters, James instructed his literary executor that there ought to be a provision in his will containing 'a curse no less explicit than Shakespeare's own on any such as try to move my bones'.

James's earliest exposure to the authorship controversy may date back to the 1880s, when a New York neighbour and family friend, John Watts de Peyster, published *Was THE Shakespeare After All a Myth?* While James visited Shakespeare's birthplace several times, he didn't write much about the experience, though, as we shall see, he seems to have shared his brother William's opinion, expressed in 1902, that 'a visit to Stratford now seems to be the strongest appeal a Baconian can make':

[the] absolute extermination and obliteration of every record of Shakespeare save a few sordid material details, and the general suggestion of narrowness and niggardliness with the way in which the spiritual quantity of Shakespeare has mingled into the soul of the world, was most uncanny, and I feel ready to believe in almost any mythical story of the authorship.

The tension between the 'spiritual' and the 'sordid material' elements of the Shakespeare myth was becoming intolerable.

In June 1901, Henry James recorded in his notebook a story idea – 'a little *donnée*' – inspired by an anecdote he had heard a fortnight earlier when visiting the Trevelyans at Welcombe, near Stratford. Lady Trevelyan had told him about 'the couple who had formerly (before the present incumbents) been for a couple of years – or a few – the people in charge of the Shakespeare house – the Birthplace':

They were rather strenuous and superior people from Newcastle, who had embraced the situation with joy, thinking to find it just the thing for them and full of interest, dignity, an appeal to all their culture and refinement, etc. But what happened was that at the end of 6 months they grew sick and desperate from finding it – finding their office – the sort of thing that I suppose it is: full of humbug, full of lies and superstition imposed upon them by the great body of visitors, who want the positive impressive story about every object, every feature of the house, every dubious thing – the simplified, unscrupulous, gulpable, tale. They found themselves too 'refined,' too critical for this – the public wouldn't have criticism (of legend, tradition, probability, improbability) at any price – and they ended by contracting a fierce intellectual and moral disgust for the way they had to meet the public. That is all the anecdote gives – except that after a while they could stand it no longer, and threw up the position.

James immediately saw potential in this tale of bardolatry turned sour – 'something more, I mean, than the mere facts. I seem to see

[162]

them – for there is no catastrophe in a simple resignation of the post, turned somehow, by the experience, into strange sceptics, iconoclasts, positive negationists.' As he turned the story over in his mind he imagined the pair as they are forced over to the opposite extreme and become rank enemies not only of the legend, but of the historic *donnée* itself.' His story, as initially conceived, was to have a ending more shocking than the 'intellectual and moral disgust' that led to their resignation in Lady Trevelyan's account: 'Say they end by denying Shakespeare – say they do it on the spot itself – one day – in the presence of a big, gaping, admiring batch. Then they must go.'

James worked on 'The Birthplace' the following summer and autumn before publishing it in his 1903 short-story collection *The Better Sort*. Around this time he was also discussing the authorship question with at least two friends, Manton Marble and Violet Hunt. Marble was an American friend and former editor of the *New York World* who had settled in Brighton. James wrote from London in early December 1902, thanking Marble for forwarding a copy of a book on the authorship controversy that they had already discussed: 'I surmise that this valuable volume is the Webb volume of which we spoke – and I feel how I drop far below the argument in merely saying that I rejoice to possess it, and to be able to read it again in the light of your eulogy; also that I heartily thank you for it.' The 'Webb volume' was almost surely Judge Thomas Ebenezer Webb's *The Mystery of William Shakespeare: A Summary of Evidence*, just published in England. Webb's style and conclusions sound downright Jamesian and it's easy to see the appeal the book held for him: 'In spite of all that has been written, there is a vague feeling of unrest as to Shakespeare in the public mind . . . Whoever the great dramatist was, we can form no adequate conception of his mind.' Webb cautiously concludes that in the absence of persuasive external evidence, the plays themselves point to Bacon rather than Shakespeare; only in his case are 'the works as we possess them and the man as we know him in strict accord'.

While Marble was clearly a committed Baconian, James himself demurred, insisting on his authority as a writer that it couldn't have been Bacon, for the man and the works were not, as Webb might put it, in 'strict accord': 'Still, all the same, take my word for it, as a dabbler in fable and fiction, that the plays and the sonnets were never written but by a Personal Poet, a Poet and Nothing Else, a Poet, who, being Nothing Else, could never be a Bacon.' Yet James was also unwilling to concede that Shakespeare wrote the plays. The gap between the poetry and what was known about the man from Stratford was simply too great: 'The difficulty with the divine William is that he isn't, wasn't the Personal Poet with the calibre and the conditions, any more than the learned, the ever so much too learned, Francis.' James never quite explains what this calibre or these conditions might be, but promises Marble that 'we will talk of these things again'.

Nine months later James was still wrestling with the problem. On 11 August 1903 he wrote to his friend Violet Hunt, who had recently visited him in Rye, challenging her defence of Shakespeare. Hunt's letter, which he describes as 'ferocious', doesn't survive, so all we have to go by is James's paraphrase of one of her elaborate metaphors:

Your comparison of genius to the passenger on the 'liner' with his cabin and his 'hold' luggage is very brilliant and I should quite agree with you – and do. Only I make this difference. Genius gets at its own luggage, in the hold, perfectly (while common mortality is reduced to a box under the berth); but it doesn't get at the Captain's and the First Mate's, in their mysterious retreats. Now William of Stratford (it seems to me) had no luggage, could have had none in any part of the ship, corresponding to much of the wardrobe sported in the plays.

Again, it's not easy knowing exactly what James is arguing here, though it feels like the claim that Shakespeare 'had no luggage' is another way of expressing what he had recently told Marble: that Shakespeare of Stratford lacked the 'calibre and the conditions' – presumably the background, training and equipment – to have written the plays. In both letters James also seems to hint that Shakespeare's humble origins argue against his having been equipped with the right 'wardrobe'.

Around the time that this exchange took place, James sent Hunt a book on the controversy, perhaps Webb's, in an effort to put more 'pressure' on her defence of Shakespeare. It failed to have the desired effect, as we can tell from James's disappointed reply of 26 August. Hunt may have recoiled from the suggestion that Shakespeare didn't write Shakespeare, but James, who admits to being haunted by the conviction that Shakespeare was a fraud, doesn't flinch at all from this possibility:

Also came the Shakespeare-book back with your accompanying letter – for which also thanks, but for which I can't now pretend to reply. You rebound lightly, I judge, from any pressure exerted on you by the author – but I don't rebound: I am 'a sort of' haunted by the conviction that the divine William is the biggest and most successful fraud ever practiced on a patient world. The more I turn him round and round the more he so affects me.

Having confessed, it seems, to a bit more than he was comfortable admitting (that colloquial and bracketed "sort of" haunted' speaks worlds), James stops himself at this point, and makes clear, in the qualified language typical of his thoughts on the subject, that this is as far as he is willing to go:

But that is all – I am not pretending to treat the question or to carry it any further. It bristles with difficulties, and I can only express my general sense by saying that I find it almost as impossible to conceive that Bacon wrote the plays as to conceive that the man from Stratford, as we know the man from Stratford, did.

Bacon was an unlikely candidate, but Shakespeare unlikelier still. When he published 'The Birthplace' in 1903, James left out the public repudiation of Shakespeare's authorship that had been the climax of the version sketched out in his notebook. Shakespeare and Stratford-upon-Avon, while clearly implied, are no longer named, Morris Gedge, the central figure of the story, struggles to live with the lie that he is paid to tell, day in, day out, to the endless stream of pilgrims who come to visit the birthplace of the divine poet. He shares his growing doubts with his wife, who is terrified of losing their livelihood if he begins to tell the truth. Like his creator, Morris Gedge chooses to share his misgivings privately, unburdening himself to a young and sympathetic American pair, who wonder why the tourists won't just accept that 'the play's the thing' and let 'the author alone'. "That's just what They won't do," Gedge excitedly confesses, "nor let me do. It's all I want – to let the author alone. Practically" – he felt himself getting the last of his chance – "there is no author; that is for us to deal with."

Gedge masks his disenchantment and turns his performance into an art. His reputation soars and visitors flock to hear him. His wife is still panicked though, worried now that he has gone 'too far' in his enthusiastic, if ironic, embrace of the myth. His confidants, the young American couple, return a year later, partly to see if what they have heard of Gedge's performance, given his doubts, could possibly be true. They conclude that his sardonic bardolatry is a thing of 'genius', though they worry that he is in danger of being exposed and losing his job. Their concerns are misplaced: Gedge's act is so successful that receipts soar and his salary is doubled. He has managed to turn his radical doubts about the Bard into art – and is rewarded for it. And he can count on those with whom he has shared his scepticism to keep his secret safe.

James can hardly be blamed for subsuming his own beliefs to the higher interest of creating powerful fiction, which is why many more people now read 'The Birthplace' than Twain's *Is Shakespeare Dead?* His story, as originally conceived, would have been more revealing biographically, but a less compelling work of fiction. The closest James comes to acknowledging an affinity with Gedge is in the prefatory remarks to the story that he supplied for the 1909 New York Edition, where James admits that the appeal of the

CONTESTED WILL

[166]

story was 'the more direct, I may add, by reason, as happened, of an acquaintance, lately much confirmed, on my own part, with the particular temple of our poor gentleman's priesthood' – implying that his own recent and disenchanting experience of visiting the divine Shakespeare's birthplace confirmed Gedge's. Again, this is as directly as James is willing to express himself, for posterity, on the subject. When James travelled to New York to visit his own birthplace near Washington Square in the spring of 1905, he discovered that the house in which he had been born six decades earlier had been 'ruthlessly suppressed' and demolished – no trace left on which to affix even 'a commemorative mural tablet'. It left James with the sensation he later describes in *The American Scene* of having been 'amputated of half my history'.

James had another opportunity to address the Shakespeare mystery when he was invited by William Dana Orcutt to write an introduction to *The Tempest*. It was 'the only one of Shakespeare's plays', Orcutt told him, 'in which we directly touch Shakespeare the man, and I believe that your analysis of him would be a contribution to Shakespeariana'. Though buried in his work on the New York Edition, James agreed to do it: 'I accept the commission with great anticipation,' he told Orcutt, before adding with uncharacteristic boldness, 'I will challenge this artist – the monster and magician of a thousand masks, and make him drop them, if only for an interval.'

The essay captures a decisive moment in the history of the authorship debate, a moment when a set of shaky biographical (and autobiographical) assumptions had hardened into fact and collided with equally entrenched nineteenth-century beliefs about artistic genius. James took as a given a set of beliefs that had not existed a century earlier though by the late nineteenth century were almost universally shared: that *The Tempest* was Shakespeare's last play, most likely written specifically for a courtly occasion; that Prospero's renunciation of his art was a veiled allusion to Shakespeare's own; that the biographical facts confirmed that Shakespeare of Stratford was a man obsessed with money; and that the play was a work of genius by an author at the height of his powers. James was also writing in the autumnal moment of the Baconian movement, when enough was now known about Francis Bacon's life, work and sensibility to fatally weaken his case, yet at a time when a convincing alternative for the authorship of the plays had yet to be advanced. It is no coincidence that his essay also marks the high-water mark in reading *The Tempest* as Shakespeare's most autobiographical play.

James would have understood why Delia Bacon invoked Prospero and *The Tempest* in her own farewell essay, for, like her and many others, he read the play as Shakespeare's great leave-taking. But this, for James, was the most troubling thing about *The Tempest*: how could the genius who wrote it renounce his art at the age of forty-eight and retire to rural Stratford to 'spend what remained to him of life in walking about a small, squalid country-town with his hand in his pockets and ear for no music but the chink of the coin they might turn over there'? He poses this central question in an unusually tortured way: 'By what inscrutable process was the extinguisher applied and, when once applied, kept in its place to the end? What became of the checked torrent, as a latent, bewildering presence and energy, in the life across which the dam was constructed?'

James had dutifully read the Shakespeare biographies of Georg Brandes and Halliwell-Phillipps yet refused to accept their popular if 'arbitrary' distinction between the author's 'genius' and 'the rest of his identity', which they reduce to a 'a man of exemplary business-method'. Shakespeare's biographers have perversely maintained, as James puts it, that 'The Poet is there, and the Man is outside.' It's an 'admirable' view, he trenchantly concludes, 'if you can get your mind to consent to it'. James could not. He found the recorded facts of Shakespeare of Stratford's life 'supremely vulgar' and ill-suited to the artist who wrote *The Tempest*. While he would not go as far as Twain's reductive views about the necessarily autobiographical nature of great writing, James nonetheless dismisses the possibility that a split between man and poet was possible: the two parts of the artist were necessarily 'one', for the 'genius is a part of the mind, and the mind a part of the behaviour'.

This rift between the received biography and the poetic genius James had encountered over the course of a lifetime of reading the works attributed to Shakespeare was clearly unbridgeable, the most 'insoluble' mystery 'that ever was'. Either something was terribly wrong about the biography of the author of *The Tempest* or James misunderstood something fundamental about literary genius. The stakes here couldn't be higher, for as many distinguished Henry James scholars have shown, the essay is as much about James's own genius and legacy as about Shakespeare's, and in that sense can usefully be read alongside the prefaces to the New York Edition he was writing at the time about how he himself should be read and valued by posterity.

It's a subtle essay by a critic at the height of his analytic and rhetorical powers. One of the most fascinating things about it is watching Shakespeare slowly recede from view. He is named only a half-dozen times or so in the twenty-three-page essay – no mean feat, since the essay concerns the authorship of his play. By the closing pages Shakespeare's name has disappeared completely, replaced by the deliberately ambiguous 'he', 'our hero' and 'the author of *Hamlet* and *The Tempest*'. The sordid biographical facts of Shakespeare's life that have no observable bearing on the works are jettisoned as well.

The essay's closing lines can either be read neutrally or as a more purposeful wish that this mystery will one day be resolved by 'the criticism of the future': 'The figured tapestry, the long arras that hides him, is always there . . . May it not then be but a question, for the fullness of time, of the finer weapon, the sharper point, the stronger arm, the more extended lunge?' Is James hinting here that one day critics will hit upon another, more suitable candidate, identify the individual in whom the man and artist converge and are 'one'? If so, his choice of metaphor – recalling Hamlet's lunge at the arras in the closet scene – is unfortunate.

Could James have forgotten that the sharp point of Hamlet's weapon finds the wrong man?

In the end, any post-mortem of the Baconian movement must acknowledge that the failure to find a cipher and the subsequent ridicule directed at the decoders and gravediggers hastened its demise. So too, did the failure, despite strenuous efforts, to show that Bacon's style resembled Shakespeare's. But given the erosion of Francis Bacon's cultural significance, the demise of the movement was probably inevitable.

In retrospect, the Baconians also lost support because they had erred in identifying their hero with the wrong authorial self-portrait, though, again, it was one that they had borrowed from mainstream scholars. That great image of authority, Prospero as Shakespeare – or as they saw it, Prospero as Bacon – had outlived its moment. Too aloof, bookish and a bit cold, he was hardly a Shakespeare for the twentieth century. A new biographical stand-in was needed, and Hamlet was waiting in the wings – for those who believed that Shakespeare wrote the plays as well as for those who didn't. Philosophy and politics were out, Oedipal desires and mourning for dead fathers in. It would still be a story of failure; but rather than Delia Bacon's account of how the plays emerged in response to political isolation and blunted republican dreams, the failure would now be more personal, and the plays an outlet for the anguish of being undervalued and overlooked. A new search was on, one that depended more than ever on finding the life in the work. It was just a different life. Whoever wrote the plays had to be someone less forbidding than a Prospero or a Bacon, someone more suited to the times: introspective, nostalgic for a lost past, psychologically complex, misunderstood, someone, like Hamlet, with 'a wounded name'.

Edward de Vere, seventeenth Earl of Oxford, by Joseph Brown,
after George Perfect Harding, 1848

Freud

In December 1929, in the course of psychoanalysing an American doctor named Smiley Blanton, Sigmund Freud asked Blanton whether he thought 'that Shakespeare wrote Shakespeare?' The question rattled Blanton, who, not quite believing what he was hearing, answered Freud's question with one of his own: 'Do you mean the man born at Stratford-upon-Avon – did he write the plays attributed to him?' When Freud said 'Yes,' Blanton, who idolized Freud but also knew his Shakespeare, did his best to explain that he 'had specialized in English and drama for twelve years' before he became a doctor, 'had been on the stage for a year or so, and had memorized a half dozen of Shakespeare's dramas'. Given all this, he 'could see no reason to doubt that the Stratford man had written the plays'. This was not the answer Freud wanted to hear. 'Here's a book I would like you to read,' he told Blanton; 'this man believes someone else wrote the plays.'

Poor Smiley Blanton. Four months into analysis – with Sigmund Freud, no less – he is urged to explore his therapist's obsessions. In a diary of his analysis with Freud, Blanton records

Sigmund Freud with Otto Rank, Karl Abraham, Max Eitingon, Ernest Jones,
Hanns Sachs, and Sándor Ferenczi, 1922

that he 'was very much upset': 'I thought to myself that if Freud believes Bacon or Ben Jonson or anyone else wrote Shakespeare's plays, I would not have any confidence in his judgment and could not go on with my analysis.' When the session ended, Blanton took with him the book that Freud had handed over – '*Shakespeare' Identified in Edward De Vere, 17th Earl of Oxford* – and joined his wife Margaret in the Viennese cafe where they custom-arily met after he saw Freud. She later recalled that he seemed 'depressed and spoke of his qualms about continuing with Freud'.

Unable to bring himself to read the book, Blanton asked his wife if she would do so for him. She agreed to, and after finishing it reassured him that it was 'obviously a book to command respect-ful attention.' Margaret Blanton was enjoying her time in Vienna, writing regularly for the *Saturday Review of Literature* and the *New York Herald Tribune*, and had little interest in breaking off and sailing home. Moreover, she was in analysis herself with a young disciple and close associate of Freud, Ruth Brunswick. Brunswick, an Oxfordian, had recently given Freud an inscribed copy of '*Shakespeare' Identified* as a birthday present. We don't know whether this was the very copy that Freud had shared with Smiley Blanton. If it was, we end up with a scenario in which Margaret Blanton was handed the inscribed copy of the book that her analyst had given to Freud who in turn gave it to her husband – shades of the spotted handkerchief that passes through so many hands in *Othello*. Perhaps Freud knew just what he was doing.

Smiley Blanton finally read the book himself, and while 'he remained unconvinced by its argument', was pleased to see that it wasn't 'just another Baconian exercise in secret ciphers and codes'. He was getting a lot out of his sessions and was relieved that he didn't have to consider his therapist a crackpot. Within a few months Blanton was having dreams identifying Freud with Shakespeare. Their initial exchange over the authorship of the plays stayed with him, long enough for him to consider including it in a lecture he planned some years later. In the end, it became something that bonded the Blantons and Freud: 'Thereafter,'

Margaret Blanton writes, 'we sent the professor new books on this subject whenever they were published in the United States. Freud always wrote to thank us for the books.'

The Blantons met Freud for the last time in London in 1938, not long after Freud arrived there after fleeing Vienna and Nazi persecution. Smiley's sessions ended sooner than expected when Freud had to undergo an operation on his jaw. Margaret spoke briefly with Freud then as well, and he apologised to her for bringing Smiley 'all the way across the Atlantic and then having to cut short the work with him'. Freud asked Margaret about their plans. She told him that before returning to New York they would spend a few days in Stratford-upon-Avon' so that her husband might 'poke around a bit and add to his Shakespeare lore'. Freud responded to this news with 'sudden and uncharacteristic sharpness': 'Does Smiley really still believe those plays were written by that fellow at Stratford?' Reading *Shakespeare' Identified* had not had the desired effect. While it was clear to Margaret that Freud 'really knew and loved the plays as much as we could possibly have', he did not believe in 'that fellow at Stratford'. She was sorely tempted, she writes, to tell Freud about her husband's 'trial by fire' eight years earlier, when Freud had first tried to make an Oxfordian of him, but 'suddenly realized that if the professor had a sense of humor' she had 'never seen it', and decided that it was best not to bring it up now: 'I think he would not have been amused.' She held her tongue.

Freud died in September 1939, promoting Oxford's cause to the very end. His admirers, when they haven't quietly suppressed what they take to be an embarrassment, have struggled to explain why in his late years he became so ardent an Oxfordian. Ernest Jones, his authorised biographer, believed that something 'in Freud's mentality led him to take a special interest in people not being what they seemed to be'. There's no denying that Freud, who embraced Lamarckism and claimed that Moses was an Egyptian, was drawn to unconventional views. What he said about Moses applies equally well to Shakespeare: 'To deprive a people of the man whom they take pride in as the greatest of their sons is not a thing to be gladly or carelessly undertaken.'

But surely there's more at stake here than thinking counter-intuitively, a habit of mind that accounted for Freud's intellectual breakthroughs as well as the occasional dead end. Jones concedes as much, though the furthest he ventures is that Freud's rejection of Shakespeare was 'some derivative of the Family Romance', a 'wish that certain parts of reality could be changed' – that we might not be who we think we are. Peter Gay, another of Freud's major biographers, dismisses Jones's explanation in favour of an alternative psychoanalytic one, that at the bottom of it all was mother love: Freud's attempts at riddle solving, which included his interest in Shakespeare's identity, were 'necessary exercises through which he could reiterate his claim to paternal and, even more, maternal love.' For Gay, the 'move from the indistinct figure of the man from Stratford to the presumed solidity of the Earl of Oxford was part of a lifelong quest' – one he associates with the 'erotic element in Freud's greed for knowledge'. This seems rather desperate to me and says more about the seductiveness of psy-chobiographical explanations than it does about why one of the great modern minds turned against Shakespeare. The answer might well lie elsewhere: Freud's devotion to Oxford's cause was no psychic riddle but a response to a threat to his Oedipal theory, the cornerstone of psychoanalysis – which in turn rested in no small way upon a biographical reading of Shakespeare's life and work. From this perspective, Freud's rejection of Shakespeare of Stratford seems both inevitable and necessary – though, like the claims of many others, it reveals more about the sceptic than it does about the authorship of Shakespeare's plays.

Freud was born in 1856, the year Delia Bacon's article in *Putnam's* kindled a debate over Shakespeare's authorship that quickly swept through Britain, America and the Continent. He was born into a world in which Shakespeare was celebrated as the greatest of modern writers, yet also one in which many questioned whether a glover's son could have created such towering works of art. This unresolved tension would play out in Freud's lifelong ambivalence about Shakespeare's identity. By the age of eight, Freud was reading and soon quoting from Shakespeare's plays and would continue to do so for the rest of his life. He was well read in English literature (for a decade he 'read nothing but English books') and ranked *Hamlet* and *Macbeth* among the 'ten most magnificent works of world literature'.

It wasn't easy remaining neutral about whether Francis Bacon had written those plays. One of Freud's mentors, the distinguished brain anatomist Theodor Meynert, was convinced that Bacon was the plays' true author and apparently tried to win Freud over. Freud was not persuaded (in later years he would tell Lytton Strachey that he 'always laughed at the Bacon hypothesis') but felt compelled to justify his reluctance to share Meynert's enthusiasm.

Much of what we know about what Freud was thinking at this time comes from his letters to Wilhelm Fleiss, the closest friend he would ever have, as well as the letters Freud exchanged with his fiancée Martha Bernays over the course of the three and a half years that they were separated (her mother had moved her from Vienna to Hamburg in an attempt to keep them apart). His letters to Fleiss have been published. Those to and from Martha Bernays are in the Freud Archives in the Library of Congress, but are sealed for many years to come. A handful of people, including Ernest Jones, have been permitted to read them and a few of the letters have been excerpted or published.

In one of these excerpts (from a letter written to Martha Bernays in June 1883), Freud mentions Meynert's conviction that Bacon wrote Shakespeare's plays. Freud disagrees, but rather than acknowledging Shakespeare's authorship argues instead that the plays were the product of several hands: 'there is more need to share Shakespeare's achievement among several rivals'. No single intelligence could have encompassed such a literary and philosophical range; if Bacon had written the plays along with his great philosophical works, he 'would have been the most powerful brain the world has ever produced'. Unfortunately, we have no context for these remarks, no clue as to how Martha Bernays responded, and, because their letters remain off-limits, don't know to what extent they reveal a young and ambitious Freud struggling with the limits of his own powerful brain and prodigious creative gifts. His attraction to group authorship may say more about his own creative anxieties at this time – as well as the cultural bias that made it hard for the urbane and highly educated Freud to believe that a man from rural Stratford, lacking much formal education, could have accomplished so much alone.

The Baconian claims of Meynert and others long gnawed at Freud. In an effort to resolve the authorship question once and for all, shortly before the First World War he invited his disciple Ernest Jones to make 'a thorough study of the methods of inter- pretation employed by the Baconians, contrasting them with psy- choanalytic methods. Then the matter would be disproved' and his mind 'would be at rest'. Jones, who steadfastly believed that Shakespeare alone wrote the plays, and who would have put at risk his own work on *Hamlet* and Oedipus, refused. It would be help- ful to know exactly when and why Freud eventually abandoned his belief in the collective authorship of the plays, and whether this development coincided with his growing interest in individual psychology, how unconscious forces shaped creativity, and the kinship between artists and analysts.

Freud's letters to Fliess convey the turbulence in his life follow- ing his father's death in 1896, a decisive year in the development of psychoanalysis, for it was at just this time that Freud abandoned his seduction theory in favour of an Oedipal one in accounting for his patients' hysteria and claims of sexual abuse. Freud's reflections during these months about Shakespeare and *Hamlet* are usually mentioned as a by-product of this theoretical shift, but the ques- tion of cause and effect turns out to be more complicated than that.

At this time Freud was strongly influenced by Georg Brandes's just published *William Shakespeare* (a book that meant so much to Freud that he brought it with him, decades later, when he had to flee Austria). The connections that Brandes drew between Shakespeare's life and his art offer the fullest flowering of the approach popularised by the German and English Romantics: 'In giving expression to Hamlet's spiritual life', Brandes writes, Shakespeare

was enabled quite naturally to pour forth all that during the recent years had filled his heart and seethed in his brain. He could let this creation drink his inmost heart's blood; he could transfer to it the throbbing of his own pulses . . . It is true that Hamlet's outward fortunes were different enough from his. He had not lost his father by assassination; his mother had not degraded herself. But all these details were only outward signs and symbols. He had lived through all of Hamlet's experience – all.

Brandes's very chapter headings – 'The Psychology of Hamlet' and 'The Personal Element in *Hamlet*' – spoke directly to Freud's interests. And Freud was won over by Brandes's account of Shakespeare's psychological state as he began writing *Hamlet*: 'Many and various emotions crowded upon Shakespeare's mind in the year 1601,' Brandes writes, most of all John Shakespeare's death: 'All the years of his youth, spent at his father's side, revived in Shakespeare's mind, memories flocked in upon him, and the fundamental relation between son and father preoccupied his thoughts, and he fell to brooding over filial love and filial reverence.' For Brandes, the death of Shakespeare's father led directly to the birth of *Hamlet*: 'He lost his father, his earliest friend and protector, whose honor and repute were so close to his heart. In the same year, *Hamlet* began to form in Shakespeare's imagination.'

When in 1900 Freud described in *The Interpretation of Dreams* how he had arrived at his insights into the Oedipal complex and the workings of the unconscious, he acknowledged a debt:

it can of course only be the poet's own mind which confronts us in Hamlet. I observe in a book on Shakespeare by Georg Brandes (1896) a statement that *Hamlet* was written immediately after the death of Shakespeare's father (in 1601), that is, under the immediate impact of his bereavement and, as we may well assume, while his childhood feelings about his father had been freshly revived. It is known, too, that Shakespeare's own son who died at an early age bore the name of 'Hamnet,' which is identical with 'Hamlet.'

While there's no evidence to support Brandes's assertion that Shakespeare was deeply affected by his father's death, the same cannot be said of Freud's reaction to a similar loss. In early November 1896, two weeks after burying his father, Freud confessed to Fliess that by 'one of these dark pathways behind the official consciousness the old man's death has affected me deeply . . . By the time he died, his life had long been over, but in [my] inner self the whole past has been reawakened by this event. I now feel quite uprooted.'

In the ensuing months Freud wrestled with conflicted feelings about his dead father, even as he undertook a sustained and unprecedented self-analysis. His ruthlessly honest letters to Fliess from this time – letters that he never dreamed would see the light of day, and the replies to which he destroyed – record his creative leaps and stumbles as he moved toward a new theory of the unconscious. By the summer of 1897, Freud was experiencing what he might have described as Hamlet-like symptoms:

I have never yet imagined anything like my present spell of intellectual paralysis. Every line I write is torture . . . I have been through some kind of neurotic experience, with odd states of mind not intelligible to consciousness – cloudy thoughts and vague doubts, with barely here and there a ray of light.

By August 1897, after visiting his father's grave, Freud was feeling more paralysed than ever. He was haunted by a dream about his father in which a sign appeared which read: 'You are requested to close the eyes.' Freud interpreted these words as an act of self-reproach, having to do with his 'duty to the dead'. Freud was in mourning, wrestling with intellectual paralysis, trying to determine whether he had badly misunderstood himself, his father and how the mind worked.

The following month Freud abandoned the seduction theory. He confided his 'great secret' to Fleiss: 'I no longer believe in my *neurotica*,' for to accept it, Freud realised, meant implicating his own father in sexual abuse: 'In all cases, the *father*, not excluding my own, had to be accused of being perverse.' Having rejected this as the cause of his own 'little hysteria' – and that of his patients as well – Freud found himself once again at sea: 'I have no idea of where I stand because I have not succeeded in gaining a theoretical understanding of repression and its interplay of forces.' He recognised his affinities with Hamlet at this moment, quoting to Fleiss the Prince's words about being 'in readiness'. October would at last bring clarity, a new theory enabled and confirmed by the literary examples of *Oedipus Rex* and *Hamlet*. Freud writes excitedly to Fleiss that

[a] single idea of general value dawned on me. I have found, in my own case too, [the phenomenon of] being in love with my mother and jealous of my father, and I now consider it a universal event in early childhood . . . If this is so, we can understand the gripping power of *Oedipus Rex*. [The] Greek legend seizes upon a compulsion which everyone recognizes because he senses its existence within himself. Everyone in the audience was once a budding Oedipus in fantasy and each recoils in horror from the dream fulfillment here transplanted into reality.

Sophocles' play provided the theory with a name, but it was *Hamlet* that grounded it in the workings of the author's mind:

Fleetingly, the thought passed through my head that the same thing might be at the bottom of *Hamlet* as well. I am not thinking of Shakespeare's conscious intention, but believe, rather, that a *real event* stimulated the poet to his representation, in that his unconscious understood the unconscious of his hero.

This is an astonishing claim. Freud suggests that Shakespeare didn't borrow or invent what Hamlet experiences, he lived it. A 'real event', the death of Shakespeare's father shortly before he wrote the play, triggered the ambivalent, Oedipal experiences in Shakespeare that were akin to those that Freud himself had recently experienced following the death of his own father.

Self-analysis had enabled Freud, by extension, to analyse Shakespeare and identify in his play – much as he identified in the residue of his own dreams – traces of the deep Oedipal ambivalence Shakespeare experienced in the aftermath of his own father's death. His psychic kinship with both Hamlet and Shakespeare gave Freud confidence that he had successfully diagnosed the hysteria each had experienced. For Ernest Jones, it was 'but fitting that Freud should have solved the riddle of this Sphinx, as he has that of the Theban one'.

Freud was convinced that his Oedipal theory provided the long-sought explanation for Hamlet's delay: 'How better than through the torment he suffers from the obscure memory that he himself had contemplated the same deed against his father out of passion for his mother, and – "use every man after his desert, and who should 'scape whipping?" Other pieces of the Hamlet puzzle quickly fell into place:

His conscience is his unconscious sense of guilt. And is not his sexual alienation in his conversation with Ophelia typically hysterical? . . . And does he not in the end, in the same marvelous way as my hysterical patients, bring down punishment on himself by suffering the same fate as his father of being poisoned by the same rival?

Freud may have gone on to more famous case studies – Little Hans, Anna O., the Rat Man, Dora – but Shakespeare was in many ways his most consequential.

In our post-Freudian age all this may seem unremarkable, but Freud himself was keenly aware how bizarre this would sound to contemporaries, who were divided between two prevalent explanations for Hamlet's delay. Either the prince was paralysed by excessive thought or he was 'pathologically irresolute'. Freud believed that until he came along, 'people have remained completely in the dark as to the hero's character' – necessarily so, for none had ever undergone the kind of self-analysis he had just pioneered.

Freud insisted on an essential distinction between *Oedipus* and *Hamlet*: while the Oedipal complex may be timeless, it manifested itself differently in the modern world. So that while 'Shakespeare's *Hamlet* has its roots in the same soil as *Oedipus Rex*', the 'changed treatment of the same material reveals the whole difference in the mental life of these two widely separated epochs of civilization: the secular advance of repression in the emotional life of mankind'. In Sophocles' play, 'the child's wishful fantasy that underlies it is brought into the open and realized as it would be in a dream. In *Hamlet* it remains repressed; and – just as in the case of a neurosis – we only learn of its existence from its inhibiting consequences.' *Oedipus Rex* belongs to an older stage of civilisation. *Hamlet*, in contrast, is the product of a modern mind, and can therefore tell us much more about ourselves. But because of the 'secular advance of repression' in our psychic lives, only psychoanalysis allows us to get to the underlying causes of neurotic behaviour. Freud might have conceded that Shakespeare, and the early modern culture in which he lived and worked, stood somewhere between Sophocles' world and our own. He couldn't, though, if Shakespeare were to prove a star witness for his new theory. Freud's Hamlet had to be a truly modern man – and Shakespeare our contemporary.

The insights that led Freud to reject the seduction theory and solve the problem of *Hamlet* are not easily untangled. Freud couldn't readily abandon his view of *Hamlet* and what its author experienced following the death of his father without calling into question that which confirmed the rightness of his Oedipal theory. That was a lot to ask of a reading that stands or falls on whether *Hamlet* had been written after the death of John Shakespeare.

Years passed. Followers and patients flocked to Freud and psychoanalysis thrived. *Hamlet* became a canonical psychoanalytic text as well as a favourite subject of the Wednesday Psychological Society meetings, where Freud explored with his disciples how Shakespeare had written the play as 'a reaction to the death of his father'. Ernest Jones, the only native English speaker in Freud's inner circle, had committed himself to elaborating on this theory, first in a brief article in 1910 and eventually in his popular book, not published until 1949, *Hamlet and Oedipus*. He was at work on the subject in the early 1920s when he received an unwelcome letter. 'By an "accident," Freud wrote to him, 'I was able to find out the notice of a new document about *Hamlet*, which must concern you as much as me.' Freud had read Georg Brandes's latest book, *Miniaturen* (1919), in which Brandes repudiated his earlier and for Freud crucial claim that Shakespeare had written *Hamlet* in 1601 in the wake of his father's death. It now appeared that their dating of the play, on which Freud's theory precariously rested, was wrong. Brandes had changed his mind following the discovery of marginal notes, scribbled by the Elizabethan writer Gabriel Harvey, which showed that *Hamlet* was written by early 1599 or at the very latest early 1601. Freud felt forced to concede that '*Hamlet* was enacted before the death of Spenser, in any case before the death of Essex, that is to say much earlier than was believed hitherto. Now, remember Shakespeare's father died in the same year 1601! Will you think of defending our theory?'

Jones wrote back coolly, promising to 'investigate and report' on this development, which also threatened to undermine his own work. Before replying, he looked into what other literary scholars had made of this new evidence, especially Sidney Lee, the leading British Shakespearean of the day. Lee, for his own reasons, was also unwilling to abandon a late date for *Hamlet*, so came up with the ingenious if strained suggestion that it only *seemed* like Harvey was speaking about the deceased Spenser and Essex as if they were alive, because he was using 'the present tense in the historic fashion' – which allowed him to conclude that 'No light is therefore thrown by Harvey on the precise date of the composition or of the first performance of Shakespeare's *Hamlet*.' This, perhaps, explains Jones's confidence, and terminology, in reassuring Freud that 'I do not find that the passages you quote absolutely prove the date, for they may be written in the historic present'.

Freud agreed that the evidence of Harvey's marginalia remained 'far too incomplete' to 'settle the matter'. But unlike Jones, Freud was unwilling to dig in his heels, knowing 'that there is much slippery ground in many of our applications from psycho-analysis to biography and literature'. He had already been forced to retract some speculative biographical conclusions about Leonardo da Vinci, and recognised that he might have to do the same with Shakespeare: 'It is the danger inherent in our method of concluding from faint traces, exploiting trifling signs.'

Freud's conviction that the author of *Hamlet* had written the play in the aftermath of an Oedipal struggle remained unshaken; but the revised dating of the play now called Shakespeare of Stratford's authorship into question. Perhaps some conspiracy had taken place after all, and 'Shakespeare' was a pseudonym. That might explain why he and his disciples had had so little success in psychoanalytic explorations of the rest of the canon: besides *Hamlet*, only *Macbeth*, *Lear* and *The Merchant of Venice* had yield-ed much, and these analyses were nowhere near as groundbreak-ing.

Freud's doubts were exacerbated by his longstanding difficulties reconciling the facts of Shakespeare's humble origins with the worldliness one expects of such a genius. As he admitted in *Civilization and Its Discontents*, his sense of the 'cultural level' of so accomplished an artist as Shakespeare was hard to reconcile with that of a man who grew up with 'a tall dungheap in front of his father's house in Stratford'. When Freud stood face to face with the Chandos portrait of Shakespeare hanging in the National Portrait Gallery in England on a visit there in 1908 his doubts about the playwright's Warwickshire roots only grew stronger, for he saw Latin rather than English features staring back at him. He record-ed that 'Shakespeare looks completely exceptional, completely un-English,' and that 'face is race'. Freud began to suspect that Shakespeare was of French descent, his name a corruption of 'Jacques Pierre'. As Jones ruefully noted after Freud became an Oxfordian, the Earl of Oxford's family name, de Vere, was a

Norman name, which reinforced Freud's belief that the writer of the plays was not, originally, of English extraction. It seems that Freud was never quite able to shake those doubts first raised by Meynert – though he could never reconcile himself to the possibility that Bacon wrote the plays. It was a mystery, still waiting to be solved. Not long after his exchange with Jones in 1921 over the dating of *Hamlet*, Freud confessed to his friend and disciple Max Eitingon that he had always been thrown by the authorship controversy, as he was by the occult. As badly as Freud, now aged sixty-five, wanted to resolve the authorship question, he just wasn't sure. His words to Eitingon – half declaration, half question – capture this indecision: 'I believe in a conspiracy then, whether concerning the authors or Bacon himself?'

Looney

Many in the closing years of the nineteenth century admired Shakespeare (as Ben Jonson first put it) 'this side idolatry'; a handful crossed over to the other side. Among them were the congregants of a small branch of the Religion of Humanity in Newcastle upon Tyne, who sang hymns in praise not of God but of Shakespeare and other 'religious teachers of mankind'. Their

John Thomas Looney

prayer-book included an 'Act of Commemoration' venerating those who 'have raised Humanity from her original weakness to her actual power' – with Homer, Dante and Shakespeare mentioned in the same breath as Moses and St Paul.

Shakespeare's familiar visage could be seen among the Church of Humanity's 'customary . . . busts and symbols' adorning their house of worship. In their revised calendar, they celebrated a month called Shakespeare, which fell, every autumn, between the months of Gutenberg and Descartes. Some years earlier, members of the Religion of Humanity who were based in London had even travelled to Stratford-upon-Avon 'as pilgrims, to render homage to Shakespeare'. The entry on Shakespeare that appeared in the movement's *New Calendar of Great Men* offers some insight into why they worshipped Shakespeare, who both anticipated and embodied their church's precepts. Their Shakespeare was 'born into a society still rich with the outward and inward beauty created by centuries of Catholic Feudalism'. Yet while he admired the conservative ethos of this 'decaying' medieval world, their Shakespeare was nonetheless 'in small sympathy with any official Christianity which he knew, or with the intriguing politicians around the Tudor throne'. Though 'no lover of war', Shakespeare was 'certainly a fervent lover of his country's inward peace'. His plays, moreover, did 'not pretend to be religious and no religion can claim them but the Religion of Humanity', for 'he took the Human Soul to be his province'.

Cut through the pious language and theirs was a post-Catholic, nationalistic, reactionary Shakespeare, deeply invested in degree, nostalgic for a world in which everyone knew his and her place. Shakespeare was a key transitional figure in their history of human progress, rooted in a traditional past yet capable of glimpsing the future; while he 'could not reach the conception of social and moral science, he stretched out eager hands towards it'. What was true of Shakespeare held equally true of his greatest character. Like Shakespeare, who 'lived sufficiently near to the moral order bequeathed by the Middle Ages to spontaneously submit himself to much of it', Hamlet recognised the importance of submission. For what else could Hamlet have meant when reflecting on 'What is a man?' other than an acknowledgement that 'selfish desires are unceasingly striving to prevail' and 'need control – not only individual control, they need social control; above all, religious control'.

The churchgoers in Newcastle and the pilgrims to Stratford were English Positivists, adherents of a newly formed Religion of Humanity modelled on the teachings of the French philosopher Auguste Comte. Though Comte's work goes largely unread today, in late nineteenth-century Europe, especially in Victorian England, his influence was extraordinary. The hallmark of Comte's work was a commitment to progress and order. Having grown up in the wake of the French Revolution, Comte retained a lifelong aversion to anarchy. Early on, he had lost his faith in the Catholic Church as well as in a metaphysical God. Reconciling the principles of religion, science and morality for Comte came at a steep but acceptable price – one that John Stuart Mill (who corresponded with him) summed up in his essay *On Liberty* as 'a despotism of society over the individual'. Comte's late work took a religious turn – progress now took a back seat to order – as he conceived of a Religion of Humanity that would replace the worship of God. If Humanity was to be worshipped, a formal religion with sacraments, ceremony, secular saints, festivals, a religious calendar and a priesthood had to be invented, or rather cobbled together out of bits and pieces of traditional Christian practices (no wonder that Comte's Positivist Church was mocked by T. H. Huxley as 'Catholicism *minus* Christianity').

Most of Comte's English disciples were Oxford-trained intellectuals interested in promoting the philosophical and political principles systemised in his early writings; they steered clear of the spiritual drift of the late Comte. A smaller and less visible English faction focused its energies on establishing a church that would promote Comte's Religion of Humanity. Despite their shared loyalty to Comte's Positivist principles, by 1878 the differences between the two groups had become unbridgeable and they went their separate ways. It is the less influential and short-lived sect, led by Richard Congreve, that concerns us here.

Within a few short years, Congreve transformed what had been a 'Positivist School' into a 'Church of Humanity' and designated himself as the movement's highest priest. Under his leadership, Sunday meetings became Sunday worship, and a liturgy, festivals and sacraments, based on Comte's principles and calendar, were put in place. In an effort to win more converts, Congreve supported satellite churches in a half-dozen or so English cities. Conversions were few, especially among members of the working class, and expansion painfully slow. A small outpost was established in Newcastle in 1882, thanks to the efforts of Malcolm Quin, an energetic and ambitious convert who built up the congregation over the next two decades.

In 1899, Congreve suddenly died – and Quin soon after tried to wrest control of the national movement, based in London. He wasn't going to leave his Newcastle flock leaderless, however, and announced in October 1901 that he had hand-picked as his successor the twenty-nine-year-old J. T. Looney, a congregant who had been 'destined to the priesthood by Dr. Congreve' himself. Indeed, Congreve's final Sacramental Address had been delivered while presiding over Looney's 'Destination to the Priesthood' on Easter Sunday 1899. Looney, Quin adds, has already provided 'occasional assistance' in his 'Apostolic work', and 'is prepared to assume the charge of the Newcastle Church and Apostolate'. Quin also hoped that eventually enough money would be raised to support him, 'for it would be to the advantage of our cause to free Mr. Looney for the prosecution of his studies, and the continuance of our northern propaganda'.

Quin's attempted coup failed and he resumed his leadership role in Newcastle. Looney's great moment, his promotion to priestly leader of the Newcastle congregation, had come and gone. Congreve's death marked the beginning of the end of the movement. Over the new few years Looney helped Quin out with 'public teaching' and even tried to establish his own flock by undertaking what no English Positivist had done before, 'open-air preaching' in the marketplace of the nearby town of Blyth. Looney was praised for his 'courageous initiative in a new field and method of Positivist propaganda'. It was also reported that his preaching was 'patiently and sympathetically listened to by large audiences'. But little or nothing came of his efforts to win converts.

The Church of Humanity never recovered from its succession crisis. In retaliation for Quin's actions, the London membership cut off funding to the provincial churches and by 1904 these began to close down, with the Newcastle branch one of the last to fold. Alienated members had already begun drifting away from a movement in steep decline. In 1910 the doors finally shut on the Newcastle church and the site was 'taken over by the Jews, who built a synagogue on it'. Shakespeare's bust, along with most of the others, was donated to the Newcastle Grammar School.

Ordinarily the story of the rise and fall of a religious sect wouldn't merit much attention, least of all in a book about Shakespearean authorship. Yet had Malcolm Quin taken over in London, enabling J. T. Looney to succeed him as leader of a still thriving Church of Humanity in Newcastle, the odds are that nowadays the Shakespeare authorship controversy would be little more than a historical footnote, a story of yet another Victorian enthusiasm — much like Lamarckism, phrenology, and the Religion of Humanity itself — that had outlived its moment.

Virginia Woolf may have been only half-serious when, reflecting on the social and political transformations that modern culture was then undergoing, she wrote that 'on or about December 1910 human character changed', but for J. T. Looney, the closure in that year of a church he had been chosen to lead, a church committed to reversing the turn toward individualism and modernism that Woolf embodied, was a wrenching turn of events. Shortly after the Newcastle church was sold off, Looney began writing a book, one that he worked on through the course of the First World War, finished by 1918 and finally published in 1920. In it, he turned against his object of veneration, something it's hard to imagine him doing had he retained a position of leadership in the Church of Humanity, toppling the idol whose bust had adorned his church and declaring Shakespeare of Stratford to be an impostor. It was the very book – *Shakespeare' Identified* – that Freud had asked Smiley Blanton to read, the book that had made a convert of Freud, one that to this day remains the bible of all those who subscribe to the belief that the Earl of Oxford was the true author of the plays.

Not much is known about John Thomas Looney (whose family name, the subject of much unwarranted abuse, rhymes with 'bony'). Though he gained many followers in the quarter-century between the publication of '*Shakespeare' Identified* in 1920 and his death in 1944, and many corresponded with him, none of them wrote a detailed account of his life – nor did any full biographical sketch appear when his book was posthumously reprinted with new introductory material, first in 1949 and then again in 1975. Looney seems to have been unusually private and only published on the subject of Oxford and the Shakespeare question: a book, an edition of Oxford's poems and a handful of articles in minor journals. Most of what is now known of his life and his beliefs, aside from the few autobiographical hints in his published work, derives from what Looney wrote to Oxfordian disciples – letters that were selectively published after he died, with his blessings, in the pages of the obscure *Shakespeare Fellowship Quarterly.*

In them, Looney relates that his family came from the Isle of Man and traced his ancestry back to the Earls of Derby (though he didn't want too much made of this aristocratic connection). He himself was born in northeast England in the coastal town of South Shields and raised in a 'strongly evangelical' Methodist household. At the age of sixteen he prepared to enter the ministry and subsequently attended Chester Diocesan College. Within a few years, however, he abandoned this calling and spent years in search of a 'philosophy of life'. What he failed to discover in the traditional church he found in 1896, at age twenty-six, in the writings of Comte. Looking back upon this formative period, Looney was especially proud of his friendship with Richard Congreve, which put him but one step removed from Comte himself. He also writes of how Congreve had encouraged him to take 'a leading place in the English Positivism movement'.

This version of his upbringing is supplemented by a pair of Looney's letters now housed in the British Library, written in response to Congreve's questions about his intellectual preparation for the priesthood as well as the depth of his commitment to the Positivist cause. Looney reassured Congreve that he was 'fully and earnestly' committed, though painfully aware of 'the disadvantages in my education and circumstances', given the breadth of knowledge that a Comtean priest should have. In addition to mathematics, astronomy, physics, chemistry and physiology, his strengths included both European and English history, especially 'the Tudor and Stuart Periods'. Sufficiently assured, Congreve went ahead with the ceremony, in which Looney promised to 'accept the obligation imposed on me by the Sacrament of Destination as an aspirant to the Priesthood of Humanity, my definitive choice of a destination'.

Perhaps fearful of losing or alienating readers, Looney never acknowledged in *'Shakespeare' Identified* how deeply his Positivist experience informed the book. Only years later would he finally confirm what he had withheld: 'for forty years I have been a student of the works of Auguste Comte, and associated with the Positivist movement in England; and that this has determined more than any other single force, my attitude to every problem and interest of importance, not excepting the Shakespeare problem itself'. It was therefore as an exercise in applied Positivism that his book needed to be valued: 'Positivism may be said to have contributed appreciably to the discovery of "Shakespeare" and it is 'from this standpoint, that I should wish my Shakespeare researches to be judged'.

'Shakespeare' Identified was also a product of Looney's profound distaste for modernity: 'I have for very many years', he explained, 'had a settled sense of our own age as one of increasing social and

OXFORD

moral disruption tending towards complete anarchy.' On the eve of the Second World War, Looney reflected back upon how the chaos and destructiveness of the Great War had informed the writing of his book. Repelled by what he saw – as he understood both 'Shakespeare' and Comte had been before him – Looney also wanted to make a difference, combat these anarchic tendencies. The authorship controversy was a means to this larger end: 'My great wish has been to make some kind of contribution towards the solving of a problem much vaster, and more serious in its incidence, than the "Shakespeare" or any merely literary problem, could possibly be.' But, as he came to see it, 'Destiny has honoured us with this particular task, and though it may not be the work we could have wished to do, we are glad to have been able to do so much.' This, in turn, explains why he writes that those 'who can read between the lines of 'Shakespeare' Identified will not have much difficulty in detecting the direction' of his larger interests.

Yet for all the praise and calumny heaped upon his landmark book, few have bothered to read between the lines or pursue Looney's hints. Mainstream Shakespeareans couldn't be bothered, refusing to take this formidable book seriously, preferring instead to poke fun at Looney's name. His followers, for their own reasons, have also chosen not to probe too deeply, uncomfortable, perhaps, with what they already sensed. The founding myth of the Oxfordian movement – as one of the most ardent Oxfordians, Charlton Ogburn, put it – is that Looney, a scholarly schoolmaster, 'approached the quest for the author systematically, and with *a completely open mind*'.

Looney certainly sounds open-minded at the beginning of '*Shakespeare' Identified*, where he explains that he became interested in the authorship question when he could no longer reconcile what he knew of the facts of Shakespeare's life with the ethos of *The Merchant of Venice*, a play he taught regularly. Even if only half-true, the story of the curious schoolmaster who unravels the mystery of the plays still has tremendous appeal. Could someone who prosecuted others 'for the recovery of petty sums', Looney

[193]

wondered, have written a play that condemned such avarice? Surely the play's author more closely resembled Antonio than Shylock, and had himself 'felt the grip of the money-lender'. Looney also found it 'impossible' to believe that Shakespeare could have quit the stage and 'retired to Stratford to devote himself to houses, lands, orchards, money and malt, leaving no traces of a single intellectual or literary interest'. No writer of this stature could have cared that much about money. Shakespeare of Stratford was either a hypocrite or an impostor.

His logic is unassailable – but only if you believe that great authors don't write for money and that the plays are transparently autobiographical. Looney believed both unquestioningly. In support of his views he warmly quotes from the popular biographer Frank Harris, whose influential *The Man Shakespeare* treated Shakespeare's protagonists as a series of self-portraits: in Brutus, for example, Shakespeare offers 'an idealised portrait of himself'; it 'can hardly be denied that Shakespeare identified himself as far as he could with Henry V'; and in Hamlet, Shakespeare goes furthest of all, having 'revealed too much of himself'.

Unlike those who had previously investigated the authorship question, Looney began his quest with no particular writer in mind. He frankly admitted that he was no literary expert, but didn't see this as necessarily a hindrance, for the 'solution required the application of methods of research which are not, strictly speaking, literary'. The great virtue of Looney's work and the source of much of his book's appeal is the modesty of his approach, as he takes us step by step through the process that inexorably led him to Oxford. While Looney didn't begin with a particular candidate, he nonetheless brought to the problem a set of questionable assumptions about Elizabethan playwriting that sharply circumscribed his approach. Most of these were nineteenth-century commonplaces, and while they have had a long half-life, would not find support in scholarly circles today, when we know a lot more about early modern authorship and how Shakespeare worked than Looney and his contemporaries did.

Like many in his day, Looney believed that so accomplished a writer as Shakespeare could never have stooped to collaborating with lesser playwrights. And there had long been a division between those who believed that Shakespeare mainly wrote for Elizabethan playgoers and those convinced he wrote for posterity; Looney fell into the latter camp, arguing that plays so dense with meaning and allusion had to have been thoroughly overhauled. Such complex works of art could never have been understood by ordinary Elizabethan theatregoers: 'To pack with weighty signifi-cance each syllable of a work meant only to amuse or supply thrills for two or three hours would, moreover, defeat its own ends.' So Looney felt 'justified in claiming then that the best of the dramas passed through two distinct phases, being originally stage-plays – doubtless of a high literary quality – which were subsequently transformed into the supreme literature of the nation'. It was an inaccurate and anachronistic notion of Shakespeare's craft, one more suited to Henry James's revisions in his New York Edition than to a collaborative Jacobean playwright.

Armed with such assumptions, Looney established a profile that everyone could agree defined the writer of such remarkable plays and sonnets: a recognised genius as well as a talented poet, a man who was also mysterious, eccentric and well educated. Building on this foundation, Looney appended a more contro-versial list of traits: whoever wrote the plays was necessarily a man with feudal connections, an aristocrat, a lover of falconry and music, an enthusiast about Italy, improvident in money mat-ters and conflicted in his attitude toward women. The author also had Catholic sympathies and was fundamentally sceptical (here citing Comte as his authority, who had labelled Shakespeare 'a sceptic').

Looney still insists – and it's hard not to believe him – that he had as yet no specific candidate or slate of potential candidates in mind. So he began at the beginning, with what 'Shakespeare' him-self had called 'the first heir of my invention': *Venus and Adonis*. With this poem in hand, he sought a match in the most popular poetry anthology of the day, Palgrave's *Golden Treasury of English Songs and Lyrics*. He soon found a poem written in the same stanzaic form. Its author was Edward de Vere, seventeenth Earl of Oxford, of whom Looney knew next to nothing. He quickly set about making up for that ignorance, learning everything he could about Oxford's life and work. Looney recalls his growing excitement as every biographical fact and casual reference he uncovered about Oxford – and there wasn't much published material to go on at that time – confirmed not only that he perfectly fitted every established criterion with which he had begun his search, but also that Oxford's life and outlook perfectly corresponded with what was in the plays.

Only a churlish reader would stop to wonder why Looney didn't cast his net further, compare *Venus and Adonis* to the works of other poets writing in similar stanzaic forms, look at Shakespeare's early plays as well as poetry, or consider the possibility that the plays were written collaboratively. The remainder of *'Shakespeare' Identified* is devoted to establishing Oxford's claim, to illustrating how his discovery alters how we ought to read the plays and grasp their social, political and spiritual purpose, and, finally, to overcoming potential objections to the Oxfordian case.

Looney's approach was a tour de force. Rhetorically, it was the most compelling book on the authorship controversy to have appeared, and in this respect it has yet to be surpassed. A good deal of editorial credit for its literary quality has gone unacknowledged, part of the mythologising of Looney's accomplishment. When his publisher Cecil Palmer insisted that the initial manuscript submitted to him be overhauled if he were to accept it, Looney told him to 'do what he liked' with it. Palmer did so, as he acknowledged some years after Looney's death, making it 'less like a schoolboy's essay, and more resembling an undergraduate's thesis'.

Looney's sleight of hand of insisting that he began with no particular candidate in mind distracts us from what he did start with: questionable assumptions about the nature of authorship and a deeply held conviction that whoever wrote the plays shared his

Positivist worldview. His 'Shakespeare' would have been familiar to fellow members of the Church of Humanity: 'essentially a medievalist' who 'has preserved for all time, in living human characters, much of what was best worth remembering and retaining in the social relationship of the Feudal order of the Middle Ages'. This Positivist argument for Shakespeare's medievalism and his crucial role in the march of human progress goes hand in hand with Looney's Comtean claims for Shakespeare's anti-materialistic, anti-democratic and deeply reactionary social vision.

Because the author of the plays was someone 'whose sympathies, and probably his antecedents, linked him more closely to the old order than to the new', he was 'not the kind of man we should expect to rise from the lower middle-class population of the towns'. For Looney, the plays' author could never have subscribed to middle-class values, especially the pursuit of wealth for its own sake. One could either worship Mammon or serve Humanity. To 'represent him as a man who, having made a snug competency for himself, left dramatic pursuits behind him voluntarily . . . to devote himself more exclusively to houses, lands and business generally, is to suggest a miracle of self-stultification in himself and an equal miracle of credulity in us'.

If further proof were needed, the plays themselves showed that their author 'did not understand the middle classes'. His ordinary 'citizens' are like 'automata walking woodenly on to the stage to speak for their class' while his "lower-orders" never display that virile dignity and largeness of character'. Looney doesn't pause to consider the vividness and 'largeness of character' of the Fool in *Lear*, the loyal old servant Adam in *As You Like It*, Feste in *Twelfth Night*, the Nurse in *Romeo and Juliet*, Falstaff's followers, and dozens of others from the lower or middling classes that populate the plays. And he is adamant that 'Shakespeare's' greatest characters, and the ones for whom he shows the deepest sympathy, are kings and queens — which leads to the only 'logical conclusion' that the author of the plays was 'an aristocrat . . . in close proximity to royalty itself'. Once the 'theory' that 'Shakespeare' wrote for money 'is repudiated we are bound to look for an author who believed with his whole soul in the greatness of drama and the high humanising possibilities of the actor's vocation'.

Looney insists, time and again, that the author of the plays stood firmly against the forces of individualism and materialism, which threatened 'the complete submergence of the soul of civilised man'. As he completed his book towards the end of the Great War, Looney saw his argument confirmed in what was going on around him: "The fatness of these pursy times," as 'Shakespeare' put it in *Hamlet*, 'against which his whole career was a protest, has settled more than ever upon the life of mankind, and the culminating product of this modern materialism is the world war that was raging whilst the most of these pages were being penned.' In arguing for the deep sympathies of the plays' author with the 'chivalries of feudalism' and his 'affection for these social relationships', Looney closely follows the thinking of his mentor, Richard Congreve, who had written a book about Queen Elizabeth's reign in order to challenge 'individualism, the gospel of the literary classes of the present day', and to praise Elizabeth's top-down rule. Congreve hotly rejected the accusation that to do so was showing 'sympathy with despotism'; Elizabeth was an absolute monarch, and England 'was safer in the hands of one rather than of the few', let alone the many. Her reign, from this perspective, was a model for the Church of Humanity. Looney also seems to have shared Congreve's view that Elizabeth was England's 'last great hereditary governor' and that her 'reign closes one great epoch of English history' – an end-point that conveniently corresponded with the death of the Earl of Oxford. Delia Bacon's tyrant was Looney's model ruler.

Looney found the most unassailable evidence for the author's embrace of authoritarian values in Ulysses' great speech about the dangers of chaos in Act 1 of *Troilus and Cressida*. 'No more terrible condemnation of revolutionary equality', Looney concluded, 'was ever uttered':

O, when degree is shaked,
Which is the ladder to all high designs,
The enterprise is sick. How could communities,
Degrees in schools, and brotherhoods in cities,
Peaceful commerce from dividable shores,
The primogenity and due of birth,
Prerogative of age, crowns, sceptres, laurels
But by degree, stand in authentic place?

(1.3.101–8)

Lifting these words out of context, and italicising the lines that highlight his hierarchical views, Looney ignores how wily Ulysses mouths these pieties to manipulate his superior, the buffoonish Agamemnon, who has ample reason to want to hear degree and 'due of birth' defended so aggressively. In the 1940s, E. M. W. Tillyard would make this speech the centrepiece of a nostalgic and influential *Elizabethan World Picture.* But not even the conservative Tillyard goes as far as Looney, who was convinced that the 'scene as a whole is a discussion of state policy, from the standpoint of one strongly imbued with aristocratic conceptions, and conscious of the decline of the feudal order upon which social life had hitherto rested'. Looney knew that the clock could not be turned back, 'that we cannot, of course, go back to "Shakespeare's" medievalism, but we shall need to incorporate into modern life what was best in the social order and social spirit of the Middle Ages'.

It wasn't enough for Looney that the author of the plays held such views; he had to advocate them, use his plays to promote an explicit political agenda. This is where Oxford's candidacy made so much sense and why Looney couldn't just write a book arguing that a socially conservative Shakespeare of Stratford had written the plays. The true author had to be a man whose aristocratic lineage made him a natural leader, one who – if he had been properly recognised in his time – could have changed the world. Like Comte's great teachings, 'Shakespeare's' collected works were a textbook for both social and political reform: 'How differently might the whole course of European history have unfolded,' Looney laments, 'if the policy of "Shakespeare" had prevailed instead of that of the politicians of his time.'

In pursuing this idea, Looney had to argue that the plays that Oxford wrote were sophisticated political allegories (he interpreted *Henry the Fifth*, for example, as Oxford's attempt to urge a conciliatory rather than imperialist course in Elizabethan foreign policy). Underlying such claims are far-fetched assumptions about how and why the playwright went about creating his characters. For Looney, these *dramatis personae* weren't creations of the writer's fertile imagination; they were rather 'living men and women, artistically modified and adjusted to fit them for the part they had to perform'. And many of them turn out to be well-known courtiers or privy councillors in the dramatist's immediate orbit. Here, too, Looney was simply appropriating a topical methodology occasionally employed by mainstream Shakespeare scholars from Malone on down, though he took it to new extremes.

Enough incidents in Oxford's life uncannily corresponded to events in the plays to support Looney's claims that the plays were barely veiled autobiography. Like Hamlet, Oxford's father died young and his mother remarried. Like Lear, he had three daughters – and his first wife was the same age as Juliet when they married. Oxford also didn't refrain from recycling in his plays appalling events from his own life, from having been deceived by a bed-trick into sleeping with his wife (like Bertram in *All's Well*) to stabbing to death an unarmed man (as Hamlet did to Polonius).

Until now, critics had failed to identify these 'cunning disguises' because they had the wrong man. Oxford's authorship, Looney was convinced, made everything clear. *Hamlet* offered the best example and Looney matches its cast of characters with those in Oxford's courtly circle: Polonius is Lord Burghley, Laertes, his son Thomas Cecil, Hamlet is Oxford himself and Ophelia is Oxford's wife Anne. But such claims about representing on the public stage some of the most powerful figures in the realm betray a shallow grasp of Elizabethan dramatic censorship. Looney didn't understand that Edmund Tilney, the Master of the Revels, whose job it was to read and approve all dramatic scripts before they were publicly performed, would have lost his job – and most likely his nose and ears, if not his head – had he approved a play that so transparently ridiculed privy councillors, past and present. Looney's scheme also defies common sense, for Lord Burghley was dead by the time *Hamlet* was written, and nothing could have been in poorer taste, or more dangerous, than mocking Elizabeth's most beloved councillor soon after his death, on stage or in print.

Yet there were things in favour of Oxford's candidacy. He had been praised in his lifetime as both poet and playwright, and his verse was widely anthologised. Since relatively little was known about Oxford's life when Looney undertook his research, he can hardly be faulted for not knowing more about him. Looney relied heavily on the romantic portrait of Oxford in the late nineteenth-century *Dictionary of National Biography*, written, as it happens, by the Shakespeare scholar Sidney Lee. He learned there that Oxford was born in 1550, briefly studied at Cambridge, succeeded his father as Earl of Oxford in 1562, was a ward under the guardianship of William Cecil and married Cecil's eldest daughter Anne in 1571 (remarrying after her death in 1588), and subsequently found himself in and mostly out of Elizabeth's favour at court. According to Lee, from 1592 or so until his death in 1604, Oxford's life 'was spent mainly in retirement'. Looney also discovered from Lee's account that Oxford wrote poetry 'of much lyric beauty', 'squandered some part of his fortune upon men of letters whose bohemian mode of life attracted him', and was the patron of a playing company.

A century later, much more information about Oxford had been unearthed, and can be found in the updated *Dictionary of National Biography* entry written by Alan Nelson, as well in as Nelson's authoritative and harsh documentary biography of de Vere, *Monstrous Adversary*. Nelson's Oxford is a far less attractive figure than Lee's, and by extension, Looney's. It had become much clearer that Oxford was 'notorious in his own time' for 'his irregular life, and for squandering virtually his entire patrimony on personal extravagance'. 'Eternally short of funds, he did not scruple to burden lesser men with his debts.' His 'eccentricities and irregularities of temper grew with his years'. Oxford had stabbed a servant to death, but was exonerated when the authorities decided that it wasn't murder but suicide: the servant had willingly impaled himself on Oxford's sword's point.

Where Looney imagines what Lee calls Oxford's 'retirement' spent reworking theatrical drafts into high art, Nelson documents instead how 'Oxford devoted his declining years to the endless pursuit of supplementary income, petitioning for the monopoly on fruit, oils, and wool; for the gauging of beer; for the preemption of tin in Cornwall and Devon' as well as 'for the governorship of Jersey' and 'the presidency of Wales'. Oxford's surviving letters 'reflect his endless disappointments. Bitter to the end, he plotted against the royal succession by a Scot.' Nelson's portrait of Oxford is close to that painted by Gabriel Harvey in 1580 in his *Speculum Tuscanismi*: 'delicate in speech, quaint in array, conceited in all points', he was 'a passing singular odd man'. As far as Positivist values were concerned, Oxford turned out to be a very poor choice – though again, given the paucity of information available about Oxford at the time, Looney could not have known that. And the seventeenth-century biographer John Aubrey hadn't helped de Vere's legacy by retailing an embarrassing and probably apocryphal anecdote about him: 'This Earl of Oxford, making of his low obeisance to Queen Elizabeth, happened to let a fart, at which he was so abashed and ashamed that he went to travel seven years. On his return the Queen welcomed him home, and said, "My lord, I had forgot the fart."'

The greatest challenge Looney had to meet was the problem of Oxford's death in 1604, since so many of Shakespeare's great Jacobean plays were not yet written, including *Macbeth, King Lear, Coriolanus, Antony and Cleopatra, Timon of Athens, Pericles,*

The Winter's Tale, Cymbeline and *Henry the Eighth*. Looney concluded that these plays were either written before Oxford died (and posthumously released one by one to the playgoing public) or left incomplete and touched up by lesser writers (which explains why they contain allusions to sources or events that took place after Oxford had died). It was a canny two-part strategy, one that could refute almost any counter-claim.

Looney also concluded that *The Tempest* – a play that scholars confidently date to well after 1604 – didn't belong in the canon and was entirely the work of another hand. In rejecting 'Shakespeare's' authorship of *The Tempest* he was also repudiating the widespread nineteenth-century biographical tradition which held that it was Shakespeare's last play and when Prospero breaks his staff and abandons his 'rough magic' it's really Shakespeare giving up his art. Looney's grounds were again Positivist: 'Shakespeare' could never have expressed such metaphysical nonsense as can be found in Prospero's speech, 'We are such stuff as dreams are made on, and our little life is rounded with a sleep.' And although *The Tempest* contains a king and a duke, 'no one can feel in reading it that he is in touch with the social structure of a medieval feudalism'.

Surely, Looney writes, 'Shakespeare' believed that 'human life is the one great objective reality' and 'his world is peopled by real men; not *dreamy stuff*'. His argument here echoes that made a few years earlier by Lytton Strachey, who in an influential and reprinted essay signalled a turn against the Romantic reading of the play: 'In *The Tempest*, unreality has reached its apotheosis. Two of the principal characters are frankly not human beings at all.' Looney's timing was perfect, for he was able to ride the tide of opinion turning against *The Tempest* and of Prospero as its autobiographical hero. Prospero, Strachey notes, 'is the central figure of *The Tempest*, and it has often been wildly asserted that he is a portrait of the author – an embodiment of that spirit of wise benevolence which is supposed to have thrown a halo over Shakespeare's life'. But 'if Prospero is wise, he is also self-opinionated and sour . . . his gravity is often another name for pedantic severity . . . and there is no character in the play to whom, during some part of it, he is not studiously disagreeable.'

Where influential Victorian biographers such as Edward Dowden had seen in Shakespeare-as-Prospero the very image of a serene and benign artist, a man who had achieved self-mastery and with that a 'remoteness from the common joys and sorrows of the world', Strachey can only find a boring protagonist and a writer who was himself 'getting bored' – 'bored with people, bored with real life, bored with drama'. By the early twentieth century the great reign of *The Tempest* as the crowning achievement of the career, and of the wise and patriarchal Prospero as the way people wanted to imagine Shakespeare, had lost much of its appeal. So too did the image of Shakespeare as a man of books, of magic, and as a repository of political wisdom. Looney's great achievement was proposing an alternative candidate to Bacon-as-Shakespeare while at the same time offering a portrait of Shakespeare that perfectly satisfied the desires of the new century: Shakespeare as Prince Hamlet. A hundred years later Hamlet still holds that autobiographical pride of place – thanks in no small part to Looney's early devotee, Freud. Where Oxford's death in 1604 had once been an almost insuperable obstacle to Looney's theory of authorship, it now proved to be providential, insofar as *Hamlet*, rather than *The Tempest*, Looney imagined, proved to be 'Shakespeare's' final play. For Looney, Hamlet's last words speak directly to the disgraced Oxford's own situation, and 'may almost be accepted as Oxford's dying words': 'what a wounded name / Things standing thus unknown, shall live behind me!' Looney's peroration captures his vision of the dying artist at work:

The picture of a great soul, misunderstood, almost an outcast from his own social sphere, with defects of nature, to all appearances one of life's colossal failures, toiling on incessantly at his great tasks, yet willing to pass from life's stage leaving no name behind him but a discredited one: at last dying, as it would seem, almost with the pen between his fingers, immense things accomplished, but not all he had set out to do.

It's difficult to resist the temptation to read between the lines here and see signs of the dismay Comte's disciples felt as the Religion of Humanity slipped from public view, leaving no name behind but a discredited one.

Looney didn't begin with a candidate; he began with a call to arms, in which he enlists 'Shakespeare' – or rather imagines 'Shakespeare' enlisting us – in this cause. Only at the end of the book does Looney drop his guard and admit to this agenda, to how he saw 'Shakespeare' playing a crucial role in the restoration of the socially and politically repressive 'new order' in which superiors rule over their inferiors, and one over all, while a spirit of *noblesse oblige* prevails. It's a sobering vision of what Looney thought the Oxfordian cause was ultimately about, and as such, worth quoting at length:

If the new order for which the 'prophetic soul' of 'Shakespeare' looked is to arise at last through a reinterpretation and application to modern problems, of social principles which existed in germ in medievalism, then 'Shakespeare', in helping to preserve the best ideals of feudalism, will have been a most potent factor in the solution of those social problems which in our day are assuming threatening proportions throughout the civilised world. The feudal ideal which we once more emphasise is that of noblesse oblige; the devotion of the strong to the weak; the principle that all power of one man over his fellows, whether it rests upon a political or industrial basis, can only possess an enduring sanction so long as superiors discharge faithfully their duties to inferiors. In this task of 'putting right', Hamlet or 'Shakespeare', who we believe was Edward de Vere, through the silent spiritual influences which have spread from his dramas, will probably have contributed as much as any other single force.

Any residual doubts about the core beliefs held by Looney – and shared and anticipated by 'Shakespeare' – are put to rest by his response to an American admirer, Flodden W. Heron, who in July 1941 wrote a letter of solidarity expressing kinship between their two democracies in that dark hour when it looked as if England faced destruction at the hands of the Nazis. It was the wrong thing to say to Looney and provoked this sharp response:

I often regret therefore that the war is represented as a struggle between dictatorship and democracy. At the bottom it is one between the human soul and elemental brute force; it just happens that the present dictatorships stand for brutal domination and spiritual tyranny, and that to the democracies has fallen the defence of the soul's freedom. The opposite is, however, quite conceivable. 'Majority rule' might be as tyrannically repressive of spiritual liberty as any other form of government.

Looney, who had to leave his home because of massive German air-raids in the Gateshead-on-Tyne area, whose unsold copies of *Shakespeare' Identified* were destroyed by German bombs in London, and who was disgusted by Hitler and the Nazis, nonetheless preferred to 'think of our two nations as being united in a struggle for the preservation of spiritual liberty rather than the maintenance of what is called "democratic government". He remained – as his book and his 'Shakespeare' remain – dead set against the forces of democracy and modernity to the very end.

Looney's Oxfordianism was a package deal. You couldn't easily accept the candidate but reject his method. You also had to accept a portrait of the artist concocted largely of fantasy and projection, one wildly at odds with the facts of Edward de Vere's life. Looney had concluded that the story of the plays' authorship and the feudal, anti-democratic and deeply authoritarian values of those plays were inseparable; to accept his solution to the authorship controversy meant subscribing to this troubling assumption as well.

Freud, Again

Freud celebrated his seventieth birthday in 1926 in the company of his old friends Max Eitingon, Sándor Ferenczi and Ernest Jones. They talked late into the night, with Freud holding forth on whether the Earl of Oxford was the true author of Shakespeare's plays. Jones later recalled his 'astonishment at the enthusiasm he could display on the subject at two in the morning'. It soon became a sore point between them. They had been drifting apart in recent years, when, in early March 1928, Jones wrote an anguished letter informing Freud that his beloved child had just died. His letter ends with a plea for some comforting thoughts – 'a word from you might help us'. Rather than offering consolation, Freud thought it better to 'do something to distract' the grief-stricken Jones. Acknowledging that his disciple was 'closest to the Shakespeare problem', Freud, who had been rereading *Shakespeare' Identified*, urged Jones to get his mind off his loss by investigating Looney's claims – 'It would surely repay an analyst's interest to look into the matter.' Warming to the subject, he added that he was especially curious about the reception of Looney's book in England. He himself was 'very impressed by Looney's investigations, almost convinced'.

Jones waited over a month before replying, and, given the circumstances, handled Freud's callous response surprisingly well, though he admits to having expected a bit more sympathy. He reminded Freud that he well remembers 'your telling us all about Looney in May 1926', and is willing to concede that 'Shakespeare was probably interested in de Vere and well informed about him.' But Jones drew the line there: he found Looney's argument unpersuasive and assured Freud that *'Shakespeare' Identified* 'had made no impression in London', where the 'only literary man I spoke to about it was disparaging'. 'So many books', Jones added, 'consist in the first half of excited promises to reveal and prove something, and in the second half of triumph at what they think they have proved.'

Freud wrote back, stung. It would be the last of their exchanges about Shakespeare: 'I was dissatisfied with your information about Looney. I recently read his book again and this time I was even more impressed by it.' Jones's remark that exciting theories don't always achieve all they promise had struck a nerve: 'I believe it is unfair', Freud replied, 'to say that he only triumphs after making promises, like so many other riddle solvers.' Freud insisted on having the final word, reminding Jones of the untapped vein of

Shakespeare analysis that was now made available through an Oxfordian perspective:

The explanation of the sonnets and the contributions to the analysis of Hamlet seem to me – besides others – to justify his conviction well . . . The existence of de Vere provides material for new investigations which can yield interesting positive and negative results. We know Lady Oxford remarried after her husband's death, but do not know the date. What would our position be if this justified the reproach of unseemly haste which Hamlet makes to his mother?

Why did Freud, who had lived with ambivalence about the authorship question for so long, commit in his final years so fully to Oxford's cause? He had read Looney's book closely enough to have found its nostalgia for a repressive and authoritarian medieval past dangerously naïve. For there's no question he saw the thrust of Looney's argument. When he wrote to Lytton Strachey, author of *Elizabeth and Essex*, advocating Looney's cause, he noted that Oxford, like Essex, 'embodied . . . the type of the tyrannical nobleman.' Freud, if anyone, was in a position to read between the lines and knew enough about Comte's ideas (one of his earliest teachers in the 1870s, Ernst Brücke, had been a committed Positivist). Freud's own view of the cost of repression in human society – especially that imposed by religion – was clear, and it was at just this time, after all, that he was wrestling in *The Future of An Illusion* (1927) with many of the social issues raised by Looney, concluding that it 'is doubtful whether men were in general happier at a time when religious doctrines held unrestricted sway; more moral they certainly were not'. Freud had also thought long and hard about the irresolvable tension between individual desire and societal will, searching in *Civilization and Its Discontents* (1930) for some sort of accommodation between the two, one that offered the best prospects for human happiness.

Freud's rejection of Shakespeare could not have been easy. It disturbed him, as his letter to Theodor Reik in March 1930 indicates: 'I have been troubled by a change in me which was brought about under the influence of Looney's book, '*Shakespeare*' *Identified*. I no longer believe in the man from Stratford.' Yet Freud stopped short of sharing with Reik any deeper, psychic explanations for the troubling change – so that they must remain inaccessible to us, if they were even accessible to him.

What is even more puzzling about his embrace of Looney's cause is that forty years earlier Freud had reinvented Hamlet (and Shakespeare too) in the image of neurotic and cosmopolitan modern man. Yet the only way he could sustain this view was by relying on an argument that turned Shakespeare, and by extension Hamlet, into a pro-feudal reactionary. It's hard to avoid concluding that Freud's decision to embrace the Oxfordian cause was, at best, self-deceiving. While until the end of his life he continued to modify and elaborate on Oedipal dynamics and would even alter his thinking about aspects of the seduction theory, in the end, his core belief in the Oedipal theory was never shaken. It must have proved deeply reassuring that Looney's book independently corroborated his solution to the *Hamlet* problem, confirming that the play had been written following the death of the author's father. For if Looney was right, and Freud apparently needed to believe so, it now made no difference whether *Hamlet* was written as early as 1598 or even 1588, for Oxford had lost his father back in 1562 and then saw his mother, like Gertrude, remarry.

Other aspects of Looney's reading of *Hamlet* were easily assimilated into Freud's. One can only imagine Freud's growing excitement when reading in '*Shakespeare' Identified* how Hamlet's 'loss of such a father, with the complete upsetting of his young life that it immediately involved, must have been a great grief to one so sensitively constituted'. Looney, like Freud, also saw Hamlet as 'the dramatic self-revelation of the author, if such a revelation exists anywhere'. In other ways, too, Freud found Looney's argument rich in possibilities. Looney had concluded, after all, that Oxford's mother's remarriage bore directly 'upon questions of Shakespearean interpretation'. Looney's Oxfordian reading of *Hamlet* – which for him was about both 'the love and admiration of a son for a dead father' and the 'grief and disappointment at his mother's conduct' which 'lie at the root of all the tragedy of his life' – allowed, at last, for a fuller exploration of both the maternal *and* paternal aspects of the Oedipal scheme, one long denied to Freud. He made much of this argument in a note that appeared in the next edition of his *Outline of Psychoanalysis*, where he declared that 'Edward de Vere, Earl of Oxford, a man who has been thought to be identifiable with the author of Shakespeare's works, lost a beloved and admired father while he was still a boy and completely repudiated his mother, who contracted a new marriage very soon after her husband's death.'

Even as he grew increasingly excited by the psychoanalytic potential of Looney's arguments, the ageing Freud became more and more impatient with those in his circle he had tried and failed to convert, including Hanns Sachs, upon whom he pressed a copy of *'Shakespeare' Identified*. Freud tried even harder with the novelist Arnold Zweig. After failing to win Zweig over to Oxford's cause, Freud asked him to return his book: 'You must bring Looney back with you. I must try him on others, for obviously with you I have had no success.' But he wasn't finished with Zweig yet and months later was still chastising him: 'I do not know what still attracts you to the man of Stratford,' Freud writes: 'He seems to have nothing at all to justify his claim, whereas Oxford has almost everything secondhand – Hamlet's neurosis, Lear's madness, Macbeth's defiance and the character of Lady Macbeth, Othello's jealousy, etc. It almost irritates me that you should support the notion.'

After reading Looney's book Freud was also convinced that the Sonnets – works that he had never seriously considered – could prove especially fertile ground for future psychoanalytic research. He was sufficiently persuaded by Looney's account of their auto-biographical nature to believe that these compact lyrics were like recorded dreams or confessions that offered access to the author's thoughts and through them to his otherwise unrecorded experiences. When the Austrian Shakespeare scholar Richard Flatter sent Freud his German translation of the Sonnets, Freud wrote back, correcting Flatter's 'obsolete' views and assuring him that 'there are no doubts any longer about their serious nature and their value as self-confessions'. The evidence for this was obvious, for the poems 'were published without the author's co-operation and handed on after his death to a public for whom they had not been meant'. Freud urged Flatter to get hold of the latest Oxfordian scholarship, which he was himself reading: '*Shakespeare's Sonnets and Edward de Vere* by Gerald H. Rendall'.

Lear too now seemed much more open to psychoanalytic explanation. Freud wrote excitedly to James S. H. Branson that 'the figure of the father who gave all he had to his children must have had for him a special compensatory attraction, since Edward de Vere was the exact opposite, an inadequate father who never did his duty by his children'; so even when de Vere's life took the opposite course of what happens in the plays, it confirmed for Freud his authorship of them. Freud also tried to persuade Bramson that the play was written by Oxford during his late years – before the date scholars usually assigned the play – and was narrowly based on Oxford's two elder and married daughters, Elizabeth and Bridget, as well as their younger, unmarried sister, Susan ('our Cordelia'). Freud saw confirmation of Oxford's authorship in the fact that in the sources all three of Lear's daughters were unmarried – and that Oxford altered this so that Lear's relationships more closely resembled his own. *Othello* could now also be explained in psycho-analytic and familial terms: Oxford's 'marriage with Anne Cecil turned out very unhappily. If he was Shakespeare he had himself experienced Othello's torments.' All told, Oxford turned out to be a far richer subject – in terms of psychopathology – than Shakespeare ever had been, which may explain, as Freud wrote to Smiley Blanton, why he was so 'strongly prejudiced' in favour of Looney's theory, though acknowledging that it doesn't totally resolve the authorship 'mystery'.

Freud wrote an acceptance speech when he was awarded the Goethe Prize in 1930. He was too frail to attend the award ceremony himself; his daughter Anna delivered his remarks in his stead. Freud took this opportunity to expand on his views of literary biography in general and on Oxford's authorship of Shakespeare's plays in particular – his first public declaration of this view (other than an aside in the 1927 American edition of *An Autobiographical Study*, where he writes that after 'reading "Shakespeare" Identified by J. T. Looney, I am almost convinced that the assumed name conceals the personality of Edward de Vere'). As far as literary biography was concerned, 'two questions which alone seem worth knowing about' any author are 'the riddle of the miraculous gift that makes an artist' and how that helps us 'comprehend any better the value and effects of his works'. Freud acknowledges that these are things we badly want to know, and that we feel this 'powerful need' most when its satisfaction is denied to us – as 'in the case of Shakespeare'. He shifts smoothly here to the authorship question:

It is undeniably painful to all of us that even now we do not know who was the author of the Comedies, Tragedies and Sonnets of Shakespeare, whether it was in fact the untutored son of the provincial citizen of Stratford, who attained a modest position as an actor in London, or whether it was, rather, the nobly-born and highly cultivated, passionately wayward, to some extent *déclassé* aristocrat Edward de Vere.

Put this way, it's not much of a choice.

In exile in London a few years later, witnessing so much that he had struggled to build threatened by the rise of an ideology concocted of a heady mixture of the cult of personality, a romanticising of a distant past, the vilification of a materialism associated with Jews, and an insistence on discipline and the subordination and submission of the masses to dictatorial will, did Freud ever stop to reflect upon how much of Looney's social vision overlapped with that which had driven him from Vienna?

More than ever in the coming years shall we need the spirit of 'Shakespeare' to assist in the work of holding the 'politician' and the materialist, ever manoeuvring for ascendancy in human affairs, to their secondary position in subordination to, and under the discipline of, the spiritual elements of society. We cannot, of course, go back to 'Shakespeare's' mediaevalism, but we shall need to incorporate into modern life what was best in the social order and social spirit of the Middle Ages.

Looney's retrograde vision comes too close for comfort to Freud's account of the Nazi rise to power in 1933, when he described 'the ideal of Hitlerism' as 'purely medieval and reactionary'. That year Freud had also written to Ernest Jones that 'We are in a transition toward a rightist dictatorship, which means the suppression of social democracy. That will not be an agreeable state of affairs and will not make life pleasant for us Jews.' It may be unfair on my part, but I cannot help but feel that Freud, who confessed himself to be Looney's 'follower', seems to have turned a blind eye to the broader implications of what Looney advocated.

Looney's daughter, Mrs Evelyn Bodell, reported that a few days before he died on 17 January 1944, her father confided that 'My great aim in life has been to work for the religious and moral unity of mankind; and along with this, in later years, there has been my desire to see Edward de Vere established as the author of the Shakespearean plays – and the Jewish problem settled.' That last phrase can be easily misread, especially in 1944 when it was becoming clearer what horrors the Nazis had inflicted on the Jews (among the victims were four of Freud's five sisters, who died in extermination camps). What Looney meant by this is clarified in a letter he sent to Freud in July 1938, shortly after he had fled Vienna and arrived in London. Rather than discussing the Shakespeare problem, Looney wanted to enlist Freud's support in resolving the Jewish one. He explains that he writes as a Positivist, as a nationalist and as someone with no quarrel with dictatorship. While highly critical of the Nazis, he is also impatient with the Jews' refusal to abandon their racial distinctiveness and assimilate fully into the nation-states in which they lived – the ultimate source, for Looney, of their persecution. He rejects the possibility of a Jewish homeland as impractical; the only solution, from his Positivist perspective, is their 'fusion', which, sooner or later, 'must come'. Looney might have added that Oxford had foreseen as much in having both Shylock and Jessica 'fuse' through conversion with the dominant Venetian society by the end of *The Merchant of Venice.*

Looney was consistent to the end. He had begun his authorship quest decades earlier after equating Shakespeare of Stratford's 'acquisitive disposition' and habitual 'petty money transactions' with Shylock's. For Looney, the idea that a money-hungry author had written the great plays was impossible. His originality, then, was in suggesting that while Shakespeare of Stratford was portrayed in Shylock, the play's true author, the Earl of Oxford, had painted his self-portrait in Antonio. Looney's solution to the authorship problem, like the resolution of the play's 'Jewish problem', and indeed, 'the religious and moral unity of mankind', was of a piece.

Oxfordians

Almost overnight, the publication of *'Shakespeare' Identified* in 1920 established Oxford as a leading candidate for the authorship of the plays. With Bacon in decline, de Vere's main competitors were now other aristocrats; the case for other professional playwrights or poets, including Marlowe, never really got off the ground. In 1905 the Earls of Southampton and Essex had each been proposed, but neither generated much interest. There was considerably more enthusiasm two years later for the candidacy of Roger Manners, fifth Earl of Rutland. He had strong literary connections, having married Sir Philip Sidney's daughter, had travelled widely and had served as an ambassador to the Danish court at Elsinore, giving him intimate knowledge of Hamlet's world. While on the young side (he would have published *Venus and Adonis* at age seventeen) his death in 1612 roughly corresponded to the end of Shakespeare's playwriting career. Rutland's advocates, who soon included

Germans, Swiss, Belgians, Russians, Americans and Argentinians, also believed that the experiences of some of the plays' most memorable characters – especially Romeo, Jaques, Hamlet and Prospero – were closely modelled upon Rutland's tumultuous life. When Sherlock Holmes was brought out of retirement to solve the mystery of who wrote Shakespeare's plays, the famous detective concluded that it was Rutland who did it.

Before Looney's book appeared, Rutland's chief aristocratic rival had been the Earl of Oxford's son-in-law, William Stanley, Earl of Derby. During the heyday of the Baconians in the 1890s, it had come to light that a Jesuit spy had reported in June 1599 that Derby was 'busied only in penning comedies for the common players'. A couple of decades later, in the wake of renewed interest in aristocratic candidates, researchers began to follow up on this tantalising information and by 1919 Derby's candidacy had attracted an international and even academic following. Besides this report, there were many points in his favour: Derby shared Shakespeare's first name and initials (so could easily have written those punning 'Will' sonnets), and his dates fit well enough, for he was born three years before Shakespeare and died the year the theatres closed, in 1642. Derby too was well travelled, especially in France, and there was considerable internal evidence in the plays that suggested they were based on what Derby had seen and done.

It's not entirely clear why Oxford emerged as the most plausible of these aristocratic contenders. Some at the time were convinced that had the case for Derby been established a few years earlier a consensus would have gathered around his candidacy. In retrospect, Looney proved to be a more effective advocate than those supporting rival claimants, his book more heartfelt, his disciples more prominent and committed, and the autobiographical connections established between Oxford's life and Shakespeare's plays more persuasive. What ultimately tipped the scales in de Vere's favour was that he alone among these earls had been recognised in his own day as an accomplished writer and praised by contemporaries for both his poetry and comedies. Though few poems and no plays that Oxford had written under his own name were extant, it was still possible to compare what survived with that attributed to Shakespeare, and argue (as the Baconians had long done) for stylistic and thematic parallels between the two bodies of work.

In order to capitalise on Looney's groundbreaking study, a proper biography as well as a scholarly edition of Oxford's acknowledged verse were needed. Looney took it upon himself to edit *The Poems of Edward de Vere*, while B. M. Ward devoted himself to completing *The Seventeenth Earl of Oxford*, the first full-length account of de Vere's life. A torrent of scholarship followed: thirty or so Oxfordian volumes poured from presses over the next two decades.

H. H. Holland led the way in 1923 with *Shakespeare through Oxford Glasses*, connecting plays previously dated to the early seventeenth century to topical events in the 1570s and 1580s. A trio of enthusiastic Oxfordians, each one a small publishing industry, soon followed. Eva Turner Clark, one of the few Americans to join the movement this early on, published four Oxfordian books. Building on Holland's work, and seeking to do for Oxford what Edmond Malone had done for Shakespeare, Clark mapped out an alternative chronology of Oxford's plays, placing their initial composition decades earlier. Her work was highly influential and Freud, who read it closely, was especially impressed. In Britain, drama critic Percy Allen was even more prolific, with five titles to his credit. He also had privately printed *My Confession of Faith* (1929), affirming how akin to a religious conversion his embrace of Oxford had been. Not to be outdone, Canon Gerald H. Rendall, a professor of Greek at University College Liverpool and already eighty years old when he became an Oxfordian, turned out four Oxfordian titles. Others, including Gilbert Slater in *Seven Shakespeares* (1931) and Montagu William Douglas in *The Earl of Oxford as 'Shakespeare'* (1931), proposed that Oxford was actually the mastermind of a group of writers responsible for Shakespeare's works. Douglas also suggested that Queen

OXFORD

Elizabeth had entrusted Oxford to oversee a propaganda department that would produce patriotic plays and pamphlets. All told, it was a rich harvest, and mainstream Shakespeareans, who refused – as did the Baconians – to acknowledge the early success of the Oxford movement, had to scramble to compete with the sheer volume of this scholarship.

Though he lived until 1944, Looney never wrote another book. He nevertheless corresponded with his followers and contributed a few Oxfordian articles, including one that appeared in the lavish quarterly *The Golden Hind*, in which he shared a new reading of *The Merry Wives of Windsor*. Once again, characters were understood to be barely concealed historical figures: the play's dashing young lover, Fenton, was another of Oxford's self-portraits, while the woman he woos, Anne Page, was an obvious stand-in for the young woman Oxford married, Anne Cecil. The doltish Slender, whom Fenton outmanoeuvres, is Oxford's rival Sir Philip Sidney, who had unsuccessfully sought Anne Cecil's hand in marriage. Even the setting in Windsor corresponded exactly with where the events on which the play was based had taken place three decades earlier. The stories matched so perfectly that Looney doubted 'whether another case could be cited in which a dramatist so closely followed facts of this nature and placed an identification so entirely outside the range of reasonable dispute'.

Oxford's loss of Anne, who died of fever in 1588, when the outpouring of drama began, turned out to be our gain, for her untimely death inspired a succession of the plays' remarkable heroines: 'After the death of Lady Oxford he went into retirement, during which came the great "Shakespearean" outburst, involving plays in which, as we have just seen, the most private affairs of his youth and early manhood were represented.' The 'sweet little Countess of Oxford' lives on 'as Ophelia, Juliet, Desdemona, and Anne Page' – and 'what Beatrice was to Dante, such, under widely different circumstances, did Anne Cecil become to our great English "Shakespeare"'. It was a romantic story of inspiration that both anticipated and surpassed the one

[217]

enacted in *Shakespeare in Love*.

Looney knew well that Oxford was buried in an unmarked grave in the churchyard of St Augustine, Hackney – which meant that those who worshipped his work had no proper shrine to visit, nothing like that which continued to lure pilgrims to Stratford-upon-Avon. But Anne was buried in Westminster Abbey, and the deification of Oxford could be realised if, as Looney proposed, her grave became the couple's shared shrine:

It is a great thing for us, then, that she lies in Westminster Abbey, and one day, when the world has done justice to Edward de Vere, her monumental tomb there will doubtless become a shrine, where, binding in one the memory of both, fit public honours will be paid to him who has become the glory of England.

With this, Looney's argument to supplant Shakespeare with Oxford was complete. He may have been unaware when he proposed it that – as the new *Dictionary of National Biography* entry bluntly puts it – de Vere's marriage to the fourteen-year-old Anne had been 'a disaster'. Oxford's father-in-law, Burghley, was soon muttering 'that Oxford had been "enticed by certain lewd persons to be a stranger to his wife"' after learning that Oxford had dodged 'the sweet little Countess' on his return from foreign travels. The couple was estranged for years. Even after they were reunited – and this Looney knew – Oxford impregnated Anne Vavasour, one of the queen's maids of honour. Four years after Anne's death, Oxford remarried. Looney's fantasy of Edward de Vere and Anne Cecil as England's Dante and Beatrice was a bit of a stretch.

Recognising the need for a central organisation to promote 'research and propaganda', a Shakespeare Fellowship was founded in 1922, with Sir George Greenwood (whose work had so influenced Twain and other sceptics) as its first president. Founding vice-presidents included Professor Abel Lefranc and Looney himself. Greenwood leaned toward Oxford as the mastermind of a group of writers, while Lefranc was an advocate of the Earl of

Derby, so at least at the outset, the organisation hoped to unite 'in one brotherhood all lovers of Shakespeare who are dissatisfied with the prevailing Stratfordian orthodoxy'. Its ends were to 'encourage and to organise research among parish registers, wills, and other documents likely to throw light on the subject'. By year's end over forty individuals had joined the organisation. With scholarly energies redirected toward candidates other than the man from Stratford, there was great confidence that the archives would soon yield unassailable evidence of who had actually written the plays.

At some now forgotten moment over the next two decades – after support for Rutland, Derby and others had faded – the organisation's mandate was quietly rewritten to give 'special consideration of the claims that Edward de Vere, the 17th Earl of Oxford, in sympathetic association with others personally connected with him, was the poet Shakespeare'. Books published by commercial presses, especially that of the sympathetic publisher Cecil Palmer, remained the coin of the Oxfordian realm, and it was only in the mid-1930s that it was thought necessary to publish a newsletter to get the word out. The first twenty years of the movement were so successful and Oxfordians so prolific that the circumstantial case was fairly complete.

The intense interest of Freud and his circle is but one indication that Oxford's cause was alive and well on the Continent; word also spread to the United States, where in 1937 Louis Bénézet, an English professor at Dartmouth College, published the first of his many Oxfordian volumes, *Shakspere, Shakespeare and de Vere*. That same year Charles Wisner Barrell popularised Looney's theory in the pages of the *Saturday Evening Post*. Soon after, Barrell created a sensation when he published an article in *Scientific American* arguing that the Ashbourne portrait – discovered in the nineteenth century, later purchased by the Folger Library, and believed by some to be of Shakespeare – had been tampered with, and that X-ray and infrared photography revealed that the figure painted over was Edward de Vere. While Oxfordians worked to bolster their circumstantial case for de Vere, considerable energy was also devoted to undermining the case for Shakespeare.

By the early 1940s, the Oxfordian movement had achieved a surprising degree of visibility, most famously in the 1941 British war movie *Pimpernel Smith* (released in the United States as *Mister V*), which starred Leslie Howard, who also produced and directed the film, in the role of an archaeologist who foils the Nazis. When Shakespeare's name comes up in conversation, Leslie Howard casually mentions that he had 'been doing a little research work . . . on the identity of Shakespeare' which 'proves conclusively that Shakespeare wasn't really Shakespeare at all . . . He was the Earl of Oxford.' Later in the film, holding up a skull at an excavation site, Howard recites the famous 'Alas, poor Yorick' speech from *Hamlet*, then adds – 'The Earl of Oxford wrote that, you know.' The Oxfordian cause had clearly arrived.

Yet for all the smoke, Oxfordian research had produced little fire. The Shakespeare Fellowship's goal of uncovering a paper trail linking Oxford to the plays had failed to turn up a single relevant document in English archives and great houses. Back in 1921 Looney had written that 'circumstantial evidence cannot accumulate for ever without at some point issuing in proof'. Yet proof remained elusive – as did widespread acceptance. While Oxfordians were fully persuaded by what they saw as overwhelming circumstantial evidence, others remained stubbornly unmoved. As their books repeated the same claims again and again, publishers lost money, then interest. Looney admitted to a supporter in 1927 that 'Naturally, I expected a more rapid spreading of the new theory than has taken place.'

With archival digging a failure and circumstantial claims linking de Vere's life to events in the plays and Sonnets at the saturation point, Oxfordian scholars in search of fresh areas of investigation found themselves at a loss. Constrained by the need to confirm rather than qualify Looney's great discovery, they began making increasingly implausible claims. The first was greatly extending the range of Oxford's literary achievement. If authorship was masked, and Oxford's genius unrivalled, it stood to reason that he not only wrote Shakespeare's plays but also the works of other great Elizabethan writers. The Baconians had gone down this slippery path; now it was their turn. They were partly driven to it by the need to show that de Vere must have written *something* between his acknowledged lyric poetry of 1570s and the plays and poems attributed to Shakespeare that began to appear a decade or so later. But what? Looney himself led the way in his edition of de Vere's poetry, accepting as axiomatic that 'Oxford is the key to Elizabethan literature', the 'personal thread which unifies all'. Looney revisited the poetry and drama of writers as various as Arthur Golding, Anthony Munday and John Lyly, then turned on mainstream scholars for having 'failed to perceive that what was linking all together was the person of Edward de Vere, the relative and pupil of Golding, and the employer in turn of both Anthony Munday and John Lyly'. Oxford, clearly, was responsible for all of their literary output. Lyly's court drama of the 1580s was, for Looney, the missing link, the 'bridge between Oxford's early lyrics and the Shakespeare work'.

It wasn't long before disciples began to hail Edward de Vere as the author of everything from Arthur Brooke's *Romeus and Juliet* and the plays of Christopher Marlowe and Thomas Kyd to the poetic works of Edmund Spenser and George Gascoigne. Some went even further, speculating that de Vere had also found time to compose such monumental works as Florio's translation of Montaigne's *Essays* and North's translation of Plutarch's *Lives*. Over time, the list would expand to include the Marprelate tracts, *Leicester's Commonwealth*, the works of Thomas Nashe, Robert Greene, and a good many others.

Given the fundamental premises of all those who doubt that Shakespeare of Stratford wrote the plays – that the true author was hidden, his genius unmatched, and his role central in creating the golden age of Elizabethan literature – expanding the boundaries of the canon was perhaps inevitable. But just as the Baconians had made exaggerated claims for their man, the hands of Shakespeare's defenders weren't exactly clean either, with mainstream scholars attributing to Shakespeare such works as *The Second Maid's Tragedy*, *Edward the Third*, *Edmund Ironside* and other plays and lyrics of contested authorship. Indeed, in the early nineteenth century, well before anyone thought to claim the works of Shakespeare for Marlowe, the very opposite – that Shakespeare had actually written all of Marlowe's works – had been suggested. Nonetheless, the recklessness with which Oxfordians set about looting Elizabethan literature in search of new works to add to de Vere's hoard was startling.

When Cecil Palmer marketed *'Shakespeare' Identified*, one of his main selling points was that Looney's book contains 'no cipher, cryptography, or hidden message connected with his reason or his discovery'. But the urge to emulate the Baconian cipher hunters proved too great for some Oxfordians, who turned to codes and ciphers in order to link de Vere to Shakespeare's works. After all, even to the casual eye, anagrams of Edward de Vere's name – 'E. Vere' – were scattered everywhere in Shakespeare's works, from the '*ever* writer to the *never reader*' of *Troilus and Cressida* to the word 'ever' that recurs with such frequency throughout the canon. Conveniently, 'never' occurs over eleven hundred times in Shakespeare's works; 'ever' and 'every' over six hundred times each. Once alert to this barely-veiled signature, it's readily identified in works others had independently reassigned to de Vere. It wasn't long before George Frisbee found this coded signature – clear evidence of Oxford's authorship – in the poetry of Christopher Marlowe, George Gascoigne, Sir John Harrington, Edmund Spenser, George Puttenham and even King James.

The argument that Oxford sought anonymity because of the usual aristocratic misgivings about print only went so far. There had to be a better explanation for why the greatest of poets suppressed his identity. The answer was soon found: Oxford was Queen Elizabeth's secret lover and their union produced an illegitimate son, the Earl of Southampton. The argument, first advanced by Percy Allen in 1933, came to be known in Oxfordian circles as the 'Prince Tudor' theory and proved deeply appealing to sceptics already convinced that conspiracy and concealment had defined Oxford's literary life. Looney, while valuing Percy Allen's loyalty, loathed his Prince Tudor theory and feared that it would 'bring the whole cause into ridicule'. Freud hated it too, and even sent a chastising letter to Allen. To this day it has deeply divided Oxfordians.

Despite objections, the Prince Tudor theory gained adherents, especially in America. It was perhaps inevitable that the theory gave way to an even bolder one, known in Oxfordian circles as 'Prince Tudor, Part II'. According to its proponents, Oxford was not only Elizabeth's lover but her son as well. The man who impregnated the fourteen-year-old future queen was probably her own stepfather, Thomas Seymour. So it was incest, and incest upon incest when Oxford later slept with his royal mother and conceived Southampton. There is more: Southampton was only the last of the Virgin Queen's children; by then she had already given birth to the Earl of Essex as well as Mary Sidney and Robert Cecil.

Nowadays, Oxfordians tend to steer clear of such loaded terms as 'conspiracy' and 'cover-up', but it's impossible to avoid them when discussing the Prince Tudor theories. As Roger Stritmatter, one of the leading advocates of Oxford at work today, puts it: 'Stratfordianism is little different . . . than the original "conspiracy" of the Tudor Crown to place Oxford in the dark,' so that 'the Stratfordian ideology is an extension of Tudor policy under another name, an extension inspired by motives that become more and more prosaic, comical and unconscious as the controversy proceeds towards the inevitable denouement of the Tudor lie'. Oxfordianism was thus a reaction to an initial lie about Oxford's connection to the crown that spawned others, all to the detriment of de Vere – the lie that Elizabeth was a virgin queen led inevitably, though indirectly, to the lie that Shakespeare of Stratford wrote the plays. An unbroken sequence of cover-ups on the part of those in authority could be traced from the Tudor court down through modern academic scholarship, which remained no less committed to keeping Oxford hidden, denying him his right-ful place and recognition.

The Prince Tudor theories help explain both what motivated Oxford and what motivates Oxfordians, whose efforts and mar-ginalisation recapitulate Oxford's own compensatory, creative struggle. We are left then, with a great 'What if?' If Oxford had been given his due in his own day, and his son Southampton had ascended the throne upon their mother's death in 1603, perhaps Britain might have avoided an irreversible breakdown of hierarchy and order that led to a wrenching civil war, and subsequently to the rise of modernity, imperialism and capitalism (the bugbears of the Positivists). In lieu of such a utopian world, we are bequeathed some remarkable and compensatory plays. For as Stritmatter elo-quently puts it, Oxford recreated 'a kingdom of the imagination in which the complexes and traumas of his life's experience and read-ing could be represented, bequeathing it to an unknowing and often vulgarly ungrateful world – a world that still does not want to acknowledge the psychological price Oxford paid for what he represents dramatically'. A theory so deeply rooted in political suppression and modern notions of psychic trauma makes it hard, almost impossible, to learn just how much was concealed or repressed. The Prince Tudor theories underscore the extent to which there is, at the heart of the Oxfordian movement, a wish to rewrite through the story of a traumatic life, as revealed in the plays, both the political and literary histories of England.

The intense desire to resolve the authorship controversy once and for all led one of Looney's most devoted followers to even more extreme measures. In 1946, Percy Allen, who had recently been elected President of the Shakespeare Fellowship, called for a vote of confidence on his leadership, after declaring that he would now seek 'a solution of the mystery of the authorship by psychic means'. Allen's advocacy of the Prince Tudor theory was barely tolerable; his speaking with the dead was beyond the pale. All but one of those in attendance immediately accepted his resignation.

Allen then announced that as 'the result of communication made to him directly and personally at many spiritual séances, he was sure of being in possession of the full solution of the question'. A year later Allen published his finding in *Talks with Elizabethans*, a detailed account of his conversations with Oxford, Bacon and Shakespeare.

It's easy to mock Allen's approach, but in truth, communicating with the dead is what we all do, or try to do, every time we pick up a volume of Milton or Virgil or Dickens – all of whom achieve a kind of immortality by speaking to us from beyond the grave. Every literature professor is in the business of speaking with the dead – though few have been as honest about it as Stephen Greenblatt, whose influential *Shakespearean Negotiations* opens with the famous confession: 'I began with the desire to speak with the dead,' then argues for the universality of this desire, 'a familiar, if unvoiced, motive in literary studies, a motive organized, professionalized, buried beneath thick layers of bureaucratic decorum: literature professors are salaried, middle-class shamans'. While brilliantly anatomising this desire to speak with the dead, Greenblatt acknowledges that the conversation is necessarily one way (as he puts it, 'all I could hear was my own voice').

But when Percy Allen spoke with the dead, the dead spoke back. His is a poignant story, perhaps the inevitable outcome of a man so deeply invested in a cause that he could not otherwise prove. It also replays many of the famous episodes of the authorship controversy, from William-Henry Ireland's announcement that he was in possession of Shakespeare's memoirs to Delia Bacon's conviction that the lost manuscripts could be found by prying up Shakespeare's gravestone. Allen had been drawn to psychic matters after hearing an acquaintance, Arthur Conan Doyle, speak on the subject in the 1920s. His interest intensified after seeing a play by Aldous Huxley on spiritualism. Years later, following the devastating news in 1939 of the death of his twin brother Ernest, Allen sought the help of one of the most celebrated mediums of the day, Hester Dowden. Her success in enabling Percy

Allen to reach his dead twin prompted him to seek her assistance in resolving the authorship controversy.

Hester Dowden was unusually well suited to the task. Her father was the Shakespeare biographer Professor Edward Dowden. Like Percy Allen, she was fully conversant with Shakespearean drama and had known, from her youth, many of the great performers of the day, including Sir Henry Irving and Ellen Terry. There was one complicating factor: three or four years earlier, another student of the authorship controversy, Alfred Dodd, had sought her help and in 1943 published *The Immortal Master*, in which he described what he learned through her: that Francis Bacon was the true author of Shakespeare's plays (unbeknownst to Dodd, his methods and conclusion had been anticipated by John Lobb in his 1910 book *Talks with the Dead*, where Shakespeare himself claimed from the grave full authorship of the works attributed to him).

Hester Dowden succeeded in putting Allen in touch not only with Bacon but also with Shakespeare and Oxford. It soon emerged that Alfred Dodd had been misinformed, as Allen learned upon putting the question directly to Bacon himself (as usual, Hester Dowden transcribed the conversations, using automatic writing, assisted through her main 'control' with the beyond, an ancient Athenian named Johannes). The truth, Bacon told him, was that

the Shakespeare plays and poems are principally the works of Lord Oxford. All the work of shaping them for the stage, and much of the comedy, are the work of Will of Stratford. You have to remember that *We are two, Oxford and Shakespeare, with Bacon always behind, as a kind of critical and general advisor.*

This was a great relief to Percy Allen, who had suspected as much. Shakespeare, at first a bit shy, soon warmed up and communicated freely with Allen (and Allen's estimation of him grew over time). Their conversations went so well that Allen, curious about his personal story, told him: 'Look here; we know almost nothing about your earthlife. Will you dictate your autobiography for me?' Shakespeare graciously agreed, and Allen provides a transcript of it, with occasional 'interpolations' by Oxford. Allen was assured by all three men of the truth of the Prince Tudor story – that Southampton 'was really the Queen's son'. Shakespeare and Oxford then went through the plays one by one, explaining to Allen in considerable detail who wrote which parts, which works were juvenilia, and so on.

Eager to share his discoveries with the world, Allen asked his interlocutors from beyond for 'more documentary proof', and wondered whether the manuscripts of the plays had survived. After some initial hesitation, Francis Bacon came through at last, and said: "They are in the tomb – the stone tomb." At this point Shakespeare and Oxford chimed in, explaining that six manu-scripts were hidden in Shakespeare's grave in Stratford: *Hamlet, Lear, Othello, Macbeth, Richard the Second,* and *Henry the Fifth* 'wrapped in parchment. Two at the head, two at the feet, and two at the breast' including *Hamlet.* The Earl of Derby had placed them there. When Allen told them that he would visit the tomb, Oxford warned him 'I will make your flesh creep!' And so he did. When Allen travelled to Stratford-upon-Avon to review some plays in April 1945 he visited Shakespeare's gravestone. Just as Oxford had predicted, he suddenly felt 'a hot, pleasant tingling coming up my fingers to the elbows in both arms'. A few days later he returned to Mrs Dowden, who picked up her pen and resumed her automatic writing, whereupon Shakespeare immediately got in touch with Allen: 'I want to thank you for coming. We were both there, and very glad to see you.'

Allen rushed off to his publishers with this astounding news, but they 'did not seem much impressed' and wanted what they called 'real evidence': 'Give us some poetry, if you can.' So Allen returned to Mrs Dowden and put in the special request to Oxford through her. He waited three weeks and was rewarded with an envelope from Mrs Dowden containing the first of Oxford's newly dictated sonnets. Four posthumous sonnets in all were composed and subsequently included in Allen's *Talks with Elizabethans*. It had taken Mrs Dowden about forty minutes to transcribe each sonnet, as Oxford composed them line by line ('if Oxford had known the verses by heart they would have taken only about three or four minutes to dictate'). The one prefacing *Talks with Elizabethans* doesn't quite measure up to those collected in 1609, and ends as follows:

The plays they played on Earth they play once more.
E'er the cock crows, and from the earth they fly,
Learn what you may – your patience they implore.
Thus from the tomb its secret you may steal,
Stirring no dust, no bones can you reveal.

In retrospect, the outbreak of the Second World War derailed an Oxfordian movement that had already begun to lose its momentum, if not its bearings. With invasion feared, meetings of the British Shakespeare Fellowship were suspended. The baton was passed to the United States, where Eva Turner Clark formed an American branch in 1939, but that organisation folded shortly after her death in 1947. By then there wasn't much left to the British wing of the Fellowship either. Looney was dead, along with such stalwarts as B. M. Ward and Canon Rendall. So too was the movement's most famous recruit, Freud. Membership had dropped to seventy – roughly two members for every Oxfordian book that had been published.

For the next forty years, the remnant of the once flourishing movement in both Britain and America hung on. In 1949 an American edition of '*Shakespeare' Identified* came out, enabling a new generation of readers to get hold of Looney's by now rare book. A brief flare of enthusiasm led to the establishment of a Shakespeare Oxford Society in America in 1957 – though it remained, according to the organisation's newsletter, 'almost dormant, as far as active members, until 1964'. Even then, prospects seemed dismal. As its newsletter acknowledged in 1968, 'the missionary or evangelical spirit of most of our members seems to be at a low ebb, dormant, or non-existent'. The British Shakespeare Fellowship tried reinventing itself as the Shakespearean Authorship Society in 1959 and for a few years published a *Shakespearean Authorship Review*, but the organisation was a shadow of its former self. Oxfordians looked on jealously when the self-promoting Calvin Hoffman generated far more attention than they could muster with his claims for Christopher Marlowe's authorship of the plays – first with the publication in 1955 of *The Murder of the Man Who Was 'Shakespeare'*, then with his success in securing permission to open the grave of Elizabethan spymaster Sir Francis Walsingham in a failed attempt to unearth Marlowe's long-hidden manuscripts of Shakespeare's plays. For a time it looked as if Marlowe might even supplant Oxford as the chief claimant to the plays.

As the years slid by, expectations dwindled. Barrell's claims in *Scientific American* about the Ashbourne portrait were exposed as an embarrassing case of wishful thinking: the overpainted figure wasn't Oxford after all, and restoration work revealed that the date of the original portrait was 1612, eight years after Oxford's death. Meanwhile, in the pages of their newsletter, American supporters of de Vere's cause could only wring their hands: 'What about the hopes of us Oxfordians? When can we reasonably expect to see light at the end of the tunnel? In 1969? Hardly; barring a miracle.' While Oxfordians put on a cheerful public face, they privately admitted that they were on the verge of failure. The language was blunt: 'We are talking to each other, converting the already converted,' and they doubted whether there were 'as many active propagandists, lecturers, and writers for the cause, as there were in the Thirties, Forties, and Fifties'. The odds of having an Oxfordian book 'accepted and published' were put at 'None'.

While convinced that their case was the stronger one, they understood that the 'general public, the uncommitted, are in millions, but the means to reach them are unavailable to us now, and bid fair to remain so, unless there is some dramatic "breakthrough"'. As the fiftieth anniversary of the publication of

Looney's book approached, the Oxfordians conceded that the 'rate of our progress in recent years toward gaining recognition of Lord Oxford as Shakespeare among the uncommitted and open-minded, can best be described as one small step forward, and two giant steps backwards'. Despite the attention generated by a sharp exchange with Harvard professors in the pages of the *Harvard Magazine* in 1974, the movement was on life-support. Membership in the Shakespeare Oxford Society now stood at eighty – and an attempt to generate new ideas and enthusiasm through a conference in 1976 drew only twenty members. Oxfordians would subsequently speak of this post-war period of decline and stagnation as their 'Dark Ages'.

Mainstream scholars could hardly wait for their adversaries to die off before publishing their obituaries. In 1959, Louis B. Wright, director of the Folger Shakespeare Library, couldn't resist a parting shot in 'The Anti-Shakespeare Industry and the Growth of Cults', in which he sneeringly described what it took to write a book that denied Shakespeare's authorship; 'the capacity to climb into a soap-bubble and soar away into Cuckoo-land.' And in 1970, the leading Shakespeare biographer, Samuel Schoenbaum, his patience sorely tested by having to slog through so many books that questioned Shakespeare's authorship, administered what must have seemed a death-stroke in his *Shakespeare's Lives*. The 'sheer volume of heretical publication appals', Schoenbaum writes, its 'voluminousness ... matched only by its intrinsic worthlessness'. It was 'lunatic rubbish', the product of 'mania'.

Imagine the disbelief that would have greeted a contributor to the *Shakespeare Oxford Newsletter* in the early 1980s, who, rejecting all the hand-wringing, urged fellow Oxfordians to be patient and predicted that in twenty-five years their movement would be thriving:

By 2010, universities in the US and UK will be offering advanced degrees in the authorship question. Stars of the stage and screen, including the likes of Derek Jacobi and Mark Rylance, will be standard-bearers for the Oxfordian cause. Books about Edward de Vere will once again find a place in publishers' lists – at a time when mainstream scholars will be hard-pressed to publish monographs on Shakespeare. Children's bookstores will stock Oxfordian titles suitable for impressionable young readers and high-school students will compete for prizes in an annual contest for the best Oxfordian essay. Prestigious magazines – including *Harper's* and *The Atlantic* – will feature the Oxfordian cause and invite readers to choose sides in the authorship dispute. The *New York Times* will regularly run articles sympathetic to Oxford's claim and eventually urge that 'both sides' of the authorship question be taught. National Public Radio will go a step further and devote a programme to promoting Oxford's case. Supreme Court justices, several of whom will declare themselves committed Oxfordians – and their opposite numbers in Britain – will try the case of 'Shakespeare *v.* Oxford' in publicised moot courts (where even if we lose we'll win, because henceforth we'll be seen as the only viable alternative to the glover's son from Stratford). Oxfordians will, like mainstream academics, have their own peer-reviewed literary journals, hold international conferences and be able to teach from an 'Oxford' edition of Shakespeare's plays. Supporters around the world will be able to participate in discussion groups accessible to millions as well as contribute to encyclopaedia entries on the authorship question – entries compiled collectively rather than by so-called experts. *And all this will come to pass without the discovery of a single new document experts would accept that confirms Oxford's claim or undermines Shakespeare's!*

No such letter was ever written, but everything described here, and more, has happened since 1985. The resurrection of the Oxfordian movement has been little short of miraculous – one of the most remarkable and least remarked episodes in the history of Shakespeare studies. What brought it about? Oxfordians usually point to the publication in 1984 of Charlton Ogburn's *The Mysterious William Shakespeare*. It would be more accurate to say that Ogburn's timely book rode the wave of some sweeping cultural changes.

Charlton Ogburn was well connected in both the political and publishing worlds. He had seen his parents' collaborative book on de Vere fail to generate much attention and had been disappointed once again when a follow-up book he co-authored with his mother – *Shake-speare; The Man Behind the Name* (1962) – met with similar neglect. The problem wasn't with the message or the messenger; it was getting enough people, especially scholars, to listen. More aggressive measures were needed to combat what he saw as a 'shoddy, tacit conspiracy' on the part of the official orthodoxy.

Ogburn elaborated on this after he was elected president of the Shakespeare Oxford Society in 1976: 'English faculties, abetted by a generally subservient press, show how far entrenched authority can outlaw and silence dissent in a supposedly free society ... We are dealing here with an intellectual Watergate, and it greatly behooves us to expose it.' Ogburn fought back. He tried and failed to secure federal funding for Oxfordian research in England. He tried and failed to get Louis B. Wright to debate with him. He tried and failed to get the *New Yorker* to run an article sympathetic to the Oxfordian cause. And he tried and failed to get the Folger Library to publish his scholarship (they claimed a three-year backlog of submissions). Even as he fought for public recognition for Oxford's candidacy, Ogburn began writing his nine-hundred-page *The Mysterious William Shakespeare*. The genius of his book was its interweaving de Vere's travails with those of modern-day Oxfordians facing an 'intellectual Watergate' – yet one more instance of how authorities engage in conspiracy and cover-up, only, in the end, to be exposed.

As Ogburn understood it, there were two sides to the authorship question and his side was being denied a fair hearing. He had come of age at a time in America when there was nothing one could do about that. That came to an end in the late 1940s, when a 'fairness doctrine' was made the law of the land – under the jurisdiction of the United States Federal Communications Commission – in order to ensure that media coverage was both fair and balanced. The doctrine was fiercely contested (for many, it ran counter to the freedoms assured by the First Amendment), and finally overturned by the mid-1980s, but by then, it had become habitual in the media to give both sides of any controversy an equal hearing. When Ogburn learned in the late 1970s that the National Geographic Society planned a television programme on Shakespeare – with Louis B. Wright, that scourge of the sceptics, involved, he appealed for equal time on the grounds of the fairness doctrine. His initial demands were 'smiled off', as he put it, but he persisted, since 'under the law we had a right to time on the air to reply'. In the end, the project was shelved; but the Oxfordians were learning how to use the levers of democracy to fight back.

Shakespeare on Trial

Convinced that the best place to challenge academics was in court, Ogburn called for a 'trial at law' overseen by a 'qualified judge'. But his opponents continued to stonewall. His strategy was not all that surprising; many of those who didn't believe that Shakespeare was the author of the plays were lawyers and the courts had been one of the few places where sceptics had held their own. Three years after the publication of *The Mysterious William Shakespeare*, the Oxfordians finally had their day in court. On 25 September 1987, three United States Supreme Court Justices – William Brennan, Harry Blackmun and John Paul Stevens – heard their case, '*In re* Shakespeare: The Authorship of Shakespeare on Trial', before a thousand spectators in Washington, DC. The moot court was major news, with the *New York Times* reporting in advance that 'the ruling could go either way', with the handicappers figuring that Brennan, the most liberal of the three, would lean toward Oxford, Blackmun 'likely to be torn by the decision' and the ruling of an 'enigmatic' Stevens difficult to predict. David Lloyd Kreeger had made it happen; member of the US Supreme Court Bar and Chairman of the Board of the Corcoran Gallery of Art, he was happy to bankroll the event.

Brennan, serving as chief justice, surprised Blackmun and

[233]

Stevens by declaring at the outset that the burden was on the Oxford side to prove its case – then overrode Blackmun's objection that 'you didn't clear that with the rest of us'. The deck was now stacked in Shakespeare's favour. Arguments were presented in the morning and the justices deliberated at midday. They handed down their decision that afternoon. Brennan spoke first, ruling that the Oxford side 'did not prove that he was the author of the plays'. Blackmun, who spoke next, conceded that while he agreed that this was the 'legal answer . . . whether it is the correct one causes me greater doubt than I think it does Justice Brennan'. Stevens also ruled for Shakespeare, making the judgement unanimous, but added a significant qualification: 'If the author was not the man from Stratford, then there is a high probability that it was Edward de Vere . . . I think the evidence against the others is conclusive.'

The Oxfordians had failed to convince them that de Vere, who died in 1604, could have been the author of plays written after that date. The justices also make clear that they believed that the case before them was essentially 'a conspiracy theory' – but the various accounts of why this conspiracy took place were incoherent and unpersuasive. For some Oxfordians, it had been a private arrangement known only to de Vere and Shakespeare. For others, it was a far-ranging plot, beginning with the Queen and extending through the Earl of Derby and Ben Jonson's active roles in maintaining the hoax. Still others were sure that it was common knowledge, with so many Elizabethans aware that de Vere was the true author of the plays that nobody even bothered commenting on it. And of course, there were those convinced of the politically motivated Prince Tudor theory. There was no consensus and little likelihood of arriving at one. The Oxfordians had nonetheless succeeded in raising serious doubts in the minds of the justices about Shakespeare's authorship. Stevens in particular found the evidence in Shakespeare's favour 'somewhat ambiguous', adding that 'one would expect to find more references in people's diaries or correspondence about having seen Shakespeare somewhere or talked to someone who had seen him'. He was left with a 'sort of gnawing uncertainty'.

At the end of the moot court, Stevens unexpectedly turned to the disappointed Oxfordians and offered them 'a bit of advice': 'I would like to suggest that the Oxfordian case suffers from not having a single, coherent theory of the case.' Stevens had a solution: 'In my opinion, the strongest theory of the case requires an assumption for some reason we don't understand, that the Queen and Prime Minister [*sic*] decided: "We want this man to be writing plays under a pseudonym."' If they wanted to prevail, the Oxfordians had best scrap their confusing and contradictory accounts of the conspiracy and stick to the defensible claim that de Vere's secrecy was the result of an executive order, 'a command from the monarch'.

A dejected Charlton Ogburn took the justices' decision as 'a clear defeat' and insisted that the moot court 'hadn't been his idea in the first place'. He wrote to the president of American University calling Professor James Boyle, who had defended Shakespeare at the moot court, 'an outright liar'. Ogburn might have had in mind not what Boyle said at the proceedings but what he told James Lardner, who was covering the story for the *New Yorker*. 'The Oxfordians have constructed an interpretive framework that has an infinite capacity to explain away information': 'all the evidence that fits the theory is accepted, and the rest rejected'. When Boyle added that it was impossible 'to imagine a piece of evidence that could disprove the theory to its adherents', Lardner asked, 'What about a letter in Oxford's hand . . . congratulating William Shakespeare of Stratford on his achievements as a playwright?' Boyle didn't skip a beat, mimicking an Oxfordian response: 'What an unlikely communication between an earl and a common player! . . . Obviously, something designed to carry on the conspiracy of concealment. The very fact that he wrote such a letter presents the strongest proof we could possibly have!'

Joseph Sobran, who wrote for the *National Review*, was among the few Oxfordians at the time to grasp how signal an event the moot court had been. Crucially, even while ruling against de Vere, 'the justices effectively dismissed the other candidates for Shakespearean honors from serious consideration'. From now on, as far as the press and public were concerned, there would only be two viable candidates: the Earl of Oxford and the glover's son from Stratford. Sobran also recognised that there 'is no such thing as bad publicity'. He was right. Major newspapers and television networks had covered the trial. And the moot court was structured so that literary experts weren't even represented. Even losing was a form of victory, since by having judges rather than scholars with decades of expertise evaluate the evidence, amateurs and experts were put on equal footing, both subordinate to the higher authority of the court and to legal rather than academic criteria for what counted as circumstantial evidence.

The moot court proved to be a turning point in the decades-long struggle to promote Oxford's cause. More than anything else, the Supreme Court justices had provided legitimacy; the Oxfordians were no longer the 'deviants' vilified by Schoenbaum (and one immediate effect of the moot court was that this harsh language was considerably toned down when Schoenbaum revised *Shakespeare's Lives* in 1991). If Supreme Court justices could take them seriously and deem them the only serious rivals to Shakespeare, so could others.

The Oxfordians, having learned some lessons from their defeat in the US, hoped that a retrial in England would reverse the decision. Once again David Lloyd Kreeger sponsored the event. The novelist Jeffrey Archer helped facilitate it, and Sam Wanamaker, founder of the as yet unbuilt Shakespeare's Globe Theatre, was willing to arrange it as a fund-raiser. Charles Beauclerk – who was descended from the de Veres – played an important role, too, helping to co-ordinate the Oxfordian side. Two years earlier, while a student at Oxford University, he had founded the De Vere Society hoping to reinvigorate the case for his ancestor. From the perspective of the Society, even staging the English trial was tantamount to a victory, since 'three of the most senior judges of appeal of the realm . . . have agreed to provide the framework for bringing Shakespeare to court, and have by that very act conceded that there are grounds for doubting the traditional ascription of authorship to the unlettered William Shaksper of Stratford'.

This moot court was held on 26 November 1988, with roughly five hundred in attendance in London's Inner Temple, presided over by Lords Ackner, Oliver and Templeman. Once again, there was extensive media coverage. The initial plan was to have Charlton Ogburn square off against his nemesis, Samuel Schoenbaum. But despite their eagerness to do battle, both men were too ill to make the trip, and seconds were found. This time, academics were represented: the formidable pair of British scholars Stanley Wells and Ernst Honigmann served as expert witnesses for Shakespeare; Oxfordians Gordon C. Cyr (of the American Shakespeare Oxford Society) and L. L. Ware (of the British Shakespearean Authorship Trust) stepped in for the other side.

The outcome was no different; in the words of one supporter of de Vere, it was an 'Oxfordian disaster'. The Lords were especially dismissive of the notion that Oxford had taken the name of a man acknowledged as an 'actor manager' in the theatre. And they couldn't understand why it took until 1920 for someone to propose that the Earl of Oxford was the true author of the plays. The Oxfordians fulminated. The biggest lesson they had learned from this latest setback was that 'there was neither time nor opportunity within the format of a court proceeding to puncture many of the Stratfordian balloons'.

There would be no more trials. Though privately acknowledged as a stinging defeat, the event gave an unexpected lift to doubters and especially to the Oxfordian cause in the UK, much as the Washington trial had done in the US. Both the moribund Shakespeare Authorship Trust and the De Vere Society (according to Beauclerk, its activities now supported by the wealthy Chicagoan, William O. Hunt, to the tune of £2,000 a term) were invigorated. In 1988 Beauclerk would also edit and see into print an abridged version of Ogburn's book, which 'signals a literary revolution of unprecedented proportions' – emphasising in his introduction both his ancestor's biographical fit ('de Vere was every inch a Hamlet') and his place among English aristocratic writers (as 'the natural precursor to Byron and the Romantic tradition in English literature').

While plans to make a film or a book of the English moot court proceedings fell through, it didn't take long for the British media to seize upon a now legitimate and newsworthy story. Where judges tried to resolve controversial issues, television hosts enjoyed stoking them. In April 1989, *Frontline* aired 'The Shakespeare Mystery', produced by Yorkshire Television in conjunction with American Public Television station WGBH. In the US alone, over three and a half million television viewers were offered their first glimpse of the authorship controversy, and the programme's title (indebted to Ogburn's) as well as Al Austin's opening voiceover made clear that things had begun to tilt in Oxford's favour: 'Who was the real Shakespeare? The son of a Stratford glovemaker? Or was he a forgotten nobleman, the seventeenth Earl of Oxford?' The programme was a triumph for Ogburn, as well as for his English counterpart, Charles Beauclerk. The academics who spoke on behalf of Shakespeare – Schoenbaum and A. L. Rowse – sounded stuffy, the Oxfordians impassioned. Al Austin's narration did the rest, filling in the blanks by connecting events in Oxford's life to key passages in the plays. *Frontline* followed it up with an even more in-depth, three-hour live videoconference, 'Uncovering Shakespeare: An Update', moderated by William F. Buckley, Jr, which aired in September 1992, and included some sharp sparring between Charles Beauclerk and Professor Gary Taylor. The programme ended with a prerecorded animation of the Stratford monument breaking up and revealing the Earl of Oxford.

The BBC wasn't far behind, providing a one-hour film on the controversy in 1994, with Charles Beauclerk again playing a prominent role. Proponents of de Vere's cause weren't happy about having to share airtime with 'poorly supported Baconians and Marlovians', but believed that 'Oxford came out well ahead in the programme'. The charismatic Beauclerk continued to promote

Oxford's cause, especially in the United States, where he appeared at over 170 venues, from college campuses to the Folger and Huntington Libraries, in the early 1990s. The Shakespeare Oxford Society was now reporting a surge of new members from as far away as Estonia and Australia.

Oxfordian success on television was reinforced by major magazine and newspaper coverage. In October 1991 the *Atlantic Magazine* gave prominent attention to the debate, inviting two independent scholars – Tom Bethell for Oxford and Irving Matus for Shakespeare – to present a case and rebut his opponent's. *Harper's* followed in April 1999 with a cover story of its own – 'Who in fact was the bard, the usual suspect from Stratford, or Edward de Vere, 17th Earl of Oxford?' Again, it was the fairness doctrine exemplified: this time, ten contributors in all, five in favour of Oxford's candidacy and five in favour of Shakespeare's. It was clear by now that Bacon, Marlowe, Derby and the dozens of other rival claimants were no longer viable competitors – no small victory for the Oxford camp.

In justifying this extensive coverage, Lewis H. Lapham, the editor of *Harper's*, recalled how he had first become interested in the controversy after editing a piece by Charlton Ogburn in the early 1970s. He found the Oxfordian hypothesis 'congenial . . . because I could more easily imagine the plays written by a courtier familiar with the gilded treacheries of Elizabethan politics than by an actor peeping through the drop curtains', and also 'because 1972 was not a year conducive to belief in the masterpieces of official doctrine'. Lapham was no longer willing, as he had been in his college days, to 'ask no questions of the standard mythography' on which claims for Shakespeare's authorship had long rested. He now found himself far more sympathetic to a theory based on governmental cover-up at a time when

Richard Nixon was busy telling lies about a war in Vietnam; the unanswered questions about the assassination of John F. Kennedy had been declared inadmissible by the custodians of the country's respectable opinion; [and] the Central Intelligence Agency was papering the walls of Berlin and Panama City with the posters of disinformation.

Lapham may well have been the first to identify why long-ridiculed Oxfordian claims about Elizabethan political conspiracies had gone from a hindrance to a selling point. The rise of Oxfordianism in the closing years of the twentieth century coincided with a greater willingness to believe in governmental cover-ups of all kinds. To cite but one example, a CNN/*Time* poll taken two years before Lapham wrote this editorial reported that '80 percent of Americans think the government is hiding knowledge of the existence of extraterrestrial life forms'. Theories soon circulated widely on the Internet about secret government involvement in the 1988 Pan Am flight 103, the World Trade Center bombing of 1993, the downing of TWA flight 800 in 1996, the deadly tsunami in the Indian Ocean in 2004, the London bombings in 2005, and most notoriously of all, the attacks on 11 September 2001. In such a climate, a minor act of conspiratorial suppression on the part of Tudor authorities made perfect sense – and in comparison, was small beer.

The Oxfordian case had the added advantage of appealing not only to anyone suspicious of governmental conspiracies, but also to those alert to gaps, anomalies and doctored or missing evidence when very public figures died. Who was responsible for the death of Diana, Princess of Wales? Or behind the alleged suicide of Marilyn Monroe? What really happened to Kurt Cobain and Tupac Shakur? For many, these remain mysteries waiting to be solved – even as the Oxfordians struggled to solve similar mysteries of what happened to de Vere's missing will and of why the Jacobean authorities decided to imprison Southampton (and perhaps confiscate his papers) the day that de Vere died. There were no coincidences.

Conspiracy theorists chalked up another victory on 11 July 2002. On that day in Poets' Corner at Westminster Abbey, a memorial window was unveiled in Christopher Marlowe's honour. His date of birth and death are given as '1564–?1593'. Why the question mark? In his own day, and for the next four centuries, there had been no doubt about the year of Marlowe's death. After he was killed on 30 May 1593, an Elizabethan inquest took place confirming the exact day and manner in which he died. The original document survives. The only reason to question the year of his death is if you believe that the Elizabethan coroner's report was fabricated and that those at the highest levels of government substituted another body in his stead and smuggled Marlowe away, allowing him to spend the next two decades writing the plays now attributed to William Shakespeare. Oxfordians took note. If Marlovian conspiracy theorists could pull off something like this with so far-fetched a claim, surely they could secure a deserved place for Oxford in Westminster – and soon began the laborious fund-raising and campaigning needed to realise Looney's dream of a pilgrimage site worthy of Edward de Vere.

The sympathetic coverage in *Atlantic* and *Harper's* was nothing compared with the stories that now began to appear in the *New York Times*, thanks to the efforts of William Niederkorn, a self-professed 'agnostic' on the authorship question. Readers browsing through the *New York Times* on 10 February 2002 may have been caught short by his surprising lead: 'It was not the Bard of Stratford-on-Avon. It was Edward de Vere, the 17th Earl of Oxford. For Oxfordians, this is the answer to "Who Wrote Shakespeare."' Much of what followed in that story reads like promotional material. Niederkorn assures his readers that the Oxford theory 'has never been stronger', touts the 'Edward de Vere Studies Conference, a beachhead in academia', provides contact information for the Shakespeare Oxford Society and quotes the remarkable if undocumented claim that 'Oxford as a likely candidate is taught in more universities and colleges than we can begin to imagine'.

America's paper of record was finally making up for its many past slights. Niederkorn's biggest news was that the Supreme Court justices who had presided over the moot court had more or

[241]

less overturned their decision. While it was widely known Justice Blackmun had subsequently written sympathetically about the Oxfordian case, Niederkorn broke new ground by reporting that Justice Stevens told him over the phone that if he 'had to pick a candidate today, I'd say it definitely was Oxford'. Even more surprising was the revelation that Justice Brennan, who had been so dead-set against Oxford at the moot court, had 'modified' his position before his death in 1997; reportedly, the more he read about the controversy, 'the more skeptical he became about the Stratfordian position'.

De Vere's supporters were properly grateful. The editors of *Shakespeare Matters* acknowledged in an editorial that ran in the Spring 2002 issue that

Oxfordians everywhere owe the *Times*' William S. Niederkorn a vote of thanks for his many months of reading and research that led up to this article, and, just as importantly, his tireless efforts within the *Times* to keep his fellow writers and editors apprised of the strength of the Oxfordian case.

They may also have suppressed a knowing smile at the surprising news of Justice Brennan's otherwise undocumented defection – for Niederkorn cited as his source the word of William F. Causey, a lawyer who had recently organised an authorship debate at the Smithsonian – reportedly, after reading Diana Price's attack on the traditional attribution of the plays in *Shakespeare's Unorthodox Biography*. And they were happier still when Renée Montagne, one of the most familiar radio voices in America, hosted a programme on the case for Oxford on National Public Radio that drew on Niederkorn's reporting and took his undocumented claim a half-step further, saying that 'all three' Supreme Court justices 'came to doubt their decision'. Oxfordians were so pleased by her programme, which reached millions of listeners, that they honoured her with their annual Distinguished Achievement in the Arts Award. A story subsequently ran in the *Wall Street Journal* setting the record straight about Justice Brennan; but it also added

Justice Antonin Scalia to the ranks of committed Oxfordians.

Oxfordians were no less delighted when Niederkorn spoke to them at their annual Oxford Day banquet in April 2002 about 'his personal journey in studying the authorship question and on bringing it to the attention of his colleagues at the *Times*'. Niederkorn was becoming something of a regular at Oxfordian gatherings, attending the annual meeting in October 2004, where he lectured on 'Abel Lefranc and his case for William Stanley, Earl of Derby, as the author of the canon', based on archival research he had conducted. His next *Times* piece on the controversy appeared ten months later, on 30 August 2005. This time there would be no more hedging: 'The controversy over who wrote Shakespeare's works has reached a turning point of sorts. A new biography of the Earl of Oxford improves on the unorthodox argument that he was Shakespeare, while fantasy has now been firmly established as a primary tool of other, more traditional Shakespeare studies.' The wheel had come full circle: now the Shakespeare scholars were the fantasists. Niederkorn offered the following pronouncement on how things stood: 'On both sides of the authorship controversy, the arguments are conjectural. Each case rests on a story, not on hard evidence.' He ends with a proposal that infuriated Shakespeareans, for whom his rhetoric smacked of that employed by creationists eager to see intelligent design taught in the schools alongside evolution: 'What if authorship studies were made part of the standard Shakespeare curriculum?'

The articles in the *New York Times* revealed the extent to which the Oxford movement had undergone a makeover, had grown, in Niederkorn's words, 'from a handful to a thriving community with its own publications, organizations, lively online discussion groups and annual conferences'. Oxfordians now sought to portray themselves as a mirror-image of their rivals. To outsiders, how much difference could there be between *Shakespeare Matters* and *Shakespeare Studies*? And they were abetted in their efforts by scholars in English departments content to ignore questions that mattered to non-academics but not to them.

This became especially clear when the University of Massachusetts at Amherst awarded a PhD in 2001 to Roger A. Stritmatter for an avowedly Oxfordian dissertation on 'The Marginalia of Edward de Vere's Geneva Bible'. For many Oxfordians, the missing link between their candidate and the plays had at last been found. An annotated Geneva Bible from around 1570 that Oxford once owned had been acquired by the Folger Shakespeare Library. Most of its annotations consisted of underlinings, which Stritmatter argued closely corresponded to allusions to Biblical passages in Shakespeare's plays, thereby confirming that de Vere was their author. Stritmatter also argued that some of the underlined passages also had an autobiographical component, conveying the familiar Oxfordian 'inner story' of 'a man whose name has been erased from history and which set forth the divine promise of his eventual redemption'.

When independent scholars David Kathman, Tom Veal and Terry Ross looked at the evidence, they pointed out a good deal that Stritmatter's dissertation committee had apparently failed to notice. For starters, the conclusion that the underlining matched Biblical allusions in Shakespeare was unwarranted, since 'only about 10 percent of Shakespeare's Biblical allusions are marked in the Bible, and only about 20 percent of the verses marked in the Bible are alluded to in Shakespeare'. Moreover, the Bible's annotator, or annotators, were interested in Scripture that Shakespeare rarely drew on (especially Samuel I through Kings I, Maccabees, Esdras, Ecclesiasticus and Tobit), and paid comparatively scant attention to passages actually alluded to in the plays (from Genesis, Job, the Gospels and Revelation, in particular). And, on closer examination, it wasn't even obvious that de Vere himself had underlined these passages, since the marginalia appeared in different-coloured inks and might have easily been made by anyone who owned the Bible after de Vere's death in 1604. Doubts had already been raised after Alan Nelson, the leading expert on Oxford's handwriting, examined the marginalia and concluded that the 'hand is simply not the same hand that wrote [Oxford's] letters'.

No matter. Oxfordians dismissed the naysayers and remained convinced of this link between de Vere and the plays. And they were greatly encouraged by the legitimacy that the dissertation had secured within the academic establishment. It was a milestone. Stritmatter's abstract proudly declared that it is the first 'dissertation in literary studies which pursues with open respect the heretical thesis of John Thomas Looney (1920), B. M. Ward (1928), Charlton Ogburn Jr (1984) and other "amateur" scholars, which postulates de Vere as the literary mind behind the popular nom de plume "William Shakespeare"'. His findings were now part of the Oxfordian story. Others have subsequently consulted de Vere's Bible in hopes of strengthening the Oxfordian claim, including Supreme Court Justice John Paul Stevens, who told a reporter for the *Wall Street Journal* how, seeing a possible connection between 'an incident using the bed trick' in Shakespeare's work and an 'incident in the Old Testament where the same event allegedly occurred', he reasoned that de Vere 'would have underlined' the relevant passage in his Bible. So he went to the Folger Library and asked 'them to dig out the Bible' so he could check. Unfortunately, the passage – Genesis 29:23 – wasn't underlined. Stevens added that 'I really thought I might have stumbled onto something that would be a very strong coincidence,' but 'it did not develop at all'.

The Oxfordian makeover came at some cost. Explicit talk of conspiracy had to be toned down, replaced by the more neutral language of an 'open secret' or 'concealed' authorship. Shelved, temporarily, was talk of Oxford's sexual dalliance with Queen Elizabeth or mention of their son, the Earl of Southampton, as the Tudor Prince to whom de Vere dedicated the Sonnets. As Peter Moore bluntly told his fellow Oxfordians at their annual conference in 1996: 'Face reality on this "Prince Tudor" business, and submit it to proper historical scrutiny . . . If you can't make or listen to the strongest arguments that can be made against your own theories, then you'd better keep them to yourself.' Oxford's advocates also knew better than to debate in public the full extent of Oxford's literary range – even if they believed he deserved credit for the literary output of a dozen or so Elizabethan poets and playwrights. Finally, there would be no more calls for prying open graves in the hopes of exhuming missing manuscripts.

Back in the 1960s and 1970s, Oxfordians wondered whether a publisher would ever again accept another book on de Vere. Now that their movement had regained legitimacy, commercial presses were willing to take that chance. And for Oxfordian authors who couldn't secure a commercial publisher, self-publishing was always an option, with Oxfordian electronic newsletters in Britain and the United States setting up one-click connections to Amazon.com or their own bookshops to promote sales. Before long, there was an embarrassment of riches, and complaints in Oxfordian newsletters that so many new studies were finding their way into print that some sort of oversight process ought to be established.

Having been spurned by publishers for so long, and having been denied ready access to the young minds that Shakespeare professors indoctrinated in their classrooms, Oxfordians were well ahead of their rivals when it came to exploiting alternative ways of getting the word out. Books may offer their writers status and legitimacy, as well as a path to tenure, but the Oxfordians saw clearly enough that most people didn't have access to expensive academic monographs. By the early years of the twenty-first century, anyone interested in Shakespeare or the authorship question would probably turn first to Google or Wikipedia. And on both these Internet sites, the Oxfordians appeared more professional and impressive than their adversaries. In this new battleground for hearts and minds, academic authority no longer counted for much; the new information age was fundamentally democratic.

Nine of the top ten hits in a recent Google search for 'Shakespeare' and 'authorship' directed the curious to sites that called into question Shakespeare's authorship. Even the neutral-sounding 'A Beginner's Guide to the Shakespeare Authorship Problem' steered readers through an 'Honor Roll of Skeptics', past a history of the doubts surrounding the authorship of Shakespeare's works and through a brief section dismissing the claims of Bacon, Marlowe and Derby, before arriving at the 'case for Edward de Vere, 17th Earl of Oxford, as "Shakespeare"'. The sole pro-Shakespeare hit is to the 'Shakespeare Authorship Page', a nuts-and-bolts site intended to rebut the claims of sceptics. The site is formidable in terms of content but far less seductive. To any objective observer, the Oxfordians, with a more passionate investment and a more narrow set of objectives, had a clear edge when the battle over authorship was waged online.

Wikipedia was fast becoming the default resource of those in search of reliable information about the authorship controversy. Its extensive coverage of the subject put to shame anything that ever appeared in standard resources, let alone reference works traditionally produced by Shakespeare scholars and accessible in public and university libraries. The Oxfordian case turned up everywhere on Wikipedia, from articles on 'Shakespeare' and the 'Shakespeare Authorship Controversy' to more specialised ones on 'Edward de Vere', 'Oxfordian theory', 'Chronology of Shakespeare's Plays – Oxfordian', and even the 'Prince Tudor Theory'. Marlovians, Baconians, Derbyites and a handful of other alternative candidates had brief entries devoted to their claims, though whenever these rivals were discussed together, Oxfordians were assiduous about maintaining top billing. For there is always a risk that new media will reorient attention to a rival and more attractive candidate – and indeed, the recent proliferation of sites on Christopher Marlowe, no doubt energised by interest in the government conspiracy at the heart of the case for Marlowe's faked death, may be a sign that the dominance of the Oxfordian camp may not extend much longer than the Baconian one, roughly seventy years or so. Just as the Oxfordians could attract their share of celebrities, so too could rival camps. Marlovians were pleased to announce a new recruit when film director Jim

Jarmusch told the *New York Times* that 'I think it was Christopher Marlowe' who wrote Shakespeare's plays.

Most people who turn to Wikipedia for information are content to read the articles. But accessible with just a click are rolling and often recriminatory exchanges – rife with insults, charges of sock-puppetry and occasionally sputtering rage – about contributions that were altered or deleted. The beauty of Wikipedia is that entries are compiled and revised by anyone interested in contributing. Persistence and the ability to get in the last word, rather than expertise, are rewarded. And Wikipedia ruled out of bounds potentially controversial explanations of *why* people believed what they did. Wikipedia was thus a godsend for those who were sceptical about Shakespeare's authorship, for the first time allowing them to compete on equal footing with their opponents. The forces of democracy and equality and the overturning of hierarchy, the very things that drove Looney to argue that Oxford wrote Shakespeare's plays, now, ironically, had come to the rescue of the movement he had founded.

On 9 September 2007, a recently formed website – 'The Shakespeare Authorship Coalition' – received six hundred thousand hits. That extraordinary response followed a well-orchestrated campaign that had culminated in a press release announcing that a pair of major figures of the British stage, Sir Derek Jacobi and Mark Rylance, had signed a petition now circulating on the Internet, a 'Declaration of Reasonable Doubt about the Identity of William Shakespeare'. They had done so following a performance of Rylance's play questioning Shakespeare's authorship – *I Am Shakespeare* – and had timed the announcement to coincide with the news that a graduate programme in Shakespeare authorship studies had been established at Brunel University in London.

It was a skilfully drafted document, the collaborative effort of some of the best minds committed to casting doubt on Shakespeare's authorship. Its title was inspired, combining the uplift of an historical declaration with that long-established sense of fairness that guided juries to just verdicts: 'reasonable doubt'. A whiff of the courtroom is apparent throughout, as 'the *prima facie* case for Mr Shakspere' is shown to be 'problematic' and the 'connections between the life of the alleged author and the works' no less 'dubious'. The testimony of a score of expert witnesses – including Mark Twain, Henry James, Sigmund Freud and Justice Blackmun – is introduced into the record. And by not specifying a single candidate, it brought together under one roof proponents of all of them. The declared purpose was to get as many people as possible to sign on to the commonsensical position that 'it is simply not credible for anyone to claim, in 2007, that there is no room for doubt about the author'.

But as John M. Shahan, chairman of the Coalition created to disseminate the 'Declaration', explained in the Oxfordian newsletter *Shakespeare Matters*, there were other, unspoken motives as well: 'We can organize Declaration signing ceremonies to try to attract media attention' and 'when we have enough signatories, especially prominent ones, we can formally challenge the orthodox to write a counter-declaration' explaining 'why they claim there is "no room for reasonable doubt"'. By October 2007, 1,161 signatures had been gathered – admittedly a modest return, given the traffic on the site, though their ranks included another pair of leading actors, Jeremy Irons and Michael York. As much as the Declaration was a challenge to defenders of Shakespeare, it was also a test of whether the Oxfordians could translate a quarter-century of success in the mainstream media and online into a movement with broad public support. Shahan admits as much:

We have nine years until 2016, the 400th anniversary of the death of the Stratford man. Unless we succeed in raising serious doubt that he was really the great author, humanity will celebrate him in ignorance, and the generation of authorship doubters that came into being following the publication of Ogburn's *The Mysterious William Shakespeare* will have failed.

Twenty months later, according to the Coalition website's official tally, four hundred new signatures had been added.

FOUR

SHAKESPEARE

Schoolroom, Guildhall, Stratford-upon-Avon

The evidence for Shakespeare

It's one thing to explain how claims that others wrote the plays rest on unfounded assumptions; it's another to show that Shakespeare of Stratford really did write them. When asked how I can be so confident that Shakespeare was their author, I point to several kinds of evidence. The first is what early printed texts reveal; the second, what writers who knew Shakespeare said about him. Either of these, to my mind, suffices to confirm his author–ship – and the stories they tell corroborate each other. All this is reinforced by additional evidence from the closing years of his career, when he began writing for a new kind of playhouse, in a different style, in active collaboration with other writers.

The sheer number of inexpensive quartos of Shakespeare's works that filled London's bookshops after 1594 was staggering and unprecedented. No other poet or playwright came close to seeing seventy or so editions in print – and that's counting only what was published in Shakespeare's lifetime and doesn't include *Othello*, first printed in 1622, or any of the eighteen plays first published in the First Folio a year later. Print runs were usually restricted to fifteen hundred copies. If cautious publishers printed and sold only a thousand copies of each of these early quartos, it's likely that fifty thousand books bearing Shakespeare's name (for some were published anonymously) circulated during his lifetime – at a time when London's population was only two hundred thousand. As an actor, playwright and sharer in the most popular playing company in the land – which performed before as many as three thousand spectators at a time in the large outdoor theatres – he was also one of the most familiar faces in town and at court. If, over the course of the quarter-century in which Shakespeare was acting and writing in London, people began to suspect that the man they knew as Shakespeare was an impostor and not the actor-dramatist whose plays they witnessed and purchased, we would have heard about it.

One of those who recognised Shakespeare and knew him by name was George Buc. Buc was a government servant, historian, book collector and eventually Master of the Revels – the official to whom Shakespeare's company would submit all playscripts for approval. A familiar acquaintance of the Earl of Oxford, Buc also knew Shakespeare well enough to stop and ask him about the authorship of an old and anonymous play published in 1599, *George a Greene, the Pinner of Wakefield*, a copy of which he had recently obtained. He might have sought out or run into Shakespeare at the Curtain or Globe playhouses, or at a court performance, or perhaps at London's bookstalls, concentrated around St Paul's and the Royal Exchange, where Shakespeare must have been a familiar sight, browsing through titles – for he could not possibly have owned all the books that echo through his plays. Nobody could or did own that many, no bibliophile, no aristocrat, not even the Queen of England, with her sumptuous library housed at Whitehall Palace. Shakespeare did his best to help Buc, recalling that the play had been written by a minister, but at this point his memory apparently failed him. The lapse was excusable; it had been many years since *George a Greene* was first staged. But Shakespeare did volunteer an unusual bit of information: the minister had acted in his own play, performing the part of the pinner (someone who impounds stray animals). A grateful Buc wrote down his finding on the quarto's title page, leaving space to insert the author's name later: 'Written by . . . . a minister, who acted the pinner's part in it himself. *Teste* [that is, witnessed by] W. Shakespeare.' Buc's flesh and blood encounter with a man he knew as both actor and playwright suggests that once you begin to put Shakespeare back into his own time and place, the notion that he actively conspired to deceive everyone who knew or met him about the true authorship of the works that bore his name seems awfully far-fetched.

Those who question Shakespeare's authorship of the plays never get around to explaining how this alleged conspiracy worked. There's little agreement and even less detail about this, despite how much depends on it, so it's not easy to challenge. Some suppose that only Shakespeare and the real author were in the know. At the other extreme are those who believe that it was an open secret, so widely shared that it wasn't worth mentioning. Most doubters also brush off the overwhelming evidence offered by the title pages of these dozens of publications by claiming that 'Shakespeare' – or as some would have it, 'Shake-speare' – was simply the pseudonym of another writer – that hyphen a dead giveaway.

But such arguments are impossible to reconcile with what we now know about how publishing worked at the time. This was not a world in which a dramatist could secretly arrange with a publisher to bring out a play under an assumed name. In fact, Shakespeare had almost no control over the publication of his plays, because – strange as it may sound today – he didn't own them. They belonged to his playing company, and once sold and entered in the Stationers' Register, ownership passed to the publisher. Modern notions of authorial copyright were a distant dream. Shakespeare certainly had a voice as shareholder, and perhaps a disproportionate one. But if the history of the publication of his plays during his lifetime is any indication, he showed little interest in when or even whether his plays were published and even less in the quality or accuracy of their printing. If he had cared a bit more, or had more say in the matter, we'd be booking seats for performances of such lost Shakespeare plays as *Cardenio* and *Love's Labour's Won*.

Poetry was a different story. Early in his career Shakespeare showed great care in seeing into print his two great narrative poems, *Venus and Adonis* and *Lucrece*, bestsellers that went through many editions. While his name didn't appear on the title pages of these volumes, dedicatory letters addressed to the Earl of Southampton and signed 'William Shake-speare' are included in italics in the front-matter of both. It's the first time that the no-torious hyphen appeared in the printed version of his name, a telling sign, for sceptics, of pseudonymous publication. Elizabethan compositors, trying to protect valuable type from breaking, would have smiled at that explanation. They knew from experience that Shakespeare's name was a typesetter's nightmare. When setting a 'k' followed by a long 's' in italic font – with the name Shakespeare, for example – the two letters could easily collide and the font might snap. The easiest solution was inserting a let-ter 'e', a hyphen, or both; as we'll soon see, compositors settled on different strategies. And as the title pages of the 1608 quarto of *Lear* and the 1609 *Sonnets* indicate, it's a habit that carried over when setting roman font as well.

Shakespeare had been writing plays for five or six years before one of them, *Titus Andronicus*, was finally published in 1594. Its title page advertised the names of the playing companies who had per-formed it, not who wrote it. This was typical. Even the most cele-brated plays by the most popular Elizabethan dramatists appeared anonymously. We have no documentary evidence that Christopher Marlowe wrote *Tamburlaine*, and if not for a casual allusion by Thomas Heywood in the early seventeenth century, Thomas Kyd's name would not be linked to his masterpiece from the late 1580s, *The Spanish Tragedy*. We still don't know who wrote some of the finest plays of the period – including *Mucedorus*, *Arden of*

Faversham and *Edward the Third*. Still, we are lucky that they have survived at all, for only six hundred or so of the estimated three thousand plays staged between the accession of Queen Elizabeth in 1558 and the closing of the theatres in 1642 were ever printed. A large percentage of those that found their way into print nonetheless remained anonymous and none of these, so far as anyone knows, was published under an assumed name. It would have been pointless to do so. For a playwright anxious about being identified on the title page of a play – fearing punishment for seditious words or imagining that publishing carried a social stigma – the simplest and obvious course of action was to do nothing: allow the play, like so many others, to reach London's bookstalls without a name attached to it. Nobody would notice and nobody would care.

If an Elizabethan writer insisted on having a pseudonym appear on a title page of a published quarto, and could somehow persuade a publisher to put it there, the worst possible moment to do so was 1598. In that year the Privy Council briefly shut down the public playhouses in the wake of *The Isle of Dogs*, a scandalous play that landed both Ben Jonson and Thomas Nashe, who collaborated on it, in serious trouble. And if you were going to put someone else's name on a play, nothing could be more foolish than to use a real person's name, especially that of someone highly visible, such as an actor who could easily be hauled in and questioned. The memory of Thomas Kyd's brutal interrogation by the authorities five years earlier would have weighed heavily on anyone who might contemplate serving as a front for another writer. Kyd, who unluckily had shared writing quarters with Marlowe, was put on the rack and tortured, and died within a year or so, but not before telling interrogators hunting down the source of anti-alien propaganda all that they wanted to know about Marlowe and his beliefs.

Yet 1598 turned out to be the very year that two publishers independently decided that Shakespeare's popularity had reached the point where it was profitable to put his name on the title page of his plays. That year, Cuthbert Burby brought out a 'newly corrected and augmented' edition of *Love's Labour's Lost* by 'W.

Shakespere', while Valentine Simmes published second editions of *Richard the Third* and *Richard the Second* (both by 'William Shake-speare'). If anyone wanted to signal through a wink and nod that a name was pseudonymous, confirmed by that hyphen, it would have helped to be consistent. Yet Burby and Simmes didn't spell Shakespeare's name the same way, and it wasn't because only one of them had been tipped off about inserting that hyphen. If there really was a conspiracy and 'Shake-speare' a pseudonym, a score of publishers who at various times over a quarter-century owned and published Shakespeare's works, and then their various printers and compositors, and then those to whom they sold their rights, would each in turn have had to be let in on the secret — and carried it to the grave. Pseudonymous publication requires both consistency and a degree of control over the printed word; the uneven publication of Shakespeare's plays didn't allow for either. Some plays, like *Richard the Third* and *The Merry Wives of Windsor*, bore Shakespeare's name from the outset. Others, like *Richard the Second*, first lacked it, then added it. Still others, including *Romeo and Juliet* and *Henry the Fifth*, were never published under Shakespeare's name during his lifetime.

Where his name does appear on the title pages of these early editions, it was variously spelled 'Shakspere', 'Shakspere', 'Shake-speare' and 'Shakespeare'. There's no pattern. Spelling simply wasn't uniform at the time. Shakespeare himself didn't even spell his own name the same way. On his will alone (which bears his signature on each page) he spelled it 'Shakspere' on the first two pages and 'Shakspere' on the last one. As Marlovians and Oxfordians well know, the names of their candidates were also spelled variously at the time. Alan Nelson has pointed out that Oxford spelled a word like 'halfpenny' eleven different ways, but this doesn't suggest that de Vere was barely literate, any more than claims about Shakespeare's spelling habits should. The author's name on the first quarto of *Hamlet* is spelled 'William Shake-speare'; the second quarto, published a year later, reads 'William Shakespeare'. Others heard and spelled his name differently, including whoever recorded the Revels Account for performances at Whitehall Palace during the Christmas season of 1604. Listed there alongside the ten plays performed by the King's Men are the names of the 'poets which made the plays': 'Shaxberd' is written alongside *Measure for Measure, The Comedy of Errors* and *The Merchant of Venice* – yet another inventive spelling and at the same time powerful evidence ascribing to him the authorship of these plays.

Early editions of Shakespeare's plays contain additional clues about the identity of their author. Playing companies turned over to printers different sorts of manuscripts. Scholars have spent lifetimes poring over the resulting printed texts, reconstructing from the smallest details the lost originals – whether one play or another was printed from 'foul papers' (an early modern term for an author's rough draft), 'fair copy' (an author's or more likely a scribe's neater transcription of that earlier draft) or 'prompt copy' (either foul or fair copy that would have been marked up and used in the playhouse). Plays set from 'foul papers' often reveal a great deal about an author's writing habits.

An Elizabethan playwright had to devote a good deal of his attention to mundane concerns: which actors in the playing company were available, how many roles had to be doubled (for there were far more roles than performers in each of his plays), and how to get them onstage and offstage, or from a balcony to the main stage, or through costume changes, on time. All this is vastly more complicated than it seems, and as someone who for much of his career acted in the plays he wrote alongside those for whom he wrote the other parts, Shakespeare had a decided advantage over freelance dramatists.

For most of his professional life, Shakespeare wrote for an unusually stable and prosperous company, named the Chamberlain's Men from their formation in 1594, and after King James came to the throne in 1603, rechristened the King's Men. Shakespeare knew that every play he wrote had to include significant roles for the half-dozen or so shareholders in the company, actors all, including himself. Other roles would go to hired men, some of whom worked with the company for years, others sporadically. And then, of course, there were the two or three boys who played female roles, since women were not allowed to perform on the Elizabethan stage. These boys were only around until maturity, when their voices and bodies changed; so there was quite a bit of turnover, making life especially difficult for a playwright who had to depend on the capabilities of those working for the company at any given moment. You couldn't write Rosalind's part in *As You Like It* unless you had absolute confidence that the boy who spoke her seven hundred lines, a quarter of the play, could manage it. You couldn't write a part requiring the boy playing Lady Percy in *The First Part of Henry the Fourth* to sing in Welsh unless you knew that the company had a young actor who could handle a tune and was a native of Wales. Whoever wrote these plays had an intimate, first-hand knowledge of everyone in the company, and must have been a shrewd judge of each actor's talents.

There were times when Shakespeare was thinking so intently about the part he was writing for a particular actor that in jotting down the speech headings he mistakenly wrote the actor's name rather than his character's. We know this because compositors passed on some of these slips when typesetting his foul papers. Take, for example, the stage direction in the First Folio edition of that early history play, *The Third Part of Henry the Sixth*, which reads: 'Enter Sinklo and Humfrey'. John Sinklo was a regular hired-man for whom Shakespeare wrote lots of skinny-man parts. Shakespeare would slip again and start thinking of Sinklo rather than the character he was playing in the draft that was used to produce the quarto edition of *The Second Part of Henry the Fourth*, where his stage direction reads: 'Enter Sinclose and three or four officers'. It's clear that the scene was originally written as a star turn for Sinklo, and wouldn't be half as funny or make as much sense without him, for he is brought onstage mostly to be teased about his waistline. The others take turns calling him names: 'nuthook', 'starved bloodhound', and, in case we miss the point, 'thin thing'.

The author of Shakespeare's plays could not have written the great roles of Richard III, Romeo, Hamlet, Othello and Lear unless he knew how far he could stretch his leading tragedian, Richard Burbage. Writing parts for the company's star comedian was even tougher. How could anyone but a shareholder in the company know to stop writing comic parts for Will Kemp the moment he quit the company in 1599 – and start writing parts in advance of the arrival of his replacement, Robert Armin, whose comic gifts couldn't have been more different? Kemp was another one of those actors Shakespeare kept confusing with his characters – easy enough to do, since Kemp always partly played himself no matter what role Shakespeare had written for him. The 1599 quarto of *Romeo and Juliet* identifies the Nurse's comic sidekick Peter first as 'The Clown' and then in an ensuing stage direction as 'Will Kemp'. The same sort of slip occurs in the quarto of *Much Ado about Nothing*, where we learn that the comic roles of Dogberry and Verges had been written for Kemp and Richard Cowley.

Rehearsing with a small group of fellow actors every morning, performing that same play with them that afternoon, and meeting regularly after that with shareholders for business decisions and to hear and purchase new plays could not have been stress-free. There are even recorded instances in which Elizabethan actors and playwrights came to blows – but not, so far as we know, members of Shakespeare's company. One reason, perhaps, is that the sharers were all enriched by their enterprise. It wasn't just Shakespeare who became successful enough to seek the status of gentleman, or invested in real estate. By focusing unforgivingly and relentlessly on Shakespeare's accumulation of wealth, Victorian biographers overlooked the extent to which his interest in financial matters was typical of his fellow sharers. And the successful sharers of the Chamberlain's Men, in turn, could only look on in envy at the far vaster fortune accumulated by their rival from the Admiral's Men, Edward Alleyn.

The evidence is of a piece: the surviving texts confirm that whoever wrote the plays had to have been a long-term partner in an all-absorbing theatrical venture. The plays could not have been written by a Christopher Marlowe squirrelled away to the Continent or an aristocrat who secretly delivered the plays to the actors. And they certainly could not have been written by somebody who, like Edward de Vere, was not alive in March 1613, when, a month or two after the Globe Theatre caught fire during a performance of a 'new' play, *Henry the Eighth*, 'Mr Shakespeare' and 'Richard Burbage' were each paid forty-four shillings by Thomas Screvin, steward to Francis Manners, sixth Earl of Rutland (the younger brother of the fifth Earl of Rutland, the one believed by some to have written the plays of Shakespeare), for collaborating on an *impresa* for the earl to use at the court celebrations honouring King James's Accession Day on 24 March. An *impresa* was a painted and ceremonial pasteboard shield on which an enigmatic saying, usually in Latin, was written. There was considerable pressure on courtiers to come up with something unusually witty, since gossip about one's *impresa* was sure to follow. Who better than Shakespeare to come up with something imaginative and apt – and the several examples of this courtly art form in *Pericles* were good advertising, confirming that he had a talent for this sort of thing, and that his Latin was strong enough. Burbage, a talented artist, was paid for 'painting and making it'. *Imprese* were ephemeral, so we don't know what Shakespeare wrote for Rutland. But Rutland was sufficiently pleased by their work to rehire Burbage three years later, when he was paid £4 18s on 25 March 1616 'for my lord's shield and for the emblance'. This time, Shakespeare wasn't available; he lay dying in Stratford, that very day affixing his signature to the successive pages of his will.

Even if we lacked all other textual evidence of Shakespeare's authorship, there is one incident that ought to persuade even the most hardened sceptic: the special epilogue written for a court performance of *The Second Part of Henry the Fourth*, where Shakespeare speaks for himself as the author of the play. Before it was performed at court, *The Second Part of Henry the Fourth* had been staged for popular audiences at the Curtain Theatre in

Shoreditch. There, the play had ended with an epilogue spoken by Will Kemp. Moments before that Falstaff, played by Kemp, is hauled off to the Fleet prison and it looks for once like Falstaff, that great escape artist, will not be able to wriggle out of trouble. But Kemp suddenly dashes back onstage and a few moments pass before playgoers realise that the play really is over and that Kemp is delivering an epilogue not as Falstaff but more or less as himself:

One word more, I beseech you. If you be not too much cloyed with fat meat, our humble author will continue the story, with Sir John in it, and make you merry with fair Katherine of France, where (for anything I know) Falstaff shall die of a sweat, unless already a' be killed with your hard opinions. For Oldcastle died martyr, and this is not the man. My tongue is weary; when my legs are too, I will bid you good night.
(Epilogue, 24–32)

Kemp's repeated mention of his legs and dancing signals that a jig – an often raunchy Elizabethan song-and-dance act that followed both comedies and tragedies – was about to commence. Kemp also announces that Shakespeare, 'our humble author', promises to 'continue the story', so that his admirers can rest assured they'll be seeing Kemp again soon.

But this epilogue wouldn't do at court, where plays didn't end with salacious jigs. So Shakespeare had to write an alternative one appropriate for the command performance at Whitehall Palace, where the Queen herself was in attendance. Taking centre stage himself, Shakespeare replaced Kemp and delivers his own lines ('what I have to say is of my own making'). It's the closest we ever get in his plays to hearing Shakespeare speak for and as himself. It's a brassy and confident speech, one that may even have caught his fellow players off guard:

First, my fear; then, my curtsy; last my speech. My fear is your dis-pleasure. My curtsy, my duty. And my speech, to beg your pardons. If you look for a good speech now, you undo me. For what I have to say is of my own making. And what indeed (I should say) will (I doubt) prove my own marring. But to the purpose and so to the venture. Be it known to you, as it is very well, I was lately here in the end of a displeasing play, to pray your patience for it, and to promise a better. I meant indeed to pay you with this, which if (like an ill venture) it come unluckily home, I break, and you, my gentle creditors, lose. Here I promised you I would be, and here I commit my body to your mercies. Bate me some, and I will pay you some, and (as most debtors do) promise you infinitely. And so I kneel down before you; but indeed, to pray for the Queen.

(Epilogue, 1–15)

This time around there's no mention of what the next play will be about and no promise that Kemp will return as Falstaff. The apology for Oldcastle in *The First Part of Henry the Fourth* (if that's the 'displeasing' if enormously popular play he never quite gets around to naming) is nicely finessed, as Shakespeare offers in compensation the Falstaff play they have just applauded as a way of making amends. Beyond this point, the epilogue's initial acceptance of social deference – all that begging and curtsying, appropriate to someone of Shakespeare's lower social station – gives way to the novel suggestion that playwright and spectators are bound in a partnership, sharers in a venture. If Shakespeare offers himself as merchant adventurer, his plays as treasure and his audience as investors, then it must needs follow that an 'ill venture' which breaks or bankrupts him will prove as costly to his creditors. When Shakespeare describes his courtly audience as 'gentle creditors' he means not only that they provide the credit or licence to let him write what he wants, but also that they credit or believe in him. Pursuing the implications of this metaphor, he redefines the basis of their understanding: accept his terms, then, and they'll be repaid with plays for a long time to come.

The episode is less well known than it should be, because for the past four centuries it has been effectively buried by generations of editors. In 1600 the Chamberlain's Men handed over a manuscript of *The Second Part of Henry the Fourth* to Andrew Wise and William Aspley to publish. They in turn asked Valentine

Simmes to print it – and the title page of this quarto, like the entry in the Stationers' Register that assigned copyright to the publishers, confirms that the play was written 'by William Shakespeare'. But when passing along the playscript, the company must have inadvertently handed over a copy containing both the Curtain and Whitehall epilogues. The compositor working for Simmes printed them both, one right after the other, resulting in the speaker first kneeling in prayer, then leaping up and resuming his speech. The Folio editors, trying to repair this, made a further hash of it in 1623, moving the kneeling bit to the end, which is how it has been printed ever since, running together two speeches with wildly different purposes. Untangled, they tell a very different story.

It's inconceivable that any of the rival candidates for the authorship of the plays associated with the court – Francis Bacon, the Earls of Oxford, Derby and Rutland, Mary Sidney, to name but a few – could possibly have stood upon that stage at Whitehall Palace, publicly assuming the socially inferior role of player, and spoken these lines. And it is even harder, after reading these powerful and self-confident lines, to imagine the alternative, that the speaker, who claims to have written the play they just saw, was merely a mouthpiece for someone else in the room, and lying to both queen and court.

'Here's Our Fellow Shakespeare'

London's literary community at the turn of the seventeenth century was small and remarkably tight-knit. Authors shared publishers, patrons, and in a few instances even lodgings or writing quarters. They often worked collaboratively. Shakespeare frequently crossed paths with many of them. He co-wrote plays with several dramatists, acted in the plays of many others and would have heard still others pitch their plays to his company's sharers. Even as a lyric poet he didn't work in isolation, sharing his Sonnets, we are told, with his 'private friends' and, along with such other 'modern writers' as Ben Jonson, George Chapman and John

Marston, contributing poetry to a volume called *Love's Martyr* in 1601.

Then, as now, writers gossiped about each other. Fortunately, a good deal of what his fellow writers thought about Shakespeare has survived. Some wrote or spoke directly to each other about him, some chose to share their thoughts with a broader reading public and some privately jotted down their observations, never expecting them to be read by anyone else. Their comments about him stretch without interruption from his early years in the theatre to his death in 1616, and after.

The first notice of Shakespeare appears in a pamphlet, about which much remains unclear, attributed to a university-trained writer named Robert Greene. In 1592, Greene (or possibly his fellow playwright Henry Chettle, who was involved in the volume's posthumous publication) warned established dramatists that there is an upstart crow, beautified with our feathers, that with his *Tiger's heart wrapt in a player's hide*, supposes he is as well able to bombast out a blank verse as the best of you: and being an absolute *Johannes fac totum*, is to his own conceit the only Shake-scene in a country.

The objection here is not so much to an actor aspiring to write plays, but to his confidence that he can do so better than they can, that he thinks himself 'the only Shake-scene in a country'. Worse still, he does so 'beautified with our feathers', that is, shamelessly appropriating the popular styles they had forged. A lot is packed into this attack, a good deal more than we can understand four hundred years later. But we are left with the impression of a veteran writer shrewdly taking the measure of an upstart he doesn't much like, even parodying a line from his recent *True Tragedy of Richard Duke of York* (better known by its Folio title, *The Third Part of Henry the Sixth*), where Shakespeare, showing a fine ear for bombastic blank verse, had written, 'O tiger's heart wrapped in a woman's hide'.

The publication of Shakespeare's *Venus and Adonis* in 1593 and *Lucrece* in 1594 elicited far more flattering responses, especially from aspiring poets. Shakespeare is also named for the first time in 1594 in the commendatory verses to *Willobie His Avisa*, which alludes to how 'Shakespeare paints poor Lucrece['s] rape'. A year later, Cambridge scholar William Covell also praised 'Sweet Shakspeare' for 'his Lucrecia'. The pair of narrative poems soon won Shakespeare other admirers, none more devoted than young Richard Barnfield, whose 'A Remembrance of Some English Poets' in 1598 provides the first extended critical appreciation of Shakespeare:

And Shakespeare thou, whose honey-flowing vein
(Pleasing the world) thy praises doth obtain.
Whose Venus, and whose Lucrece (sweet, and chaste)
Thy name in fame's immortal book have placed.

The rhymes are a bit wooden, but the message is clear: Shakespeare was a writer to be reckoned with.

Even as Barnfield was praising his lyrical gifts, Francis Meres was cementing Shakespeare's reputation as both poet and playwright in *Palladis Tamia* (1598), an invaluable account of what Shakespeare had achieved a decade into his career. Meres, just a year or so younger than Shakespeare, had earned degrees from both Cambridge and Oxford before moving to London by the mid-1590s to make a living as a writer and translator. The most exciting section of *Palladis Tamia* is his 'Comparative Discourse of Our English Poets', in which Meres touches on eighty English writers. He is surprisingly astute about the great talent at work all around him, and his judgements have stood the test of time. No contemporary writer earned as much praise from Meres as Shakespeare.

Meres likens modern English writers to ancient Roman ones (so that, for instance, 'the sweet witty soul of Ovid lives in mellifluous and honey-tongued Shakespeare'). When it came to finding a match for both Plautus and Terence, 'the best for comedy and tragedy' among the Roman dramatists, he concludes that only Shakespeare 'among the English is the most excellent in both kinds for the stage' – and to underscore his point, Meres lists a dozen of Shakespeare's popular comedies and tragedies. Crushingly, for those who want to believe that the Earl of Oxford and Shakespeare were one and the same writer, Meres names both and distinguishes between them, including both 'Edward Earl of Oxford' and Shakespeare in his list of the best writers of comedy (while omitting Oxford from the list of leading tragedians). Meres also ranks Shakespeare among the best of English lyric poets as well as among those who are 'the most passionate among us to bewail and bemoan the perplexities of love'.

Shakespeare caught the attention of both older and younger generations of writers. Around 1600, the veteran author and controversialist Gabriel Harvey wrote in his copy of Chaucer's *Works* about Shakespeare's growing popularity, as well as the split between what we might call highbrow and lowbrow responses to his works: 'The younger sort takes much delight in Shakespeare's *Venus and Adonis*; but his *Lucrece*, and his *Tragedy of Hamlet, Prince of Denmark*, have it in them, to please the wiser sort.' In another private note, Harvey lists Shakespeare along with his old friend Edmund Spenser 'and the rest of our flourishing metricians' – high praise from a university man.

Barnfield was not the only young poet captivated by Shakespeare's style. In 1599, John Weever paid homage to his source of inspiration in a full-length Shakespearean sonnet:

Honey-tongued Shakespeare, when I saw thine issue
I swore Apollo got them and none other.

Weever praises both of Shakespeare's narrative poems as well as his plays, which he admits he doesn't know as well ('*Romeo, Richard*,' more whose names I know not'). Shakespeare attracted young admirers outside of London too, including the author or authors of the three anonymous *Parnassus* plays performed at St John's College, Cambridge between 1599 and 1601. In the second of these often slyly mocking scripts, Shakespeare is made much of. A character named Ingenioso says 'We shall have nothing but pure Shakespeare' – and refers to him again as 'Sweet Mr Shakespeare!' – while another repeats that praise and adds: 'I'll have his picture in my study at the court', and concludes: 'Let this duncified world esteem of Spenser and Chaucer, I'll worship sweet Mr Shakespeare.'

In the third and final *Parnassus* play, actors impersonating Burbage and Kemp make cameo appearances. After claiming that university-trained playwrights are second-rate, the actor playing Kemp adds: 'Why here's our fellow Shakespeare puts them all down, aye, and Ben Jonson too.' In this up-to-date reference to the 'Poets' War' raging at the time in the London theatres, Kemp also notes 'that Ben Jonson is a pestilent fellow, he brought up Horace giving the poets a pill, but our fellow Shakespeare hath given him a purge that made him bewray his credit'. For these Cambridge undergraduates, Shakespeare was a living, breathing presence, one whose poetry they knew by heart, whose literary sparring they followed closely, and a copy of whose portrait they could imagine displaying in their rooms.

It wasn't just poets who took note. In 1605, in his *Remaines Concerning Britaine*, the leading historian of the day, William Camden, included Shakespeare among the greatest of contemporary writers: 'what a world could I present to you out of Sir Philip Sidney, Edmund Spenser, Samuel Daniel, Hugh Holland, Ben Jonson, Thomas Campion, Michael Drayton, George Chapman, John Marston, William Shakespeare, and other most pregnant wits of these our times, whom succeeding ages may justly admire'. Are we to suppose that as reputable a historian as Camden must have been in on the conspiracy as well – and willing to lie in print? Not long after, a twenty-one-year-old Scot named William Drummond arrived in London. He started reading a lot of Shakespeare that year, especially the sexy stuff: *Romeo and Juliet, A Midsummer Night's Dream, Love's Labour's Lost* and *Lucrece*. When in 1611 Drummond compiled a list of the books in his library, he included both *Venus and Adonis* and *Lucrece*, attributing both to 'Schaksp.'. His copy of *Romeo and Juliet* survives and can be found in the Edinburgh University Library; in it, Drummond supplies the author's missing name: 'Wil. Sha.'. As Alan Nelson has shown, Drummond was not the only book-buyer at the time to identify Shakespeare by name. Their ranks include the author of *The Anatomy of Melancholy*, Robert Burton; the chief actor of the Admiral's Men, Edward Alleyn (who purchased a copy of the Sonnets); Richard Stonley, a Teller of the Exchequer under Queen Elizabeth; the Queen's nephew and godson, John Harrington, a major author in his own right; and Humphrey Dyson, who had extensive connections in the theatre world. If there were any place that we might hope to find these well-connected figures re-attributing Shakespeare's works to their 'true' author it would surely be in such private documents. But each of these writers put down Shakespeare's name rather than someone else's because each one knew who Shakespeare was and didn't doubt that he had written these works.

It would be surprising if other dramatists had left no record of what they thought of Shakespeare. It is they, after all, who had worked most closely with him, seen his plays, seen him act, and taken his full measure. It wasn't until Shakespeare had nearly retired from the stage that they began to share their views, pro-ducing a nice symmetry: even as a veteran playwright like Robert Greene was responsible for Shakespeare's earliest notice, drama-tists were prominent among those who would provide some of the last that he would read or hear about. John Webster, whose 1612 play *The White Devil* owes so much to Shakespeare that it often hovers between plagiarism and parody, was happy to acknowledge the debt to 'the right happy and copious industry of Master Shake-speare, Master Dekker, and Master Heywood' and to 'wish what I write may be read by their light'. Michael Drayton, fellow native of Warwickshire and a leading poet and dramatist, may have known Shakespeare longer than most. Born within a year of Shakespeare, Drayton didn't write about him until well after his death, when he praises him warmly:

And be it said of thee,
Shakespeare, thou hadst as smooth a comic vein,
Fitting the sock, and in thy natural brain,
As strong conception, and as clear a rage,
As any one that trafficked with the stage.

Thomas Heywood, who had his hand in over two hundred plays over the course of a very long career, also had high praise for

Mellifluous Shake-speare, whose enchanting Quill
Commanded Mirth or Passion, was but Will.

The youngest rival playwright to write about Shakespeare was Francis Beaumont. An undated letter Beaumont wrote to his friend and mentor Ben Jonson, in verse – from 'F.B.' to 'B.J.' – survives and seems to have been written around 1608. In it, Beaumont alludes to several playwrights, including in passing their mutual rival, Shakespeare. The letter was only discovered in 1921 and is less well known than it ought to be:

Here I would let slip
(If I had any in me) scholarship,
And from all learning keep these lines as clear
As Shakespeare's best are, which our heirs shall hear
Preachers apt to their auditors to show
How far sometimes a mortal man may go
By the dim light of Nature.

Beaumont flatters both Jonson and himself by invoking Shakespeare as the great anomaly: an exemplary poet of Nature, one who exemplifies how far a writer can go, lacking sufficient learning and scholarship.

Jonson left the most personal and extensive tributes to Shakespeare. For many, his testimony alone resolves any doubts about Shakespeare's authorship of the plays. Their relationship dates at least as far back as 1598, when Jonson's breakthrough play – *Every Man in His Humour* – was purchased and staged by the Chamberlain's Men. Jonson proudly lists Shakespeare among those who performed in it. While Shakespeare didn't act a year later in the follow-up, *Every Man out of His Humour*, he did have a role in Jonson's Roman tragedy *Sejanus* in 1603. In 1619, three years after Shakespeare's death, Jonson had occasion to speak about his old rival when visiting that other admirer of Shakespeare's work, William Drummond, in Scotland. Drummond kept extensive notes of Jonson's table-talk, including his judgement that 'Shakespeare wanted art' and his disapproval of his rival's weak grasp of geography in *The Winter's Tale*: 'Shakespeare in a play brought in a number of men saying they had suffered shipwrack in Bohemia, where there is no sea near by some hundred miles.'

More of Jonson's unguarded comments survive in the notes found after his death, edited and published in 1641 as *Timber, Or Discoveries; Made upon Men and Matter*. Jonson here recalls the disagreement he had, decades earlier, with members of Shakespeare's company who thought it praiseworthy that Shakespeare never revised:

I remember, the players have often mentioned it as an honour to Shakespeare, that in his writing (whatsoever he penned) he never blotted out line. My answer hath been, would he have blotted a thousand. Which they thought a malevolent speech. I had not told posterity this, but for their ignorance, who choose that circumstance to commend their friend by, wherein he most faulted.

An old man now, writing long after Shakespeare's death, Jonson wants to set the record straight; he has nothing to lose and there's no point in either holding back unspoken praise or taking secret grievances to the grave. It's as generous as anything Jonson ever wrote, notwithstanding the final qualification:

I loved the man, and do honour his memory, on this side Idolatry, as much as any. He was (indeed) honest, and of an open, and free nature; had an excellent fancy; brave notions, and gentle expressions; wherein he flowed with that facility, that sometime it was necessary he should be stopped.

Jonson concludes with praise and blame mixed in equal measure, once again remembering those old times and the differences in their styles and sensibilities:

His wit was in his own power; would the rule of it had been so too. Many times he fell into those things, could not escape laughter. As when he said in the person of Caesar, one speaking to him: 'Caesar, thou dost me wrong.' He replying: 'Caesar did never wrong but with just cause,' and such like, which were ridiculous. But he redeemed his vices with his virtues. There was ever more in him to be praised, than to be pardoned.

I find it difficult to read these recollections and imagine how anyone could believe that Jonson was a double-dealer and somehow put up to writing this, his tribute intended to further a conspiracy to delude the world into thinking that Shakespeare had written the plays.

Sceptics frequently point to what they see as the suspiciously long lapse of seven years between Shakespeare's death in 1616 and the belated appearance of the First Folio in 1623. It confirms for them that nobody took any notice of Shakespeare of Stratford's death since he had nothing to do with the authorship of the plays. What they overlook is that just three years after his death a set of Shakespeare's selected plays, ten in all – including tragedies, comedies and histories – was already for sale in London, issued by a pair of enterprising London publishers, Thomas Pavier and William Jaggard. These volumes could be purchased individually or as a set, and we know that some discriminating buyers bought all ten and had them bound together as a kind of collected works. It was a legitimate enterprise, since Pavier by this time owned or had obtained the copyright to five of the ten plays, and he and Jaggard may have believed, or persuaded themselves, that the rights to other plays were derelict. By this time a dozen or so different publishers could claim ownership of one or another of the eighteen plays by Shakespeare that had already been published – and before a more ambitious collection could be published, a syndicate would have to be formed that included them all, a time-consuming business. Pavier and Jaggard's collection may well have been intended to whet the appetite for a more comprehensive edition of Shakespeare's works, toward which end Jaggard was already working. Alternatively, it may have spurred members of the King's Men to produce such a volume. In either case, in 1619 the playing company asked the Lord Chamberlain to order the Stationers' Company to put a stop to the publication of any more of Shakespeare's plays – or as they saw it, their plays. This request may have been intended to block other publishers, for they may already have joined forces with Pavier and Jaggard (and would subsequently use Pavier's quartos and Jaggard's press in producing the 1623 Folio). Shakespeareans are still a bit mystified by the motives behind the Pavier quartos. Whatever led to their publication, it's obvious that surprisingly little time elapsed from news of Shakespeare's death to determined efforts to see his collected plays into print.

In addition to the thirty-six plays, the 1623 Folio contained a woodcut of Shakespeare, dressed in a very expensive doublet. According to Jonson, the portrait was a likeness. He added that it was a shame that the artist couldn't draw Shakespeare's wit as accurately:

Could he but have drawn his wit
As well in brass, as he hath hit
His face; the print would then surpass
All, that was ever writ in brass.

The Folio also included memorial verses, most famously Jonson's own long poem 'To the Memory of My Beloved, The Author Mr William Shakespeare, and what He Hath Left Us'. Hugh Holland, Leonard Digges and 'I.M.' (probably James Mabbe) contributed poems as well. In his poem, Jonson links Shakespeare to his place of birth, addressing him as 'Sweet Swan of Avon', while Digges explicitly identifies the man who wrote the plays with the one who lies buried in Stratford:

Shakespeare, at length thy pious fellows give
The world thy Works; thy Works, by which, outlive
Thy tomb, thy name must. When that stone is rent,
And Time dissolves thy Stratford monument,
Here we alive shall view thee still.

The monument Digges mentions was already erected by 1623. If he hadn't visited it himself, he may have heard about it from the players, for in 1622, members of the King's Men were paid *not* to perform in Stratford-upon-Avon when passing through Shakespeare's birthplace while touring. They must have known that the Puritan-leaning town had long been inhospitable to players; but they nonetheless paid Stratford-upon-Avon a visit, perhaps to pay their respects at the gravestone and monument of the man who had made their fortune.

After completing most of the research for this chapter, I came across one additional bit of evidence. Had I included every stray comment about Shakespeare made by other writers at the time, this chapter would have swelled to twice its size. But I thought I'd add one more, not only because it shows that evidence confirming Shakespeare's authorship continues to be discovered, but also because it underscores that no matter how many documents turn up, there will always be those who continue to interpret them in light of an unprovable and fantastic hoax.

William Camden's 1590 edition of *Britannia*, written in Latin, contains a brief description of Stratford-upon-Avon. Camden describes (here rendered into English) how the town 'owes all of its reputation to its two foster sons, John of Stratford, the Archbishop of Canterbury who built the church, and Hugh Clopton, the magistrate of London who began the stone bridge over the Avon supported by fourteen arches, not without very great expense'. There's a copy of this book in the Huntington Library that was owned by Richard Hunt. Hunt, born around 1596 and educated at Oxford, went on to become vicar in Bishop's Itchington, ten miles or so east of Stratford-upon-Avon. In this copy a reader, in all probability Hunt himself, had come across that passage and added, in Latin, next to the words about Stratford's most famous sons: '*et Gulielmo Shakespear Roscio planè nostro*' ("and to William Shakespeare, truly our Roscius"). Roscius was a widely admired Roman actor who achieved great fame and amassed a considerable fortune before retiring from the stage. To compare someone to Roscius in Shakespeare's day – as Thomas Nashe had praised Edward Alleyn of the Admiral's Men in the 1590s – was to acknowledge that he was a star of the stage.

The marginalia were discovered by Paul Altrocchi. But for Altrocchi, a committed Oxfordian, they only served to confirm, rather than refute, the idea that someone other than Shakespeare had written the plays:

The annotation, likely written so soon after Shaksper of Stratford's death in 1616, does confirm the remarkable early success of what Oxfordians view as William Cecil's clever but monstrous connivance: forcing the genius Edward de Vere into pseudonymity and promoting the illiterate grain merchant and real estate speculator, William Shaksper of Stratford, into hoaxian prominence as the great poet and playwright, William Shakespeare.

Debating such a conclusion is pointless, given the radically different assumptions governing how this document ought to be read.

Virtually every piece of evidence offered by Shakespeare's fellow writers has been similarly explained away. Sceptics now produce a handy chart, which first appeared in Diana Price's *Shakespeare's Unorthodox Biography*, that migrates from book to book, and from arguments for one new candidate for the authorship of the plays to another, denying that *any* literary evidence exists for Shakespeare's authorship. It has taken on iconic status – now known simply by the acronym CLPE, 'Chart of Literary Paper Evidence'. Price and her followers define authorship in such a way that Shakespeare is always narrowly excluded, if need be on semantic grounds. According to the CLPE, there's no evidence of Shakespeare having had a *direct relationship* with a patron, though he wore the livery of the Lord Chamberlain, served King James both as a King's Man and as a Groom of the Chamber, and directly addressed a patron, the Earl of Southampton, in the letters prefacing both *Venus and Adonis* and *Lucrece*. Price's CLPE also insists that Shakespeare had no 'Notice *at death* as *a writer*'. I'm not sure how those who wrote memorial tributes to him, or paid for or carved his monument, or laboured to create the Pavier editions or the First Folio, might feel about that. But according to the CLPE, time had apparently expired before all these memorial efforts were realised. And though Price knows that Shakespeare was a shareholder and therefore not paid directly for each play by his playing company (and knows about the *imprese* payment as well), her CLPE assures us that there is no evidence of his 'having been paid to write'. Readers are invited to make up their own minds.

Jacobean Shakespeare

I was in London on 5 November 2008, Guy Fawkes Day, that time-honoured celebration of King James's miraculous escape from a terrorist plot. There had been fireworks exploding in the skies of London all week, a legacy of four hundred years of bonfires and bells, though I wondered how much those setting off these explosives knew about what they were commemorating. I thought I'd pay my own respects to King James more quietly by viewing his portrait at the National Portrait Gallery. I passed through the Tudor galleries, rich in portraits of Elizabeth I and her courtiers, but became confused when I entered the next gallery and couldn't find the familiar images of James and his courtiers, where they had long been displayed. I walked around in circles before finally asking a guard to direct me to the Jacobean portraits. He explained that they were temporarily in storage, their place now taken up by 'Shakespeare and His Circle'. The King's Men without the king felt a bit like *Hamlet* without the prince.

Discouraged, I headed to Foyles, that wonderful bookshop, in search of recent books about King James – also in vain; only one was in stock. I couldn't understand why historians, commercial publishers and booksellers had largely given up on someone who ruled in England for twenty-two years (after having reigned in Scotland for thirty-six). Adjoining shelves sagged under the weight of books about the Tudors, especially Queen Elizabeth. It was the same everywhere I turned: there was a popular television series on 'The Tudors' and any number of lavish films I could rent about Elizabeth – but not one sequel on her royal successor (the very subject, I later learned, of Ronald Hutton's witty essay 'Why Don't the Stuarts Get Filmed?').

Shakespeare in Love is one of the most delightful movies ever made about Shakespeare. In one of its best scenes we get to watch Queen Elizabeth, played by Judi Dench, sitting in the galleries at the outdoor playhouse at a performance of *Romeo and Juliet*, and telling Shakespeare afterwards to come by the palace, 'where we will speak some more'. Imagine replacing her in this scene with, say, Simon Russell Beale in the role of King James. It wouldn't work. Though almost half of his creative life was spent as a King's Man, Shakespeare has for the longest time been powerfully and irrevocably linked with Queen Elizabeth, so much so that we seem to have forgotten Ben Jonson's even-handed recollection of how Shakespeare's plays 'so did take Eliza, and our James!'

Things have been this way since at least the early eighteenth century, when writers began inventing an intimacy between playwright and queen that had no documentary foundation. In 1702, John Dennis claimed that *The Merry Wives of Windsor* 'was written at her command'. A few years later, Nicholas Rowe added that Elizabeth 'without doubt gave him many gracious marks of her favour'. The last time anyone tried to establish a direct connection between Shakespeare and his other monarch was 1709, when Bernard Lintott wrote that 'King James the First was pleased with his own hand to write an amicable letter to Mr Shakespeare;

which letter, though now lost, remained long in the hands of Sir William D'Avenant, as a credible person now living can testify.' No such letter has survived and it's unlikely that it ever existed (D'Avenant also bragged that he was Shakespeare's illegitimate son). By the end of the eighteenth century, letters from James to Shakespeare were long forgotten; as the Ireland forgeries confirm, those from Elizabeth now captured the popular imagination. When it has been an article of faith for so long that Shakespeare was an Elizabethan writer, who can blame the Oxfordians for succumbing to the widespread conviction that Shakespeare's plays were the creations of a Tudor playwright and restrict their story almost entirely to life under Elizabeth?

We have also had drummed into us that he was Shakespeare of the Globe – though that playhouse was only built in the closing years of Elizabeth's reign. Long forgotten are the other playing spaces in and around London in which he had built his reputation over the previous decade: the Theatre, the Curtain, Newington Butts, the Rose, Richmond, Whitehall, perhaps a brief stint at the Swan. I'm as blameworthy as the next in this respect, having spent years researching and writing about the construction of the Globe and what was taking place in the closing years of Elizabeth's reign. The Globe has become an icon, a once-again familiar sight on Bankside in London. I'm not sure if it's an urban legend, but I have heard that dozens of replicas of it have sprouted round the world.

But had you asked anyone on the streets of London in the winter of 1610 where you could go to see Shakespeare's latest play, there would have only been one answer: 'Blackfriars.' The Blackfriars Theatre means little today to most admirers of Shakespeare; so far as I know, only a single replica of it has ever been erected, in rural Virginia, which attracts both spectators and scholars. The story of the Blackfriars Theatre is also the story of the Jacobean Shakespeare, and of the particular challenges he faced toward the end of his playwriting career. And that, in turn, helps explain why only Shakespeare could have written his late plays that were staged there.

The story dates back to February 1596, when James Burbage purchased a building in the fashionable London precinct of Blackfriars. Burbage's lease on Shakespeare's company's outdoor playhouse in Shoreditch, the Theatre, was about to expire, and his plan was to transfer the company to a permanent playing space. The new site had a lot going for it. For one thing, it was located in the heart of the City, which was much more convenient for London playgoers. For another, it was indoors, so that players could perform in inclement weather, year-round. And because of the site's ecclesiastical origins – it had been a Dominican priory before the dissolution of the monasteries – Blackfriars was technically not under the jurisdiction of London's City fathers, which meant that professional actors, who at the time were relegated to London's suburbs, could perform in the centre of town without fear of retribution. Burbage sank a lot of money into turning the building into an intimate playhouse, capable of holding perhaps six hundred spectators in a crammed rectangular playing chamber that was forty-six by sixty-six feet. But he failed to anticipate the stiff resistance to his plans by influential locals, including the company's own patron, the Lord Chamberlain, who did not want a theatre in the neighbourhood that would attract unruly crowds. The rest of the story is familiar: in 1599 the company moved instead to Southwark and began playing in an outdoor playhouse built out of the timbers of the dismantled Theatre, which they named the Globe.

Many years passed before the dream of inhabiting Blackfriars became a reality for Shakespeare and his fellow players. Soon after the Globe was up and running, hoping to recoup some of his late father's enormous outlay, Richard Burbage leased the Blackfriars site to Henry Evans, an enterprising scrivener who had been working with various children's companies since the 1580s and who wagered correctly that those living near the Blackfriars stage wouldn't object to a children's company performing there a few times a week. Evans now had a theatre but he didn't have enough boy actors, so he brought in Nathaniel Giles, Master of the

Children of the Chapel Royal at Windsor, who had the legal authority to abduct potential 'choristers', much as sailors were impressed to man the English fleet. By late 1600 the children were thriving at Blackfriars and threatening the dominance of the adult players. Shakespeare was well aware, as he writes in *Hamlet*, that the 'public audience' are 'turned to private plays, / And to the humour of children'.

By 1604, however, following a terrible outbreak of plague that closed the theatres and swept away a sixth of London's population, Evans became 'weary and out of liking' with his long-term lease and approached Richard Burbage about cancelling it, but they never came to terms. Evans must have been relieved, for his company's fortunes soon improved after a patent was issued placing the company under the patronage of Anna of Denmark, James's queen. Renamed the Children of the Queen's Revels, the company soon attracted the most talented young dramatists of the day, including John Marston, George Chapman, Thomas Middleton, Francis Beaumont and John Fletcher. The repertory of the adult companies tended to range over all genres, and included a lot of old crowd-pleasers. The Children of the Queen's Revels, lacking a backlist of old favourites to draw upon, stuck to a more restricted fare, mixing tragicomedies with irreverent satires. Its novel offerings catered to upscale playgoers willing to pay sixpence for the cheapest seat (six times the entry price charged at the Globe) and as high as two shillings and sixpence for those who wanted a box seat adjoining the stage. Gallants could pay more and sit on stools on the stage itself, to see and be seen, just a few feet from the action.

The adult players kept a close eye on these developments. There was concern that the satiric bent of the dramatic fare at Blackfriars crossed the line and might land all of London's players in trouble – a point made around 1608 by the veteran Thomas Heywood, who warned in his *Apology for Actors* of the new breed of writers who hurl 'liberal invectives against all estates', and do so in 'the mouths of children, supposing their juniority to a be a privilege for any railing, be it never so violent'. It wasn't long before a string of outrageous plays – including *Eastward Ho*, *The Isle of Gulls* and especially a lost play called *The Silver Mine* that mocked the King himself as a foul-mouthed drunk – angered James enough to call for the dissolution of the children's company (the King had reportedly 'vowed they should never play more, but should first beg their bread'). Henry Evans, now paying £40 a year rent but forbidden to stage any plays at Blackfriars, decided that it was time to move on, and surrendered his lease to the Burbages in August 1608.

It's at this point that Shakespeare and his fellow King's Men re-enter the picture, having tacitly secured the permission that had been denied them a dozen years earlier to perform in this space. Shakespeare, Richard Burbage, Henry Condell, Thomas Evans, John Heminges and William Sly formed a syndicate and became housekeepers in the potentially lucrative indoor playhouse. They chose not to abandon the Globe, however, playing at Blackfriars from October until Easter and outdoors at the Globe during late spring and summer. The first few years of the new venture saw both challenges and setbacks. In contrast to the Globe venture nine years earlier, they were moving into an established playhouse with a regular and demanding clientele who brought certain expectations about the kind of drama they wanted to see. In addi-tion, Blackfriars needed significant renovation. More troublingly, plague now returned with renewed force and it wasn't until 1610 that the King's Men began performing at Blackfriars on a regular basis.

The King's Men had motives for the move beyond finding a dry place to play in winter. The core of their veteran company was get-ting on in years and an infusion of fresh blood was badly needed. The attrition of late had been severe. Thomas Pope, one of the founding members of the Chamberlain's Men and a co-owner of the Globe, had died by 1604. We hear no more of Sinklo after that year, either. Shakespeare, we can be pretty sure, had stopped act-ing regularly for the company around this time as well. Augustine Phillips, another member of the original fraternity and a co-owner of the Globe, died in 1605. William Sly died in 1608 soon after signing on to the Blackfriars syndicate. The survivors were ageing, and the Jacobean theatre – no less for professional playwrights than for actors – was, they knew, a young man's game. That the King's Men were keen on absorbing some of the young talent on display at Blackfriars is confirmed in a lawsuit in which the Burbages acknowledged as much:

In process of time, the boys growing up to be men, which were Underwood, Field, Ostler, and were taken to strengthen the service, the boys daily wearing out, it was considered that house would be as fit for ourselves, and so purchased the lease remaining from Evans with our money, and placed men players, which were Heminges, Condall, Shakespeare, etc.

Richard Field, William Ostler and John Underwood were the pick of the litter – and having reached the age of twenty or so were ready to take on adult roles. All three would soon become sharers in the King's Men (though it took the enterprising Field a few more years before his move became final). This was a full partnership, combining the next generation of star actors with some of London's most beloved and established players. We can see the result in one of the few cast lists from the period to survive. Audiences lucky enough to watch the King's Men perform John Webster's *The Duchess of Malfi* at Blackfriars saw the parts of Ferdinand, the Cardinal, Antonio and Delio performed by Burbage, Condell, Ostler and Underwood respectively. While no cast lists for individual Shakespeare plays survive, Underwood, Field and Ostler are listed in the 1623 Folio among those who acted in his plays.

In taking over Blackfriars, the King's Men also took on board playwrights who had made their reputations writing for its coterie audiences. The company could now boast that the five leading playwrights in the land – Shakespeare, Ben Jonson, Thomas Middleton, John Fletcher and Francis Beaumont – were now writing for them. Biographical critics like to imagine that some mid-life crisis or a longing to reunite with his wife and daughters led Shakespeare to turn to romance and tragicomedy at this time. It's more likely that his turn to romance and tragicomedy in his late and collaborative plays was dictated by the popularity of these kinds of plays at Blackfriars, amounting to a house style.

By 1610, then, Shakespeare was writing for a new group of actors and alongside (as often as not collaboratively) a new generation of playwrights. And he was doing so in a new playing space. He had always written plays that could be converted from one venue to another, expecting that many of the plays first performed at the outdoor amphitheatres would be restaged at various royal palaces, at aristocratic houses and in touring provincial productions in all kinds of venues. That's one reason that there are so few props and so little fancy stage business in his plays. But Blackfriars brought a particular set of challenges. Gone are the fight scenes — like the thrilling duel at the end of *Hamlet*. The cramped stage at Blackfriars, crowded with playgoers on stools, couldn't accommodate them (which explains why, for example, a much anticipated fight at the end of *The Two Noble Kinsmen* is only reported, not staged). Another great difference had to do with lighting. While Blackfriars plays were performed in the afternoon, the playhouse windows didn't admit enough light. So performances were illuminated by candlelight. In addition to creating a different mood in the intimate space, the candles needed to be trimmed in the course of a three-hour performance. This was handled at Blackfriars by intermissions between the acts, a far cry from the situation at the Globe, where action onstage was uninterrupted. By the time he wrote *The Winter's Tale*, with its sudden passage of sixteen years in mid-play, Shakespeare had clearly begun to make creative use of these breaks.

Audiences at Blackfriars expected to be entertained during the time it took to trim or replace candles. So when the King's Men took over from the children's company, they wisely acquired the skilled musicians who had accompanied them at Blackfriars. As a result, the plays that Shakespeare was now writing for the company included a great deal more music. Gone, then, from Shakespeare's works from 1610 on, are the trumpets and drums of his earlier plays from *Titus Andronicus* onward, instruments which the actors themselves could easily handle, replaced by far more subtle musical effects. You can hear it in *Cymbeline's* call for 'solemn music', the music that awakens Hermione in *The Winter's Tale*, the 'sad and solemn music' in *Henry the Eighth*, the 'sudden twang of instrument' in *The Two Noble Kinsmen*, and especially in *The Tempest*, with its repeated calls for 'solemn and strange music' and 'soft music'. Dancing, too, began to figure regularly in Shakespeare's plays. Only six of his first thirty-three plays incorporated dancing scenes; after the move to Blackfriars, dancing would figure in all of Shakespeare's plays.

Most of these dance sequences revolve around a formal masque, a court-centred art form that drew together dance, music and the spoken word. Ben Jonson, one of the innovators of this genre, was also the first to introduce elements of the Jacobean court masque onto the Blackfriars stage in 1605. Shakespeare's first attempt at a masque, written not long after, appeared in *Timon* at the Globe. After the move to Blackfriars they start appearing with surprising regularity, in *Cymbeline*, *The Tempest*, *Henry the Eighth* and *The Two Noble Kinsmen*.

The Jacobean court masques attracted some of the most talented artists in the land. Shakespeare never wrote a masque for court, but as his late works make clear, he had a keen eye for the form, and members of his company were familiar enough with the genre, having been recruited to play the part of anti-masquers at court performances after 1609. It wouldn't be long before Shakespeare offered his own version of the anti-masque, which Caliban and his mates provided after the dance of the Spirits in *The Tempest*, a play aptly described by Stephen Orgel as 'the most important Renaissance commentary' on the masque. Playgoers at Blackfriars may have been privileged relative to those at the Globe, but only a small number of playgoers at either theatre had the chance to witness the lavish masques performed before King

James's court; the masques Shakespeare incorporated into his plays were the next best thing.

The move to Blackfriars coincided with and may have accelerated what critics have long characterised as Shakespeare's turn to a distinctive late style – though the reasons for the changes in his verse habits cannot simply be attributed to the new venue or the kinds of plays he was writing. I'm as wary of developmental or evolutionary arguments about style as I am about the life-stages of Shakespeare's career, but there's no getting around the evidence offered by the plays themselves after 1608 or so. The change in how he composed blank verse marks a watershed, excluding potential candidates like Oxford who died long before Shakespeare's style took this turn.

One of the curious things about his late style is that most critics (and I suspect most actors) don't like it much: it's often too difficult, too knotty, and for some too self-indulgent on Shakespeare's part. Here's a brief example from the opening scene of the late play *Henry the Eighth*, where Norfolk defends a seemingly hyperbolic description:

As I belong to worship and affect
In honour honesty, the tract of every thing
Would by a good discourser lose some life
Which action's self was tongue to.

(1.1.39–42)

Even the best Shakespeare editors throw up their hands in despair at passages like this. With patience, the sense of it can be unpacked. Norfolk has taken a very roundabout way of saying, 'Look, I'm noble and bound to tell the truth; but no matter how well a skilled reporter can describe something, it would fall short of what those who were there experienced.' For Frank Kermode, whose ear for Shakespearean language is as keen as anyone's, the 'personification of action' in this passage, as well as 'the redundant affirmation of his honour and honesty, the affected "tract" are all 'typical of the muscle-bound contortions of the late Shakespeare's language'. It feels more like prose than blank verse, an effect in part achieved by abandoning a regular pause or breath at the end of lines.

Russ McDonald, who has treated this subject elegantly in *Shakespeare's Late Style*, runs through all the tricks that make up this new sound, and his account dovetails with Kermode's. Shakespeare's verse is now a lot more clipped and elliptical. It's much tougher to follow because he removes the connections between clauses, wreaks havoc with conventional syntax and keeps interrupting speeches (and lengthening them) with parenthetical thoughts or qualifiers. Metaphors spill over one another, and letters, sounds, words and phrases re-echo. As scholars as long ago as Malone were quick to note, rhyme is all but banished, in its place far more enjambment and lines that have what's called an extra-metrical or eleventh unstressed syllable.

Here's another example, from one of the last scenes Shakespeare ever wrote, Arcite's speech to his knights in *The Two Noble Kinsmen*, which contains in abundance almost all of these stylistic innovations:

Thou mighty one, that with thy power hast turned
Green Neptune into purple;
Whose approach in vast field comets prewarn,
Unearthed skulls proclaim; whose breath blows down
The teeming Ceres' foison; who dost pluck
With hand armipotent from forth blue clouds
The masoned turrets that both mak'st and break'st
The stony girths of cities: me thy pupil,
Youngest follower of thy drum, instruct this day
With military skill, that to thy laud
I may advance my streamer and by thee
Be styled lord o'th'day.

(5.1.49–60)

These lines are a nightmare to annotate or even paraphrase. Yet, as with even the knottiest passages from the late plays, playgoers

[287]

don't seem to object. Shakespeare somehow writes lines that sound pleasing enough to the ear when delivered at full speed in the theatre, yet defy easy analysis in the study. 'Masoned turrets' is a compressed way of describing who built them. City walls are now 'stony girths'. 'Unearthed' in the sense of excavated had never been used this way before in English literature. Shakespeare's eye drifts toward strange words, such as the one he lifts from Chaucer — 'armipotent' — who in a similar way had lifted it from his source, Boccaccio. It's hard to disagree with Kermode's conclusion that at this point in his career Shakespeare 'is simply defying his audience, not caring to have them as fellows in understanding'.

Lytton Strachey noted another change in these late plays: Shakespeare is no longer as interested in 'who says what'. He's right. There's clearly a shift away from individuated voices in these works. By 1610 or so giving each speaker a distinctive voice seemed to stop mattering so much to Shakespeare, or perhaps other things just mattered more. Anyone who wants to claim that Shakespeare can write in such radically distinct styles simultaneously — that, say, he composed *Henry the Eighth* and *Henry the Fifth* at the same time, or *The Winter's Tale* and *As You Like It* — is to my mind proposing the impossible. Nobody was writing in this often impenetrable style during the Elizabethan years; during the Jacobean period, many would, as admirers of Chapman and Fletcher can attest. It was a period style as much as a personal one.

By March 1613, Shakespeare felt comfortable enough in the Blackfriars neighbourhood to purchase lodgings a hundred yards from the indoor theatre, though whether he saw this as a long-term residence, an investment or simply a place to stay in London while commuting from Stratford, we don't know. Whatever his intentions, they probably changed three months later, when at the end of June disaster struck. The thatch of the Globe caught fire by accident during what several contemporaries tellingly described as a *new* play, *Henry the Eighth*, and the theatre quickly burned to the ground. The Globe was rebuilt, this time with tiles rather than the more flammable thatch roofing, but a year would pass before the new structure was finished. In the meantime, Shakespeare would write his last two collaborative plays, *The Two Noble Kinsmen* and the now lost *Cardenio*, exclusively for Blackfriars. No playwright who had died in 1604 could have anticipated or responded to these unfolding opportunities and events as Shakespeare did.

When I began teaching in the early 1980s, I didn't know that three of the plays on my Shakespeare syllabus – *Titus Andronicus, Timon of Athens* and *Pericles* – were co-authored. I never taught *Henry the Eighth* or *The Two Noble Kinsmen* so didn't give much thought to the extent to which they were collaborative efforts as well. Like many other Shakespeareans at the time, I also didn't pay much attention to the largely forgotten attribution studies of the nineteenth century. Serious work in that field had all but died out after the greatest Shakespeare scholar of the twentieth century, E. K. Chambers, had roundly dismissed the enterprise as the work of 'disintegrators'. The leading authorities on whose judgement in these matters I relied, especially the editors of the authoritative Arden, Oxford and Cambridge series, all agreed with Chambers and firmly rejected the possibility that Shakespeare collaborated in any significant way.

That now seems very long ago. A revolution has since occurred in how Shakespeare professors think about collaboration, largely as a result of the investigations of a new and creative generation of scholars interested in attribution, especially MacDonald Jackson, Ward Elliott, Jonathan Hope, David Lake and Gary Taylor. Working for the most part independently, they established irrefutable cases for Middleton's, Wilkins's and Fletcher's contributions to Shakespeare's Jacobean plays, as well as for George Peele's hand in the much earlier *Titus Andronicus*. They did so by painstakingly teasing out the habits, conscious and unconscious, that characterise each writer's style. Some of these researchers focused on versification, others on vocabulary, still others on the minutest of verbal tics, the kind of thing you would never catch while reading or watching a play, such as the use of auxiliaries, a preference for contractions, and so on. Following their analyses and statistics can be mind-numbing, but there's no denying their conclusions about Shakespeare and his fellow playwrights' stylistic preferences. Look closely enough at each writer's body of work and then turn to their collaborative efforts, and their differences leap out. These studies also reached nearly identical conclusions about which parts of plays were Shakespeare's and which his co-authors'. Building on these findings, Stanley Wells and Gary Taylor's 1986 Oxford edition of Shakespeare's *Works* broke new ground by acknowledging almost all these collaborations. And in 2002, the scattered insights of various editors and researchers were collected and freshly set forth in *Shakespeare Co-Author* by Brian Vickers, who took delight in mocking editors who had ignored these studies or continued to insist in defiance of the evidence that Shakespeare had worked alone.

By the time that Vickers's book came out, a few editors had already begun to acknowledge on title pages that a given play was by 'Fletcher and Shakespeare' or 'Shakespeare and Middleton.' But this news has barely begun to trickle out of the academic world. It may take a decade or two before the extent of Shakespeare's collaboration passes from the graduate seminar to the undergraduate lecture, and finally to popular biography, by which time it will be one of those things about Shakespeare that we thought we knew all along. Right now, though, for those who teach the plays and write about his life, it hasn't been easy abandoning old habits of mind. I know that I am not alone in struggling to come to terms with how profoundly it alters one's sense of how Shakespeare wrote, especially toward the end of his career when he co-authored half of his last ten plays. For intermixed with five of those that he wrote alone, *Antony and Cleopatra*, *Coriolanus*, *The Winter's Tale*, *Cymbeline* and *The Tempest*, are *Timon of Athens* (written with Thomas Middleton), *Pericles* (written with George Wilkins), and *Henry the Eighth*, the lost *Cardenio* and *The Two Noble Kinsmen* (all written with John Fletcher).

I don't want to exaggerate what these attribution studies have achieved. They certainly haven't brought us any closer to unravelling Shakespeare's literary DNA. While we now have a pretty clear sense of which scenes were first drafted by Shakespeare and which by his co-authors – and all of those knotty passages I quoted above were written by Shakespeare – we are still in the dark about some of the most pressing questions about the nature of each collaborative effort. Did Shakespeare invite others to work together on a play, or did they approach him? Who worked out the plot? Why do these collaborations seem inferior to Shakespeare's solo-authored plays? The new attribution studies also aren't of much help when collaborations became more intensive, when playwrights engaged in give-and-take over a particular passage or simply borrowed from or imitated each other's styles, perhaps unconsciously.

One of the great challenges, then, to anyone interested in the subject is that we know so little about how dramatists at the time worked together. We just know – primarily from Philip Henslowe's accounts of theatrical transactions from 1591 to 1604 – that they did, and that in the companies that performed in his playhouses, it was the norm, not the exception. But it is risky to extrapolate too much from that evidence how Shakespeare himself worked. And it seems obvious that collaborations during his early years were significantly different from those after 1605 or so, when he seemed to have resumed the practice after a long hiatus (perhaps best explained by the fact that he was no longer acting, so had both mornings and afternoons now free to engage in more sustained collaborations). We don't even have an adequate language to describe co-authorship ('collaboration' still carries a whiff of co-operating with the enemy). Writers at the time aren't much help either, even Ben Jonson, a veteran collaborator, who boasts in the Preface of his *Volpone* how he wrote the play by himself in only five weeks,

> fully penned it
> From his own hand, without a coadjutor,
> Novice, journeyman, or tutor.

While we don't know precisely what each of these terms means, it seems pretty clear that there was a pecking order, based on experience, among writers who worked together.

Only a few other scraps of information have come down to us, such as Nathan Field's letter in 1614 pitching a new play to Henslowe, where he writes that 'Daborne and I have spent a great deal of time in conference about this plot, which will make as beneficial a play as hath come these seven years'. A richer anecdote was recorded by Thomas Fuller in 1684, who had heard that John Fletcher and one of his fellow authors had met 'in a tavern, to contrive the rude draft of a tragedy; Fletcher undertook *to kill the king* therein, whose words being overheard by a listener (though his loyalty not to be blamed herein), he was accused of high treason'. Luckily for Fletcher and his collaborator, the felony charges were dropped after it became clear 'that the plot was only against a dramatic and scenical king', and 'all wound off in merriment'. The story, fictional or not, allows us a fleeting glimpse of what is otherwise almost entirely lost to us – writers working out a plot together. But how, when and where Shakespeare conferred about the plot and characters of *Pericles, Henry the Eighth, The Two Noble Kinsmen* or *Timon of Athens* we'll never know.

Attribution studies are good at telling us how evenly the labour was divided as well as what parts of plays each dramatist preferred to write. The evidence suggests that most of Shakespeare's joint efforts were equal, active partnerships. The most evenly split play was *Pericles*, with Wilkins contributing 835 lines and Shakespeare 827. Fletcher was responsible for a slightly larger share of both *Henry the Eighth* and *The Two Noble Kinsmen* (1,604 lines to Shakespeare's 1,168 in the former; 1,398 to 1,124 in the latter). And Shakespeare was responsible for the lion's share of both *Titus Andronicus* (1,759 to Peele's 759) and *Timon of Athens* (1,418 to Middleton's 897). Again, though I'm using Vickers's precise figures, these numbers need to be taken as approximations, as the odds are high that collaboration extended further, to the point where two writers may have been responsible for parts of individual speeches, and perhaps, depending on whether one was responsible for smoothing out the final version, even lines.

No less fascinating is the breakdown of who was primarily responsible for which sections. With *Titus Andronicus*, where Shakespeare was the less established writer, Peele wrote the opening third of the play as well as a terrific scene at the beginning of Act 4. Shakespeare handled the rest. The other collaborations are Jacobean, and Shakespeare is in each case the more experienced partner. Wilkins seems to have written the first half of *Pericles*, Shakespeare the second half. *Timon* is more complicated: Shakespeare apparently wrote the opening scene and the closing act, but much of the rest is shared – with individual scenes at times divided between the two, suggesting that the collaboration with Middleton was unusually close. In *Henry the Eighth*, his first collaboration with Fletcher, Shakespeare again begins the play; Fletcher ends it, but as with Middleton, there's considerable back-and-forth along the way. And in *The Two Noble Kinsmen*, Shakespeare once again handles the opening and this time gets the last word in as well, along with most of the fifth act.

Stanley Wells, in *Shakespeare and Co.*, has suggested that Shakespeare's practice here may have been fairly typical, if one of the few scraps of evidence to survive – a lawsuit concerning a collaborative play from 1624, *Keep the Widow Waking*, jointly written by Thomas Dekker, John Webster, John Ford and William Rowley – can be taken as representative. Dekker gave evidence that he wrote eight pages of the first act, along with one speech that came much later, and it's clear that he established the plot line for his colleagues to follow. Dekker also testified that he 'often' saw the play (or at least part of it) acted, suggesting some sort a professional obligation on the part of the playwright to be present on days when the play was rehearsed then performed. I suspect that in a decade's time the account of the field as it now stands will sound sketchy and elementary. More scholars are turning their attention to these issues and more sophisticated approaches are being developed; it will take some time, but in due course

Shakespeare's editors and biographers will offer a truer portrait of this late, collaborative stage of his career.

If mainstream scholars have been uncomfortable acknowledging the degree to which attribution studies have transformed our understanding of how Shakespeare worked, one can only imagine how those who don't believe he wrote the plays feel. To date they have been almost silent on this question. It's not hard to see why. It's impossible to picture any of their aristocrats or courtiers working as more or less equals with a string of lowly playwrights, especially with Wilkins, who kept an inn and may have run a brothel. For Oxfordians in particular, attribution studies are a nightmare. Their strategy has long been to argue that after de Vere's death in 1604, any unfinished works were touched up or completed by other playwrights. Orthodox Shakespeareans deride this as a 'jumble sale' scenario. You'd have to imagine something along the lines of Middleton, Wilkins and Fletcher coming upon Oxford's estate sale in 1604, finding these unfinished plays for the having and each making a grab for them, with the dextrous Fletcher making off with three, the others with one each.

The Oxfordian claim that lesser playwrights touched up the works attributed to Shakespeare but written by de Vere by 1604 had until now proved quite difficult to refute. But editors of the collaborative plays have recently shown that some of these late plays could not have been started by one writer and later finished by another. A representative example appears in Lois Potter's Arden edition of *The Two Noble Kinsmen*, where Potter shows that Fletcher wasn't adequately aware of what Shakespeare was up to in the previous scene. In Act 2, scene 1, Shakespeare's has a Jailor's Daughter describe how Palamon and Arcite 'discourse of many things, but nothing of their own restraint and disasters' (2.1.40–1). The friends appear on the upper stage at the end of the scene but never exit – and that's where Shakespeare leaves them. Fletcher, independently writing the scene that immediately follows, clearly had only a rough idea of what Shakespeare was busy writing in his assigned section, and has Palamon and Arcite appear on the main stage. And when they start to speak they contradict what the Jailor's Daughter has just told us in the scene Shakespeare wrote, for the pair act as if they are meeting for first time since the battle, with Palamon asking 'How do you, noble cousin?' and Arcite replying 'How do you, sir?' (2.2.1–2). Such discrepancies, while no doubt ironed out by the company in production, are still visible in the surviving script – and render highly improbable the argument that Fletcher is completing an old unfinished playscript that fell into his hands. Things were a lot easier in the old days for those who doubted Shakespeare's authorship, when it was still possible to imagine the 'real' author having his latest play delivered surreptitiously to the stage door at the Globe.

Epilogue

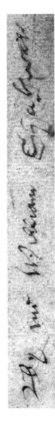

The controversy over Shakespeare's authorship has proven to be, in retrospect, a long footnote to the larger story of the way we read now. We've inherited many ideas about writing that emerged in the eighteenth century, especially an interest in literature as both an expression and an exploration of the self. This development – part of what distinguishes the 'modern' from the 'early modern' – has shaped the work of many of our most celebrated authors, whose personal experiences indelibly and visibly mark their writing. It's fair to say that the fiction and poetry of many of the finest writers of the past century or so – and I'm thinking here of Conrad, Proust, Lawrence, Joyce, Woolf, Kafka, Plath, Ellison, Lowell, Sexton, Roth and Coetzee, to name but a few – has been deeply autobiographical. The link between the life and the work is one of the things we're curious about and look for when we pick up the latest book by a favourite author.

Over the past decade or so, interest in writers' lives has only intensified. Creative-writing programmes and bestseller lists confirm how pervasive self-revelation has become in our literary culture. An author photo and few sentences of biography on the dust jacket are no longer enough; readers now turn to a writer's home page and blog. Hardly a year goes by without a scandal in which yet another writer is vilified for peddling fiction that could never sell except in the guise of a memoir. If the life fails to correspond to the work, something is wrong, and we feel cheated when invention masquerades as hard-earned experience.

'By me William Shakespeare,' from Shakespeare's Will, 1616

The extent to which so much that now gets written is autobiographical can easily alter the expectations we bring to all kinds of imaginative writing. We now assume that novels necessarily reveal something about a writer's life (so that, for example, it has become a truth universally acknowledged that Elizabeth Bennet's romantic longings in *Pride and Prejudice* are a barely-disguised version of Jane Austen's). At the same time, many literary biographies are supplanting the fictional works they are meant to illuminate, to the point where *Ariel* and *The Bell Jar* struggle to find a readership that books about Sylvia Plath's marriage and suicide now command. In such a climate, it's hard not to assume that literary works — of the past no less than of the present — are inescapably autobiographical.

This has been a blessing for those who deny Shakespeare's authorship, whose claims stand or fall on the core belief that literature is, and always has been, autobiographical. Consult the works of recent sceptics and you'll learn from Diana Price that 'creative writers cannot help but reveal themselves in their work', and from Hank Whittemore that the works attributed to Shakespeare are 'nonfiction dressed as fiction'. At one point or another, every writer who rejects Shakespeare's authorship says much the same thing. As the editor of the Oxfordian newsletter *Shakespeare Matters* recently conceded, 'without the evidence of the plays and poems of Shakespeare, there would be no authorship debate', for the 'works themselves are the primary evidence in the whole matter'. While I have focused in this book on the Baconians and Oxfordians, this holds true for the case made for *every* rival candidate.

For most of the twentieth century, C. J. Sisson's withering attack in 1934 on the excesses of Victorian biographers — 'The Mythical Sorrows of Shakespeare' — deterred scholars tempted to interpret Shakespeare's works as overtly autobiographical. Sisson's warnings were reinforced in the 1970s by Samuel Schoenbaum, whose *William Shakespeare: A Documentary Life* offered a model of literary biography that refused to stray beyond the documented facts. But this reluctance to speculate about autobiography embedded within the works failed to satisfy modern readers hungry for a different sort of life of Shakespeare, one more suited to popular notions of literary self-revelation.

The turn of the millennium witnessed a revival of claims that hadn't appeared in mainstream studies of Shakespeare since the Victorian age. Michael Wood's *In Search of Shakespeare*, which first aired as a BBC television series in 2003, led the way, assuring us that the Sonnets were 'mainly private records of real events and emotions, however much reshaped for publication'. Wood adds that Shakespeare's 'sexual jealousy has a subtext of his own physical decline and anxiety about his sexual performance'. Shakespeare's infatuation with a young man was no less fraught; take 'Sonnet 33', for example: 'a modern psychologist would certainly be interested in Shakespeare's passionate, almost desperate love for a seventeen-year-old in the year after his son's death. In today's terms, it was very adaptive, a kind of transference.' Wood admits that some of his claims are speculative. Though he concedes, for example, that 'we have no evidence' for what Shakespeare was thinking while at work on *The Tempest*, he nonetheless concludes that 'for a writer as intelligent, and as conscious of the illusion of theatre, as he was, it is hardly possible that an autobiographical edge to the plot was not in his mind'.

A year later, Stephen Greenblatt's bestselling *Will in the World* gave this approach the seal of approval of the leading American Shakespearean of the day. Greenblatt admits straight away that 'the whole impulse to explore Shakespeare's life arises from the powerful conviction that his plays and poems spring not only from other plays and poems but from things he knew firsthand, in his body and soul'. Rather than consider what historical developments gave rise to this conviction, he focuses instead on how firsthand experience can be retrieved from Shakespeare's surviving works, allowing extraordinary access into the poet's desires and anxieties. As Greenblatt sees it, Shakespeare 'turned everything life had dealt him – painful crises of social standing, sexuality, and

[299]

religion — into the uses of art . . . He had managed even to transform his grief and perplexity at the death of his son into an aesthetic resource.'

Shakespeare's wooing of Anne Hathaway 'offered a compelling
dream of pleasure' enacted in plays like *Two Gentlemen of Verona*
and *Taming of the Shrew*, while the story of their subsequent,
unhappy marriage is replayed in the 'frustrated craving for intimacy' found in so many later plays. This sour portrayal of married life
— confirmed for him in how Shakespeare treated Anne Hathaway
in his will — makes it difficult for Greenblatt '*not* to read his works
in the context of his decision to live for most of a long marriage
away from his wife'. And if 'there is one thing that the sonnets,
taken as biographical documents, strongly suggest, it is that he
could not find what he craved, emotionally or sexually, within his
marriage'. Two hundred years on we have come full circle, back to
where Malone began.

Greenblatt is far from the only prominent academic to speculate about the life. In his 2007 biography *Shakespeare Revealed*
(tellingly subtitled *Decoding a Hidden Life* by his American publishers) René Weis, a leading British scholar and editor, similarly
concludes that 'the plays and poems contain important clues'
about 'Shakespeare's inner life'. The Sonnets, for Weis as well, are
particularly revealing. Their metaphors about 'strength by limping
sway disabled' and being 'made lame by Fortune's dearest spite',
for example, suggest that Shakespeare himself may have walked
with a limp, perhaps a result of a childhood illness or 'an accident
like a fall from a horse'. Again and again, for Weis, things that
happened in Shakespeare's life resurface in the plays: there 'is
every reason for Shakespeare to have modelled his younger heroines on his own daughter'; in *Twelfth Night* 'Shakespeare indulges
in the fantasy of resurrecting a lost male twin'; and in *Othello*,
'Iago's latent homosexuality may also connect guiltily with
Shakespeare'. Like Freud, Greenblatt and many others, Weis
believes that it was the death of his father that prompted
Shakespeare 'to write a play named after his dead son' — leading

him to break from scholarly consensus and conclude, improbably, that *Hamlet* was written as late as 1602.

This sort of speculation has become commonplace in popular biographies of Shakespeare, filtering down to the classroom and serving as a model for studies of other Renaissance dramatists. It's clearly an occupational hazard, and I flinch when I think of my own trespasses in classrooms and in print, despite my best efforts to steer clear of biographical speculation. Nobody describes this problem better than Jonathan Bate in his recent reflections on the Sonnets, published in *The Times*:

Don't be drawn into the trap of supposing that they are autobiographical: that is an illusion of Shakespeare's art. But it's very hard to stop yourself. When I worked on them for my book *The Genius of Shakespeare* in the 1990s, I became convinced that I had identified the dark lady: she was the wife of John Florio, the Italian tutor in the household of the Earl of Southampton. When I returned to them recently for my book *Soul of the Age*, I became convinced that I had identified the rival poet: he was John Davies of Hereford, the greatest calligrapher in England and a hanger-on in the circle of the Earl of Pembroke.

'Each time,' Bate concludes, 'the poems had worked their magic: they had made me project a story of my own into their narrative. They work like love itself by making you want to join your story to that of another.'

Bate's remarks were seized upon as a direct challenge to those who doubted that Shakespeare wrote the plays. William Niederkorn immediately responded to Bate in a *New York Times* editors' blog: 'Why do exalted Shakespeare scholars want us to think the Sonnets are purely imaginative invention?' For Niederkorn, professors who refuse to accept that the Sonnets 'depict the life of the author' as well as those who 'cast their lot with the biography of Shakespeare as an unmatched literary genius arising from undistinguished circumstances' have 'good reason to deny the Sonnets' reality'. Niederkorn coyly leaves this good reason unspoken – that the man from Stratford had nothing to do with the Sonnets' composition — choosing instead to steer *New York Times* readers to a rival paper's story about prominent Shakespeare sceptics as well as to the weblink to the 'Declaration of Reasonable Doubt'.

The more that Shakespeare scholars encourage autobiographical readings of the plays and poems, the more they legitimate assumptions that underlie the claims of all those who dismiss the idea that Shakespeare wrote the plays. And every step scholars have taken toward embracing such readings has encouraged their adversaries to make even more speculative claims. The recent publication of Hank Whittemore's Oxfordian reading of the Sonnets, *The Monument*, offers a glimpse of where things may be heading. Even other Oxfordians (as William Boyle, the editor of *Shakespeare Matters*, put it when news of Whittemore's work first circulated) saw that they were 'undoubtedly journeying into new territory', one that was both 'controversial — and risky'. The Sonnets could now be read not as primarily fictional creations but as 'documentary evidence every bit as important and potent as any letters, any diary, or anything to be found in the Calendar of State Papers. In fact, in some instances the Sonnets provide historical information that exists nowhere else.'

In November 2008, I joined ninety or so people gathered at London's Globe Theatre to hear Whittemore share his work. It turned out to be an elegant revival of the Prince Tudor theory. The story of the Sonnets could be traced back to when Elizabeth, enamoured of the young Earl of Oxford, slept with him. The product of their union was the Earl of Southampton. The Sonnets — especially numbers 27 through to 126 — turn out to be a series of missives from Oxford to their royal child. This sequence of poems was written from 1601, in the aftermath of the abortive Essex rebellion (for which Southampton, a friend of Essex, was imprisoned), through to 1603 and the accession of King James, who displaced Southampton, the true heir to the throne. Interwoven with this suppressed history was an imaginative reading of the Sonnets in which Oxford serves as an advocate for his son, securing his release from prison in exchange for renouncing any claims to the throne. For Whittemore, 'Oxford used the sonnets as a genuine outlet for his grief, expressing the personal torment of having to blame himself for Southampton's fate.'

It was a spellbinding performance, as perfect a marriage of conspiratorial history and autobiographical analysis as one could imagine. If the enthusiastic response of the audience that evening was any indication, Oxfordian concerns about the riskiness of Whittemore's approach were misplaced. I looked around the room and saw the same kind of people – middle-aged, sensibly dressed, middle-class – who regularly attend lectures about Shakespeare, nodding their heads in agreement and laughing aloud at the funny parts. I found it all both impressive and demoralising, a vision of a world in which a collective comfort with conspiracy theory, spurious history and construing fiction as autobiographical fact had passed a new threshold.

I left the Globe wondering what mainstream biographers might say in response to Oxfordians who insist that Edward de Vere had a stronger claim to have written *Hamlet* and *Lear*, since – unlike the glover's son from Stratford – he had been captured by pirates and had three daughters. I can readily understand why this is a conversation that Shakespeareans who believe that autobiographical evidence counts are reluctant to have. But refusing to acknowledge that they have been doing similar things in their own books – even if their topical readings are far less fanciful and the author whose life they read out of the works is the one named on the title pages – rightly infuriates those who don't believe that Shakespeare of Stratford had the life experience to write the plays. I was left wondering whether Shakespeare scholars ignore their adversaries (when not vilifying them) because they share with them more unspoken assumptions about the intersection of life and literature than they care to admit – and indeed, were the first to profess. If they would concede as much, they might well conclude, as Prospero said of Caliban, 'This thing of darkness I acknowledge mine.' Perhaps it's time to shift our attention from debating who wrote Shakespeare's works to whether it's possible to discover the author's emotional, sexual and religious life through them.

The evidence strongly suggests that imaginative literature in general and plays in particular in Shakespeare's day were rarely if ever a vehicle for self-revelation. With the exception of confessions of faith and some lyric poetry, autobiography as a genre and as an impulse was extremely unusual. And even in instances when sixteenth-century lyric poets like Edmund Spenser or George Gascoigne speak about themselves, it is in the tradition of the invented persona adopted by Chaucer in his *Canterbury Tales* or Dante in his *Divine Comedy*, as characters in their own fictions rather than anything resembling what we now understand as autobiographical. Those who have scoured the period for evidence of autobiographical writing have come up almost empty-handed. In his pioneering study of the origins of British autobiography, Paul Delaney found little in the sixteenth century, and even when he turned to the seventeenth century he could find only two hundred examples, half of which were 'religious autobiographies'. In her recent and promisingly titled *Tudor Autobiography*, Meredith Skura has revisited this barren ground, but even with a considerably looser definition of autobiographical writing she located only a dozen or so Tudor writers 'who found ways to incorporate their lives into a sermon, a saint's life, courtly and popular verse, a history book, a traveler's report, a husbandry book' – everything, it seems, but a play.

Those who believe that Elizabethan plays were autobiographical ought to be able to show that contemporaries were on the lookout for confessional allusions, as we know some were for topical ones. Yet not a single such contemporary observation survives for any play in the period, including Shakespeare's; however much on the minds of modern biographers, it doesn't appear to have occurred to Elizabethan playgoers. It's hard to avoid concluding that autobiographical details Shakespeare is alleged to have embedded in the plays are a lot like Baconian ciphers: something hidden there for posterity, about which contemporaries were oblivious, but that hundreds of years later brilliant detective work can uncover and decode.

Even if Shakespeare occasionally drew in his poems and plays on personal experiences, and I don't doubt that he did, I don't see how anyone can know with any confidence if or when or where he does so. Surely he was too accomplished a writer to recycle them in the often clumsy and undigested way that critics in search of autobiographical traces – advocates and sceptics of his authorship alike – would have us believe. Because of that, and because we know almost nothing about his personal experiences, those moments in his work which build upon what he may have felt remain invisible to us, and were probably only slightly more visible to those who knew him well.

It's wiser to accept that these experiences can no longer be recovered. We don't know what we are looking for in any case, and even if we did, I'm not at all sure we would know how to interpret it correctly. In the end, attempts to identify personal experiences will only result in acts of projection, revealing more about the biographer than about Shakespeare himself. It's worth recalling the experience of T. S. Eliot, who was struck by the inability of contemporary biographers to untangle the personal from the fictional: 'I am used . . . to having my personal biography reconstructed from passages which I got out of books, or which I invented out of nothing because they sounded well; and to having my biography invariably ignored in what I *did* write from person-al experience.'

If we can't get the autobiographical in Eliot's poetry and drama right – though there are many still alive who knew him, as well as a trove of letters and interviews to draw upon – what hope have we of doing so with Shakespeare? You would think that the endless alternatives proposed by those reading his life out of the works – good husband or bad, crypto-Catholic or committed Protestant, gay or straight, misogynist or feminist, or for that matter, that the works were really written by Bacon or Oxford, Marlowe and so on

— would cancel each other out and lead to the conclusion that the plays and poems are not transparently autobiographical.

A more serious objection to hunting for the life in the works is that it assumes that what makes people who they are now made people who they were back in Shakespeare's day. Social historians have shown how risky such an assumption can be. There's little evidence that the lives of early modern men and women resembled our own. Their formative years certainly didn't. Childhood was brief and most adolescents, rich and poor, were sent from home to live and serve in other households. As a result, children — even royal ones — didn't live under the same roof as their parents for very long. Households, far more than families, were the domestic unit people considered themselves part of; these went beyond simple ties of blood or marriage, and one might pass through several households in the course of a lifetime. Despite all this, it's not easy to break that preconception so central to psychobiography, that the modern, nuclear family and the developmental struggles intrinsic to it were the norm back then too.

Family dynamics that we find in Shakespeare's fictions are not necessarily what we find in his world. Likewise we should not assume that people married at thirteen just because Juliet did (both men and women waited, on the average, until they were twenty-five, and a surprising proportion, perhaps as many as one in five, including Shakespeare's three brothers, never married at all). It's odd that those who think they have discovered Shakespeare's life in his works focus so exclusively on his relationships with his father, son, wife and daughters — all of whom he lived apart from for most of his adult life. The whole business is so circular as to be suspect. For all we know (and the point is that we don't know) Shakespeare's most meaningful relationships might have been with fellow writers, actors, sharers, patrons, landlords, neighbours, lovers, friends or household members with whom he interacted in the course of the quarter-century in which he was writing, but for which no evidence survives.

The lives of women within Elizabethan households have been

especially misunderstood, when not ignored. Thanks to studies like Germaine Greer's *Shakespeare's Wife*, it's now clear that many of the documents relating to Shakespeare's economic activities in Stratford – from processing malt to petty debts – concerned matters that were under Anne Hathaway's jurisdiction, part of the complicated business of overseeing a household for close to thirty years while her husband was mostly off in London. Here, too, biographers – obsessed with the notion of Shakespeare as malt dealer and unable to imagine Anne Hathaway as anything but a spurned, passive and possibly adulterous wife – have got it wrong.

There's also reason to be sceptical about the extent to which early modern emotional responses resemble ours. For one thing, recurrent and devastating outbreaks of plague, death in childbirth, harvest failures and high infant-mortality rates may have taken a toll on social and familial bonds. For another, these bonds didn't last as long. People lived on the average until their mid-forties. Some, like Shakespeare's parents and daughters, lived quite long lives. But six of Shakespeare's seven brothers and sisters didn't survive past the age of forty-six and he died at fifty-two. Extraordinary claims have been made about Shakespeare's grief over his young son Hamnet's death. But there's a good chance that he only saw his son a handful of times after leaving Stratford-upon-Avon for London not long after Hamnet was born.

Other imagined constants such as love and marriage weren't the same then either. Stratford records indicate that Shakespeare's decision to marry at eighteen was exceptional. Given the late age at which people got married and the extremely low illegitimacy rates at the time, sexual desire must have either been sublimated or found an outlet in non-procreative sex – perhaps both. People didn't think in terms of modern binaries of 'heterosexuality' or 'homosexuality' either. Moreover, the degree of personal privacy and hygiene we enjoy today would have been foreign to Shakespeare and his contemporaries, who shared rooms and even beds, and lived at a time when the use of objects like the fork, the handkerchief and the nightdress were only beginning to become widespread.

Even the meaning of key concepts, such as what constitutes an 'individual', weren't the same. Writers, including Shakespeare, were only beginning to speak of individuality in the modern sense of 'distinctiveness' or 'specialness' – the exact opposite of what it had long meant: 'inseparability'. You can search in vain through the handful of Elizabethan works that even touch on the subject for anything that resembles modern notions of social or psychological development. Henry Cuffe, writing about *The Differences of the Ages of Man's Life* in 1600, can't get much beyond choosing between Pythagoras' division of life into the four stages of 'childhood, youth, manhood, old age' and Aristotle's tripartite division into 'childhood, flourishing man-age, and old-age'. Cuffe doesn't think in terms of individual psychology; people fall into types, and types behave according to imbalances in heat or moisture in their bodies, which, for Cuffe, explains why children can't reason, fretful ones die young and old men are suspicious. While Cuffe may be dismissed as a stodgy scholar trapped within inherited theoretical categories, someone who would be more comfortable with Ben Jonson's humour plays than the complex psychology of Shakespeare's, his work, and that of others like him, suggests that Elizabethans didn't think of motivation, individuality or behaviour in the ways we do now. Nor did they subscribe to modern notions of coming of age, which define so many cradle-to-grave biographies of Shakespeare, imposing on him sexual, religious or familial traumas, and sometimes all three, for which no substantive evidence, barring that imported from the plays, survives.

Pre-modern conceptions of self and of one's place in the world were not identical to our own, and though social historians are still defining the differences, those who view the lives of early modern men and women through the lens of modernity ought to proceed with caution. Moreover, given that this was an age of faith (or at least one in which church attendance was mandatory), religion too played a far greater role in shaping how life, death and the afterlife were imagined. As much as we might want Shakespeare to have been like us, he wasn't – and biographers lead us astray when they invite us to imagine that he was.

A friend recently shared with me a terrific review in the *Financial Times* by Susan Elderkin about novels set in places that their authors had never visited. Elderkin writes:

A few years ago on Radio 4's *Front Row*, Mark Lawson conducted a memorable interview with the author Sid Smith who had won the Whitbread First Novel award for his book *Something Like a House.* Set in China during the Cultural Revolution, the novel was widely praised for its evocation of peasant life . . . Lawson, impressed by Smith's depiction, asked if he spoke fluent Mandarin. Smith said no, he didn't speak Chinese. Lawson asked if he had worked in China. No, he hadn't. At this point Lawson became agitated. 'But you've been to China,' he said. There was a short pause, followed by Smith's calm assertion that no, actually, he had never been to China. Lawson was right to be astounded. *Something Like a House* is full of odd details about life in China that you'd think would take years of first-hand experience to note . . . What was most enjoyable about the interview, though, was not Lawson's surprise but Smith's refusal to be even slightly apologetic. He found his China in the London Library, and from films, newspapers and the internet.

The same week, while at work in the British Library, I called up one of the two surviving copies of a volume of Elizabethan poetry called *Licia, or Poems of Love.* It was published anonymously in 1593 and contains fifty-one sonnets, along with an ode, an elegy and an unusual poem about 'The Rising to the Crown of Richard the Third', told as if 'written by himself'. It was just the kind of thing that might have caught Shakespeare's eye, busy at this time on his own Sonnets and perhaps on his *Richard the Third* as well. The author of *Licia* appended a longish preface, in the middle of which is a remarkable sentence that anticipates Sid Smith's conversation with Mark Lawson by four centuries: 'A man may write of love, and not be in love, as well of husbandry, and not go to plough, or of witches and be none.' It's as apt a description of the author of Shakespeare's Sonnets, *As You Like It* and *Macbeth* as any I know.

It's unlikely that the identity of *Licia*'s author was widely known in his own day. Scholars have since learned (from a stray remark of his son) that it was written by Giles Fletcher, who in 1593 was a far cry from the persona of the young lover conveyed by these sonnets: married and middle-aged, father to at least seven children, he was also a veteran diplomat who had recently returned from a dangerous mission to the court of the Tsar. Fletcher had hoped to write a history of Elizabeth's reign, but shelved plans for that after Lord Burghley refused to approve such a politically sensitive project. So he tried his hand at something completely different – 'this kind of poetry wherein I wrote, I did it only to try my humour'. He borrows heavily (we might say plagiarises, though the concept would have been foreign to Fletcher) from Latin poetry, especially Angerianus' *Poetae Tres Elegantissimi*, with a nod here and there to Sidney's *Astrophel and Stella*. And it's likely that the unusual name Licia is taken from Sidney as well, whose *Arcadia*, published three years earlier, describes at some length, and a bit tongue-in-cheek, paintings of 'eleven conquered beauties', including the 'Queen of *Licia*'. Sonnets don't have to be autobiographical; they don't even have to be original. Poets assume personae. Mistresses can be fictional (though that didn't stop a young Cambridge scholar from bragging, after Fletcher's book appeared, that he had slept with Licia).

If Giles Fletcher could compose sonnets to 'try' his 'humour', Shakespeare could have done so too. If Sid Smith could have asked around or read enough to write convincingly about China, Shakespeare could easily have done the same with Venice and Verona. We know that he was voracious in his pursuit of sources: rather than rest content with what he found in one or two books about the reign of Richard II, he managed to get his hands on almost everything written about him. The argument that he could never have had access to so many books unless he was a wealthy aristocrat is nonsense. Nobody asks this question about Thomas

Dekker, who in 1599 alone worked on eleven plays (with a dizzying number of printed sources) after his release from prison for debt. How did professional playwrights like Dekker and Shakespeare gain access to so many books? We don't know for sure. They may have owned some, borrowed others and browsed in London's many bookstalls in search of additional sources of inspiration. Elizabethan playing companies spent upward of £10 for a single elaborate costume, though only £6 for a finished play. It may well be that they also maintained a stock of comparatively inexpensive books, since it was in their interest to provide dramatists whose proposed scripts they had purchased with the necessary materials to research and write their promised plays.

Shakespeare's knowledge of the world was not limited to what he found in books. It was not difficult in Elizabethan London, where thousands of 'strangers' or foreign-born individuals were living, to encounter all sorts of travellers – both those from abroad visiting or living in London, and English merchants or voyagers who had seen a good bit of the world. A curious Shakespeare could have learned everything he needed to know about the Italian settings of his plays from a few choice conversations.

This obsession with hands-on experience extends to the playwright's familiarity with hawking, hunting, tennis and other aristocratic pursuits. It would be surprising if, during his years as a travelling player, performing at various aristocratic households around England, Shakespeare hadn't frequently observed the rich at play. As for the ways of the court: Shakespeare visited royal palaces scores of times and was ideally placed to observe the ways of monarchs and courtiers. Insisting that Shakespeare could only write about what he had felt or done, as Steevens warned Malone two hundred years ago, can lead to some very unsettling conclusions. If the blood-splattered plays are truly to be taken as autobiographical evidence, whoever wrote them had to have unusual access to the mind of a murderer. They are also full of scoundrels, liars, cheats, adulterers, cowards, orphans, heroes, rapists, pimps, bawds and madmen. The plays are not an à la carte menu, from which we pick characters who will satisfy our appetite for Shakespeare's personality while passing over less appetising choices. He imagined them all.

One of the most habitual charges made against Shakespeare is that he didn't have enough formal education to have written the plays – and, some have argued, there's no record that he received *any* formal education. What they fail to add is that no evidence survives that anybody in Shakespeare's day was educated in Stratford, since the records for all pupils at that time have been lost (though we know the names of the schoolmasters and the Tudor schoolroom in the town's Guildhall survives to this day). Are we to imagine that the London publisher Richard Field, Shakespeare's age-mate, went uneducated as well because there's no record of his attending school? Or that the sons of other leading figures in Stratford, some of whom went on to Oxford, were unlettered before arriving at university? Scholars have exhaustively reconstructed the curriculum in Elizabethan grammar schools and have shown that what Shakespeare and Field would have learned there – and for that matter, what the many playgoers who had a comparable education would have been taught in similar schools – was roughly equivalent to a university degree today, with a better facility in Latin than that of a typical classics major.

No less groundless is the argument that Shakespeare's vocabulary was far greater than someone with only a grammar-school education could have possessed. As David Crystal, the leading expert on Shakespeare's language, has shown, the myth that 'Shakespeare had the largest vocabulary of any English writer' is hard to dispel. Impressive claims are often tossed about, such as that Shakespeare used as many as thirty thousand different words. It's true if you count variants (both 'cat' and 'cats', or 'say' and 'says'); otherwise, his vocabulary was about twenty thousand words. It's a sizeable figure but not all that surprising, given the vast range of subjects treated in his plays and poems as well as how much of his work survives (the complete *Works* runs to just under nine hundred thousand words). Crystal also notes that 'most of us use at least 50,000 words' out of the roughly one million that are available in English today – and yet few of us with working vocabularies twice Shakespeare's can boast of having written anything of the order of *Romeo and Juliet*.

Ignorance of what a grammar-school education offered has also led sceptics to claim that the true author of the plays intentionally wrote over the heads of most of those who went to see them: 'what is all that culture and erudition doing in the plays', Diana Price wonders, if Shakespeare is merely writing 'primarily for the general public over at the Globe?' This isn't snobbery so much as an impoverished sense of how much playgoers who paid to see Shakespeare's plays – and for that matter the even more erudite ones of Marlowe, Jonson, Webster, Marston and Chapman – readily understood. Ignored, too, in attacks on Shakespeare's limited if typical formal education, is the kind of informal study of books and foreign tongues that aspiring writers, then, as now, engage in long after classroom education has come to an end. We have no idea how much of this Shakespeare undertook in the decade or more between the time he finished school and he began writing and acting professionally.

What I find most disheartening about the claim that Shakespeare of Stratford lacked the life experience to have written the plays is that it diminishes the very thing that makes him so exceptional: his imagination. As an aspiring actor, Shakespeare must have displayed a talent for imagining himself as any number of characters onstage. When he turned to writing, he demonstrated an even more powerful imaginative capacity, one that allowed him to create roles of such depth and complexity – Rosalind, Hamlet, Lear, Juliet, Timon, Brutus, Leontes and Cleopatra, along with hundreds of others, great and small – that even the least of them, four centuries later, seems fully human and distinctive. What's especially fascinating is that he didn't actually invent most of these characters: he found almost all of them, half-formed, not in the people he knew but in the works of other writers – including

North's translation of Plutarch's *Lives* and Holinshed's *Chronicles*, sources he turned to again and again. The stories and portraits they contained stuck in his mind, sometimes for years, until he was able to see what was needed to transform them utterly and breathe life into them.

The argument for writing from personal experience is implicitly an argument for a kind of realism. When it served his purposes, Shakespeare wrote realistically; but when realism fell short, he never hesitated to bring divinities onstage, have a character enter invisible, make time run backwards, or bring a statue to life. If Shakespeare really had been interested in writing about what he knew first-hand, he would have done what Jonson, Dekker, Middleton and many other playwrights at the time chose to do: set his plays where he grew up, or in his adopted city, London. But he chose instead to give his imagination freer reign, locating his plots in distant lands and former times – Vienna, Verona, Venice, and ancient Britain, Athens, Troy, Tyre and Rome. In *Cymbeline*, he even has modern-day Italians and ancient Romans rub elbows. Even when he is closest to personal experience and sets much of *As You Like It* in a version of Warwickshire's Forest of Arden, it turns out to be a magical landscape inhabited not only by shepherds and hermits but also by lions, snakes and a divinity, Hymen.

'Imagination', the *Oxford English Dictionary* reminds us, means 'forming a mental concept of what is not actually present to the senses', one that 'does not correspond to the reality of things'. In simple terms, then, imagination begins where experience – what we see, hear or feel – ends. Shakespeare may not tell us a lot about his personal life in the plays, but he often shares what he thinks about the workings of the imagination. It's no accident that Hamlet, the character widely acknowledged as his greatest creation, argues most cogently for the power of imagination, confiding to Ophelia: 'I am very proud, revengeful, ambitious; with more offences at my beck than I have thoughts to put them in, imagination to give them shape, or time to act them in.' Where Hamlet most resembles his creator is not in the fact that he was captured by pirates or mourned his father's death, but in his capacity to give shape and words to often wild thoughts: as he demands of Horatio, 'Why may not imagination trace the noble dust of Alexander till he find it stopping a bunghole?'

Helena, Lear, Antonio, Miranda, Vincentio, Gower, Malvolio and Polixenes are among the many other characters – rulers and lovers, the puritanical and the guileless, the self-deluded and the self-knowing – who reflect upon imagination in the plays. Fittingly, it's the character most sceptical about the power of imagination, Theseus in *A Midsummer Night's Dream*, to whom Shakespeare assigns its most memorable definition:

> I never may believe
> These antique fables, nor these fairy toys.
> Lovers and madmen have such seething brains,
> Such shaping fantasies, that apprehend
> More than cool reason ever comprehends.
> The lunatic, the lover and the poet
> Are of imagination all compact.
> One sees more devils than vast hell can hold;
> That is the madman. The lover, all as frantic,
> Sees Helen's beauty in a brow of Egypt.
> The poet's eye, in fine frenzy rolling,
> Doth glance from heaven to earth, from earth to heaven;
> And as imagination bodies forth
> The forms of things unknown, the poet's pen
> Turns them to shapes and gives to airy nothing
> A local habitation and a name.
> Such tricks hath strong imagination
> That, if it would but apprehend some joy,
> It comprehends some bringer of that joy.
> (5.1.2–20)

One of the great pleasures of this speech is that Theseus is him-self 'an antique fable'. Along with lovers and lunatics, writers share a heightened capacity to imagine the 'forms of things unknown'. But only writers can turn them 'to shapes' and give 'to airy nothing / A local habitation and a name'. It's hard to imagine a better definition of the mystery of literary creation. Not long after delivering this speech, Theseus watches a play performed by Bottom and the other rude mechanicals and finds himself transformed by the experience. His reaction to their play ranks among the most wonderful speeches in Shakespeare: 'The best in this kind are but shadows; and the worst are no worse, if imagination amend them.' His captive bride-to-be Hippolyta is quick to remind him, as well as us: 'It must be your imagination then, and not theirs' (5.1.210–12).

When I first explored the idea of writing this book some years ago, a friend unnerved me by asking, 'What difference does it make who wrote the plays?' The reflexive answer I offered in response is now much clearer to me: 'A lot.' It makes a difference as to how we imagine the world in which Shakespeare lived and wrote. It makes an even greater difference as to how we understand how much has changed from early modern to modern times. But the greatest difference of all concerns how we read the plays. We can believe that Shakespeare himself thought that poets could give to 'airy nothing' a 'local habitation and a name'. Or we can conclude that this 'airy nothing' turns out to be a disguised something that needs to be decoded, and that Shakespeare couldn't imagine 'the forms of things unknown' without having experienced them first-hand. It's a stark and consequential choice.

Bibliographical Essay

The literature on the Shakespeare authorship controversy is vast. A full accounting, if it were even possible, would multiply the length of this book several times over. What follows, then, is a guide limited to the specific sources I have drawn on in print, manuscript and electronic form, so that anyone interested can retrace or follow up on my research.

For those seeking an overview of the controversy, there are a number of fine surveys, all of which I have found helpful and reliable: R. C. Churchill, *Shakespeare and His Betters* (London, 1958); H. N. Gibson, *The Shakespeare Claimants* (London, 1962); Warren Hope and Kim R. Holston, *The Shakespeare Controversy* (Jefferson, North Carolina, 1992); and John F. Michell, *Who Wrote Shakespeare?* (London, 1996). See, too, William Leahy, ed., *Shakespeare and His Authors: Critical Perspectives on the Authorship Question* (London, 2010). For early bibliographies of the controversy, see W. H. Wyman, *Bibliography of the Bacon–Shakespeare Controversy* (Cincinnati, 1884), and Joseph S. Galland's dissertation, *Digesta Anti–Shakespeareana* (Evanston, Illinois, 1949).

Those interested in the strongest arguments in favour of Shakespeare's authorship should consult Irvin Matus, *Shakespeare, in Fact* (New York, 1994) and Scott McCrea, *The Case for Shakespeare* (Westport, Conn., 2005). The best scholarly account remains S. Schoenbaum, *Shakespeare's Lives* (Oxford, 1970), extensively revised in 1991. Particularly recommended, and to which I am deeply indebted, are discussions of the authorship controversy that appear in F. E. Halliday, *The Cult of Shakespeare* (London, 1957), Marjorie Garber, *Shakespeare's Ghost Writers* (New York, 1987), Gary Taylor, *Reinventing Shakespeare* (New York, 1989), Harold Love, *Attributing Authorship* (Cambridge, 2002) and especially Jonathan Bate, *The Genius of Shakespeare* (London, 1997). Those seeking a point-by-point defence of Shakespeare's authorship should consult the website of David Kathman and Terry Ross, www.shakespeareauthorship.com, as well as Alan Nelson's: socrates.berkeley.edu/~ahnelson/authorsh.html.

Literature in support of alternative candidates – both print and digital – dwarfs that defending Shakespeare's claim. A few of the titles that I have found most useful are, in chronological order: George Greenwood, *The Shakespeare Problem Restated* (London, 1908); Gilbert Slater, *Seven Shakespeares* (London, 1931); Calvin Hoffman, *The Murder of the Man Who Was Shakespeare* (London, 1955); Charlton Ogburn, Jr, *The Mysterious William Shakespeare* (New York, 1984); Richard Whalen, *Shakespeare, Who Was He?* (Westport, Conn., 1994); Joseph Sobran, *Alias Shakespeare* (New York, 1997); Diana Price, *Shakespeare's Unorthodox Biography* (Westport, Conn., 2001); Brenda James and William D. Rubinstein, *The Truth Will Out: Unmasking the Real Shakespeare* (New York, 2006); Mark Anderson, *'Shakespeare' by Another Name* (New York, 2005); and Brian McClinton, *The Shakespeare Conspiracies* (Belfast, 2007). I'll refer to others as occasion demands. Those in search of a full array of arguments that challenge Shakespeare's claim and bolster those of other candidates have a host of online alternatives to choose from, the best of which include the 'Shakespearean Authorship Trust' (www.shakespeareanauthorshiptrust.org.uk); 'Francis Bacon's New Advancement of Learning' (www.sirbacon.org); the 'Shakespeare Fellowship' (www.shakespearefellowship.org); the 'Shakespeare Oxford Society' (www.shakespeare-oxford.com); the 'Marlowe-Shakespeare Connection' (marlowe-shakespeare.blogspot.com); and the 'De Vere Society' (www.deveresociety.co.uk).

When referring to specific facts about William Shakespeare's life in these pages, my sources, unless otherwise specified, are E. K. Chambers, *William Shakespeare: Facts and Problems*, 2 vols (Oxford, 1930); S. Schoenbaum, *William Shakespeare: A Documentary Life* (Oxford, 1975) and S. Schoenbaum, *William Shakespeare: Records and Images* (London, 1981). I have also made extensive use of the *Oxford Dictionary of National Biography* throughout. Unless I'm quoting the exact title of a book or article or need to quote the original spelling for a specific reason I have modernised spelling and punctuation. Quotations from the plays and poems are taken from *The Complete Works of Shakespeare*, ed. David Bevington, updated 4th edn (New York, 1997).

PROLOGUE

Cowell's lectures, which have never been published, are quoted from the manuscript in the Durning-Lawrence collection housed in Senate House Library, University of London, Durning-Lawrence Library, MS 294. *Some Reflections on the Life of William Shakespeare. A Paper Read before the Ipswich Philosophic Society by James Corton Cowell, February 7, 1805* [And a second paper, April 1805].

I have singled out a few of the many notable sceptics; James, Freud, Keller and Twain are discussed at length in chapters that follow. For Charlie Chaplin, see his *My Auto-Biography* (New York, 1964), where he writes 'I can hardly think it was the Stratford boy. Whoever wrote them had an aristocratic attitude.' Malcolm X relates in *The Autobiography of Malcolm X* (New York, 1965), that

Another hot debate I remember I was in had to do with the identity of Shakespeare . . . I just got intrigued over the Shakespearean dilemma. The King James translation of the Bible is considered the greatest piece of literature in English . . . They say that from 1604 to 1611, King James got poets to translate, to write the Bible. Well, if Shakespeare existed, he was then the top poet around. But Shakespeare is nowhere reported connected with the Bible. If he existed, why didn't King James use him?

According to Orson Welles, 'I think Oxford wrote Shakespeare. If you don't agree, there are some awfully funny coincidences to explain away' (quoted in Kenneth Tynan, *Persona Grata* [London, 1953]). Sir Derek Jacobi said that he was "99.9 per cent certain" the actual author of the plays and sonnets was Edward de Vere, the Earl of Oxford' (*Evening Standard*, 23 April 2009). For Elise Broach's young adult novel, see *Shakespeare's Secret* (New York, 2005).

For the suggestion that there is a conspiracy at work in the Shakespeare industry, see, for example, Charlton Ogburn, who writes that to 'prevent the unthinkable must be the primary concern of the Shakespeare Birthplace Trust', and adds that the Trust draws on a handsome budget, and that the National Endowment for the Humanities, Mellon and Guggenheim foundations contribute to the orthodox Shakespeare cause as well. He also writes: 'Of much greater importance, I feel sure, is the professional, economic, and psychological investment in Shakespeare orthodoxy by academicians on both sides of the ocean', and goes on to speak of the 'diabolical elements' in the case 'which make it exceedingly difficult for such authorities to divest themselves of their ties to him' (Ogburn, *The Mysterious William Shakespeare*).

For the discovery of the Cowell manuscript, see Allardyce Nicoll, 'The First Baconian', *Times Literary Supplement*, 25 February 1932. The wonderfully named William Jaggard pointed out in a letter to the *TLS* that Cowell placed Wilmot's residence in 'Barton-on-the-Heath', which he describes visiting 'six miles north of Stratford-on Avon' when in fact it is 'sixteen miles due south' (3 March 1932). The only previous effort I know of to examine the Cowell manuscript is described in Nathan Baca's report of Daniel Wright's unpublished research on Cowell and his suspicion that the document may be a forgery, in *Shakespeare Matters* 2 (Summer 2003). For more on the Durning-Lawrence collection, see K. E. Attar, 'Sir Edward Durning-Lawrence: A Baconian and His Books', *The Library* 5 (September 2004), pp. 294–315; K. E. Attar, 'From Private to Public: The Durning-Lawrence Library at the University of London', in *The Private Library*, 5th ser, vol. 10 (Autumn 2007), pp. 137–56; and Alexander Gordon, *Memoir of Lady Durning-Lawrence* (Privately printed, 1930). The forger (or forgers) clearly incorporated arguments set forth in Sidney Lee, 'A New Study of *Love's Labour's Lost*', *Gentleman's Magazine* (October 1880). For the receipt for the Cowell manuscript, see Senate House Library, University of London, DLL/1/10, which contains a half-sheet, perhaps eight by four inches, on which is written: 'Cowell M.S.S. £8 = 8 – 0 Lady Durning-Lawrence holds the Receipts.' The half-sheet offers no date or any other information about where it came from, from whom it was purchased or where these receipts are. There's a hole in the top right corner suggesting that something may have been attached.

For the earliest published claims that Shakespeare lent money or hoarded grain, see R. B. Wheler, *History and Antiquities of Stratford-upon-Avon* (Stratford, 1806); and vol. 1 of John Payne Collier, *The Works of William Shakespeare* (London, 1844). For the letter from Richard Quiney to Shakespeare, see Alan Stewart, *Shakespeare's Letters* (Oxford, 2008).

For more on Serres, see Olivia Wilmot Serres, *The Life of the Author of the Letters of Junius, the Rev. James Wilmot* (London, 1813); her entry in the *Dictionary of National Biography*; Bram Stoker, *Famous Imposters* (London, 1910); and Mary L. Pendered and Justinian Mallett, *Princess or Pretender?* (London, 1939).

SHAKESPEARE

IRELAND

For facts about Shakespeare (and when specific documents were discovered by scholars) see Chambers, *William Shakespeare*, and Schoenbaum, *William Shakespeare: A Documentary Life* as well as his *William Shakespeare: Records and Images*. For an overview of early modern diaries and biographies, see William Matthews, *British Diaries: An Annotated Bibliography of British Diaries Written between 1442 and 1942* (Berkeley, 1950), and Donald A. Stauffer, *English Biography before 1700* (Cambridge, Mass., 1930). Malone made his plea to search more widely for documents about Shakespeare in *Gentleman's Magazine* 65 (1795). See too, Sir James Prior, *Life of Edmond*

BIBLIOGRAPHICAL ESSAY

Malone, Editor of Shakespeare (London, 1860).

The Ireland story has been especially well documented. I have drawn on the following contemporary accounts: Samuel Ireland, *Miscellaneous Papers and Legal Instruments under the Head and Seal of William Shakspeare* (London, 1796); James Boaden, *A Letter to George Steevens, Esq. Containing a Critical Examination of the Papers of Shakespeare* (London, 1796); Edmond Malone, *An Inquiry into the Authenticity of Certain Miscellaneous Papers and Legal Instruments . . . Attributed to Shakespeare* (London, 1796); Samuel Ireland, *Mr Ireland's Vindication of His Conduct, Respecting the Publication of the Supposed Shakspeare MSS* (London, 1796); William-Henry Ireland, *An Authentic Account of the Shaksperian Manuscripts* (London, 1796); Francis Webb, *Shakespeare's Manuscripts, in the Possession of Mr Ireland, Examined* (London, 1796); Samuel Ireland, *An Investigation of Mr Malone's Claim to the Character of Scholar, or Critic, Being an Examination of His Inquiry into the Authenticity of the Shakspeare Manuscripts, &c., by Samuel Ireland* (London, 1797); George Chalmers, *An Apology for the Believers in the Shakspeare-Papers* (London, 1797); George Chalmers, *A Supplemental Apology for the Believers in the Shakspeare-Papers* (London, 1799); George Chalmers, *An Appendix to the Supplemental Apology for the Believers in the Suppositious Shakespeare-Papers* (London, 1800); William-Henry Ireland, *The Confessions of William Henry Ireland* (London, 1805); and William-Henry Ireland, *Vortigern: An Historical Play with an Original Preface* (London, 1832).

I have also drawn on the following modern accounts: Clement M. Ingleby, *The Shakespeare Fabrications* (London, 1859); Bernard Grebanier, *The Great Shakespeare Forgery* (New York, 1965); S. Schoenbaum, 'The Ireland Forgeries: An Unpublished Contemporary Account', *Shakespeare and Others* (Washington DC, 1985), pp. 144–53; Jeffrey Kahan's excellent *Reforging Shakespeare: The Story of a Theatrical Scandal* (London, 1998); Paul Baines, *The House of Forgery in Eighteenth-Century Britain* (Brookfield, Vermont, 1999); Patricia Pierce, *The Great Shakespeare Fraud: The Strange, True Story of William-Henry Ireland* (Phoenix Mill, 2004); and Tom Lockwood, 'Manuscript, Print and the Authentic Shakespeare: The Ireland Forgeries Again', *Shakespeare Survey* 59 (Cambridge, 2006), pp. 108–23. Finally, for what the small number of surviving early modern dramatic manuscripts looked like, see William Long, 'Precious Few: English Manuscript Playbooks', in *A Companion to Shakespeare*, ed. David Scott Kastan (Oxford, 1999), pp. 414–33, and Grace Ioppolo, *Dramatists and Their Manuscripts in the Age of Shakespeare, Jonson, Middleton and Heywood* (London, 2006).

[321]

SHAKESPEARE DEIFIED

For the deifying performances at Drury Lane, see Richard Fitzpatrick, *The Occasional Prologue, Written by the Rt. Hon. Major General Fitzpatrick, and Spoken by Mr Kemble, on Opening the Theatre Royal, Drury Lane, with Shakespeare's Macbeth, Monday, April 21st 1794* (London, 1794). See too, vol. 1 of *Biographia Dramatica*, ed. David Erskine Baker, Isaac Reed and Stephen Jones, 3 vols (London, 1812), and *The London Stage 1660–1800*, part 5, ed. Charles Beecher Hogan (Carbondale, 1968). On the deification of Shakespeare in general, see Robert Witbeck Babcock, *The Genesis of Shakespeare Idolatry 1766–1799* (Chapel Hill, 1931); Péter Dávidházi, *The Romantic Cult of Shakespeare* (Houndmills, 1998); Charles Laporte, 'The Bard, the Bible, and the Victorian Shakespeare Question', *English Literary History* 74 (2007), pp. 609–28; and Marcia Pointon, 'National Identity and the Afterlife of Shakespeare's Portraits', in *Searching for Shakespeare*, ed. Tarnya Cooper (London, 2006). Dryden's remarks about the divine Shakespeare can be found in *Aureng-Zebe* (1676), *The Tempest, or The Enchanted Island* (1670) and *All for Love* (1678). For Voltaire, see Thomas R. Lounsbury, *Shakespeare and Voltaire* (London, 1902). For an account of deifying Shakespeare in the visual arts, see William L. Pressly, *The Artist as Original Genius: Shakespeare's 'Fine Frenzy' in Late-Eighteenth-Century British Art* (Newark, 2007).

The literature on Garrick and the Jubilee is considerable. I have relied on Christian Deelman, *The Great Shakespeare Jubilee* (New York, 1964); Johanne M. Stochholm, *Garrick's Folly; the Shakespeare Jubilee of 1769 at Stratford and Drury Lane* (London, 1964); Martha W. England, *Garrick's Jubilee* (Columbus, Ohio, 1964); Halliday, *Cult of Shakespeare*; and Vanessa Cunningham, *Shakespeare and Garrick* (Cambridge, 2008); I quote from Samuel Foote, *Letter . . . to the Reverend Author of the Remarks, Critical and Christian* (London, 1760).

For the emergence of the Shakespeare expert, see Simon Jarvis, *Scholars and Gentlemen: Shakespearian Textual Criticism and Representations of Scholarly Labour, 1725–1765* (Oxford, 1995); Peter Seary, *Lewis Theobald and the Editing of Shakespeare* (Oxford, 1990); Marcus Walsh, *Shakespeare, Milton, and Eighteenth-Century Literary Editing* (Cambridge, 1997); Arthur Sherbo, *The Birth of Shakespeare Studies* (Michigan, 1986); Jonathan Bate, *Shakespearean Constitutions: Politics, Theatre, Criticism 1730–1830* (Oxford, 1989); Michael Dobson, *The Making of the National Poet* (Oxford, 1992); and Gary Taylor, *Reinventing Shakespeare*.

'LIKE A DECEIVED HUSBAND'

The best biography of Malone is Peter Martin, *Edmond Malone, Shakespearean Scholar* (Cambridge, 1995). On Malone's attempts to establish the plays' chronology and topicality, see his 'Attempt to Ascertain the Order in Which the Plays of Shakespeare were Written' (London, 1778); his 'A Second Appendix to Mr Malone's Supplement' (London, 1783); and 'Mr Malone's Preface,' as quoted in *The Plays of William Shakespeare*, ed. Samuel Johnson and George Steevens, 4th edn (London, 1793). Margreta de Grazia writes about Malone in *Shakespeare Verbatim: The Reproduction of Authority and the 1790 Apparatus* (Oxford, 1991). William Oldys's manuscript notes, which Malone consulted, can be found in British Library Add. MSS 22959. For the emendation to 'brown best bed', see Malone's account in vol. 1 of the 1793 edition of Johnson and Steevens, where he writes: that 'Mr Theobald and other modern editors have been more bountiful to Mrs Shakespeare, having printed instead of these words, "– my brown best bed, with the furniture".' See, too, Kenneth Gross's inventive and often brilliant *Shylock is Shakespeare* (Chicago, 2006).

For Heywood's unfinished or lost literary biographies from the early seventeenth century, see vol. 2 of Edmond Malone, ed., *The Plays and Poems of William Shakespeare* (London, 1821), where he cites Heywood's note to *Hierarchy of Blessed Angels* (1635) where he is still promising this work over twenty years after Richard Brathwaite first mentioned in 1614 that his 'judicious friend, Master Thomas Heywood, hath taken in hand, by his great industry, to make a general, though summary, description of all the poets'. For the rise of literary biography in eighteenth-century England, see, in addition to *Biographia Britannica: Lives of the Most Eminent Persons Who have Flourished in Great Britain and Ireland*, 7 vols (London, 1747–66), Roger Lonsdale's outstanding introduction to his edition of Samuel Johnson, *The Lives of the Most Eminent English Poets*, 4 vols (Oxford, 2006). On the missing inventory of Shakespeare's will, see J. O. Halliwell-Phillipps, *Outlines of the Life of Shakespeare*, 3rd edn (London, 1883), pp. 235 ff. The quotation from Capell is from 'Mr Capell's Introduction', in *The Plays of William Shakespeare*, ed. Johnson and Steevens.

'WITH THIS KEY'

For autobiographical readings of the Sonnets cited here, see *A New Variorum Edition of Shakespeare: The Sonnets*, ed. Hyder Edward Rollins, 2 vols (Philadelphia, 1944). On Wordsworth in particular, see *The Letters of William and Dorothy Wordsworth: The Early Years 1787–1805*, ed. Ernest De

Selincourt, rev. Chester L. Shaver (Oxford, 1967). Anna Jameson is quoted from her *The Loves of the Poets*, 2 vols (London, 1829). For Keats, see *The Letters of John Keats, 1814–21*, ed. Hyder Edward Rollins, 2 vols (Cambridge, Mass., 1958). And for Coleridge, see *Specimens of the Table Talk of the Late Samuel Taylor Coleridge*, ed. H. N. Coleridge, 2 vols (London, 1835); Samuel Taylor Coleridge, *Lectures 1808–1819 on Literature*, ed. R. A. Foakes, 2 vols (Princeton, 1987); and Samuel T. Coleridge, *Shakespearean Criticism*, ed. Thomas Middleton Raysor, 2 vols (London, 1960). Gary Taylor's account of this autobiographical turn in *Reinventing Shakespeare* is especially helpful. For the backlash against reading Shakespeare's life through his works, see C. J. Sisson, 'The Mythical Sorrows of Shakespeare', Annual Shakespeare Lecture of the British Academy, *Proceedings of the British Academy* 20 (1934).

For an early response to collaboration, see Edward Ravenscroft, *Titus Andronicus* (London, 1687). For Theobold, Hanmer and other editors on plays they deemed collaborative or not by Shakespeare, see Babcock, *The Genesis of Shakespeare Idolatry*; see too Alexander Pope's Preface, included in vol. 1 of *The Plays of William Shakespeare*, ed. Johnson and Steevens; Edmond Malone, *A Dissertation on the Three Parts of King Henry VI Tending to Show that Those Plays Were Not Written Originally by Shakspeare* (London, 1787); Henry Tyrrell, *The Doubtful Plays of Shakspere* (London, 1851); and Joseph C. Hart, *The Romance of Yachting* (New York, 1848).

MONEYLENDER AND MALT DEALER

On biographical information about Shakespeare that emerged in the nineteenth century, see Schoenbaum, Chambers and Wheler. On Collier's discoveries, see J. Payne Collier, *Reasons for a New Edition of Shakespeare's Works* (London, 1841); Collier's biographical essay in vol. 1 of his edition of *The Works of William Shakespeare* (London, 1844); and the magisterial study by Arthur Freeman and Janet Ing Freeman, *John Payne Collier: Scholarship and Forgery in the Nineteenth Century*, 2 vols (New Haven, 2004). Joseph Hunter published his discovery in vol. 1 of *New Illustrations of the Life, Studies, and Writings of Shakespeare*, 2 vols (London, 1845). On Halliwell-Phillipps and his discoveries, see Halliwell-Phillipps, 'Life of William Shakespeare', in vol. 1 of his *Works of William Shakespeare* (London, 1853). See too, Arthur and Janet Ing Freeman, 'Did Halliwell Steal and Mutilate the First Quarto of *Hamlet*?', *The Library* 2.4 (2001), pp. 349–63, as well as D. A. Winstanley, 'Halliwell Phillipps and Trinity College Library', *The Library* 5.2 (1948), pp. 250–82. And for a defence of Halliwell-Phillipps, see Marvin Spevack, *James Orchard Halliwell-Phillipps: The Life and Works of the Shakespearean Scholar and Bookman* (London, 2001). For the verdicts rendered by Halliwell-Phillipps and Alexander Dyce that Shakespeare attended carefully to his financial interests, see Halliwell-Phillipps, 'Life of William Shakespeare', in his *Works of William Shakespeare*, and Dyce, 'Some Account of the Life of Shakespeare', in his *Works of William Shakespeare* (London, 1857). The essay 'Who Wrote Shakespeare?' appeared anonymously in *Chambers's Edinburgh Journal* 449 (August 1852), pp. 87–9.

HOMER, JESUS AND THE HIGHER CRITICISM

For a detailed overview of the Homeric authorship question see J. A. Davison, 'The Homeric Question', in *A Companion to Homer*, ed. Alan J. B. Wace and Frank H. Stubbings (London, 1962), pp. 234–65; see too Martin West, 'The Invention of Homer', *Classical Quarterly* 49.2 (1999), pp. 364–82. Emerson's assessment of Wolf is quoted from Moncure Daniel Conway, *Emerson at Home and Abroad* (London, 1883). See as well Robert Wood, *Essay on the Original Genius and Writings of Homer* (London, 1775), and Thomas Blackwell, *An Enquiry into the Life and Writings of Homer* (London, 1735).

For an excellent edition of Wolf, see, F. A. Wolf, *Prolegomena to Homer*, translated with introduction and notes by Anthony Grafton, Glenn W. Most and James E. G. Zetzel (Princeton, 1985). I am deeply indebted to Anthony Grafton, 'Prolegomenon to Friedrich August Wolf', *Journal of the Warburg and Courtauld Institutes* 44 (1981), pp. 101–29. For responses to Wolf's argument in the nineteenth and twentieth centuries, see, in addition to Disraeli's novel: Samuel Butler, *The Authoress of the Odyssey* (London, 1897); de Quincey's essays in vol. 13 of *The Works of Thomas de Quincey*, eds. Grevel Lindop and John Whale (London, 2001); Elizabeth Barrett Browning, *Aurora Leigh*, ed. Margaret Reynolds (New York, 1996), cited in Laporte, 'The Bard, the Bible, and the Victorian Shakespeare Question'; and E. V. Rieu's introduction to his translation of *The Iliad* (Harmondsworth, 1950).

On Strauss and his *Life of Jesus*, see David Friedrich Strauss, *The Life of Jesus*, 3 vols, [trans. George Eliot] (London, 1846); Richard S. Cromwell, *David Friedrich Strauss and His Place in Modern Thought* (Fair Lawn, New Jersey, 1974); and Horton Harris, *David Friedrich Strauss and His Theology* (Cambridge, 1973). H. Bellyse Baildon discusses the Higher Criticism in the introduction to his edition of *Titus Andronicus* (London, 1904), and Robertson speaks of it in *The Baconian Heresy* (New York, 1913). For Shakespeare as holy writ, see Joss Marsh, *Word Crimes: Blasphemy, Culture,* and Literature in Nineteenth-Century England (Chicago, 1998), and J. B. Selkirk, *Bible Truths* (London, 1862). On Carlyle, see Adrian Poole, *Shakespeare and the Victorians* (London, 2004); Arnold is quoted from *Matthew Arnold*, ed. Miriam Allott and Robert H. Super (Oxford, 1986), and George Gilfillan from 'Shakespeare – A Lecture' in *A Third Gallery of Portraits* (New York, 1855) – I'm indebted to Laporte for this reference. So far as I know, Gary Taylor, in *Reinventing Shakespeare*, is the only Shakespeare scholar to mention Samuel Mosheim Schmucker, and I'm grateful that his work alerted me to *The Errors of Modern Infidelity Illustrated and Refuted* (Philadelphia, 1848), reprinted (unchanged except for the title) as *Historic Doubts Respecting Shakespeare: Illustrating Infidel Objections against the Bible* (Philadelphia, 1853), from which I have quoted.

BACON

DELIA BACON

The Beechers' remarks about Delia Bacon are quoted in Martha Bacon, 'The Parson and the Bluestocking,' in *The Puritan Promenade* (Boston, 1964). The admirer's glowing description was offered by Sarah Edwards Henshaw; see Theodore Bacon, *Delia Bacon: A Biographical Sketch* (Boston, 1888), as well as Henshaw's article (under the pseudonym Sydney E. Holmes) that appeared in the Chicago *Advance*, 26 December 1867. Henshaw is also the source for Bacon's lecturing style, in her 'Delia Bacon as a Teacher of Shakespeare' in *Shakespeareana* 5 (February 1888). Bacon's academic range is described in an admiring letter about her lectures that appeared in the *New York Herald* on 21 December 1852. For other facts about her background described here, see the standard biography, Vivian C. Hopkins, *Prodigal Puritan: A Life of Delia Bacon* (Cambridge, Mass., 1959). See, too, Nina Baym's excellent 'Delia Bacon, History's Odd Woman Out', *The New England Quarterly* 69 (1996), pp. 223–49. For more on her association with Tree, see Charles H. Shattuck, *Shakespeare on the American Stage* (Washington DC, 1976), and Joy Hartman Reilly's Masters essay, 'Miss Ellen Tree (1805–1880), Actress and Wife to Charles Kean' (Columbus, Ohio, 1979). Letters are quoted from Hopkins's edition – except for those quoted specifically from Delia Bacon's surviving correspondence and papers that are housed in the Folger Library.

Bacon's remarks about the subject of her play are quoted from her Preface to *The Bride of Fort Edward, Founded on an Incident of the Revolution* (New York, 1839). For more on early American women dramatists, see *Plays by*

Early American Women, 1775–1850, ed. Amelia Howe Kritzer (Ann Arbor, 1995) and *The Cambridge Companion to American Women Playwrights*, ed. Brenda Murphy (Cambridge, 1999). Bacon's disappointment in seeing Shakespeare staged is recorded by Henshaw, who remembers Bacon saying that it 'is impossible to put Shakespeare on the stage in a way to satisfy one's expectations . . . Nothing can equal the imagination.' For Poe on Bacon, see *Collected Writings of Edgar Allan Poe*, ed. Burton R. Pollin, 2 vols (New York, 1985). Bacon may have been thinking about the Shakespeare authorship problem for considerably longer, if her letter of 1854 to her patron, Charles Butler, does not exaggerate: 'It is more than ten years since I have had' the 'whole business thrust upon me'.

Gary Taylor notes in his *Reinventing Shakespeare* that it wasn't until 1865 that the Harvard finally added a curriculum requirement of 'reading English aloud'; another decade would pass before there would be a composition requirement on set literary texts, including Shakespeare's. Bacon's unique approach to teaching Shakespeare is described both by Henshaw and another of her students, Rebecca Taylor Hatch, *Personal Reminiscences and Memorials* (New York, 1905). Bacon's view of the 'ignorant masses' is quoted from her *The Philosophy of the Plays of Shakspere Unfolded* (London and Boston, 1857). The only time she ever expressed the idea that Francis Bacon might somehow have been related to her was in October 1857, after she had published her last word on the authorship controversy and was quite ill. See the letter described by Hopkins, from Maria Mitchell, a scientist who visited the ailing Bacon in Stratford, and in the course of urging her family to come to England and bring her home, mentioned Delia's 'claim of descent from Francis Bacon.'

For Francis Bacon's reputation, see Graham Rees, '*Novum Organum* and the Texts of 1620: Fluctuating Fortunes', in *The Instauratio Magna Part II: Novum Organum and Associated Text*, ed. Rees and Maria Wakely, *The Oxford Francis Bacon*, vol. 11 (Oxford, 2004); Charles Webster, 'The Origins of the Royal Society', *History of Science* 6 (1967); and Richard Yeo's excellent 'An Idol of the Market-Place: Baconianism in Nineteenth Century Britain', *History of Science* 23 (1985). For Emerson on Francis Bacon, see Vivian C. Hopkins, 'Emerson and Bacon', *American Literature* 29 (1958), as well as *The Early Lectures of Ralph Waldo Emerson*, ed. Stephen E. Whicher and Robert E. Spiller (Cambridge, Mass., 1959). For Bacon's reception in antebellum America, see Theodore Dwight Bozeman, *Protestants in an Age of Science: The Baconian Ideal and Antebellum American Religious Thought* (Chapel Hill, 1977), as well as George H. Daniels, *American Science in the Age of Jackson* (New York, 1968). And on the lost sections of Francis Bacon's work, see for example, Byron Steel [pseud. for Francis Steegmüller], *Sir Francis Bacon: The First Modern Mind* (Garden City, New York, 1930).

MacWhorter's book was reviewed in *The Christian Examiner* 52 (March 1857), where his argument was dismissed as a 'cobweb'. For details of the MacWhorter affair, see Catherine E. Beecher, *Truth Stranger than Fiction* (Boston, 1850). For more about this period in Bacon's life, see, in addition to Hopkins: Eliza Ware Rotch Farrar, *Recollections of Seventy Years* (Boston, 1866); Caroline Dall, *What We Really Know about Shakespeare* (Boston, 1886); Bruce A. Rhonda, ed., *Letters of Elizabeth Palmer Peabody* (Middletown, Connecticut, 1984); and the groundbreaking work of Helen R. Deese, 'A New England Woman's Network: Elizabeth Palmer Peabody, Caroline Healey Dall, and Delia S. Bacon', *Legacy* 8 (1992), pp. 77–91; as well as Deese, ed., *Daughter of Boston: The Extraordinary Diary of a Nineteenth-Century Woman, Caroline Healey Dall* (Boston, 2005). See, too: Nancy Glazener, 'Print Culture as an Archive of Dissent: Or, Delia Bacon and the Case of the Missing Hamlet', *American Literary History* 19 (2007), pp. 329–49, and Zachary Lesser, 'Mystic Ciphers: Shakespeare and Intelligent Design: A Response to Nancy Glazener', *American Literary History* 19 (2007), pp. 350–6.

THE SHAKESPEARE PROBLEM RESOLVED

Hawthorne's *Notebooks* are a valuable source of information about Delia Bacon and the authorship question; see *Nathaniel Hawthorne, The English Notebooks, 1856–1860*, ed. Thomas Woodson and Bill Ellis (Columbus, Ohio, 1997). So too are his letters: Nathaniel Hawthorne, *The Letters, 1853–1856* and *The Letters, 1857–1864*, both volumes edited by Thomas Woodson, James A. Rubino, L. Neal Smith and Norman Holmes Pearson (Columbus, Ohio, 1987). See too Hawthorne's 'Preface' to Bacon's *The Philosophy of the Plays of Shakspere Unfolded*.

I quote Leonard Bacon's view of America's political roots from his *A Discourse on the Early Constitutional History of Connecticut* (Hartford, Conn., 1843). Also see his essay, 'The Proper Character and Functions of American Literature', *American Biblical Repository*, n.s. 3 (January 1840), as well as Hugh Davis, *Leonard Bacon: New England Reformer and Antislavery Moderate* (Baton Rouge, 1998). I am indebted to Nina Baym's argument that 'Bacon's find, displacing republicanism from bourgeois Puritans to Church of England aristocrats, deprived New England Calvinism of its originary historical claim, and, indeed, struck more generally at American exceptionalism' ('Delia Bacon: Hawthorne's Last Heroine', *Nathaniel Hawthorne*

Review 20 [1994], pp. 1–9).

For Emerson's interest in Delia Bacon, see, in addition to Hopkins, Theodore Bacon's *Delia Bacon: A Biographical Sketch*. Emerson's high praise for Delia Bacon is quoted in Helen R. Deese, 'Two Unpublished Emerson Letters: To George P. Putnam on Delia Bacon and to George B. Loring', in *Essex Institute Historical Collections* 122 (1986). For Emerson on Shakespeare, see Sanford E. Marovitz, 'Emerson's Shakespeare: From Scorn to Apotheosis', in *Emerson Centenary Essays*, ed. Joel Myerson (Carbondale, Illinois, 1982), pp. 122–55, as well as Ralph Waldo Emerson, 'Shakspeare, or the Poet', in *Representative Men: Seven Lectures*, in *The Collected Works of Ralph Waldo Emerson*, vol. 4, introduction and notes by Wallace E. Williams, ed. Douglas Emory Wilson (Cambridge, Mass., 1987), and *The Early Lectures of Ralph Waldo Emerson*, ed. Stephen E. Whicher and Robert E. Spiller (Cambridge, Mass., 1959).

For Delia Bacon's time in England see Hopkins's biography. Carlyle's response is quoted in Laporte's essay and Whitman from *November Boughs*, in *The Works of Walt Whitman*, ed. Malcolm Cowley, 2 vols (New York, 1948). Theodore Bacon quotes Carlyle's letter to Emerson on 8 April 1854 that 'Miss Bacon has fled away to St. Albans (the *Great* Bacon's place) five or six months ago; and is there working out her Shakespeare Problem, from the depths of her own mind, disdainful apparently, or desperate and careless, of all *evidence* from museums or archives'. Hawthorne recorded, after visiting Delia Bacon in England, that her working library was restricted to books that 'had some reference to her Shakespearian theory': 'Ralegh's *History of the World*, a volume of Bacon's letters, a volume of Montaigne, and a volume of Shakespeare's plays' (see his *English Notebooks*).

For Bacon's anonymous and landmark essay, see 'William Shakespeare and His Plays; An Enquiry Concerning Them', *Putnam's Monthly* 7 (1856), reprinted in *Americans on Shakespeare, 1776–1914*, ed. Peter Rawlings (Aldershot, 1999). For Richard Grant White, see his 'The Bacon-Shakespeare Craze', *The Atlantic Monthly* 51 (April 1883), and his *Memoirs of the Life of William Shakespeare* (Boston, 1865).

The story about Meigs appears in *Baconiana* 6, 3rd series (1908), pp. 193–4. For William Henry Smith, see his *Was Lord Bacon the Author of Shakespeare's Plays: A Letter to Lord Ellesmere* (London, 1856) as well as his *Bacon and Shakespeare: An Inquiry, Touching Players, Playhouses, and Play-writers in the Days of Elizabeth* (London, 1857). William Henry Smith was still at it in 1884, when he published a slight pamphlet, *Bacon and Shakespeare. William Shakespeare: His Position as Regards the Plays, etc.* (London, 1884).

Nathaniel Hawthorne tried to allay her fears about rivals in his letter of 12 May 1856. For more on this, see: John Alden, 'Hawthorne and William Henry Smith', *Book Collector* 5 (1956). Hawthorne, even more than Emerson and Carlyle before him, was fascinated by Delia Bacon; though he too didn't believe her theory, he did more to help her see her book into print than anyone else (finding her a publisher, covering the cost of publication out of his own pocket, and even acceding to the publisher's demand to write a preface to her book). Bacon had much to thank Hawthorne for, though in her increasing paranoia and mental instability, she eventually turned against him as well. See Robert Cantwell, 'Hawthorne and Delia Bacon', *American Quarterly* 1 (1949), pp. 343–60, and James Wallace, 'Hawthorne and the Scribbling Woman Reconsidered', *American Literature* 62 (1990), pp. 201–22.

For Delia Bacon's alternative titles, see her letter from London of 5 July 1855 to the American publishers, Phillips and Sampson (Folger MS Y.c.64). Hawthorne's essay, 'Recollections of a Gifted Woman', first appeared in *Atlantic Monthly* 11 (1863) and is reprinted in *Americans on Shakespeare*. Theodore Bacon quotes Delia Bacon's letter to Hawthorne in October 1856 that 'the archives of this secret philosophical society are buried somewhere, perhaps in more places than one. The evidence points very strongly this way, it points to a tomb – Lord Bacon's tomb would throw some light on it I think.'

We know about Delia's plans for opening Shakespeare's tomb from Leonard Bacon's letter to Dr George Fayrer, 8 January 1858 (Folger MS Y.c.2599, number 119). Emerson's posthumous praise for Delia Bacon appears in a letter to Caroline Sturgis Tappan on 13 October 1857, quoted in Hopkins, who also quotes a letter that Emerson wrote not long after to Caroline Healey Dall:

'Tis very tragic to have such extraordinary abilities made unavailable by some disproportion, or by a want of somewhat which everybody else has. But if one could forget that there is a suffering woman behind it, her book, as it is, is a literary feast. More ability, and of a rare kind, goes to it, than to a score of successful works.

For Schoenbaum's harsh judgement, see especially the 1970 edition of *Shakespeare's Lives*. And for Delia Bacon, 'The author's apology and claim', quoted here, see Folger MS Y.c.2599, number 311. For the international appeal of the Baconian movement, see R. W. Churchill, *Shakespeare and His Betters*.

MARK TWAIN

My account of Twain's final years draws on Hamlin Hill, *Mark Twain, God's Fool* (New York, 1973); William R. Macnaughton, *Mark Twain's Last Years as a Writer* (Columbia, Missouri, 1979); and Karen Lystra, *Dangerous Intimacy: The Untold Story of Mark Twain's Final Years* (Berkeley, 2004). See too, *Mark Twain's Autobiography*, ed. Albert Bigelow Paine, 2 vols (New York, 1924); *Mark Twain's Own Autobiography*, ed. Michael J. Kiskis (Madison, 1990); John Lauber, *The Making of Mark Twain* (New York, 1985); *The Autobiography of Mark Twain*, ed. Charles Neider (New York, 1959), and Justin Kaplan, *Mr. Clemens and Mark Twain: A Biography* (New York, 1966).

On the rise of autobiography, see *Mark Twain–Howells Letters: The Correspondence of Samuel L. Clemens and William D. Howells, 1872–1910*, ed. Henry Nash Smith and William M. Gibson, 2 vols (Cambridge, Mass., 1960); Robert Folkenflik, 'Introduction: The Institution of Autobiography', in *The Culture of Autobiography*, ed. Folkenflik (Stanford, 1993); Loren Glass, 'Trademark Twain', in *American Literary History* 13 (2001), pp. 671–93; and Loren Glass, *Authors Inc.: Literary Celebrity in the Modern United States, 1880–1980* (New York, 2004). Louis Kaplan, who first tried to tabulate them in *A Bibliography of American Autobiographies* (Madison, 1961), counted over 6,300 of them up to 1945. Also see *American Autobiography 1945–1980*, ed. Mary Louise Briscoe, Barbara Tobias and Lynn Z. Bloom (Madison, 1982), and Robert F. Sayre, 'The Proper Study: Autobiographies in American Studies', in *American Quarterly* 29 (1977), pp. 241–62. See too, Allon White, *The Uses of Obscurity: The Fiction of Early Modernism* (London, 1981). I quote Conrad from *Some Reminiscences* (London, 1912). As for Twain on autobiographical elements in his own fiction, see Michael Kiskis's *Mark Twain's Own Autobiography*, which cites a letter Twain wrote to Kate Staples in 1886. Twain said as much two years later in a headnote to *Mark Twain's Library of Humor*, where he observed (in the third person) that his 'earliest book, *The Innocents Abroad*, was the result of his experience and observation' and that his 'succeeding books continue the story of his own life, with more or less fullness and exactness', as cited in Alan Gribben's essay, to which I am much indebted, 'Autobiography as Property: Mark Twain and His Legend', in *The Mythologizing of Mark Twain*, ed. Sara deSaussure Davis and Philip D. Beidler (University, Alabama, 1984). See too Twain's letter to an unidentified correspondent in 1891, where he writes: 'As the most valuable capital or culture or education usable in the building of novels is personal experience I ought to be well equipped for that trade,' *Mark Twain's Letters*, ed. Albert Bigelow Paine (New York, 1917).

My account of the Riley adventure draws on the report of Isabel Lyon about the composition of Twain's various works now housed at the Berg Collection at the New York Public Library: '(Clemens), M. B. Isabel Lyon, "Holograph notes on books by S. L. Clemens"'. See too the correspondence at the Berg, 'Clemens, S.L., A.L.S. to J. H. Riley', 9 October 1870. An alternative version of Riley's death appears in Twain's correspondence with Bliss, to whom he writes on 15 May 1872 that 'cancer has fast hold of his vitals and he can live but a little while. Nine physicians have tried their hands on him, but the cancer has beaten the lot' (*Mark Twain's Letters to His Publishers*, ed. Hamlin Hill [Berkeley, 1967]).

For Twain's allusions to *The Tempest*, see, for example, his 'Memorable Midnight Experience', in Mark Twain, *The Complete Works* (New York, 1923). And for Twain's sense of himself as a classic, see Samuel Moffett, 'Mark Twain: A Biographical Sketch', *McClure's Magazine* 13 (October 1899), pp. 523–9, which subsequently appeared as a preface to the *Works*. For Twain's self-promotion, see, in addition to Gribben's essay, Louis J. Budd, 'A "Talent for Posturing": The Achievement of Mark Twain's Public Posturing', in *The Mythologizing of Mark Twain*; Justin Kaplan, *Mr. Clemens and Mark Twain*; and R. Kent Rasmussen and Mark Dawidziak, 'Mark Twain on the Screen', in *A Companion to Mark Twain*, ed. Peter Messent and Louis J. Budd (Oxford, 2005).

The best account of Helen Keller's life can be found in Joseph P. Lash, *Helen and Teacher: The Story of Helen Keller and Anne Sullivan Macy* (New York, 1980). See too her memoir *Midstream: My Later Life* (New York, 1929). Kittredge's review appeared in *The Nation* 75 (1902), pp. 268–70. While the review was published anonymously, Kittredge claimed it as his own: see James Thorpe, *A Bibliography of the Writings of George Lyman Kittredge* (Cambridge, Mass., 1948). Keller's account of her growing scepticism about Shakespeare's authorship appears in her unpublished and virtually unknown manuscript, 'Francis Bacon', in the Helen Keller Archives, American Foundation for the Blind, Box 223, Folder 9. Keller's review of Greenwood's book appeared in *The Matilda Ziegler Magazine for the Blind*, as cited in *Baconiana* 7, 3rd series (1909), pp. 55–6. My account of Keller, Anne Sullivan Macy and John Macy's visit to Twain at Stormfield draws heavily on the recollections of Isabel Lyon in her 'Holograph notes on books by S. L. Clemens', under the heading 'Is Shakespeare Dead?' (in the Berg Collection, New York Public Library). See William Stone Booth, *Some Acrostic Signatures of Francis Bacon* (Boston, 1909).

For how *The Testament of Love* altered biographies of Chaucer, see for example, William Godwin, *Life of Geoffrey Chaucer* (London, 1803). See too: Walter W. Skeat, *Chaucerian and Other Pieces* (Oxford, 1897), R. Allen

Shoaf, ed., *Thomas Usk, The Testament of Love* (Kalamazoo, Michigan, 1998), and Paul Strohm, 'Politics and Poetics: Usk and Chaucer in the 1380s', in *Literary Practice and Social Change in Britain, 1380–1530*, ed. Lee Patterson (Berkeley, 1990), pp. 83–112.

CIPHER HUNTERS

On the high hopes Baconians had for cracking the code and uncovering lost manuscripts at this time, see, for example, 'The Goal in Sight', *Baconiana* 7, 3rd series (1910), pp. 145–9, as well as *New Shakespeareana* 9 (1910). For a fascinating account of codes and literature, see Shawn James Rosenheim, *The Cryptographic Imagination: Secret Writing from Edgar Poe to the Internet* (Baltimore, 1997). See too, David Kahn, *The Codebreakers: The Story of Secret Writing* (New York, 1996).

Donnelly's diary entry of 23 September 1882 is quoted from Martin Ridge, *Ignatius Donnelly: The Portrait of a Politician* (Chicago, 1962). See too, vol. 1 of *Mark Twain's Notebooks and Journals*, ed. Frederick Anderson, Michael B. Frank and Kenneth M. Sanderson (Berkeley, 1975), as well as vol. 3 of *Mark Twain's Notebooks and Journals*, ed. Robert Pack Browning, Michael B. Frank and Lin Salamo (Berkeley, 1979). Twain's recollections of Donnelly's book appear in his 'Autobiographical Dictation, 11 January 1909', archived in the Mark Twain Papers, University of California, Berkeley. See Ignatius Donnelly, *The Great Cryptogram: Francis Bacon's Cipher in the So-Called Shakespeare Plays* (Chicago, 1888). For Donnelly's approach to breaking the Shakespeare code, also see R. C. Churchill, *Shakespeare and His Betters*, as well as Donnelly's *The Cipher in the Plays and on the Tombstone* (Minneapolis, 1899). The definitive book on Shakespearean codes and ciphers is William F. Friedman and Elizebeth S. Friedman, *The Shakespearean Ciphers Examined* (New York, 1958).

Walt Whitman had first called his poem 'Shakspere's Cipher'; after a half-dozen or so periodicals rejected it, the poem ran in a new magazine, *The Cosmopolitan* (October 1887). For more on Whitman and the Shakespeare authorship question, see vol. 3 of Horace Traubel, *With Walt Whitman in Camden* (New York, 1914). See too, Whitman's *November Boughs* (1888), where he writes: 'we all know how much *mythus* there is in the Shakespeare question as it stands today. Beneath a few foundations of proved facts are certainly engulfed far more dim and elusive ones, of deepest importance – tantalizing and half suspected – suggesting explanations that one dare not put in plain statement,' *The Works of Walt Whitman*, ed. Malcolm Cowley, vol. 2 (New York, 1948). And for Twain on Milton as the true author of *Pilgrim's Progress*, see vol. 3 of *Mark Twain's Notebooks and Journals*.

For more on Orville Ward Owen, see Friedman and Friedman, *The Shakespearean Ciphers Examined*, as well as John Michell, *Eccentric Lives and Peculiar Notions* (London, 1984). I also quote from Schoenbaum's account in *Shakespeare's Lives*. The New York Public Library has a manuscript archive – the 'Bacon Cipher Collection', consisting of thirty boxes of material from Owen, Gallup and the Riverbank Laboratory. See Kate H. Prescott, *Reminiscences of a Baconian* (n.p., 1949). And for Gallup's investigations, see Elizabeth Wells Gallup, *The Bi-literal Cypher of Sir Francis Bacon*, part 3 (Detroit, 1910). Sceptics still try to decode the true meaning behind Malvolio's lines in Act 2 of *Twelfth Night*; see, for example, Sundra G. Malcolm, 'M.O.A.I. Unriddled: Anatomy of an Oxfordian Reading', in *Shakespeare Matters* (Fall 2007), which takes this seriously as an Oxfordian anagram, and concludes that the anagram should read IAMO – 'I am Oxford. (I am O).'

For Helen Keller's frustrated efforts to see her work on Bacon into print, see her letter to Gilder, archived in the Henry E. Huntington Library, Francis Bacon Foundation/Arensberg Archive, Box 58, Folder for 'Keller, Helen.' For his response, see R. W. Gilder to Helen Keller, 20 April 1909, American Foundation for the Blind, Helen Keller Archives, Box 210, Folder 5. And see Lash, *Helen and Teacher*, on her frustrated efforts to write something other than memoir. For Keller's further correspondence on her authorship project, see Helen Keller to R. W. Gilder, 9 May 1909, American Foundation for the Blind, Helen Keller Archives, Box 210, Folder 4 (the lines about the 'genuine data of Shakespeare's life' are dictated, not typed by Keller herself). See, too, Helen Keller's letter to William Stone Booth, 23 May 1909, Helen Keller Archives, American Foundation for the Blind, Box 48, Folder 6. And for her additional recollections of 'Twain's response to Booth's ciphers, see Keller's 1929 memoir, *Midstream*.

IS SHAKESPEARE DEAD?

For Twain's familiarity with Shakespeare, see Howard G. Baetzhold, *Mark Twain and John Bull: The British Connection* (Bloomington, Indiana, 1970); Anthony J. Berret, *Mark Twain and Shakespeare: A Cultural Legacy* (Lanham, Maryland, 1993); Thomas J. Richardson, 'Is Shakespeare Dead? Mark Twain's Irreverent Question', in *Shakespeare and Southern Writers: A Study in Influence*, ed. Philip C. Kolin (Jackson, Mississippi, 1985), pp. 63–82; Joe Falocco, 'Is Mark Twain Dead? Samuel Clemens and the Question of

BIBLIOGRAPHICAL ESSAY

Shakespearean Authorship', *The Mark Twain Annual 2* (2004), pp. 25–40; and Alan Gribben, *Mark Twain's Library: A Reconstruction*, 2 vols (Boston, 1980). See too Mark Twain, *The Adventures of Huckleberry Finn*, ed. Walter Blair and Victor Fischer (Berkeley, 1988). And for his observation about the absence of evidence in Stratford, see vol. 1 of *Mark Twain's Notebooks and Journals*. For Twain's parody of *Julius Caesar*, see *The Works of Mark Twain: Early Tales and Sketches, vol. 2, 1864–1865*, ed. Edgar Marquess Branch and Robert H. Hirst (Berkeley, 1981); and for his 1881 burlesque of *Hamlet*, see *Mark Twain's Satires and Burlesques*, ed. Franklin R. Rogers (Berkeley, 1967).

For the composition of *Is Shakespeare Dead?* see Mark Twain, 'Autobiographical Dictation, 11 January 1909', Mark Twain Papers, Bancroft Library; Berret, *Mark Twain and Shakespeare*; Isabel Lyon, 'Holograph notes on books by S. L. Clemens'; Paine's *Mark Twain: A Biography*; and Mark Twain, *Is Shakespeare Dead? From My Autobiography* (New York, 1909). Twain complained to Macy that Booth made his case poorly. He wrote to him on 27 March 1909 that he himself had trouble with the acrostics, and, more damagingly,

[the] typical reader will puzzle over ten (10) acrostics, suffer defeat, and deliver his verdict to any that will listen: 'The acrostics are not there' – and he will not examine another one. It is too bad, too bad, *too bad!* With the acrostic letter indicated for him, the unconverted could be converted – but not by any other process.

(Helen Keller Archives, American Federation for the Blind, Box 50, Folder 12).

Twain's description of Tichborne's background and upbringing, written in the margins of a blank page of Greenwood's book, overlaps at many points with his sense of the background and attributes of the true author of Shakespeare's plays; see Mark Twain's copy of George Greenwood, *The Shakespeare Problem Restated* in the Berg Collection, New York Public Library. His comments on the Tichborne trial appear in his *Following the Equator* (New York, 1897). For more on the case, see Rohan McWilliam, *The Tichborne Claimant: A Victorian Sensation* (London, 2007).

Fiedler is quoted in Susan Gillman, *Dark Twins: Imposture and Identity in Mark Twain's America* (Chicago, 1989). Twain's view of Keller and Sullivan is found in Nella Braddy, *Anne Sullivan Macy: The Story Behind Helen Keller* (Garden City, New York, 1933). And see Leslie A. Fiedler, 'Afterword', in Mark Twain, *1601*, and *Is Shakespeare Dead?* ed. Shelley Fisher Fishkin (New York, 1996), as well as Gillman, *Dark Twins*, for Twain on twins and impostures. Twain's interest in whether Queen Elizabeth was a man is recounted in Henry W. Fisher, *Abroad with Mark Twain and Eugene Field: Tales They*

[335]

Told to a Fellow Correspondent (New York, 1922). And his sceptical remarks about Shakespeare's authorship can be found littered throughout his copy of Greenwood's *The Shakespeare Problem Restated*. Also of interest is Twain's late claim, in an imaginary dialogue, that 'Shakespeare created nothing,' in 'What Is Man?' published by Twain in 1905, begun, he says, around 1880, reprinted in Mark Twain, *Collected Tales, Sketches, Speeches, and Essays, 1891–1910*, ed. Louis J. Budd (New York, 1992).

Twain prefaced *Pudd'nhead Wilson* with a fascinating 'A Whisper to the Reader' that directly addresses the question of an author's limited legal knowledge; see Mark Twain, *Pudd'nhead Wilson and Those Extraordinary Twins* (1893–4; New York, 1922). See too Daniel J. Kornstein, 'Mark Twain's Evidence: The Never-Ending Riverboat Debate', from the 'Symposium: Who Wrote Shakespeare? An Evidentiary Puzzle', *Tennessee Law Review* 72 (2004). For more on Twain's plagiarism, see *A Bibliography of the Works of Mark Twain*, by Merle Johnson (Folcroft, Pennsylvania, 1935). See too Twain's letter to Macy on 25 February 1909, Helen Keller Archives, American Foundation for the Blind, Box 50, Folder 12, as well as Michael Bristol, 'Sir George Greenwood's Marginalia in the Folger Copy of Mark Twain's *Is Shakespeare Dead?*, *Shakespeare Quarterly* 49 (1998), pp. 411–16.

On the publication and aftermath of *Is Shakespeare Dead?*, see Lyon's 'Holograph notes'; Hill, *Mark Twain, God's Fool*; Fiedler, 'Afterword'; Alan Gribben, 'Autobiography as Property'; Justin Kaplan, *Mark Twain and His World* (New York, 1974); *Mark Twain: The Contemporary Reviews*, ed. Louis J. Budd (Cambridge, 1999), and especially Eugene H. Angert's withering review, 'Is Mark Twain Dead?' in *The North American Review* 190 (September 1909). I am grateful to William Sherman for sharing with me Macy's letter about 'Shake and Bake': Macy to Walter Conrad Arensberg, 20 October 1926, Arensberg Francis Bacon Collection, Henry E. Huntingon Library. For the afterlife of the cipher hunters, see Schoenbaum, *Shakespeare's Lives*; Virginia M. Fellows, *The Shakespeare Code* (Gardiner, Montana, 2006); Friedman and Friedman, *The Shakespeare Ciphers Examined*; and, for Friedman's military work, Rosenheim, *The Cryptographic Imagination* and Ronald Clark, *The Man Who Broke Purple: A Life of the World's Greatest Cryptographer* (Boston, 1977). For Twain's defence of *Is Shakespeare Dead?*, see his brief letter to M. B. Colcord in May 1909, Folger MS. Y.c.545.

HENRY JAMES

For James's instructions to his literary executor, see Leon Edel, *Henry James: A Life* (New York, 1985). The reference to Peyster is found in Churchill,

BIBLIOGRAPHICAL ESSAY

Shakespeare and His Betters. William James's letter to C. E. Norton, 4 May 1902, is quoted in *Shakespeare Fellowship Newsletter* (September 1953). For James's notebook entry for the anecdote that was the basis of 'The Birthplace', see Tony Tanner, 'The Birthplace', in N. H. Reeves, *Henry James, The Shorter Fiction: Reassessments* (New York, 1997), pp. 77–94. For the published story, see Henry James, *The Altar of the Dead, The Beast in the Jungle, The Birthplace, and Other Tales* (New York, 1909).

For James's correspondence on Shakespeare's authorship, see *Henry James: Selected Letters*, ed. Leon Edel (Cambridge, Mass., 1987); *Henry James: Letters. Volume IV, 1895–1916*, ed. Leon Edel (Cambridge, Mass., 1984); and *The Letters of Henry James*, ed. Percy Lubbock (New York, 1920). I am grateful to Pierre A. Walker and Greg W. Zacharias, editors of *The Complete Letters of Henry James*, for their help in securing copies of original letters. For the book to which James is clearly referring, see Judge Thomas Ebenezer Webb, *The Mystery of William Shakespeare: A Summary of Evidence* (London, 1902).

Henry James was also aware of the cipher hunters and a character in his story 'The Figure in the Carpet' stops short of dismissing the possibility of a cryptic author out of hand: 'He was like nothing, I told him, but the maniacs who embrace some bedlamatical theory of the cryptic character of Shakespeare. To this he replied that if we had had Shakespeare's own word for his being cryptic he would immediately have accepted it' (Henry James, 'The Figure in the Carpet', in vol. 2 of *Henry James' Shorter Masterpieces*, ed. Peter Rawlings (Sussex, 1984). And for James's visit to his own birthplace, see Henry James, *The American Scene*, in *Collected Travel Writings: Great Britain and America*, ed. Richard Howard (New York, 1993). The source for many of my references here, as well as my argument, draws on Gordon McMullan's illuminating discussion on Henry James and the 'elusive late Shakespeare' in *Shakespeare and the Idea of Late Writing* (Cambridge, 2007). For Orcutt's conversation with James, see William Dana Orcutt, 'Celebrities Off Parade: Henry James', the editorial page of *The Christian Science Monitor*, 23 August 1934. For James on *The Tempest*, see his Introduction to *The Tempest* in vol. 8 of *The Complete Works of William Shakespeare*, ed. Sidney Lee (New York, 1907).

For readings of James on Shakespeare that I have found unusually helpful, see Nina Schwartz, 'The Master Lesson: James Reading Shakespeare', *Henry James Review* 12 (1991), pp. 69–83; William T. Stafford, 'James Examines Shakespeare: Notes on the Nature of Genius', *PMLA* 73 (1958), pp. 123–8; Neil Chilton, 'Conceptions of a Beautiful Crisis: Henry James's Reading of *The Tempest*, in *Henry James Review* 26 (Fall 2005), pp. 218–28;

OXFORD

Peter Rawlings, *Henry James and the Abuse of the Past* (New York, 2005); Lauren T. Cowdery, 'Henry James and the "Transcendent Adventure": The Search for the Self in the Introduction to *The Tempest*', *Henry James Review* 3 (Winter 1982), pp. 145–53; and Michael Millgate, *Testamentary Acts: Browning, Tennyson, James, Hardy* (Oxford, 1992). James was approached in November 1935 by members of the British Academy to lecture on the occasion of the tercentenary of Shakespeare's death. But by then, James was far too ill – and wrote back that the 'kind invitation … comes, alas, too late'. He would take to the grave his final thoughts on the subject (see Philip Horne, *Henry James: A Life in Letters* [London, 1999]).

FREUD

See Smiley Blanton, *Diary of My Analysis with Sigmund Freud*, with biographical notes and comments by Margaret Gray Blanton (New York, 1971). For his correspondence with Freud, see the Margaret Gray Blanton Papers at the Wisconsin Historical Society, Madison, Wisconsin, MSS 93, Box 13, Folder 2. See too, the Margaret Gray and Smiley Blanton Collection, MS-0739, University of Tennessee, Special Collections Library, Knoxville, Tennessee. Brunswick's brief obituary appeared in *Shakespeare Fellowship Quarterly* 7 (1946); for more about her, see Lisa Appignanesi and John Forrester, *Freud's Women* (New York, 2000). The copy of Looney's book that Brunswick gave Freud survives as part of the library Freud took with him to London when he fled Vienna. See Harry Trosman and Roger Dennis Simmons, 'The Freud Library', *Journal of American Psychoanalytic Association* 21 (1973), pp. 646–87.

For Freud and the authorship question, see Ernest Jones, *The Life and Work of Sigmund Freud*, 3 vols (New York, 1953–7) on which I rely heavily; see too, Peter Gay, *Reading Freud: Explorations and Entertainments* (New Haven, 1990), and Harry Trousman, 'Freud and the Controversy over Shakespearean Authorship', *Journal of the American Psychoanalytic Association* 13 (1965). For Freud's views on Shakespeare, see *The Standard Edition of the Complete Psychological Works of Sigmund Freud*, trans. James Strachey, in collaboration with Anna Freud, 24 vols (London, 1953–74); for his correspondence with Strachey, see *Bloomsbury/Freud: The Letters of James and Alix Strachey, 1924–1925*, ed. Perry Meisel and Walter Kendrick (New York, 1985). Freud would have consulted the 1895–6 Munich edition of Georg Brandes, *William Shakespeare*; I quote from the English version,

BIBLIOGRAPHICAL ESSAY

William Shakespeare, translated from the Danish by William Archer, Mary Morison and Diana White (New York, 1935). For Freud's letters to Fliess – including the ones from 2 November 1896, 12 June 1897, and the crucial ones of 21 September 1897 and 15 October 1897 – see *The Complete Letters of Sigmund Freud to Wilhelm Fliess, 1887–1904*, ed. and trans. Jeffrey Moussaieff Masson (Cambridge, Mass., 1985). Freud had seen the world through Hamlet's eyes as early as 1872, writing to a friend about his inhibitions (when he was uncertain whether he was more attracted to a girl or to her mother) as 'the nonsensical Hamlet in me, my diffidence' (letter of 4 September 1872, in *The Letters of Sigmund Freud to Eduard Silberstein*, ed. Walter Boehlich and trans. Arnold J. Pomerans [Cambridge, Mass, 1990]).

For Ernest Jones's judgement, see his *Hamlet and Oedipus* (New York, 1954). Freud was more comfortable crediting the creative artists whose work both anticipated and confirmed his own: 'Not I, but the poets discovered the unconscious' (Norman N. Holland, 'Freud on Shakespeare', *PMLA* 75 [1960], pp. 163–73). It wasn't until the second edition of *The Interpretation of Dreams* was published in 1908 that Freud belatedly acknowledged his transformative insight 'revealed itself to me as a piece of my self-analysis, as my reaction to my father's death; that is, to the most important event, the most poignant loss, in a man's life'. As Jonathan Crewe has astutely argued, '*Hamlet* rather than *Oedipus Rex* [is] the crucial "Freudian" work, since it is in relation to it rather than the Greek play that the *discovery* of the oedipal structure of unconscious desire can be (re)effected' – his unpublished insight (for a paper, 'Naught so Damned') is quoted in Julia Reinhard Lupton and Kenneth Reinhard, *After Oedipus: Shakespeare and Psychoanalysis* (Ithaca, New York, 1993). See too, Peter L. Rudnytsky, *Freud and Oedipus* (New York, 1987).

On the response to the theory by Freud's disciples, see Ludwig Binswanger, *Sigmund Freud: Reminiscences of a Friendship*, trans. Norbert Guterman (New York, 1957). Binswanger was at first surprised to hear a fictional character treated as if he were a real person – but was reassured when he learned of the biographical foundations of this claim, for, he writes, 'Freud later told me personally a short life story of Shakespeare, from which it is easy to see that Shakespeare – as whom, indeed, we must always see Hamlet – had a severe mother complex' (*Freud/Binswanger Correspondence*, ed. Gerhard Fichtner and trans. Arnold J. Pomerans [London, 2003]).

For the basis of Brandes's reversal, see Gabriel Harvey's reference to Edmund Spenser (who died in January 1599) as well as to the Earl of Essex (executed in early 1601, before Shakespeare's father died) as if they were both still alive. Freud also tells Jones about Brandes's source, *Gabriel Harvey's*

[339]

Marginalia, ed. G. C. Moore Smith (Stratford-upon-Avon, 1913). Freud is here translating into English from Georg Brandes, *Miniaturen*, trans. Erich Holm [pseud.] (Berlin, 1919). For Freud's correspondence with Jones, see *The Complete Correspondence of Sigmund Freud and Ernest Jones, 1908–1939*, ed. R. Andrew Paskauskas (Cambridge, Mass., 1993). For more on the dating of *Hamlet* at the time, see the fourth edition of Sidney Lee, *A Life of William Shakespeare* (London, 1928), and Leo Kirschenbaum, 'The Date of *Hamlet*', *Studies in Philology* 34 (1937).

Jones was also troubled by another, even messier *Hamlet* problem, precisely when the Oedipal dimensions were added to the story, for it now looked likely that they were already present in the version conventionally attributed to Thomas Kyd, written long before Shakespeare's father – and for that matter his son Hamnet – had died (see Jones's letter to Freud, 3 February 1921). For Freud and the Chandos portrait, see Michael Molnar, 'Sigmund Freud's Notes on Faces and Men: National Portrait Gallery, September 13, 1908', in *Freud: Conflict and Culture*, ed. Michael S. Roth (New York, 1998). The full phrase reads: 'Face is race, family, and constitutional predisposition.' See Jones and their correspondence on Freud's view of Shakespeare's French origins. And for Freud on Bacon and authorship, see A. Bronson Feldman, 'Confessions of William Shakespeare', *American Imago* 10 (1953). The complicated wording of Freud's remarks to Eitingon, prompted by the publication of a recent essay on the Bacon question, are ambiguous enough to justify quoting in the original: '*Interessanter war mir ein vorstehender Aufsatz über Bacon-Shakespeare. Dies Thema und das Okkulte bringen mich immer etwas aus der Fassung. Meine Neigung geht durchaus auf die Verneinung. Ich glaube an ein paranoides Wahnsystem, ob bei den Autoren oder bei Bacon selbst?*' From the letter of 13 November 1922, in *Sigmund Freud / Max Eitingon, Briefwechsel, 1906–1939*, ed. Michael Schröter (Berlin, 2004).

LOONEY

I quote or draw upon the following documents on the Religion of Humanity in these opening paragraphs: *Religion of Humanity* (London: Church of Humanity, 1898); Malcolm Quin, *A Final Circular Addressed to the Supporters of His Religious Action* (Newcastle, 1910); Vernon Lushington, *Shakespeare. An Address Delivered to the Positivist Society of London on the 2nd of August 1885 (18 Dante 97), at Stratford-upon-Avon* (London, 1885); Frederic Harrison, ed., *The New Calendar of Great Men: Biographies of the 558 Worthies of All Ages and Nations in the Positivist Calendar of Auguste Comte* (London, 1892). For background on Comte, I have drawn on Frank E. Manuel, *The*

Prophets of Paris: Turgot, Condorcet, Saint-Simon, Fourier, and Comte (New York, 1962); Isaiah Berlin, *Historical Inevitability* (London, 1954); Arline Reilein Standley, *Auguste Comte* (Boston, 1981); John Edwin McGee, *A Crusade for Humanity: The History of Organized Positivism in England* (London, 1931); and especially T. R. Wright's illuminating *The Religion of Humanity: The Impact of Comtean Positivism on Victorian Britain* (Cambridge, 1986). See too, his 'Positively Catholic: Malcolm Quin's Church of Humanity in Newcastle on Tyne', *Durham University Journal* 75 (1983), pp. 11–20.

For Looney's destination to the priesthood, see British Library Add. 43844, fol. 62. For Quin on Looney, see Malcolm Quin, *A Special Circular, Addressed to the Members and Supporters of the Positivist Church and Apostolate of Newcastle-upon-Tyne, and to Other Adherents of the Religion of Humanity* (Newcastle?, 10 October 1901/3 Descartes 47); Malcolm Quin, *Religion of Humanity. Second Annual Circulate Addressed to Members and Supporters of the Positivist Church and Apostolate of Newcastle-upon-Tyne for the Year 46* (Newcastle?, 1900); and Malcolm Quin, *Religion of Humanity. Third Annual Circulate Addressed to Members of the Positivist Church and Apostolate of Newcastle-upon-Tyne for the Year 47* (Newcastle?, 1901?). Quin's Positivist writings on the Religion of Humanity, some of which – including those that mention Looney – are rare, can be found at Keele University. For more on Quin, in addition to McGee and Wright, see Quin, *Memoirs of a Positivist* (London, 1924).

For Virginia Woolf's observation about 1910, see her essay 'Character and Fiction' which first appeared in *Criterion* in July 1924. For Oxfordian sketches of Looney, see Percy Allen, *Shakespeare Fellowship News-letter* (May 1944); Looney provides additional information in a letter to Charles Wisner Barrell, 6 June 1937, *Shakespeare Fellowship Quarterly* (June 1944). Also helpful is the brief summary of Looney's career in vol. 1 of the third edition of *'Shakespeare' Identified*, ed. Ruth Lloyd Miller (Jennings, Louisiana, 1975). See too, Hope and Holston, *The Shakespeare Controversy*; and 'Discoverer of the True Shakespeare Passes', *The Shakespeare Fellowship Quarterly* 5 (1944), pp. 18–23. Finally, see Looney's letters to Congreve about his intellectual background: British Library Add. MSS 45,240, ff. 180–5, and British Library Add. 43,844, fol. 62. All this is in addition to what Looney says about himself in J. Thomas Looney, *'Shakespeare' Identified in Edward de Vere the Seventeenth Earl of Oxford* (London, 1920).

For Ogburn's remark, see *The Mysterious William Shakespeare* (the italics are mine). For the appeal of portraying Looney as a teacher, see, for example, Eddi Jolly's 'An Introduction to the Oxfordian Case', which begins:

'Nearly one hundred years ago, a schoolteacher, who had taught the plays of Shakespeare for many years, became convinced that William Shakespeare of Stratford-upon-Avon, was not their author,' in *Great Oxford: Essays on the Life and Work of Edward de Vere, 17th Earl of Oxford 1550–1604*, ed. Richard Malim (Tunbridge Wells, 2004). In later years Looney had misgivings about the exaggerated role he had assigned to his teaching rather than his Positivist convictions in the formation of *'Shakespeare' Identified*, and told his followers that he 'would place professional studies and duties amongst the minor factors of my education and preparation for this particular piece of work' (*Shakespeare Fellowship Quarterly* 5 [June 1944]).

Surveying the field of Shakespeare studies in the early pages of *'Shakespeare' Identified*, Looney approves of the growing 'tendency to put aside the old conception of a writer creating everything by the vigour of his imagination, and to regard the writings as reflecting the personality and experiences of the author'. Cecil Palmer's comments about the state of Looney's submitted manuscript appear in *Shakespeare Fellowship Newsletter* (March 1952). For Congreve's influence on Looney's view of Elizabethan politics, see Richard Congreve, *Elizabeth of England* (London, 1862), and his *Historical Lectures* (London, 1900). Strachey's remarks about *The Tempest* are quoted from Lytton Strachey, 'Shakespeare's Final Period', *Books and Characters* (New York, 1922), pp. 64–9; the essay first appeared in *The Independent Review* in 1906.

For the destruction of unsold copies of Looney's book during the war, see Hope and Holston, *The Shakespeare Controversy*. For more on Looney's vision of the Second World War, see his letter to Eva Turner Clark, quoted in the *Shakespeare Fellowship News-letter* 1 (1940): 'To me, however, it does not appear to be a struggle between democracy and dictatorship so much as between material force and spiritual interests.' On 10 June 1939 Looney had made clear his explicit disgust with the Nazis: 'In the centuries that lie ahead, when the words Nazi and Hitler are remembered only with feelings of disgust and aversion and as synonyms for cruelty and bad faith, Shakespeare, Wordsworth, Tennyson & Shelly [*sic*] will continue to be honoured as expressions of what is most enduring and characteristic of Humanity' (as quoted in vol. 1 of the third edition of Looney, *'Shakespeare' Identified*). See Looney's letter to Flodden W. Heron of San Francisco, of 5 July 1941, which is partially reprinted in 'A Great Pioneer's Ideas on Intellectual Freedom', *Shakespeare Fellowship Quarterly* 6 (1945).

FREUD, AGAIN

See vol. 3 of Jones, *Life and Work* as well as the *Correspondence of Freud and Jones*, especially the letters of 7 March 1928, 11 March 1928, 29 April 1928 and 3 May 1928. It's uncertain when Freud first read Looney's book; Jones says 'some ten years' after 1913, or roughly 1923 (*Life and Works*, vol. 3); Peter Gay, who seems to have overlooked this passage in Jones, argues for a later date, perhaps 1926 (*Reading Freud*). And see Strachey, *Bloomsbury/Freud*, for the letter of 25 December 1928. And yet in the next sentence Freud, who apparently wants to have it both ways, is unwilling to relinquish his notion, which Looney would have sharply challenged, that Oxford 'certainly emerges in Hamlet as the first modern neurotic'. Peter Gay, *Freud: A Life for Our Time* (New York, 1998), provides information about Ernst Brücke and Positivism. For Freud's correspondence with Reik, see Theodor Reik, *The Search Within: The Inner Experiences of a Psychoanalyst* (New York, 1956).

For Freud's later thoughts on the seduction theory (including his belief that the fantasies were connected not with the father but with the mother, and that actual 'seducers turned out as a rule to have been older children') see Freud's 1924 'An Autobiographical Study' as well as his paper on 'Female Sexuality' (1931). For his further exploration of the workings of the Oedipal theory, see, especially 'The Dissolution of the Oedipal Complex' (1924), all of which can be found in the standard edition of his works. For a more qualified view of Freud's rejection of the seduction theory in favour of an Oedipal one, see Paul Robinson, *Freud and his Critics* (Berkeley, 1993).

For the exchange with Sachs, see Hanns Sachs, *Freud: Master and Friend* (Cambridge, Mass., 1944), and with Zweig, see *The Letters of Sigmund Freud and Arnold Zweig*, ed. Ernest L. Freud and trans. Elaine and William Robson-Scott (New York, 1970). See too Richard Flatter, 'Sigmund Freud on Shakespeare', *Shakespeare Quarterly* 2 (1951), pp. 368–9; H. R. Woudhuysen, 'A Freudian Oxfordian', *Times Literary Supplement* 20–26 April 1990; and Freud's letter to James S. H. Branson, 25 March 1934, reproduced in 'Appendix A' of Jones, *Life and Works*.

Freud's letter in English to Smiley Blanton of 20 December 1937 can be found in the archives of the Wisconsin Historical Society, The Margaret Gray Blanton Papers, MSS 93, Box 13, Folder 2. Freud would amend his long-held views on *Hamlet* and advocate Oxford's authorship first in a footnote added in 1930 to *The Interpretation of Dreams*; then in a footnote to *Moses and Monotheism* (1939); and, finally, in a posthumous 1940 edition of his *Outline of Psychoanalysis*.

Freud added a footnote to *An Autobiographical Study* in 1935 in which he writes:

I no longer believe that William Shakespeare the actor from Stratford was the author of the works which have so long been attributed to him. Since the appearance of J. T. Looney's volume *'Shakespeare' Identified*, I am almost convinced that in fact Edward de Vere, earl of Oxford, is concealed behind this pseudonym.

His translator James Strachey was 'taken aback' at this and asked Freud to 'reconsider' in part because of Looney's 'unfortunate name'. Freud wrote back sharply on 29 August 1935, saying 'I cannot understand the English attitude to this question: Edward de Vere was as good an Englishman as Will Shakspere.' While willing to accede to Strachey's request for the English edition, he asks that the note be included in the American edition, where the 'same sort of narcissistic defence need not be feared'.

I quote from Freud's account of 'the ideals of Hitlerism' from his letter to Marie Bonaparte, quoted in Giovanni Costigan, *Sigmund Freud: A Short Biography* (New York, 1965). See too his letter of 7 April 1933 to Ernest Jones in their *Correspondence*. Freud's description of himself as Looney's 'follower' is quoted from A. Bronson Feldman, 'Confessions of William Shakespeare'. Looney's daughter's account appears in Percy Allen, John Thomas Looney (1870–1944)', *Shakespeare Fellowship Newsletter* (May 1944). For Looney's letter to Freud of 15 July 1938, see J. Thomas Looney to Sigmund Freud, Container number 36, Sigmund Freud Papers, Sigmund Freud Collection, Manuscript Division, Library of Congress, Washington D.C.

OXFORDIANS

For the rise of various aristocratic candidates, see Churchill, *Shakespeare and His Betters*; Gibson, *Shakespeare Claimants*; Michell, *Who Wrote Shakespeare?*, and Schoenbaum, *Shakespeare's Lives*. For Sherlock Holmes, see Claud W. Sykes, *Alias William Shakespeare?* (London, 1947). The first to develop the argument for Derby was James Greenstreet, 'A Hitherto Unknown Noble Author of Elizabethan Comedies' (July 1891), 'Further Notices of William Stanley' (January 1892), and 'Testimonies against the Accepted Authorship of Shakespeare's Plays' (May 1892), all published in *The Genealogist*. But it wasn't until 1915 that the case for Derby was fully articulated. Latham Davis made the case for Essex in *Shake-speare: England's Ulysses* (Seaford, Delaware, 1905); J. C. Nicol argued for Southampton's solo authorship in *The Real Shakespeare* (London, 1905). For the Derbyites, see especially: Robert Frazer, *The Silent Shakespeare* (Philadelphia, 1915) and Abel Lefranc, *Sous le masque de William Shakespeare: Vie Comte de Derby*, 2 vols (Paris, 1919). Burkhard Hermann (writing under the name Peter Alvor) first proposed in 1906 that Rutland wrote the comedies, Southampton the tragedies and histories. Rutland's solo authorship was then urged in the introduction to the German play *Der wahre Shakespeare*, by Carl Bleibtreu, who followed that up two years later with *Die Lösung der Shakespearefrage* in 1909 and again with *Shakespeares Geheimnis* (Berne, 1923). Rutland's greatest advocate was Célestin Demblon, who in 1912 published *Lord Rutland est Shakespeare* and two years later *L'Auteur d'Hamlet et son monde* (Paris, 1914). For the earliest claim about Marlowe's role in writing Shakespeare's plays, see Wilbur G. Zeigler, *It Was Marlowe* (Chicago, 1895).

For Freud's high regard for Turner's scholarship, see his letter of 20 December 1937 to Smiley Blanton in the Wisconsin Historical Society, The Margaret Gray Blanton Papers, MSS 93, Box 13, Folder 2. For Looney's essay on *The Merry Wives*, see J. Thomas Looney, 'The Earl of Oxford as "Shakespeare": New Evidence', *The Golden Hind* (1922), pp. 23–30. For biographical facts about de Vere's life, see Alan H. Nelson's entry in the *Oxford Dictionary of National Biography*, as well as his biography, *Monstrous Adversary: the Life of Edward de Vere, 17th Earl of Oxford* (Liverpool, 2003). David Chandler is one of the few critics to consider Oxfordian methodology; see his 'Historicizing Difference: Anti-Stratfordians and the Academy', *Elizabethan Review* (1991). That electronic journal is now defunct, but his important article can be found at: web.archive.org/web/20060506133739/ http://www.jmucci.com/ER/articles/chandler.htm.

For the founding of the Shakespeare Fellowship, see B. R. Ward, *The Mystery of 'Mr. W. H.'* (London, 1923); *Shakespeare Authorship Review* 1 (1959); as well as the archives of Brunel University, which includes the original Shakespeare Fellowship list of members, 'Shakespeare Fellowship Library' (SAT-0067, Brunel University). For Charles Wisner Barrell, see 'Identifying "Shakespeare"', *Scientific American* (January 1940), as well as Ogburn, *The Mysterious William Shakespeare*. For Leslie Howard, see Hope and Holston, *The Shakespeare Controversy*. Looney's words about circumstantial evidence, as well as his views of Oxford's links to other poets, appear in his edition of *The Poems of Edward De Vere* (London, 1921); his letter of 1927 to Mr Hadder is reprinted in the *Shakespeare Fellowship Newsletter* (September 1952). For an extended list of works of other writers reattributed by various supporters to Oxford, see, for example, Paul Streitz, *Oxford: Son of Queen Elizabeth I* (Darien, Connecticut, 2001); see too The Oxford Authorship Site, www.oxford-shakespeare.com; and more recently, Oxfordian editor Stephanie Hughes's claims in 'Beyond the Authorship Question: Was Shakespeare Only the Beginning?', *Shakespeare Matters* 4 (Spring 2005).

For the episode in which Marlowe's works were attributed to Shakespeare in the early nineteenth century, see David Chandler, 'Marlowe: A Hoax by William Taylor', *Notes and Queries* 239 (June 1994), 220–2. For the claim that Looney's work eschewed ciphers, see the advertisement in Looney's edition of the *Poems of Edward de Vere*. For George Frisbee's findings, see his *Edward de Vere: A Great Elizabethan* (London, 1931). Looney's remarks about Allen are recorded in his letter to Joan Violet Robinson, 3 September 1933; published in Christopher Paul, 'A New Letter by J. T. Looney Brought to Light', *Shakespeare Oxford Newsletter* 43 (Summer 2007). For Freud on Allen, see Woudhuysen, 'A Freudian Oxfordian'.

For more on the Prince Tudor theories, see Ogburn, *The Mysterious William Shakespeare*; Ogburn's letter to the editor of *The Elizabethan Review*, 5.1 (Spring 1997); and Paul H. Altrocchi, 'A Royal Shame: The Origins and History of the Prince Tudor Theory', *Shakespeare Matters* 4 (Summer, 2005). For the origins of the theory, see Percy Allen, *Lord Oxford and Shakespeare: A Reply to John Drinkwater* (London, 1933) and Allen's collaboration with B. M. Ward, *An Enquiry into the Relations between Lord Oxford as 'Shakespeare', Queen Elizabeth and the Fair Youth of Shakespeare's Sonnets* (London, 1936).

For Prince Tudor, Part II, see Paul Streitz, *Oxford: Son of Queen Elizabeth I*. As incestuous as these relationships are, Streitz drew a firm line when it comes to any homoerotic affection on Oxford's part toward his son and half-brother Southampton. Streitz provides a useful lineage extending from the union of Elizabeth and Seymour, then Elizabeth and Oxford, down through Southampton, leading in a direct line to Princess Diana. For an Oxfordian critique of the theory, see Christopher Paul, 'The Prince Tudor Dilemma: Hip Thesis, Hypothesis or Old Wives' Tale?', *Oxfordian* 5 (2002), pp. 47–69. For Roger Stritmatter's remarks, see *The Oxfordian* 2 (1999).

For the vote of confidence in Allen, see the *Shakespeare Fellowship Newsletter* (March 1946). For Stephen Greenblatt on speaking with the dead, see the opening of *Shakespearean Negotiations* (Berkeley, 1988). For more on Hester Dowden, see Edmund Bentley, *Far Horizon: A Biography of Hester Dowden, Medium and Psychic Investigator* (London, 1951). Percy Allen recounts his séances and discoveries in *Talks with Elizabethans: Revealing the Mystery of 'William Shakespeare'* (London, 1947?), which reprints the sonnet quoted here on its title page.

For the fortunes of the Oxfordian movement, see, in addition to Ogburn, *The Mysterious William Shakespeare: Shakespeare Fellowship Quarterly* 5 (1944); *Shakespeare Authorship Review* 7 (1962); *Shakespeare Oxford Society Newsletter*, 15 December 1966; and *Shakespeare Oxford Society Newsletter*, 25 May 1966.

For the challenges to Barrell's claims about the Ashbourne portrait, see Schoenbaum, *William Shakespeare, Records and Images*. For the decline of the Oxfordian movement in the 1960s and 1970s, see *Shakespeare Oxford Society Newsletter*, 28 February 1969; *Shakespeare Oxford Society Newsletter*, 31 March 1970; *Shakespeare Oxford Society Newsletter* (Fall 1976); see too the prefatory page in memory of Charlton Ogburn Jr, *The Oxfordian 2* (1999), as well as Charles Vere's comments in the *Shakespeare Oxford Society Newsletter* (1994). Louis B. Wright's remarks appear in 'The Anti-Shakespeare Industry and the Growth of Cults', *Virginia Quarterly Review* 35 (1959); and see Schoenbaum, *Shakespeare's Lives*.

For more on Ogburn, see *Shakespeare Matters* (Summer, 2007); Charlton Ogburn, 'President's Message', *Shakespeare Oxford Society Newsletter* (Fall 1976); and the *Shakespeare Oxford Society Newsletter* (30 March 1966). For the Fairness Doctrine, see Fred W. Friendly, *The Good Guys, The Bad Guys and The First Amendment: Free Speech vs. Fairness in Broadcasting* (New York, 1976), and Steven J. Simmons, *The Fairness Doctrine and the Media* (Berkeley, 1978). For Ogburn's efforts, see, in addition to *The Mysterious William Shakespeare: Shakespeare Oxford Society Newsletter* (Winter 1979), and his 'President's Message'.

SHAKESPEARE ON TRIAL

For the moot court in Washington DC, see James Lardner, 'Who Wrote Shakespeare?', the *New Yorker*, 11 April 1988, and 'Washington Talk: Briefing; In Re Shakespeare', *New York Times*, 10 September 1987. Kreeger hoped to have the justices prepare by reading Schoenbaum's *Documentary Life* and Ogburn's *Mysterious William Shakespeare*. This didn't work out, and they relied primarily on the arguments of two American University law professors: Peter Jasri for Oxford, James Boyle for Shakespeare. For a full transcript, see *American University Law Review* 37 (Spring 1988), pp. 609–826. Ogburn's letter of complaint appears in the *Shakespeare Oxford Society Newsletter* 24 (Spring 1988). And see the interview with Charlton Ogburn, conducted by Dr Sheila Tombe, in *Apostrophe* (Spring/Summer 1996). Also see Kreeger's 'Preface', *American University Law Review* 37·3 (Spring, 1988). Justice Stevens was even more explicit in suggesting how the Oxfordians should pursue their case five years later in an address he gave at Wilkes University in Pennsylvania. By then he had come around almost completely to Oxfordian assumptions about the autobiographical nature of the plays as well as their aristocratic bias. See US Supreme Court Justice John Paul Stevens, 'The Shakespeare Canon of Statutory Construction', *University of*

Pennsylvania Law Review 140 (1992).

For the moot court in London, see David J. Hanson, 'A Wildcatter Reports on the London Moot Court Hearing in an Open Letter to Russell des Cognets', *The Shakespeare Newsletter* (Spring–Summer 1989). Lord Ackner ended on a witty note, quoting James Barrie: 'I know not whether Bacon wrote the words of Shakespeare, but if he did not, it seems to me he missed the opportunity of his life' – from a transcript of the moot court case in the archives of the International Shakespeare Globe Centre, 'Shakespeare Globe Trust, Shakespeare Moot, Judges Summing Up' (file '1988 Moot'). See too Gordon C. Cyr, 'Let the Real Debate Begin! Legalisms of "Moot" Format Obscure the Authorship Question', *The Shakespeare Oxford Society Newsletter* 25 (Winter 1989). See as well the Shakespeare Moot of 26 November 1988: 'Appraisals from Anonymous Sources' that follows Cyr's account. For Hunt's financial support and for additional background into the relationship of these two British organisations, see Charles Beauclerk's correspondence in the Brunel University library archives, Shakespeare Authorship Trust, Box 0033. And for the British edition of Ogburn's book, see Charlton Ogburn, *The Mystery of William Shakespeare: An Abridgement of the Original American Edition*, ed. Lord Vere (London, 1988).

For the number of viewers, see 'News Items of Interest from Gary Goldstein', in *Shakespeare Oxford Society Newsletter* 25 (Summer 1989); WGBH-TV in Boston also reported that it was their most popular Frontline series that season. For more on the restored fortunes of the Oxfordian movement, see: the *Shakespeare Oxford Society Newsletter* (June 1992); and Lewis H. Lapham, 'Notebook: Full Fathom Five', *Harper's Magazine* (April 1999). The poll is cited from cnn.com, 15 June 1997. On Westminster, see Nathan Baca, 'Commemorating Marlowe', *Shakespeare Matters* 2 (Fall 2002); and see *Shakespeare Matters* (Summer 2003) for fundraising efforts.

On William Niederkorn's agnosticism, I quote from his unsolicited email to me of 9 January 2007. For more on Niederkorn, see *Shakespeare Matters* 1 (Summer 2002) and *Shakespeare Matters* 4 (Winter 2005). See too, William S. Niederkorn, 'The Shakespeare Code, and Other Fanciful Ideas from the Traditional Camp', *New York Times*, 30 August 2005. For a helpful analysis of Niederkorn on Shakespeare, see Ron Rosenbaum, 'The Shakespeare Code: Is *Times* Guy Kind of Bard "Creationist"?', *New York Observer*, 19 September 2005. And for a critique of Niederkorn's conclusion that each side has its own story to tell, see my 'Happy Birthday, Whoever You Were', *Telegraph* (23 April 2006). For National Public Radio and Renée Montagne, see 'The Real Shakespeare: Evidence Points to Earl', *NPR*, 4 July 2008. The award was given to her at the 13th Annual Shakespeare Authorship Studies Conference in 2009. For Oxfordians on the US Supreme Court, see Jess Bravin, 'Justice Stevens Renders an Opinion on Who Wrote Shakespeare's Plays', *Wall Street Journal*, 18 April 2009. For a sense of recent Oxfordian scholarship, see Richard Malim, ed., *Great Oxford*. And for a representative Oxfordian edition of Shakespeare's plays, see William Shakespeare, *Macbeth*, edited and 'Fully Annotated from an Oxfordian Perspective', Richard F. Whalen (Truro, Mass., 2007).

I quote from the introduction to Stritmatter's dissertation at www.shakespearefellowship.org/virtualclassroom/intro.pdf. For criticism of his argument, see Kathman's 'Oxford's Bible', which I have drawn on and quoted above, accessible at www.shakespeareauthorship.com. See too, Tom Veal's online critiques at stromata.tripod.com/id288.htm and stromata.tripod.com/id459.htm. See, as well, Scott Heller, 'In a Centuries-Old Debate, Shakespeare Doubters Point to New Evidence', *The Chronicle of Higher Education*, 4 June 1999, where Alan Nelson is quoted. For Justice Stevens, see Bravin, 'Justice Stevens Renders an Opinion', *Wall Street Journal*.

Part of the revival of interest in Marlowe has also been spurred by director Michael Rubbo's documentary, *Much Ado About Something*, created in response to seeing the 1989 Frontline documentary that had ignored Marlowe's candidacy and focused on Oxford's (www.pbs.org/wgbh/pages/frontline/shows/muchado/fine). See, too, for example, 'The Marlowe-Shakespeare Connection' (marlowe-shakespeare.blogspot.com); 'Marlowe's Ghost' (marlowesghost.com); 'The Marlowe Lives! Association' (www.marlovian.com); and Peter Farey's home page (www2.prestel.co.uk/rey). See, too, the introduction to *Hamlet*, by Christopher Marlowe and William Shakespeare, ed. Alex Jack (Becket, Mass., 2005) and William Honey's privately printed *The Life, Loves, and Achievements of Christopher Marlowe, Alias Shakespeare* (London, 1982). For Jarmusch on Marlowe, see Lynn Hirschberg, 'The Last of the Indies', *New York Times*, 31 July 2005.

For Moore's remarks, see Peter Moore, 'Recent Developments in the Case for Oxford as Shakespeare', *Ever Reader* (No. 4, Fall 1996/Winter 1997). And see William Boyle, 'Books and Book Reviewers', *Shakespeare Matters* 2 (Fall 2002). For the 'Beginner's Guide', see www.shakespeareoxford.com/?p=35. Shahan's remarks appear in *Shakespeare Matters* (Fall 2007). For the latest tally of those who have signed the 'Declaration of Reasonable Doubt', see www.doubtaboutwill.org.

THE EVIDENCE FOR SHAKESPEARE

For facts about editions of the plays and poems, see Andrew Murphy, *Shakespeare in Print: A History and Chronology of Shakespeare Publishing* (Cambridge, 2003). For Buc's acquaintance with the Earl of Oxford, see Charles J. Sisson, *Thomas Lodge and Other Elizabethans* (Cambridge, Mass., 1933). My account of Buc's encounter with Shakespeare draws on Alan H. Nelson, 'George Buc, William Shakespeare, and the Folger George a Greene', *Shakespeare Quarterly* 49 (1998), pp. 74–83; see too, James Shapiro, *1599: A Year in the Life of William Shakespeare* (London and New York, 2005). For more on typesetting, see Margreta de Grazia and Peter Stallybrass, 'The Materiality of the Shakespearean Text', *Shakespeare Quarterly* 44 (1993), pp. 255–83; Randall McLeod, 'Spellbound: Typography and the Concept of Old-Spelling Editions', *Renaissance and Reformation*, n.s. 3 (1979), pp. 50–65; and, forthcoming, Adam G. Hooks, 'Shakespeare and Narrative of Authorship: Biography, Book History, and the Case of Richard Field'. On the origins in the 1870s of the myth that Elizabethan aristocratic poets were averse to publishing their work, see Steve W. May's definitive essay, 'Tudor Aristocrats and the Mythical "Stigma of Print"', *Renaissance Papers* 10 (1980), pp. 11–18.

The kind of specificity offered by the 1604 performances is highly unusual for court payments, which are usually limited to naming the sharers who came to collect the money owed them (so that, for example, Kemp, Burbage and Shakespeare are named as those who were paid in 1595 for their company's recent performances at court), as noted in Chambers, *William Shakespeare: Facts and Problems*. For a helpful discussion of what dramatists knew about stagecraft, see Stanley Wells, *Shakespeare and Co.* (London, 2006).

'HERE'S OUR FELLOW SHAKESPEARE'

See Chambers, *William Shakespeare: Facts and Problems*, for what other writers at the time said about Shakespeare. For Beaumont and Fletcher, see Aubrey's *Brief Lives*, as quoted in Philip Finkelpearl's entry on Beaumont in the new *Dictionary of National Biography*. And for more on the dating of Beaumont's poem, see Peter R. Moore, 'The date of F.B.'s Verse Letter to Ben Jonson', *Notes & Queries* (September 1995), pp. 347–52. For an illuminating discussion of the Pavier quartos, see Sonia Massai, *Shakespeare and the Rise of the Editor* (Cambridge, 2007). See too John Jowett, *Shakespeare and*

BIBLIOGRAPHICAL ESSAY

Text (Oxford, 2007). I am indebted for the suggestion about why the King's Men visited Stratford to Deelman, *The Great Shakespeare Jubilee*. And for the annotations on the Huntington copy of Camden's *Britannia*, see Paul Altrocchi, 'Sleuthing an Enigmatic Latin Annotation', *Shakespeare Matters 2* (Summer 2003), as well as Alan Nelson's research into Hunt's background, and for his translations too (see web.archive.org/web/20051226113826/socrates.berkeley.edu/~ahnelson/Roscius.html). Nelson and Altrocchi have a collaborative article on this, 'William Shakespeare, "Our Roscius"', forthcoming in *Shakespeare Quarterly*. And see Diana Price, *Shakespeare's Unorthodox Biography*.

JACOBEAN SHAKESPEARE

For the Jacobeans on film, see Ronald Hutton, 'Why Don't the Stuarts Get Filmed?' in *Tudors and Stuarts on Film: Historical Perspectives*, ed. Susan Doran and Thomas S. Freeman (New York, 2009), pp. 246–58. I quote from the script of Marc Norman and Tom Stoppard, *Shakespeare in Love: A Screenplay* (New York, 1998). For more on Elizabeth and Shakespeare, see Helen Hackett, *Elizabeth and Shakespeare: The Meeting of Two Myths* (Princeton, 2009), as well as Rowe's *Life of Shakespeare*. For King James's letter to Shakespeare, see *A Collection of Poems . . . by Mr William Shakespeare*, ed. Bernard Lintott (London, 1709). For the boys' companies, the impressing of choristers, and their repertory, see Lucy Munro, *Children of the Queen's Revels* (Cambridge, 2005). For the quotation on the boy players from scene 7 of the 1603 Quarto of *Hamlet*, see *The First Quarto of Hamlet*, ed. Kathleen O. Irace (Cambridge, 1998). For King James's angry reaction, see the letter from Sir Thomas Lake to Lord Salisbury, 11 March 1608, quoted in Irwin Smith, *Shakespeare's Blackfriars Playhouse* (New York, 1964). For more on Blackfriars, see: Gerald Eades Bentley, 'Shakespeare and the Blackfriars Theatre', *Shakespeare Survey 1* (1948), pp. 38–50; Leeds Barroll, 'Shakespeare and the Second Blackfriars Theater', *Shakespeare Studies 33* (2005), pp. 156–70; Gerald Eades Bentley, *The Jacobean and Caroline Stage*, vol. 6 (Oxford, 1968); Andrew Gurr, *The Shakespeare Company: 1595–1642* (Cambridge, 2004); and *Inside Shakespeare: Essays on the Blackfriars Stage*, ed. Paul Menzer (Selinsgrove, 2006).

For dance in the Blackfriars plays, see, for example, the elaborate satyrs' dance sequence followed by the dance of the shepherds and shepherdesses of *The Winter's Tale*, the Morris dance of *Two Noble Kinsmen*, the dance of the celestial spirits in *Henry the Eighth*, and especially, again, *The Tempest*, with its dance of the 'Strange Shapes' in Act 3 and dance of reapers and nymphs in Act 4. My discussion of music and dancing in the Blackfriars plays draws

[351]

on the invaluable work of Irwin Smith. See too Alan Brissenden's excellent overview in his *Shakespeare and the Dance* (London, 1981).

It seems that the entertainment of *The Two Noble Kinsmen* in Act 3 is lifted from the second anti-masque of Beaumont's *Masque of the Inner Temple and Gray's Inn*, which had been performed at Whitehall on 20 February 1613 in celebration of the marriage of Princess Elizabeth to the Elector Palatine (see Brissenden, *Shakespeare and the Dance*). James liked it enough to ask to see it again. For the anti-masquers of the King's Men, see Richard Proudfoot, 'Shakespeare and the New Dramatists of the King's Men 1606–1613', in *Later Shakespeare*, ed. John Russell Brown and Bernard Harris (London, 1966), pp. 235–61. For anti-masque in *The Tempest*, see Stephen Orgel, *The Illusion of Power: Political Theater in the English Renaissance* (Berkeley, 1975). For Frank Kermode on the knotty language of the late plays, see his *Shakespeare's Language* (London, 2000). See too Russ McDonald, *Shakespeare's Late Style* (Cambridge, 2006), and Gordon McMullan, *Shakespeare and the Idea of Late Writing*.

Strachey's full sentence reads: 'He is no longer interested, one often feels, in what happens, or who says what, so long as he can find a place for a faultless lyric, or a new unimagined rhythmical effect, or a grand and mystic speech'; see Strachey, 'Shakespeare's Final Period', *The Independent Review* 3 (August 1904). For contemporary accounts of the burning down of the Globe, see for example, the reports quoted in Gordon McMullan's Arden edition of *Henry VIII* (London, 2000).

For Chambers, see his chapter on 'The Problem of Authenticity' in *William Shakespeare: Facts and Problems*, as well as his famous British Academy lecture on *The Disintegration of Shakespeare* (Oxford, 1924). And see Ben Jonson, *Volpone*, ed. R. B. Parker (Manchester, 1983). I quote Field's letter from Brian Vickers, *Shakespeare, Co-Author: An Historical Study of Five Collaborative Plays* (Oxford, 2002). The story of Fletcher's tavern affair is told in vol. 2 of Thomas Fuller, *The History of the Worthies of England* (London, 1662). For a full discussion of the division of labour between Shakespeare and his collaborators, see Vickers, *Shakespeare, Co-Author*. See too, Stanley Wells, *Shakespeare and Co.*, and C. J. Sisson, *Lost Plays of Shakespeare's Age* (Cambridge, 1936). And for a fascinating account of Shakespeare and George Wilkins, see Charles Nicholl, *The Lodger: Shakespeare on Silver Street* (London, 2008).

EPILOGUE

For the underlying autobiographical assumptions shared by those who deny Shakespeare's authorship, see, for example, Diana Price, *Shakespeare's Unorthodox Biography*, Hank Whittemore, *The Monument* (Marshfield Hills, Mass., 2005), and William Boyle, 'Can Literature Be Evidence?' in *Shakespeare Matters* 3 (Summer 2004).

See Michael Wood, *In Search of Shakespeare* (London, 2003); Stephen Greenblatt, *Will in the World: How Shakespeare Became Shakespeare* (New York, 2004); see too, Greenblatt 'A Great Dane Goes to the Dogs', *New York Review of Books*, 26 March 2009; and René Weis, *Shakespeare Revealed: A Biography* (London, 2007). See, too, *Shakespeare's Personality*, ed. Norman N. Holland, Sidney Homan and Bernard J. Paris (Berkeley, 1989). For Bate's remarks and Niederkorn's response, see Jonathan Bate, 'Is This the Story of the Bard's Heart?', *The Times*, 20 April 2009; and William S. Niederkorn, 'The Sonnets at 400', in 'Paper Cuts', the blog of the editors of the *New York Times Book Review*, papercuts.blogs.nytimes.com/2009/05/20/the-sonnets-at-400/. And see Hank Whittemore, *The Monument*. T. S. Eliot adds, 'I am inclined to believe that people are mistaken about Shakespeare just in proportion to the relative superiority of Shakespeare to myself' in his 'Shakespeare and the Stoicism of Seneca', in *Selected Essays*, second edition (London, 1934).

Much of this social history can be found in E. A. Wrigley et al., *English Population History from Family Reconstitution, 1580–1837* (Cambridge, 1997) and E. A. Wrigley and R. S. Schofield, *The Population History of England, 1541–1871: A Reconstruction* (London, 1981). For more recent overviews, see Will Coster, *Family and Kinship in England 1450–1800* (London, 2001); *The Family in Early Modern England*, ed. Helen Berry and Elizabeth Foyster (Cambridge, 2007); and Naomi Tadmore, 'The Concept of the Household-Family in Eighteenth-Century England', *Past and Present* 151 (1996), pp. 111–40. On early modern autobiography, see Paul Delany, *British Autobiography in the Seventeenth Century* (London, 1969); Meredith Skura, *Tudor Autobiography* (Chicago, 2008); Henry Cuffe, *The Differences of the Ages of Man's Life* (London, 1607); and Germaine Greer, *Shakespeare's Wife*. See too, Gail Kern Paster, *Humoring the Body: Emotions and the Shakespearean Stage* (Chicago, 2004), and *Reading the Early Modern Passions: Essays in the Cultural History of Emotion*, ed. Gail Kern Paster, Katherine Rowe and Mary Floyd-Wilson (Philadelphia, 2004).

For the story of the Mark Lawson interview, see Susan Elderkin, 'Gullible's Travels', *Financial Times*, 23 June 2007, my thanks to Rosie Blau, who commissioned the review and shared it with me. For Giles Fletcher's work, see his *Licia, or Poems of Love* (n.p., 1593); *The English Works of Giles Fletcher, the Elder*, ed. Lloyd E. Berry (Madison, 1964); and Gordon McMullan's excellent *Dictionary of National Biography* entry. And for the story of the young scholar who bragged of sleeping with Licia, see *Records of Early English Drama: Cambridge*, ed. Alan H. Nelson, 2 vols (Toronto, 1989), as well as Nelson's 'Shakespeare and the Bibliophiles,' where the story is told of young William Covell (a future clergyman and early admirer of 'sweet Shakespeare') who reportedly boasted to a Cambridge friend (who in turn told this to a married woman with whom Covell was having an affair) that Covell 'lay with Licia, and by what means he got to her bed'. For what Shakespeare would have learned in grammar school, see T. W. Baldwin, *William Shakspere's Small Latine & Lesse Greeke*, 2 vols. (Urbana, Illinois, 1944). For Shakespeare's vocabulary, see David Crystal, *'Think on My Words': Exploring Shakespeare's Language* (Cambridge, 2008).

Acknowledgements

Researching and drafting a book is a solitary business, revising and seeing it into print a deeply collaborative one. I have been blessed in my friends and colleagues – James Bednarz, Mary Cregan, Robert Griffin, David Kastan, Richard McCoy, Gail Kern Paster, William Sherman, Alvin Snider and Stanley Wells – who have been patiently reading and improving my work, some of them for decades. Collectively, they have made this a much better book than the one I first shared with them and have spared me from many errors of fact and judgement.

I have benefited greatly from the guidance of a pair of brilliant editors, Bob Bender and Julian Loose, as well as from the suggestions and support of my literary agents, Anne Edelstein and Rachel Calder. I'm also grateful for the help I've had along the way, in matters large and small, from Rosie Blau, Warren Boutcher, Jerry Brotton, Tim Brearley, Maurice Charney, Ashley Combest, Barry and Mary Cregan, Becky Fincham, Clive Fisher, Andrew Hadfield, Adam Hooks, David Kurnick, William Leahy, Hermione Lee, Zachary Lesser, Laurie Maguire, Russ McDonald, John McGavin, Gordon McMullan, James Miller, William Monroe, Alan Nelson, David Norbrook, Anne Owen, Tom Paulin, Douglas Pfeiffer, Trevor Poots, Ross Posnock, Martin Puchner, Eleanor Rees, Jacqueline Rose, Richard Sacks, Herbert and Lorraine Shapiro, Jill Shapiro, Michael Shapiro, Kevin Sharp, Laurie Sheck, Patrick Spottiswoode, Alan Stewart, Jean Strouse, Daniel Swift, Sam Swope, Jeff Talarigo, Jeremy Treglown, Pierre Walker, René Weis, Linda Woodbridge, Terence Wright and Georgiana Ziegler.

One of the unspoken arguments of this book is that electronic resources can only take scholarship so far; libraries, and their largely untapped archival riches, remain as crucial as ever. Libraries have been a second home for me while researching this book, and I'm grateful for the help provided by the following archivists and institutions: the New York Public Library; the Folger Shakespeare Library; the British Library; the National Library, Dublin; Karen Attar at Senate House Library of the University of London; Columbia University Libraries; the Huntington Library; Dartmouth

College Library; Brunel University Library; Neda Salem at the Mark Twain Project at the Bancroft Library, University of California at Berkeley; University of Tennessee Library; Harry Miller at the Wisconsin Historical Society; Helen Burton at Keele University Library; Helen Selsdon at the Helen Keller archives, American Foundation for the Blind; and the Shakespeare Birthplace Trust.

I could not have written this book without the generous support provided by a Guggenheim Fellowship; a Distinguished Visiting Fellowship at Queen Mary, University of London; and a fellowship at the Dorothy and Lewis B. Cullman Center for Scholars and Writers at the New York Public Library, an unrivalled literary community, thanks in large part to the guidance of Jean Strouse. I'm grateful, too, for the helpful feedback from audiences that have heard my work-in-progress at King's College, University of London; Penn State University; the Sun Valley Writers Conference; the Early Modern seminar at Oxford University; and Queen Mary, University of London. I'm also keenly aware of how much I have learned over the past quarter-century from my students at Columbia University.

Once again, my greatest debt is to my wife and best critic, Mary Cregan, and to our son Luke, to whom this book is dedicated.

Index

Abraham, Karl, 173
Ackner, Lord, 237
actors, 259–62, 282–3
Adams, Henry, 127
Addenbrooke, John, 12, 70
Admiral's Men, 67, 261, 276
All's Well That Ends Well, 63, 200
Allen, Ernest, 225–6
Allen, Percy, 216, 222–3, 224–8
Alleyn, Edward, 26, 50, 261, 270, 276
Altrocchi, Paul, 276
The American Scene (James), 167
Angerianus, 310
Anna of Denmark, Queen, 28
Anne Boleyn, 143–4
Antony and Cleopatra: authorship, 290;
   dating, 44, 63, 202; Looney on, 202–3
Apology for Actors (Heywood), 281
Arcadia (Sidney), 310
Archer, Jeffrey, 236
Arden of Faversham, 256–7
Arden Shakespeare series, 289
Ariel (Plath), 298
Aristotle, 308
Armin, Robert, 261
Arnold, Matthew, 85
As You Like It: Adam's character, 197;
   autobiographical readings 64; dating, 63;
   setting, 314
Ashbourne portrait, 219–20, 229
Aspley, William, 264–5
The Athenaeum, 120
The Atlantic, 231, 239
Aubrey, John, 56, 202
Austen, Jane, 298
Austin, Al, 238
authorship: early modern conventions, 194–5,
   256–7, 304–5; expectation that fiction is
   autobiographical, 125–9, 297–316; nature

of, 36–7; personae, 304
autobiography: development of genre, 127,
   304–5; expectation that fiction is autobiographical, 125–9, 297–316

Bacon, Delia, 93–100, 93, 101–24, 149–51
Bacon, Francis, 91; nineteenth-century
   reputation, 101–2; arguments against
   Baconians, 265; attempts to call up from
   dead, 225, 226, 227; and ciphers, 102, 112,
   113, 133–45, 158–60; D. Bacon's theories,
   100–24; demise of support, 170; Freud's
   view, 177–8, 186; James's view, 164; life and
   works, 100–1; link to possible motive for
   Cowell forgery, 13–14; other Baconians,
   119, 131, 132–45, 158–60, 163–4, 226; TV
   coverage of claims, 238; Twain's theories,
   131–4, 135–7, 139–40, 145–58, 160
Bacon, Leonard: education, 93; on Founding
   Fathers, 109–10; and sister's Baconian
   theories, 98, 122; and sister's play, 96–7;
   as sister's protector, 94, 95, 103–4
Bacon College, Kentucky, 101
Baconiana (journal), 135, 158
Baildon, H. Bellyse, 84
Barnfield, Richard, 267
Barrell, Charles Wisner, 219, 229
Bate, Jonathan, 4, 55, 301
Beale, Simon Russell, 278
Beauclerk, Charles, 236, 237–9
Beaumont, Francis, 271, 281, 283, 353–4
Becker, Sarah, 106
Beecher, Catherine, 93, 104
Beecher, Mary, 93
Behn, Aphra, 50
The Bell Jar (Plath), 298
Bénézet, Louis, 219
Bennett, Arnold, 127
Benson, John, 45, 56, 57

Bernays, Martha, 177–8
Bethell, Tom, 239
Betterton, Thomas, 56
Biographia Britannica, 50
Biblical scholarship, 82–9, 115–16, 151–2
biography: development of literary, 50–1; difficulties of understanding early modern people, 306–9; *see also* autobiography
'The Birthplace' (James), 161, 162–3, 165–7
Blackfriars Theatre, 71–2, 74, 279–86, 289
Blackmun, Harry, 233–5, 242
Blackwell, Thomas, 79
Blackwell's (magazine), 58, 81
Blanton, Margaret, 174–5
Blanton, Smiley, 173–5, 211
Boaden, James, 25
Boccaccio, Giovanni, 288
Bodell, Evelyn, 213
books: Elizabethan and Jacobean access to, 310–11; Elizabethan and Jacobean ownership, 254; WS's ownership, 55; *see also* authorship; printing and publishing
Booth, Edwin, 149
Booth, William Stone, 133–5, 147, 152–3, 158–9
Boswell, James, 25, 50–1, 68
Boswell, James, the Younger, 52, 53
Boyle, James, 235
Boyle, William, 302
Bradley, Henry, 134
Brandes, Georg, 168, 178–80, 184
Branson, James S. H., 211
Brathwaite, Richard, 325
Brennan, William, 233–5, 242
The Bride of Fort Edward (D. Bacon), 95–7
Britannia (Camden), 275–6
Broach, Elise, 5–6
Brooke, Arthur, 221
Brown, Charles Armitage, 59
Brown, Joseph: portraits by, 171
Browning, Elizabeth Barrett, 81
Browning, Robert, 59
Brücke, Ernst, 208
Brunswick, Ruth, 174
Buc, George, 254–5
Buckhurst, Lord, 107
Buckley, William F., Jr., 238
Bunyan, John, 139–40
Burbage, James, 71–2, 280
Burbage, Richard: as actor, 280, 281, 282, 283; and impersonations of, 269; and Rutland's *imprese*, 262; in WS's plays, 261

Burby, Cuthbert, 257–8
Burghley, Lord *see* Cecil, William
Burton, Robert, 141, 270
Butler, Charles, 111
Butler, Samuel, 80

Cambridge Shakespeare series, 289
Camden, William, 269, 275–6
Camden Society, 73
Campbell, Thomas, 59
Campion, Thomas, 269
Canterbury Tales (Chaucer), 304
Capell, Edward, 49, 56, 65
Cardenio, 68, 256, 289, 290
Carion, John, 22
Carlyle, Thomas, 85, 113–14
Causey, William F., 242
Caxton, William, 50
Cecil, Anne, 200, 201, 217–18
Cecil, Robert, 142, 223
Cecil, Thomas, 200
Cecil, William (Lord Burghley), 200, 201, 218, 276, 310
censorship, 35–6, 201
Chalmers, George, 38, 60
Chamberlain's Men *see* King's Men
Chambers, E. K., 289
Chaplin, Charlie, 321
Chapman, George: Camden on, 269; and Children of the Queen's Revels, 281; and Sonnets, 60, 265–6; style, 288; works' erudition, 313
Charles L. Webster and Company, 135
Chart of Literary Paper Trails *see* CPLT
Chaucer, Geoffrey: author's persona, 304; and authorship of The Testament of Love, 134; D. Bacon on, 96; as Sonnets' rival poet, 60; WS's lifting of words from, 288; WS's supposed ownership of books by, 27
Chettle, Henry, 266
Children of the Chapel Royal, Windsor, 281
Children of the Queen's Revels, 72, 281–2
Church of Humanity, 189–90, 197
Churchyard, Thomas, 22
cipher wheels, 136, 141, 159
ciphers and codes, 133–45, 158–60, 222
the Claimant, 153–5
Clark, Eva Turner, 216, 228
Clayton, John, 76
Clemens, Clara, 124
Clemens, Jean, 124, 152
Clemens, Livia, 124

Clemens, Samuel *see* Twain, Mark
Clopton, Hugh, 275
Clopton House, 19
codes *see* ciphers and codes
Coleridge, Samuel Taylor, 59, 61, 62–3, 81
Collier, John Payne, 12, 69, 71–4
Combe, John, 70
Combe, Thomas, 54
Combe, William, 70
Comedy of Errors, 63, 65, 259
  coming of age, 308
Comte, Auguste, 188, 191–2, 195, 208
Condell, Henry, 30–1, 39, 282, 283
Congreve, Richard, 189, 192, 198
A Connecticut Yankee in King Arthur's Court (Twain), 149
Conrad, Joseph, 127, 128
conspiracy theories, 7–8, 222–4, 239–41, 245–6, 255, 321
Cooke, Dr James, 55
copyright, 255–6
Coriolanus: authorship, 290; D. Bacon's studies, 107; dating, 63, 202; Looney on, 202–3; court cases, 233–7
Covell, William, 267
Cowell, James Corton, 1–2, 11–14
Cowley, Richard, 261
Cowper, William, 33
CPLE (Chart of Literary Paper Evidence), 276–7
Cromwell, Oliver, 20
cryptography *see* ciphers and codes
Crystal, David, 312–13
Cuffe, Henry, 308
Curtain Theatre, 262–3
Cymbeline: authorship, 290; dating, 63, 203; eyewitness account of contemporary performance, 72; Looney on, 203; music and dance in, 28; setting and characters, 314
Cyr, Gordon C., 237

Daborne, Robert, 292
Dall, Catherine Healey, 105–6
Dana, Richard Henry, 95
Daniel, Samuel, 55, 60, 72, 269
Dante Alighieri, 187, 304
D'Avenant, William, 279
Davies, John, of Hereford, 301
De Augmentis Scientiarum (F. Bacon), 137
De Passe, Simon: portraits by, 91
De Vere Society, 236–7
The Death of Marlowe, 143–4

'Declaration of Reasonable Doubt about the Identity of William Shakespeare', 248–9
Deelman, Christian, 32–3
Defoe, Daniel, 129
de Grazia, Margreta, 44
Dekker, Thomas, 30, 270, 293, 310–11, 314
Delaney, Paul, 304
Dench, Judi, 278
Dennis, John, 278
Derby, William Stanley, Earl of, 215, 218–19, 227, 265
Diana, Princess of Wales, 348
Digges, Leonard, 31, 274
Disraeli, Benjamin, 80
Divine Comedy (Dante), 304
Dix and Edwards, 115
Dodd, Alfred, 226
Donne, John, 2
Donnelly, Ignatius, 135–9, 152–3, 159
Douglas, Montagu William, 216–17
Dowden, Edward, 204, 226
Dowden, Hester, 225–8
Doyle, Sir Arthur Conan, 225
Drake, Sir Francis, 27
Drayton, Michael: contemporaries on, 269; doctor, 55; Oldys's biography, 50; plays by, 67; as Sonnets' rival poet, 60; on WS, 270–1; and WS's death, 56
Droeshout, Martin: portraits by, 251, 274
Drummond, William, 269–70, 272
Drury Lane theatre, 29, 33
Dryden, John, 31
The Duchess of Malfi (Webster), 283
Durning-Lawrence, Sir Edwin, 11
Dyce, Alexander, 73, 74, 77
Dyson, Humphrey, 270

Ealer, George, 150–1
Eastward Ho, 282
Eden, Frederick, 22
Edison, Thomas, 130
Edmund Ironside, 222
Edward the Third, 222, 257
Egerton, Lord Francis, 71
Egerton, Sir Thomas, 71
Eichhorn, Johann Gottfried, 82–3
Eitingon, Max, 173, 186, 206
Elderkin, Susan, 309
Eliot, George, 83
Eliot, T. S., 305
Elizabeth I, Queen: as addressee of Sonnets, 60; and Bacon, 100; Baconians on rela-

tionship with Bacon, 141–2, 143; Broach on relationship with Oxford, 5; Congreve on, 198; forged letter to WS from, 22–3, 23, 35, 36; forged verses to by WS, 27, 37; and Oxford, 202; Oxfordians on, 216–17, 222–3, 245–6, 302; at performances of WS plays, 72, 263; Twain's belief was man, 155–6; and WS, 278–9

Elizabeth of Bohemia (the Winter Queen), 354

Elliott, Ward, 289

Ellis, Sir Henry, 113

Emerson, Ralph Waldo: on Bacon, 101; and D. Bacon, 111–13, 114–15, 119; and Higher Criticism, 86; on the Sonnets, 59, 61; on Wolf's study of Homer, 78–9

Essex, Robert Devereux, Earl of: allusions to in WS's plays, 41–2; as author of WS's plays, 214; Baconians on relationship with Bacon, 143; rebellion (1601), 302; and *Richard the Second*, 109; Oxfordians on, 223

Evans, Henry, 280–1, 282, 283

Evans, Thomas, 282

Every Man in His Humour (Jonson), 271–2

Every Man out of His Humour (Jonson), 272

Fabyan, George, 142, 159–60

Farmer, Richard, 65

Farrar, Eliza, 105, 106

Farren, Elizabeth, 29

Fenton, Richard, 70–1

Ferenczi, Sándor, 173, 206

Fiedler, Leslie, 158

Field, Nathan, 292

Field, Richard, 283

'The Figure in the Carpet' (James), 339

Fisher, Henry W., 155–6

Flatter, Richard, 210–11

Fleiss, Wilhelm, 177, 178, 180–1

Fletcher, Giles, 309–10

Fletcher, John: and Children of the Queen's Revels, 281; co-authorship of WS plays, 68, 289, 290, 292, 293, 294–5; and King's Men, 283; other collaborations, 292; style, 288

Florio, John, 221, 301

Folger Shakespeare Library, 5, 232

Following the Equator (Twain), 154

Foote, Samuel, 32

Ford, Ford Madox, 128

Ford, John, 293

Forman, Simon, 72, 74

Forrest, Edwin, 149

Franklin, Benjamin, 127

French, George Russell, 42

Freud, Anna, 212

Freud, Sigmund, 173–86, 173, 206–13, 216, 223

Friedman, William, 159–60

Frisbee, George, 222

Frontline (TV series), 238

Fuller, Thomas, 56, 292

Fuseli, Henry, 33–4

Gallup, Elizabeth Wells, 142–5, 159, 160

Garber, Marjorie, 4

Garrick, David, 18, 32–3, 34

Gascoigne, George, 221, 222, 304

Gay, Peter, 176

George IV, King, 26

George a Greene, the Pinner of Wakefield, 254–5

Gilder, Richard Watson, 145–7

Giles, Nathaniel, 280–1

Gilfillan, George, 85

Globe Theatre: beginnings, 280; entry price, 281; fire and rebuilding, 262, 288–9; as icon, 279; and King's Men, 282; lighting, 284

Godwin, William, 134

Golding, Arthur, 221

Google, 246–7

Grafton, Anthony, 82

Greenblatt, Stephen, 225, 299–300

Greene, Robert, 66, 141, 221, 266

Greene, Thomas, 73

Greenwood, George: and Shakespeare Fellowship, 218; WS studies, 132, 148, 152, 153, 156–7, 158

Greer, Germaine, 307

Greville, Fulke, 2

Hakluyt, Richard, 50

Hakluyt Society, 73

Hall, John, 54–5

Hallam, Henry, 63–4

Halliwell-Phillipps, James Orchard, 55, 73, 74–5, 75–7, 168

Hamlet: allusions to child actors, 281; arguments for Bacon's authorship, 141–2; autobiographical readings, 49, 62, 64, 300–1; dating, 42, 63, 104, 301; duel at end, 284; Freud on, 177, 178–85, 209–10; Hamlet and imagination, 314–15; Harris on, 194; Looney on, 198, 204–5, 217; mentioned in forged letter from Peele to Marlowe, 26;

MS, 227; parallels with Oxford's life, 200–1; performances attended by Twain, 149; publishing history, 258; Religion of Humanity on, 187–8; WS's contemporaries on, 268

Hanmer, Thomas, 65
Harding, George Perfect: portraits by, 171
Harper's, 231, 239–40
Harrington, Sir John, 222, 270
Harris, Frank, 194
Hart, Joseph C., 69
Harvey, Gabriel, 184–5, 202, 268
Hathaway, Anne, 57; allusions to in WS's works, 44–8, 300; business dealings, 75, 307; forged letter from WS to, 22; marriage to WS, 8, 44–8, 300; and WS's will, 9
Hathaway, Thomas, 54
Hathway, Richard, 67
Hawthorne, Nathaniel, 110–11, 120–2, 123
Hédelin, François, 79
Heine, Heinrich, 58
Heminges, John: and Blackfriars Theatre, 282, 283; and First Folio, 30–1, 39; forged receipt from WS to, 22
Henry the Second, 26
Henry the Fourth, Part I, 260
Henry the Fourth, Part II, 262–5
Henry the Fifth: allusions to contemporary events, 41; authorship, 65; Harris on, 194; Looney on, 200; MS, 227; publishing history, 258
Henry the Sixth, Part II, 65, 66, 67
Henry the Sixth, Part III: authorship, 65, 66, 67; Greene's parody, 266; internal evidence of WS's authorship, 260
Henry the Eighth: authorship, 68, 289, 290, 292, 293; dating, 288; first performances, 262; Looney on, 203; music in, 285; style, 286–7
Henslowe, Philip: Diary, 66–8, 69, 72; Field's letter pitching new play, 292
Heron, Flodden W., 205–6
Heywood, Thomas: Apology for Actors, 281; and Kyd's authorship of *The Spanish Tragedy*, 256; literary biographies by, 54; prolificness, 271; Webster on, 30, 270; on WS, 271
High Life Below Stairs, 21
Higher Criticism, 82–9, 115–16, 151–2
The History of Thomas Lord Cromwell, 64–5
Hoffman, Calvin, 229
Holinshed, Raphael, 27, 314

Holland, H. H., 216
Holland, Hugh, 269, 274
Holmes, William, 22
Homer, 78–82, 115–16, 187
Honigmann, Ernest, 237
Hooker, Richard, 55
Hope, Jonathan, 289
Horneby, Thomas, 70
Howard, Leslie, 220
Howe, Edmund, 30
Howells, William Dean, 127
Huband, Ralph, 75
Huckleberry Finn (Twain), 149
Hunt, Richard, 275–6
Hunt, Violet, 163, 164–5
Hunt, William O., 237
Hunter, Joseph, 74
Hutton, Ronald, 278
Huxley, Aldous, 225
Huxley, T. H., 188

imprese, 262
'In re Shakespeare: The Authorship of Shakespeare on Trial', 233–6
Instauratio Magna (F. Bacon), 102
Ireland, Samuel, 19–20, 21–8, 34–8; books by, 17
Ireland, William-Henry, 19, 21–8, 34–8, 52
Irons, Jeremy, 249
Irving, Sir Henry, 226
Is He Dead? (Twain), 158
Is Shakespeare Dead? (Twain), 157–8, 160
The Isle of Dogs (Jonson and Nashe), 257
The Isle of Gulls, 282

Jackson, MacDonald, 289
Jacobi, Derek, 230–1, 248
Jaggard, William, 273–4
James I, King: accession, 302; Accession Day celebrations, 262; and Bacon, 101; and Children of the Queen's Revels, 282; and masques, 354; Oxford as author of works, 222; and WS, 72, 277–9
James II, King, 20
James, Henry, 127, 160–70, 339
James, William, 161–2
Jameson, Anna, 61–2
Jarmusch, Jim, 247–8
Jesus Christ, 83–9, 151–2
Jews, 3–4
jigs, 263
John of Stratford, Archbishop of

Canterbury, 275

Johnson, Dr Samuel: and authorship of *Richard the Second*, 65; influence on Malone, 40; *Lives of the Poets*, 50–1; on writing for money, 77; WS edition, 39; on WS's Lost Years, 71

Jones, Ernest, 173: on authorship of Hamlet, 184–5; on Baconians, 178; and Freud's correspondence with Bernays, 177; Freud's letter to about Nazis, 213; on Freud's Oedipal theory, 182; on Freud's Oxfordian theories, 206–8; on Freud's rejection of WS's authorship, 175–6

Jonson, Ben: Beaumont's letter to, 271; contemporaries on, 269; D. Bacon on, 115; *The Isle of Dogs*, 257; and King's Men, 283; and masques, 285; printed editions, 31; settings, 314; and the Sonnets, 265–6; as Sonnets' rival poet, 60; on *Volpone*, 291–2; works' erudition, 313; on WS, 31, 271–3, 274; and WS's death, 56

Josephus, 79

The Jubilee (Garrick), 33

Julius Caesar: D. Bacon's studies, 107, 108; dating, 63; forged MS, 26; Harris on, 194

Kathman, David, 244

Keats, John, 59, 62

Keep the Widow Waking (Dekker, Webster, Ford and Rowley), 293

Keller, Helen, 125, 131–3, 145, 155, 159

Kemble, Fanny, 95

Kemble, John Philip, 28

Kemp, Will, 261, 263, 269

Kermode, Frank, 286–7, 288

King John, 43, 65

King Lear: 1608 quarto, 256; autobiographical readings, 64; D. Bacon's studies, 107; dating, 63, 202; Fool's character, 197; forged MS page, 24–5, 24, 35–6, 38; Freud on, 185, 210, 211; Looney on, 202–3; MS, 227

King's Men (formerly Chamberlain's Men): and Jonson, 271–2; and Stratford, 275; theatres used by, 280, 282–6; and WS, 259–66, 264–5, 271–2, 274

Kittredge, George Lyman, 131

Knight, Charles, 73, 74

Kreeger, David Lloyd, 233, 236

Kyd, Thomas, 31, 221, 256, 257, 342

Lake, David, 289

Lamb, Charles and Mary, 161

Lapham, Lewis H., 239–40

Laporte, Charles, 84

Lardner, James, 235

Lawson, Mark, 309

The Learned Pig, 21

Leaves of Grass (Whitman), 139

Lee, Sidney, 184, 201, 202

Lefranc, Abel, 218–19

Leicester, Robert Dudley, Earl of, 22, 141

Leonardo da Vinci, 185

Licia, or Poems of Love (Fletcher), 309–10

Lintott, Bernard, 278

Lobb, John, 226

The Lodger (Nicholl), 76

The London Prodigal, 76

Looney, John Thomas, 186; background, 189–90; disappointment at slow spread of Oxfordian theories, 220; edition of Oxford's poetry, 216; Freud on, 207–9, 212–13; on Oxford as author of other contemporaries' poetry, 221; Oxfordian theories, 189–206, 213–14, 217–18, 223; on Prince Tudor theories, 222–3; US edition of 'Shakespeare' Identified, 228

Love's Labour's Lost, 65, 257–8

Love's Labour's Won, 256

Love's Martyr (contributed volume of poetry), 266

'Love's Martyr' (D. Bacon), 94, 95

Lowin, John, 22

Lucrece, 96, 256, 266–7, 268, 269

Lyly, John, 31, 221

Lyon, Isabel, 124, 131–3, 147–8, 151, 152

Mabbe, James, 31, 274–5

Macbeth: dating, 63, 202; Drury Lane opening-night performance (1794), 29; eyewitness account of contemporary performance, 72; Freud on, 177, 185, 210; Looney on, 202–3; MS, 227

McCrea, Jane, 94

McDonald, Ross, 287

Macklin, William, 39

MacWhorter, Alexander, 103–4, 105, 106

Macy, John, 132–4, 148, 153, 157, 159

Malcolm X, 321

Malone, Edmond: and authorship of individual plays, 66–9; edition and biography of WS, 39–53; and hunt for WS's papers, 18, 19, 20, 26; Ireland papers exposed as forgery by, 34–8; suppositions made from Sonnets, 60, 61; on WS's style, 287

Marble, Manton, 163–4
Marlowe, Christopher: arguments against Marlovians, 262; authorship of *Tamburlaine*, 256; Bacon as, 141; forged letter from Peele re WS, 26; Jonson on, 31; and Kyd, 257; Marlovian theories, 6–7, 214, 229, 238, 240–1, 247–8; Oxford as, 221, 222; as Sonnets' rival poet, 60; works' erudition, 313; WS as author of his plays, 222
Marshall, William: portraits by, 91
Marston, John, 265–6, 269, 281, 313
Mary Queen of Scots, 41
Mary Queen of Scots, 143–4
Masque of the Inner Temple and Gray's Inn (Beaumont), 353–4
masques, 285–6
Masson, David, 59–60
Matus, Irving, 239
Measure for Measure, 63, 259
Meigs, Return Jonathan, 119
Melville, Herman, 85
The Merchant of Venice: 1604 performance, 259; dating, 63; Freud on, 185; Looney on, 193–4
Meres, Francis, 20, 30, 53, 267–8
The Merry Wives of Windsor, 217, 258, 278
Meynert, Theodor, 177, 186
Middleton, Thomas: and Children of the Queen's Revels, 281; co-authorship of Timon, 68, 289, 290, 292, 293; and King's Men, 283; settings, 314
A Midsummer Night's Dream, 63, 315–16
Mill, John Stuart, 188
Milton, John, 51, 139–40
Mister V (film), 220
Moffett, Samuel, 129–30
Montagne, Renée, 242
Montaigne, Michel Eyquem de, 17
Moore, Peter, 245
Morse, Samuel, 95, 102, 135
Moses, 175–6
Mucedorus, 256–7
Much Ado about Nothing, 261
Munday, Anthony, 67, 221
Murdoch, Patrick, 51
Murphy, Arthur, 31

Nashe, Thomas, 221, 257, 276
National Geographic Society, 233
Neilson, William A., 131
Nelson, Alan, 4, 201–2, 244–5, 258, 270
Neville, Henry, 3

New York Times, 231, 241–2, 243
Nicholl, Charles, 76
Nicoll, Alardyce, 11, 13
Niederkorn, William, 241–3, 301–2
Nietzsche, Friedrich, 79–80
North, Sir Thomas, 221, 314
Nugent, William, 2

Oedipus Rex (Sophocles), 181, 183
Ogburn, Charlton, Jr, 231–5, 237–8, 239, 321
Oldys, William, 45, 50
Oliver, Lord, 237
Orcutt, William Dana, 167
Orgel, Stephen, 285
Orton, Arthur, 153–5
Ostler, William, 283
Othello: autobiographical readings, 46, 300; dating, 63, 72; Freud on, 210; Looney on, 217, MS, 227; performances attended by Twain, 149
Otway, Thomas, 51
Ovid, 30
Owen, Orville Ward, 140–2, 144–5, 159; cipher wheel, 136
Oxford, Edward de Vere, Earl of, 171; arguments against Oxfordians, 262, 265, 268, 286, 294–5; and Ashbourne portrait, 219–20, 229; attempts to call up from dead, 224–8; as author of other contemporaries' work, 221–2; Broach's theories, 5–6; and ciphers, 222; court cases, 233–7; D. Bacon's theories, 107; Freud's theories, 173–86, 206–13, 223; Geneva Bible, 244–5; Internet publicity, 246–9; life, 200–2, 211, 217–18; link to possible motive for Cowell forgery, 13–14; Looney's theories, 189–206, 213–14, 217–18, 223; media coverage, 238–40, 241–3; Ogburn's resurrection of movement, 231–8; other Oxfordians, 214–49, 276, 302–3; overview of Oxfordian arguments, 7; Prince Tudor theories, 222–4, 227, 240, 245–6, 302–3; spelling, 258
Oxford Shakespeare series, 289

Paine, Albert Bigelow, 125–6, 152–3
Palladia Tamia (Meres), 20, 267–8
Palgrave, Francis, 196
Palmer, Cecil, 196, 219, 222
Park Theatre, New York, 95, 96
Parker Society, 73
Parnassus plays, 268–9
Parr, Samuel, 24

Pavier, Thomas, 273–4
Peabody, Elizabeth Palmer, 105, 111
Peele, George: and authorship of *Henry the Sixth*, 66; Bacon as, 141; co-authorship of *Titus Andronicus*, 289, 292, 293; forged letter to Marlowe, 26; Keller's thesis on, 131
Percival, James Gates, 94–5
Percy Society, 73
Pericles: authorship, 64–5, 66, 67, 289, 290, 292, 293; dating, 63, 202; evidence of author's *impresa* skills, 262; Looney on, 202–3

Peyster, John Watts de, 161
Phillips, Augustine, 282–3
The Pilgrim's Progress (Bunyan), 139–40
Pimpernel Smith (film), 220
plague, 281
Plath, Sylvia, 298
Playfair, John, 101
playscripts, Elizabethan and Jacobean, 35–6
Plutarch, 221, 314
Poe, Edgar Allan, 94, 97, 135
Poets' War, 269
Pope, Alexander, 40, 43, 51, 65
Pope, Thomas, 282
Positivist movement, 186–90, 191–2, 197, 208
Potter, Lois, 294
Prescott, Kate, 142–3, 144–5
Price, Diana, 242, 276–7, 298, 313
Pride and Prejudice (Austen), 298
The Prince and the Pauper (Twain), 130, 149
Prince Tudor theories, 222–4, 227, 240, 245–6, 302–3

printing and publishing, Elizabethan and Jacobean conventions, 137–8, 255–9
The Puritan Widow, 64–5
Puttenham, George, 222
Pythagoras, 308
Quin, Malcolm, 189–90
Quincey, Thomas de, 81
Quincey, Richard, 18, 54, 70
Quincey, Thomas, 54
Ralegh, Sir Walter, 27, 107
Rank, Otto, 173
Ravenscroft, Edward, 65
Reed, Edwin, 131
Reik, Theodor, 208–9
Religion of Humanity, 186–90, 191–2, 197, 208
Rendall, Gerald H., 211, 216, 228

Richard the Second: authorship, 65; and Essex, 109; forged MS, 26; MS, 227; publishing history, 258; sources, 310
Richard the Third, 258
Rieu, E. V., 81–2
Riley, James H., 129
Riverbank Laboratories, 160
Robert, Earl of Leicester, 143–4
Robert the Earl of Essex, 143–4
Robertson, J. M., 84–5
Robinson Crusoe (Defoe), 129
Rogers, Philip, 75
Romeo and Juliet: autobiographical readings, 62, 64; Drummond's copy, 269–70; internal evidence for WS's authorship, 26; Looney on, 217; Nurse's character, 197; publishing history, 258
Romney, George: paintings by, 15, 34
Roscius, 276
Ross, Terry, 244
Roubiliac, Louis François, 32
Rowe, Nicholas, 40, 43
Rowley, William, 293
Rowse, A. L., 238
Rubbo, Michael, 351
Rutland, Roger Manners, fifth Earl of, 214–15, 265
Rutland, Francis Manners, sixth Earl of, 262
Rylance, Mark, 230–1, 248

Sachs, Hanns, 173, 210
St Albans, 114
Savage, Richard, 51
Scalia, Antonin, 243
Schlegel, August Wilhelm von, 58, 81
Schlegel, Friedrich von, 58, 81
Schmucker, Samuel Mosheim, 86–9
Schoenbaum, Samuel: on D. Bacon, 122–3; illness prevents attendance at Oxfordian moot court, 237; prolificness, 4; rejection of autobiographical view of WS's works, 298–9; on sceptics, 230, 236; TV appearances, 238
Screvin, Thomas, 262
The Second Maid's Tragedy, 222
Sejanus (Jonson), 272
Selkirk, J. B., 85
Serres, Olivia Wilmott, 11, 13–14
Seymour, Thomas, 223
Shahan, John M., 249
Shakespeare, Elizabeth (WS's grand-daughter), 54

Shakespeare, Hamnet (WS's son), 43–4, 180, 300–1, 307

Shakespeare, Joan (WS's sister), 54

Shakespeare, John (WS's father), 179, 184, 300

Shakespeare, Judith (WS's daughter), 54

Shakespeare, Susanna (WS's daughter), 45, 54, 55

Shakespeare, William (WS): as actor, 271–3, 276, 282; attempts to call up from dead, 224–8; Blackfriars lodgings, 288; business dealings, 12, 70, 73, 75–8, 307; contemporary reputation, 30, 265–73; death, 262; deification, 29–33, 84–5, 186–8; documents pertaining to life (real and fake), 18–28, 34–8, 69–70, 71–7; education, 312–13; familiarity to contemporaries, 254–5; hyphen in name, 256; imagination, 313–16; legal training, 49, 156–7; life: conceptions drawn from works, 43–53, 56–64, 298–316; life: facts, 47; 'Lost Years', 8–9, 71–3; life experience, 309–12; marriage and family, 8, 44–8, 300, 306, 307; portraits, 15, 17, 34, 57, 219–20, 229, 251, 274; reasons for lack of biographical information, 17–18, 53–6; relationship with Elizabeth and James, 277–9; signature, 297; spelling of name, 258–9; statues, 32; Stratford properties, 30, 53, 55, 69–70, 73; theatres used by, 279–86, 288–9; tomb, 121–2; vocabulary, 312–13; will, 1, 9, 18, 45, 55, 262, 297

– AUTHORSHIP CONTROVERSY: basis in belief in autobiographical nature of literature, 298–316; candidates for authorship, 2–3; evidence for WS, 253–77, 294–316; growing tendency to expect fiction to be autobiographical, 125–9, 297–316; James's theories, 160–70; literary scholarship context, 78–89, 115–16, 151–2; online discussion groups, 6; sceptics, 2, 8; sceptics' dismissal of evidence, 275–7; theological source of arguments, 86–9, 115–16, 151–2; witness from family and acquaintances, 54–6, 265–73

– PRINTED EDITIONS: First Folio (1623), 30–1, 39, 274; Johnson and Steevens (1778), 19, 39; Malone (1790), 39–53; Oxford edition (1986), 290; Pavier and Jaggard's collection (1619), 273–4; Third Folio, second impression (1664), 64–5; in WS's lifetime, 253–4, 256, 257–61

– WORKS: allusions to contemporary events, 41–3; audience, 313; authorship of individual plays, 64–6; autobiographical readings, 43–52, 56–64, 298–316; Blackfriars' effect on, 284–6; characters, 197–8, 288, 313–14, 314–15; co-authorship, 66–9, 289–95; copyright ownership, 255–6; dating, 39–43; internal evidence of his authorship, 63–4; internal evidence of his authorship, 259–65; late style, 286–8; lost plays, 256; music and dance in, 285–6; reasons for lack of props and stage business, 284; reasons for turn to tragicomedy, 284; settings, 314; WS speaking own epilogue, 263–4; see also individual plays and poems by name; Sonnets

Shakespeare, William (WS's nephew), 54

Shakespeare Authorship Coalition website, 248–9

Shakespeare Authorship Society, 229, 237

Shakespeare Fellowship, 218–19, 220, 224–5, 228, 229

Shakespeare in Love (film), 278

Shakespeare Oxford Society, 228–9, 230–1, 232, 237, 239

Shakespeare Society (Collier's), 73

Shakespeare's Secret (Broach), 5–6

Shakespeareana Genealogica, 42

Sharp, Thomas, 30

Shylock is Shakespeare (Gross), 47

Sidney, Mary, 223

Sidney, Sir Philip, 144, 217, 265, 269, 310

Silliman, Benjamin, 102

The Silver Mine, 282

Simmes, Valentine, 258, 264–5

Simpson, Edward, 96

Sinklo, John, 260, 282

Sir John Oldcastle, 64–5, 67

Sisson, C. J., 298

1601 (Twain), 149

Skeat, Walter, 134

Skura, Meredith, 304

Slater, Gilbert, 216

Sly, William, 282, 283

Smith, Benjamin: engravings by, 15

Smith, Edith Jane Durning, 11

Smith, R. A., 119

Smith, Sid, 309

Smith, William, 119–20

Sobran, Joseph, 235–6

Something Like a House (Smith), 309

Sonnets: 1609 edition, 256; autobiographical readings, 58–62, 299, 300, 301–2, 302–3; Freud on, 210–11; publishing history, 56–8;

writing of, 265–6
Sonnet 20, 61
Sonnet 37, 60–1
Sonnet 93, 44–6, 48
Sonnet III, 61
Sonnet 144, 60
Sophocles, 181, 183
Southampton, Henry Wriothesley, Earl of:
as author of WS's plays, 214; dedicatory
letters to, 256; and Essex rebellion, 302;
forged correspondence with WS, 22, 35,
36; letter mentioning WS, 72; and Prince
Tudor theories, 222, 240, 245–6, 302–3
Spedding, James, 113
Spenser, Edmund: author's persona, 304;
Bacon as, 141; contemporaries on, 268,
265; D. Bacon's theories, 107; mentioned
in D. Bacon's play, 96; Oxford as, 221, 222;
as Sonnets' rival poet, 60; WS's supposed
copy of book by, 22
Steevens, George: and conspiracy theories,
38; edition of WS's plays, 19, 39; forges
letter from Peele to Marlowe, 26; and
Ireland papers, 26; and Malone, 46–8;
and the Sonnets, 57–8
Stevens, John Paul, 233–5, 242, 245
Stonley, Richard, 270
Stow, John, 30
Strachey, Lytton, 177, 203–4, 208, 288
Stratford-upon-Avon: attitude to theatre,
275–6; Britannia on, 275–6; Garrick's WS
festival (1769), 32–3; Guildhall schoolroom, 253, 312; New Place, 30, 53, 55; other
property belonging to WS, 69–70, 73;
prominent people from, 275–6; WS's
birthplace, 161–3
Strauss, David Friedrich, 83–9
Stritmatter, Roger, 223–4, 244–5
Sullivan, Anne, 131, 133–3, 155
Swift, Jonathan, 51

The Taming of the Shrew, 65, 300
Taylor, Gary, 4, 238, 289, 290
The Tempest: arguments for Bacon's authorship, 133–4, 138; authorship, 290; autobiographical readings, 62, 64, 299; D. Bacon's
studies, 123; dating, 63, 203; James's essay,
161, 167–70; Looney on, 203–4; music and
dance in, 285; Strachey on, 203–4
Templeman, Lord, 237
Terry, Ellen, 226
The Testament of Love (Usk), 134

the Theatre, 280
theatre and theatres: cost of costumes and
plays, 311; Elizabethan and Jacobean con-
ventions, 259–62; in London, 279–86,
288–9; play performance and publication
statistics (1558–1642), 257
Theobald, Lewis, 65
Thomson, James, 51
Tichborne, Sir Roger Charles, 153–5
Tillyard, E. M. W., 199
Tilney, Edmund, 201
Timber, Or Discoveries; Made Upon Men and
Matter (Jonson), 272
Timon of Athens: authorship, 68, 289, 290,
292, 293; autobiographical readings, 64;
dating, 63, 202; Looney on, 202–3; masque
in, 285
Titus Andronicus: authorship, 65, 66, 289, 292,
293; first publication, 256
Tom Sawyer (Twain), 129
The Tragedy of Locrine, 64–5
Tree, Ellen, 95, 96–7
Trevelyan, Lady, 162–3
Troilus and Cressida, 63, 198–9, 222
Twain, Mark, 124–34, 125, 135–7, 139–40,
145–58, 160
Twelfth Night: autobiographical readings,
300; ciphers in, 143; dating, 63; Feste's
character, 197
Two Gentlemen of Verona, 65, 300
The Two Noble Kinsmen: authorship, 68, 289,
290, 292, 293, 294–5; fight at end, 284;
style, 287–8
typesetting see printing and publishing
Tyrrell, Henry, 69

Underwood, John, 283
Usk, Thomas, 134

Vavasour, Anne, 218
Veal, Tom, 244
Venus and Adonis: contemporary reception,
266–7, 268, 269; Looney on, 195–6; pub-
lishing history, 256
Vickers, Brian, 290, 292
Vico, Giambattista, 79
Volpone (Jonson), 291–2
Voltaire, 31
Vortigern (Ireland; WS forgery) 26–7, 28, 29,
38

Wall Street Journal, 242–3, 245

Wallis, Albany, 18, 20, 38
Walpole, Horace, 32
Walsingham, Sir Francis, 229
Wanamaker, Sam, 236
Warburton, Bishop, 65
Ward, B. M., 216, 228
Ware, L. L., 237
Warton, Joseph, 24
Watson, Thomas, 58
Webb, Francis, 22, 38
Webb, Judge Thomas Ebenezer, 163, 165
Webster, John, 30, 270, 283, 293, 313
Weever, John, 268
Weis, René, 300–1
Welles, Orson, 321
Wells, Stanley, 4, 237, 290, 293
Wheler, R. B., 12, 69–70
White, Allon, 127–8
White, Richard Grant, 118–19
The White Devil (Webster), 30, 270
Whitman, Walt, 114, 139
Whittemore, Hank, 298, 302–3
Wikipedia, 247–8
Wilkins, George, 289, 290, 292, 293, 294
Willmott, Robert, 61

Willobie His Avisa, 267
Wilmot, James, 1–2, 11–14
Wilson, Robert, 67
The Winter's Tale: authorship, 65, 290; Blackfriars' influence on, 284; dating, 40, 63, 203; eyewitness account of contemporary performance, 72; Jonson on, 272; Looney on, 203; music in, 285
Wirt, William, 101
Wise, Andrew, 264–5
Wolf, Friedrich August, 78–82
women, 306–7
Wood, Michael, 299
Wood, Robert, 79
Woolf, Virginia, 190
Wordsworth, William, 58, 59, 61
Wright, Louis B., 230, 232, 233
Wyclif, John, 20

York, Michael, 249
A Yorkshire Tragedy, 64–5

Zweig, Arnold, 210